Arabic

An Essential Grammar

'The book has the great advantage of introducing Arabic grammatical terminology in a manner that is clear and easy to follow . . . there is nothing like it on the market at present and I believe it will be much appreciated by teachers and students alike'

Stefan Sperl, *Senior Lecturer in Arabic*, *SOAS*, *UK*

Arabic: An Essential Grammar is an up-to-date and practical reference guide to the most important aspects of the language. Suitable for beginners, as well as intermediate students, this book offers a strong foundation for learning the fundamental grammar structures of Arabic. The complexities of the language are set out in short, readable sections and exercises and examples are provided throughout.

The book is ideal for independent learners as well as for classroom study.

Features of this book include:

- coverage of the Arabic script and alphabet
- a chapter on Arabic handwriting
- a guide to pronunciation
- examples provided throughout.

Faruk Abu-Chacra is Senior Lecturer Emeritus in Arabic at the University of Helsinki, Finland.

Routledge Essential Grammars

Essential Grammars are available for the following languages:

Chinese
Czech
Danish
Dutch
English
Finnish
German
Modern Greek
Modern Hebrew
Hungarian
Norwegian
Polish
Portuguese
Serbian
Spanish
Swedish
Thai
Urdu

Other titles of related interest published by Routledge:

Arabic–English Thematic Lexicon (forthcoming)
By Daniel Newman

Colloquial Arabic of Egypt
By Jane Wightwick and Mahmoud Gaafar

Colloquial Arabic of the Gulf and Saudi Arabia
(second edition forthcoming)
By Clive Holes

Modern Written Arabic: A Comprehensive Grammar
By El Said Badawi, Mike Carter and Adrian Gully

Arabic

An Essential Grammar

Faruk Abu-Chacra

Routledge
Taylor & Francis Group
LONDON AND NEW YORK

First published 2007
by Routledge
2 Park Square, Milton Park, Abingdon, Oxon OX14 4RN

Simultaneously published in the USA and Canada
by Routledge
270 Madison Ave, New York, NY 10016

Routledge is an imprint of the Taylor & Francis Group, an informa business

Typeset in Sabon by RefineCatch Limited, Bungay, Suffolk
Printed and bound in Great Britain by
Antony Rowe Ltd, Chippenham, Wiltshire

British Library Cataloguing in Publication Data
A catalogue record for this book is available from the British Library

Library of Congress Cataloging-in-Publication Data
Abu Shaqra, Faruq.
Arabic : an essential grammar / by Faruk Abu-Chacra.
p. cm.
1. Arabic language – Textbooks for foreign speakers – English.
I. Title.
PJ6307.A384 2007
492.7′82421—dc22

2006023828

ISBN10: 0–415–41572–1 (hbk)
ISBN10: 0–415–41571–3 (pbk)
ISBN10: 0–203–08881–6 (ebk)

ISBN13: 978–0–415–41572–9 (hbk)
ISBN13: 978–0–415–41571–2 (pbk)
ISBN13: 978–0–203–08881–4 (ebk)

Contents

Preface

This book describes the fundamental grammar and structure of modern literary Arabic. It is complete with exercises and offers a strong foundation for reading and writing the Arabic of newspapers, books, broadcasts and formal speech, as well as providing the student with a course for self-study. The exercises and examples contain modern vocabulary and expressions taken from everyday use.

The work contains thirty-nine chapters with an appendix of tables for verb forms and verb conjugation paradigms. All chapters are progressive and they complement each other. For this reason it is recommended that the student master each lesson before going on to the next.

Up to chapter 22, a full transliteration into the Latin alphabet is given for all Arabic examples and exercises. From chapter 22 onwards, the transliteration is omitted from the exercises only.

There are two types of exercise: Arabic sentences translated into English, and English sentences to be translated into Arabic. The words of the English to Arabic translation exercises are taken from the Arabic to English exercises of the same chapter.

So that readers do not have to use Arabic–English dictionaries, which a learner of Arabic would find difficult at this stage, most Arabic words in the exercises are indexed with a superscript number and the same number is given to the equivalent English word.

I am confident that this book will prove to be of great help to those who have begun or will begin the study of Arabic, and that teachers will find it a useful aid.

Acknowledgements

I would like to express my gratitude to my former colleagues at the Institute for Asian and African Studies at the University of Helsinki (Finland), especially Professor Tapani Harviainen and Dr Bertil Tikkanen, and to Professor Daniel Newman of the University of Durham (England) as well as Professor Benjamin Hoffez of Oakland University (USA). They read the original manuscript and made numerous valuable comments and suggestions for its improvement. In addition I should also like to thank the anonymous reviewers appointed by Routledge for their constructive criticism and advice.

I also acknowledge the generous financial support of the Ministry of Education of Finland, the University of Helsinki, Alfred Kordelin Foundation, Jenni and Antti Wihuri Foundation, and the Finnish Association of Non-Fiction Writers.

Faruk Abu-Chacra
Helsinki, Finland, 2007

Abbreviations

acc.	accusative
act.	active
C	consonant
def.	definite
dipt.	diptote
du.	dual
f./fem.	feminine
gen.	genitive
imperat.	imperative
imperf.	imperfect
indef.	indefinite
indic./ind.	indicative
intrans.	intransitive
juss.	jussive
lit.	literally
m./masc.	masculine
nom.	nominative
part./particip.	participle
pass.	passive
pers.	person
pl./plur.	plural
prep.	preposition
s./sing.	singular
subj.	subjunctive
trans.	transitive
V.	vowel
v.	verb

Chapter 1

Arabic script, transliteration and alphabet table

1.1 The Arabic script

The Arabic alphabet consists of 28 letters representing consonants. In addition there are three vowel signs which are used in writing both short and long vowels. Moreover, there are various other orthographic signs that are explained in the following chapters.

The 28 letters are written from right to left. When writing words, the letters are connected (joined) together from both sides, except in the case of six letters, which can only be joined from the right side. These letters are numbered 1, 8, 9, 10, 11 and 27 in the table below and are marked with an asterisk (*). It is important to remember that these letters cannot be connected to the following letter (i.e. on their left side).

Most of the letters are written in slightly different forms depending on their location in the word: initially, medially, finally or standing alone. There are no capital letters.

Arabic grammarians use three different names for the alphabet:

أَلْحُرُوفُ ٱلْأَبْجَدِيَّةُ	ʾal-ḥurūfu l-ʾabǧadiyyatu
أَلْحُرُوفُ ٱلْهِجَائِيَّةُ	ʾal-ḥurūfu l-hiǧāʾiyyatu
أَلْأَلِفْبَاءُ	ʾal-ʾalifbāʾu

1.2 *Transliteration*

The transliteration of the Arabic alphabet given below is based on the Latin alphabet, but some of the letters have an extra sign indicating some special feature of the Arabic pronunciation of the letter in question.

The **ʾalif** (ا), which is the first letter, has so far not been given any transliteration, because its sound value varies (to be dealt with in chapters 6 and 7).

1.3 *Alphabet table and transliteration*

transliteration	standing alone	final	medial	initial	name
(1) (*)	ا	..ـا	..ـا	ا	ʾAlif
(2) b	ب	..ـب	..ـبـ..	بـ..	Bāʾ
(3) t	ت	..ـت	..ـتـ..	تـ..	Tāʾ
(4) ṯ	ث	..ـث	..ـثـ..	ثـ..	Ṯāʾ
(5) ǧ	ج	..ـج	..ـجـ..	جـ..	Ǧīm
(6) ḥ	ح	..ـح	..ـحـ..	حـ..	Ḥāʾ
(7) ḫ	خ	..ـخ	..ـخـ..	خـ..	Ḫāʾ
(8) d (*)	د	..ـد	..ـد	د	Dāl
(9) ḏ (*)	ذ	..ـذ	..ـذ	ذ	Ḏāl
(10) r (*)	ر	..ـر	..ـر	ر	Rāʾ
(11) z (*)	ز	..ـز	..ـز	ز	Zayn
(12) s	س	..ـس	..ـسـ..	سـ..	Sīn
(13) š	ش	..ـش	..ـشـ..	شـ..	Šīn
(14) ṣ	ص	..ـص	..ـصـ..	صـ..	Ṣād
(15) ḍ	ض	..ـض	..ـضـ..	ضـ..	Ḍād
(16) ṭ	ط	..ـط	..ـطـ..	طـ..	Ṭāʾ
(17) ḏ̣	ظ	..ـظ	..ـظـ..	ظـ..	Ḏ̣āʾ

(18)	ʿ	ع	..ـع	..ـعـ..	عـ..	ʿAyn
(19)	ġ	غ	..ـغ	..ـغـ..	غـ..	Ġayn
(20)	f	ف	..ـف	..ـفـ..	فـ..	Fāʾ
(21)	q	ق	..ـق	..ـقـ..	قـ..	Qāf
(22)	k	ك	..ـك	..ـكـ..	كـ..	Kāf
(23)	l	ل	..ـل	..ـلـ..	لـ..	Lām
(24)	m	م	..ـم	..ـمـ..	مـ..	Mīm
(25)	n	ن	..ـن	..ـنـ..	نـ..	Nūn
(26)	h	ه	..ـه	..ـهـ..	هـ..	Hāʾ
(27)	w (*)	و	..ـو	..ـو	و	Wāw
(28)	y	ي	..ـي	..ـيـ..	يـ..	Yāʾ

1.4 *Writing letters in different positions*

Below each letter is presented as it appears in different positions in connected writing when using a computer or as written by hand.

(1)	ا ا	ااا ااا	(2) b	ب ب	ببب ببب
(3) t	ت ت	تتت تتت	(4) ṯ	ث ث	ثثث ثثث
(5) ǧ	ج ج	ججج ججج	(6) ḥ	ح ح	ححح ححح
(7) ḫ	خ خ	خخخ خخخ	(8) d	د د	ددد ددد
(9) ḏ	ذ ذ	ذذذ ذذذ	(10) r	ر ر	ررر ررر

(11)	z	ز	ززز	(12)	s	س	سسس
		ز	ز ز ز			س	سسس
(13)	š	ش	ششش	(14)	ṣ	ص	صصص
		ش	ششش			ص	صصص
(15)	ḍ	ض	ضضض	(16)	ṭ	ط	ططط
		ض	ضضض			ط	ططط
(17)	ḏ̣	ظ	ظظظ	(18)	ʿ	ع	ععع
		ظ	ظظظ			ع	ععع
(19)	ġ	غ	غغغ	(20)	f	ف	ففف
		غ	غغغ			ف	ففف
(21)	q	ق	ققق	(22)	k	ك	ككك
		ق	ققق			ك	ككك
(23)	l	ل	للل	(24)	m	م	ممم
		ل	للل			م	ممم
(25)	n	ن	ننن	(26)	h	ه	ههه
		ن	ننن			ه	ههه
(27)	w	و	ووو	(28)	y	ي	ييي
		و	ووو			ي	ييي

Chapter 2

Pronunciation of consonants

(1) **ʾAlif** ا This first letter has no pronunciation of its own. One of its main functions is to act as a bearer for the sign **hamzah**, discussed separately in chapter 7. **ʾAlif** is also used as a long vowel /ā/ (see chapter 6).

(2) **Bāʾ** ب /b/ A voiced bilabial stop as the **/b/** in English 'ha**b**it'.

(3) **Tāʾ** ت /t/ An unaspirated voiceless dental stop as the **t** in English 's**t**op'. Never pronounced as American English **tt** as in 'le**tt**er'.

(4) **Ṯāʾ** ث /ṯ/ A voiceless interdental fricative as **th** in English '**th**ick', 'too**th**'.

(5) **Ǧīm** ج /ǧ/ A voiced palato-alveolar affricate. In reality, this letter has three different pronunciations depending on the dialectal background of the speaker:

(a) In Classical Arabic and the Gulf area, as well as in many other places in the Arab world, it is pronounced as a voiced palato-alveolar affricate as the **j** in '**j**udge', '**j**ourney', or the **g** in Italian '**g**iorno'.

(b) In Lower Egypt (Cairo, Alexandria) it is pronounced as a voiced velar stop as the **g** in English '**g**reat'.

(c) In North Africa and the Levant it is pronounced as a voiced palato-alveolar fricative /ž/ as the **s** in English 'plea**s**ure', and as **j** in French '**j**our'.

(6) **Ḥāʾ** ح /ḥ/ This consonant has no equivalent in European languages. It is pronounced in the pharynx by breathing with strong friction and no uvular vibration or scrape, so that it sounds

like a loud whispering from the throat. It must be kept distinct from the sounds of خ /ḫ/ (7) and هـ.. /h/ (26).

(7) **Ḫā᾽** خ /ḫ/ This consonant occurs in many languages. It is a voiceless postvelar (before or after /i/) or uvular (before or after /a/ or /u/) fricative, quite similar to the so-called ach-Laut in German 'Na**ch**t' or Scottish 'lo**ch**' or the Spanish **j** in 'mujer', but in Arabic it has a stronger, rasping sound.

(8) **Dāl** د /d/ A voiced dental stop as the **d** in English 'lea**d**er'.

(9) **Ḏāl** ذ /ḏ/ A voiced interdental fricative, as the **th** in English 'ei**th**er'.

(10) **Rā᾽** ر /r/ A voiced alveolar trill, which differs from English **r** in that it is a rolled sound or trill, pronounced as a rapid succession of flaps of the tongue, similar to Scottish **r** in '**r**adical' or Italian **r** in 'pa**r**la**r**e' or Spanish **rr** in 'pe**rr**o'.

(11) **Zayn** ز /z/ A voiced alveolar sibilant, as the **z** in English 'ga**z**elle'.

(12) **Sīn** س /s/ A voiceless alveolar sibilant as the **s** in English '**s**tate'.

(13) **Šīn** ش /š/ A voiceless palato-alveolar sibilant as the **sh** in English '**sh**ave', 'pu**sh**'.

(14) **Ṣād** ص /ṣ/ Belongs to the group of emphatic consonants. The emphatic consonants are pronounced with more emphasis and further back in the mouth than their non-emphatic (plain) counterparts. In pronouncing them the body and root of the tongue are (simultaneously) drawn back towards the rear wall of the throat (pharynx), and also the tip of the tongue is slightly retracted. Hence the emphatic consonants are also called pharyngealized consonants. ص /ṣ/ is thus the emphatic or pharyngealized counterpart of the plain alveolar س /s/ (12) and sounds somewhat similar to the **s** in English '**s**on' or 'a**ss**umption'. For the retracting and lowering effect of the emphatic consonants on the adjacent vowels, see chapter 4.

(15) **Ḍād** ض /ḍ/ It is also an emphatic consonant, classified as a pharyngealized voiced alveolar stop. Arab phoneticians and reciters of the Quran recommend it is pronounced as a counter-

part to د /d/ (8). In current use in many dialects it is, however, also pronounced as the counterpart of ذ /ḏ/ (9), somewhat similar to the sound **th** in English '**th**us'. See also chapter 4.

(16) **Ṭāʾ** ط /ṭ/ An emphatic consonant, classified as a pharyngealized voiceless alveolar stop. It is the counterpart of ت /t/ (3), and similar to the sound /t/ at the beginning of the English word '**t**all'. See also chapter 4.

(17) **Ḏ̣āʾ** ظ /ḏ̣/ An emphatic consonant, classified as a pharyngealized voiced interdental fricative. It is the emphatic counterpart of ذ /ḏ/ (9). In some dialects it is pronounced as ض /ḍ/ (15). In some other dialects it is pronounced as pharyngealized ز /z/ (11). See also chapter 4.

(18) **ʿAyn** ع /ʿ/ This consonant has no equivalent in European languages. It is defined as a voiced emphatic (pharyngealized) laryngeal fricative, which is pronounced by pressing the root of the tongue against the back wall of the pharynx (upper part of the throat) and letting the pressed air stream from the throat pass through the pharynx with some vibration. In a way it is the voiced counterpart of ح /ḥ/ (6). It sounds as if you are swallowing your tongue or being strangled.

(19) **Ġayn** غ /ġ/ A voiced postvelar (before or after /i/) or uvular (before or after /a/ or /u/) fricative, a gargling sound, produced by pronouncing the خ /ḫ/ (7) and activating the vocal folds, similar to Parisian French **r** in 'Pa**r**is' and '**r**ouge' but with more scraping.

(20) **Fāʾ** ف /f/ A voiceless labiodental fricative as the **f** in English '**f**ast'.

(21) **Qāf** ق /q/ This has no equivalent in European languages. It is a voiceless postvelar or uvular stop, pronounced by closing the back of the tongue against the uvula as if it were to be swallowed. It is like خ /ḫ/ (7) without vibration. This sound should not be confused with ك /k/ (22), e.g. قَلْب **q**alb, 'heart', but كَلْب **k**alb 'dog'.

(22) **Kāf** ك /k/ An unaspirated voiceless velar stop as the **k** of English 's**k**ate'.

(23) **Lām** ل /l/ A voiced alveolar lateral as the **l** in English '**l**et'.

(24) **Mīm** م /m/ A voiced bilabial nasal as the **m** in English '**m**oon'.

(25) **Nūn** ن /n/ A voiced alveolar nasal as the **n** in English '**n**ine'.

(26) **Hāʾ** هـ (ه) /h/ A voiceless glottal fricative as the **h** in English '**h**ead'.

Note: This letter has another function when it occurs at the end of a word with two superscript dots: ة ، ـة... Then it is pronounced exactly like ت /t/ (3) and is called **tāʾ marbūṭah** (see chapter 10 on gender).

(27) **Wāw** و /w/ A voiced bilabial semivowel, as the **w** in English '**w**ell'.

(28) **Yāʾ** ي /y/ A voiced alveo-palatal semivowel, as the **y** in English '**y**es'.

Chapter 3

Punctuation and handwriting

3.1 Punctuation

Punctuation marks are not found in early Arabic manuscripts. The Arabs have borrowed modern European punctuation marks with some modifications in order to distinguish them from Arabic letters, as follows:

. ، : ؛ ! ؟ ( ) ″ «   »

3.2 Arabic handwriting

It is recommended that handwriting technique is practised from the very beginning, otherwise it may become difficult to learn not only to write but even to read handwritten texts. Arabs consider good handwriting a sign of erudition.

Printed and handwritten Arabic texts do not differ from each other as much as they do in European languages.

Arabic handwriting follows certain rules. The straight horizontal direction used in writing English must be modified in Arabic handwriting, since some of the letters change their form according to the preceding or following letter.

3.3 Some remarks concerning the dots with certain consonants

The most common way of marking the dots which belong to certain consonants in handwriting is to use a straight stroke ▬ instead of two dots, as in ت /t/ or ي /y/; and ^ instead of three dots, as in ث /ṯ/. One might suspect that the straight stroke replacing two dots could be confused with the vowels **fatḥah** ـَـ or **kasrah** ـِـ, but this is not the case, since these vowel signs are diagonal (slanting) strokes. As noted above, handwritten as well as printed texts are normally written without vowel signs.

Exercises

The examples below and in the next few chapters are intended mainly for practising how to read and write Arabic script.

سحق	هجم	نكره	جرح
سحق	هجم	نكره	جرح
(1) s+ḥ+q	h+ğ+m	n+k+r+h	ğ+r+ḥ
رحل	لهم	زرع	غرق
رحل	لهم	زرع	غرق
(2) r+ḥ+l	l+h+m	z+r+ᶜ	ġ+r+q
لحم	نسي	تعب	بحر
لحم	نسي	تعب	بحر
(3) l+ḥ+m	n+s+y	t+ᶜ+b	b+ḥ+r
سمع	عمل	منه	صبغ
سمع	عمل	منه	صبغ
(4) s+m+ᶜ	ᶜ+m+l	m+n+h	ṣ+b+ġ
ترك	وزع	ترجم	ميل
ترك	وزع	ترجم	ميل
(5) t+r+k	w+z+ᶜ	t+r+ğ+m	m+y+l
عزي	جحش	سكت	نجح
عزي	جحش	سكت	نجح
(6) ᶜ+z+y	ğ+ḥ+š	s+k+t	n+ğ+ḥ

عكف	دحرج	عمي	فيل
عكف	دحرج	عمي	فيل
(7) ʿ+k+f	d+ḥ+r+ǧ	ʿ+m+y	f+y+l
غرس	فهم	هجر	هرب
غرس	فهم	هجر	هرب
(8) ġ+r+s	f+h+m	h+ǧ+r	h+r+b
بهق	زعم	فهمه	درس
بهق	زعم	فهمه	درس
(9) b+h+q	z+ʿ+m	f+h+m+h	d+r+s
صبر	ضرب	طبع	بطل
صبر	ضرب	طبع	بطل
(10) ṣ+b+r	ḍ+r+b	ṭ+b+ʿ	b+ṭ+l
سرد	ظلم	قوي	مرض
سرد	ظلم	قوي	مرض
(11) s+r+d	ḏ̣+l+m	q+w+y	m+r+ḍ
وضع	شرد	مهله	ضبط
وضع	شرد	مهله	ضبط
(12) w+ḍ+ʿ	š+r+d	m+h+l+h	ḍ+b+ṭ
فرغ	شهم	سمسر	عرك
فرغ	شهم	سمسر	عرك
(13) f+r+ġ	š+h+m	s+m+s+r	ʿ+r+k
قسم	برك	شكل	فرش
قسم	برك	شكل	فرش
(14) q+s+m	b+r+k	š+k+l	f+r+š

شحم	مصور	مورد	مصدر
شحم	مصور	مورد	مصدر
(15) š+ḥ+m	m+ṣ+w+r	m+w+r+d	m+ṣ+d+r
شهر	مكث	لطم	ولده
شهر	مكث	لطم	ولده
(16) š+h+r	m+k+ṯ	l+ṭ+m	w+l+d+h
قسم	برك	شرف	شوق
قسم	برك	شرف	شوق
(17) q+s+m	b+r+k	š+r+f	š+w+q
ذبح	رحم	فندق	خوف
ذبح	رحم	فندق	خوف
(18) ḏ+b+ḥ	r+ḥ+m	f+n+d+q	ḫ+w+f
شكر	مكتب	نهد	بحث
شكر	مكتب	نهد	بحث
(19) š+k+r	m+k+t+b	n+h+d	b+ḥ+ṯ

Chapter 4

Vowels

4.1 There are three vowels in Arabic called أَلْحَرَكَاتُ ʾal-ḥarakātu. They can be both short and long (see chapter 6).

4.2 *Short vowels*

The three short vowels are written as diacritical signs above or below the consonant to which they belong. As a word always begins with a consonant, the consonant is pronounced before the vowel.

Fatḥah: ـَ /**a**/ is a small diagonal stroke above the consonant:

بَ /b**a**/, e.g. كَتَبَ **kataba**, to write.

Kasrah: ـِ /**i**/ is a small diagonal stroke under the consonant:

بِ /b**i**/, e.g. قَبِلَ qab**i**la, to accept.

Ḍammah: ـُ /**u**/ is a sign similar to a comma above the consonant:

بُ /b**u**/, e.g. حَسُنَ ḥas**u**na, to be handsome.

4.3 The sound quality of **fatḥah** ـَ /a/ tends to be slightly coloured towards /æ/, like /a/ in the word 'f**a**t' in English.

4.4 Short vowels are not normally marked in personal handwriting or in most Arabic publications. In order to avoid misunderstandings, the vowel signs are marked on unusual or foreign words, and in the Quran and children's books.

4.5 The vowel qualities of the three vowels mentioned above are influenced by the *emphatic* (pharyngealized) consonants. The emphatic consonants are most easily heard in conjuction with **fatḥah** ـَ /a/, which is then coloured towards /o/, or to American English /u/ in 'but' or /o/ in 'bottle', 'hot', etc.

Emphatic consonants	***Corresponding non-emphatic consonants***
صَ (14) towards /ṣo/ counterpart of	سَ (12) towards /sæ/ as in 'sat'
ضَ (15) towards /ḍo/ counterpart of	دَ (8) towards /dæ/ as in 'dam'
طَ (16) towards /ṭo/ counterpart of	تَ (3) towards /tæ/ in 'tat'
ظَ (17) towards /ḏ̣o/ counterpart of	ذَ (9) towards /ḏæ/ in 'that'

Example: The non-emphatic /s/ in the word سَلَبَ salaba 'to steal' sounds like sælæbæ, but the emphatic /ṣ/ in the word صَلَبَ ṣalaba 'to crucify' sounds almost like ṣolobo.

Note a: The following two consonants may sometimes also function as emphatic: ر /r/ (10), and ل /l/ (23) only with the word أَللّٰهُ ʾallāh, 'God'.

Note b: The uvular ق /q/ has almost the same effect on the adjacent vowels as the emphatic consonants. Thus the word كَلْب kalb, 'dog', with a velar /k/, sounds almost like kælb, whereas قَلْب qalb 'heart', with an uvular ق /q/, sounds almost like qolb.

Note c: Phonologically the above sounds /æ/ and /o/ both represent the **fatḥah** ـَ. However, in the transliteration system used in this book they are replaced by /a/. This is because they function as /a/ phonemically.

Exercises

Read and practise your handwriting:

	خَبَزَ	كَرِهَ	سَمِعَ	شَهِدَ	فَرِغَ
	خَبَزَ	كَرِهَ	سَمِعَ	شَهِدَ	فَرِغَ
(1)	ḫabaza to bake	kariha to dislike	samiʿa to hear	šahida to witness	fariġa to be empty
	دَرَسَ	قَرُبَ	كَرُمَ	ثَقُلَ	سَمِعَهُ
	دَرَسَ	قَرُبَ	كَرُمَ	ثَقُلَ	سَمِعَهُ
(2)	darasa to study	qaruba to be near	karuma to be noble	ṯaqula to be heavy	samiʿahu he heard him

	رَبِحَ	وَرِمَ	زَهِدَ	رَضِعَ	سَهُلَ
	رَبِحَ	وَرِمَ	زَهِدَ	رَضِعَ	سَهُلَ
(3)	rabiḥa to gain	warima to be swollen	zahida to abstain	raḍiᶜa to suckle	sahula to be easy
	رَقَصَ	قَهَرَهُ	طَبَخَ	ظَلَمَ	لَهُ
	رَقَصَ	قَهَرَهُ	طَبَخَ	ظَلَمَ	لَهُ
(4)	raqaṣa to dance	qaharahu defeat him	ṭabaẖa to cook	ḏalama to oppress	lahu for him
	عَطِشَ	ضَرَبَ	عَهِدَ	هَجَرَ	وَقَعَ
	عَطِشَ	ضَرَبَ	عَهِدَ	هَجَرَ	وَقَعَ
(5)	ᶜaṭiša to be thirsty	ḍaraba to beat	ᶜahida to entrust	hağara to emigrate	waqaᶜa to fall
	هَرَبَ	بَلَعَ	ضَعُفَ	سَكَتَ	نَدِمَ
	هَرَبَ	بَلَعَ	ضَعُفَ	سَكَتَ	نَدِمَ
(6)	haraba to escape	balaᶜa to swallow	ḍaᶜufa to be weak	sakata to be silent	nadima to regret
	رَسَمَ	شَهَرَ	حَلَفَ	رَكَضَ	خَلَطَ
	رَسَمَ	شَهَرَ	حَلَفَ	رَكَضَ	خَلَطَ
(7)	rasama to draw	šahara to make famous	ḥalafa to swear	rakaḍa to run	ẖalaṭa to mix
	طَبَعَ	فَهِمَ	عَرَضَ	صَرَخَ	وَزَنَ
	طَبَعَ	فَهِمَ	عَرَضَ	صَرَخَ	وَزَنَ
(8)	ṭabaᶜa to print	fahima to understand	ᶜaraḍa to exhibit	ṣaraẖa to scream	wazana to weigh

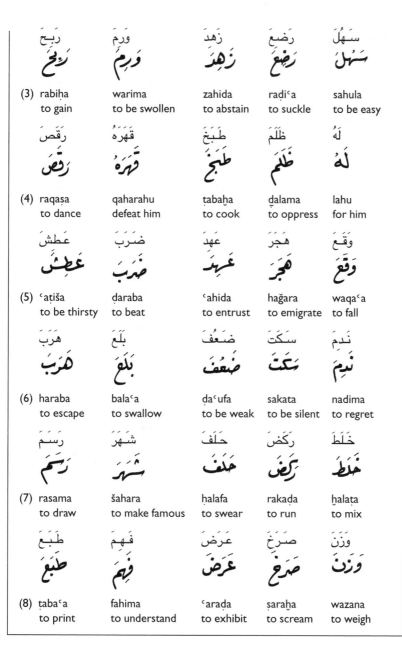

Write in Arabic:

(9)	waṯiqa to trust	baḥaṯa to search	baḫila to be stingy	kasila to be lazy	tarakahu he left him
(10)	ġaḍiba to be angry	ǧamaᶜa to collect	mariḍa to become ill	našara to publish	faqada to lose
(11)	naǧaḥa to succeed	saǧada to bow	tabiᶜa to follow	ǧaraᶜa to swallow	ḍaġaṭa to press
(12)	waṣala to arrive	raǧaᶜa to return	labisa to dress	ḥasaba to calculate	waᶜada to promise
(13)	ṭarada to dismiss	raġama to force	salima to be safe	našiqa to sniff	waḍaᶜa to put down
(14)	ġariqa to sink	barama to turn	haǧama to attack	raḥima to be merciful	šahida to witness
(15)	badala to change	taᶜisa to be miserable	fasada to be rotten	zaraᶜa to plant	ᶜaṭiba to be destroyed
(16)	ṯabata to be firm	talafa to destroy	barada to be cold	dabaġa to tan	zaᶜila to be angry
(17)	maḍaġa to chew	nabata to grow (plants)	hatafa to shout	zaḥafa to creep	baraᶜa to be skilful
(18)	ṣaᶜuba to be difficult	mazaḥa to joke	ġadara to betray	baraqa to flash	zaᶜama to pretend
(19)	rakiba to ride	ṯaqaba to drill	zaliqa to glide	ḍaǧira to be bored	zalaṭa to swallow

Chapter 5

Sukūn, šaddah, noun cases and nunation as indefinite form

5.1 *Sukūn:* ـْـ

A small circle written above a consonant indicates the absence of a vowel, e.g.

هُمْ hu**m**, they   مِنْ mi**n**, from   تَحْتَ ta**ḥ**ta, under

لَوْ la**w**, if   كَيْ ka**y**, in order to   كَيْفَ ka**y**fa, how

5.2 *Šaddah:* ـّـ *(doubling of a consonant)*

(a) When a consonant occurs twice without a vowel in between, the consonant is written only once but with the sign **šaddah** above and the pronunciation is also doubled, e.g.

عَلَّمَ ʿallama, to teach   جَرَّبَ ǧarraba, to try   عَدَّ ʿadda, to count

(b) When **kasrah** ـِـ /i/ appears together with **šaddah** ـّـ, the **kasrah** is usually placed above the consonant but under the **šaddah**, e.g.

جَرِّبْ ǧarrib, try!   عَلِّمْ ʿallim, teach!

5.3 *Noun cases*

Case inflection is called إِعْرَابُ ٱلْاسْمِ ʾiʿrābu l-ismi in Arabic. Arabic nouns and adjectives have three cases. For the most part they are indicated by adding a vowel to the last consonant, and they are called:

Nominative: مَرْفُوعٌ marfūʿun (takes the vowel **ḍammah**)

Accusative: مَنْصُوبٌ manṣūbun (takes the vowel **fatḥah**)

Genitive: مَجْرُورٌ mağrūrun (takes the vowel **kasrah**)

(There is more about cases in later chapters.)

5.4 *Nunation as indefinite form*

Nouns and adjectives are generally indicated as indefinite forms, أَلنَّكِرَةُ ʾan-nakiratu, by doubling the final vowel sign and pronouncing them with a final /...n/. The final vowel itself does not, however, become long in spite of the double vowel sign. This process of making a noun or adjective indefinite is called تَنْوِينٌ tanwīnun in Arabic and nunation in English. The indefinite forms of the three different cases are:

Nominative indef.: The word ends with a double **ḍammah**:

ـُـُ or ـٌ /**...un**/ مَلِكٌ malik**un**, a king

Accusative indef.: The word ends with a double **fatḥah** and often an extra ʾ**alif** ا which is *not pronounced* as a long vowel **ā**:

ـًا /**...an**/ مَلِكًا malik**an**, a king (object)

Genitive indef.: The word ends with a double **kasrah**:

ـٍ /**...in**/ مَلِكٍ malik**in**, a king's, of a king

Note a: The form of the double ḍammah ـٌ is the commonest of the two alternatives and will be used in this book.

Note b: In spoken Arabic the use of nunation, i.e. /...un/, /...an/ and /...in/ in nouns, is rare.

Exercises

Read and practise your handwriting:

(1)	دَخَّنَ	كَلْبًا	وَلَدًا	بَحْرٌ	جَرَّ
	daḫḫana	kalban	waladan	baḥrun	ğarra
	to smoke	dog	boy	sea	to draw
(2)	عَيَّنَ	قَوْمٌ	مُحَمَّدٌ	مُعَلِّمًا	نَهْرٍ
	ʿayyana	qawmun	muḥammadun	muʿalliman	nahrin
	to appoint	people	Muhammad	teacher	river
(3)	ثَوْبًا	يَوْمًا	مَطَرٍ	خَرْبَشَ	رَمْيًا
	ṯawban	yawman	maṭarin	ḫarbaša	ramyan
	dress	day	rain	to scratch	shooting
(4)	عَلَّمَ	عَوْنٌ	حَرْبٌ	هِيَ	هُوَ
	ʿallama	ʿawnun	ḥarbun	hiya	huwa
	to teach	help	war	she	he
(5)	عَلَمًا	قَلَمٌ	حَرِكٍ	وَطَنٌ	نَحْنُ
	ʿalman	qalamun	ḥarikin	waṭanun	naḥnu
	flag	pen	lively	homeland	we
(6)	رَجُلٍ	عَمَلٌ	جَبَلٍ	شَرَفٍ	عَرَبِيٌّ
	rağulin	ʿamalun	ğabalin	šarafin	ʿarabiyyun
	man	work	mountain	honour	Arab
(7)	قَمَرٍ	شَمْسٌ	قَصْرٍ	سَيِّدٍ	بَطْنٌ
	qamarin	šamsun	qaṣrin	sayyidin	baṭnun
	moon	sun	castle	lord, Mr	belly
(8)	رَمْلٌ	غَرْبٍ	شَرْقٌ	دَيْنٌ	نَفْسٍ
	ramlun	ġarbin	šarqun	daynun	nafsin
	sand	west	east	debt	soul
(9)	شُغْلٍ	حُكْمًا	عُذْرٌ	لَوْنًا	خُبْزًا
	šuġlin	ḥukman	ʿuḏrun	lawnan	ḫubzan
	work	rule	excuse	colour	bread
(10)	شَيْخًا	سَيْفٍ	قِسْمٌ	جَمَلٌ	عِلْمٌ
	šayḫan	sayfin	qismun	ğamalun	ʿilmun
	old man	sword	part	camel	knowledge

Sukūn, šaddah, noun cases and nunation as indefinite form

Write in Arabic:

Remember: The words below with endings /...un/, /...an/ and /...in/ should be written with a double vowel (and an extra ʾalif ا if the ending is /...an/), as mentioned above, e.g. مَلِكًا malik**an**, 'a king'.

(11)	raḥḥala to deport	baḥḥa to be hoarse	ḥassa to feel	zuhdan asceticism	ḥarraka to move
(12)	muḫaddirun anaesthetic	maḏhabiyyun sectarian	wakkala to authorize	ḥasadan envy	raddada to repeat
(13)	šahran month	ḫağalun shyness	ṣabba to pour	buʿdun distance	ḥaṭṭa to put
(14)	ḫarraba to destroy	qaṭaʿa to cut	rağğaʿa to return	šabba to grow up	mutaḥarrirun emanicipated
(15)	ḫamran wine	ḥayawiyyin lively	šahriyyan monthly	bawwaba to classify	qarnin horn
(16)	zawğan husband	ballaġa to inform	radda to return	šahiyyan tasty	rağʿiyyin reactionary
(17)	bawwala to urinate	rabbun lord	šaḥḥama to grease	šağğaʿa to encourage	ḍanna to think
(18)	šukran thanks	šaʿʿala to light	ʿabdan slave	ṭabʿan naturally	marḥaban hello
(19)	ṣaḥḥa to be healthy	muḫarribin saboteur	ḥaḍḍan fortune	qarrara to decide	šawwaqa to desire

Chapter 6

Long vowels, ˀalif maqṣūrah, dagger or miniature ˀalif, word stress and syllable structure

6.1 The three short vowels, ـَـ /a/, ـُـ /u/, and ـِـ /i/, also have long variants. They are written by adding one of the following three letters after the short vowel signs. These letters are called in Arabic حُرُوفُ الْمَدِّ ḥurūfu l-maddi 'letters of prolongation':

ˀalif	ا, which is related to **fatḥah**	ـَـ	/a/
wāw	و, which is related to **ḍammah**	ـُـ	/u/
yāˀ	ي, which is related to **kasrah**	ـِـ	/i/

Short vowels	***Long vowels***
...بَـ /ba/	بَـا /bā/, e.g. بَـابٌ bābun, door
...بُـ /bu/	بُـو /bū/, e.g. نُـورٌ nūrun, light
...بِـ /bi/	بِـي /bī/, e.g. دِيـنٌ dīnun, religion

Note: In some books long vowels are transliterated as double vowels. Here we use the macron above the vowel to indicate length.

6.2 It should be noted that the combination of the letter **lām** ...ـل followed by **ˀalif** ـا... is called **lām-ˀalif** and written as لَا or ـلَا... /lā/ (not as لا). Also, the **lām-ˀalif** لَا follows the rule of **ˀalif** (1) ـا..., which means that it cannot be connected to the following letter (to the left), e.g.

سَلَامٌ salāmun, peace   لَامَ lāma, to blame   حَلًّا ḥallan, a solution

6.3 *ʾAlif maqṣūrah*

The long vowel /ā/ at the end of a word can be written with **ʾalif** ـَا... or, in some words, with **yāʾ**, but without dots ـَى... That **yāʾ** is then called أَلِفٌ مَقْصُورَةٌ ʾalif maqṣūrah, e.g.

عَلَى ʿalā, on　　رَوَى rawā, to tell　　رَمَى ramā, to throw

Note: Certain rules explained in later chapters govern which one of the two **ʾalifs** is to be used in a word.

6.4 *Dagger or miniature ʾalif*

In some common words the long vowel /ā/ is written with a miniature **ʾalif**, also called dagger **ʾalif**. As the name suggests, this is a small vertical stroke ـٰ placed above the consonant, replacing the ordinary full **ʾalif** (ا), e.g.

هٰذَا (not: هَاذَا)	لٰكِنَّ (not: لَاكِنَّ)	ذٰلِكَ (not: ذَالِكَ)
hā<u>d</u>ā, this	lākinna, but	<u>d</u>ālika, that

6.5 *Word stress and syllable structure*

Surprisingly enough, the Arabic grammarians did not deal with the position of stress (dynamic accent) in Arabic words. Nevertheless almost all Arabic words must be stressed on one of their syllables, which may be short or long. The stress appears as an increase in vocal intensity as well as a raising of the pitch of voice.

The following general rules are mainly based on the methods of pronunciation employed by the reciters of the Quran. In some cases there are variations between different traditions, and the native dialect of the speaker may also influence the pronunciation.

Syllables are divided into short and long. A short syllable consists of a consonant plus a short vowel (CV), whereas a long syllable consists of: (1) a consonant plus a long vowel ($C\bar{V}$), (2) a consonant plus a short vowel plus a consonant (CVC), or (3) a consonant plus a long vowel plus a consonant (C$\bar{V}$C). No syllable can start with more than one consonant.

1a) The stress falls on the first long syllable counting from the end of the word. However, the final syllable cannot itself carry the stress, except when the word has only one syllable, e.g. yak-tu-**bū**-na, **qal**-bun, ʾ**uq**-tu-lū, ka-**tab**-tum, ka-tab-**tun**-na, **mam**-la-ka-tun, **ḏū**. (The hyphens here indicate syllable not morpheme junctures.)

1b) Another tradition holds that if the first long syllable is the fourth syllable counting from the end or any syllable before that syllable, then the third syllable counting from the end receives the stress, e.g. mam-**la**-ka-tun.

2) If there is no long syllable or if only the last syllable is long, the first syllable receives the stress, e.g. **ka**-ta-ba, **qa**-ta-lū, **sa**-ma-ka-tun, **sa**-ma-ka-tu-hu-mā. According to another tradition, in these cases the stress cannot be retracted to an earlier position than the third syllable counting from the end. E.g. sa-**ma**-ka-tun, sa-ma-ka-**tu**-hu-mā.

3) The stress cannot normally fall on the definite article ʾ**al**- or a prefixed preposition or conjunction, e.g. ʾal-**ya**-du, ka-**ḏā**, wa-**ra**-mat.

Note: The final short vowel or final syllable of certain word endings to be dealt with later tend to be left out in pronunciation, especially in pausa (at the end of a sentence). Yet the given stress rules still apply in most cases, if you bear in mind that the final vowel or syllable has been lost. E.g. maf-**hūm**(-un), **mad**-ra-sa(-tun), **sa**-ma-ka(-tun), lub-**nā**-nī (lub-nā-**niy**-yun).

Exercises

Read and practise your handwriting:

	حُرُوفٌ	سَفِيرٍ	كَرِيمٌ	رَمَى	حِمَارًا
(1)	ḥurūfun	safīrin	karīmun	ramā	ḥimāran
	letters	ambassador	generous	to throw	donkey

	حَزِينٌ	تَاجِرٍ	وَاسِعًا	هٰذِهِ	حَالاً
(2)	ḥazīnun	tāǧirin	wāsiʿan	hāḏihi	ḥālan
	sad	merchant	wide	this (f.)	immediately
	حَيٌّ	لَمَّا	فِي	رَوَى	جَدِيدًا
(3)	ḥayyun	lammā	fī	rawā	ǧadīdan
	living	when	in	to tell	new
	رُوحٌ	صُوفًا	جَرَى	خَبَّازًا	هُنَاكَ
(4)	rūḥun	ṣūfan	ǧarā	ḫabbāzan	hunāka
	soul, spirit	wool	to run	baker	there
	قَانُونٌ	خَيَّاطًا	حَدَّادٍ	قَرِيبًا	بَنَى
(5)	qānūnun	ḫayyāṭan	ḥaddādin	qarīban	banā
	law	tailor	blacksmith	near	to build

Read, practise your handwriting and transliterate:

	مِصْرِيٌّ	حَمَّالاً	سَمِينٌ	زُجَاجٍ	سَحَابًا
(6)	Egyptian	porter	fat	glass	clouds
	طَرِيقٌ	سُوقٍ	سِكِّينٍ	بَكَى	دَجَاجًا
(7)	road	marketplace	knife	to cry	poultry
	دُرُوسٌ	عُصْفُورٍ	كِلاَبًا	زَيْتُونٌ	كَلاَمًا
(8)	lessons	bird	dogs	olives	talk
	ضُيُوفٌ	خِنْزِيرًا	فَلاَّحًا	يَابِسٌ	وَالِدٍ
(9)	guests	pig	peasant	dry	father
	رِيحٌ	سَعَى	جَاهِلٌ	عِلْمِيٌّ	غَزَالاً
(10)	wind	to strive	ignorant	scientific	gazelle
	وَزِيرٍ	غَرِيبًا	عَجُوزٍ	عَرَبِيٌّ	شَرَابٌ
(11)	minister	strange	old	Arab	drink
	ضَعِيفٌ	لَطِيفٍ	بِلاَدًا	مَشْهُورٌ	حَالاً
(12)	weak	kind, gentle	countries	famous	immediately

	حَلَالاً	عَادِلاً	دَنَا	نَزِيهٌ	نَبِيهٍ
(13)	permitted	just	to come near	honest	smart
	سَلَاماً	نَظِيفاً	كُرْسِيٌّ	لَحَّامٍ	مِيَاهاً
(14)	peace	clean	chair	butcher	waters
	سُورِيَّا	ذٰلِكَ	سِيَاسِيّاً	صُنْدُوقٌ	ذَابَ
(15)	Syria	that	politician	box	to melt

Write in Arabic:

Note: The words below all have the ordinary **ʾalif** (ا) and not the **ʾalif maqṣūrah** ى or the dagger **ʾalif** (ʼ). This is to avoid misunderstandings at this stage.

(16)	bārīsu Paris	sūriyyā Syria	ʿādilan just	hubūṭin lowering	ṣiyāmun fasting
(17)	bāšā pasha	wāğiban duty	ğāsūsan spy	ḏurūfun circumstances	ḫirrīğan graduate
(18)	baḫḫārun sailor	ṣawwānin flint	ḏalāmun darkness	mustašārin adviser	ʿabīdan slaves
(19)	baḫīlan stingy	suʿālan cough	muʿaddātun equipment	manqūšin engraved	nahā to forbid
(20)	ḫamran wine	muhāğirun emigrant	ṣiyāḥin shouting	hāğara to emigrate	ḍubbāṭun officers
(21)	zawğan husband	ʿāman year	minšārun saw	zayyātun oil-seller	nāṭūrun guard
(22)	badawiyyin Bedouin	taʿāwunin co-operation	ġadīrin pool	fawāriqu differences	ḫuršūfun artichoke
(23)	bāraza to duel	zāra to visit	ʿaḏīmun great	faransiyyun Frenchman	tazawwağa to marry
(24)	ʿirāqiyyun Iraqi	ḫazzānan reservoir	maḫṣūṣin special	zawāriqu boats	ḫarṭūšan bullets

Chapter 7

Hamzah (hamzatu l-qaṭʿi) and the maddah sign

7.1 **Hamzah** or **hamzatu l-qaṭʿi,** هَمْزَةُ ٱلْقَطْعِ, means the cutting or disjunctive **hamzah. Hamzah** is considered to represent the first letter of the alphabet and it has a full consonantal value like other consonants. (Arabic grammarians refer to ʾ**alif** as the ʾ**alif hamzah**.)

The sign of **hamzah** was added to the Arabic script at a rather late stage. Therefore **hamzah** does not have a real independent form comparable to the other consonant letters. **Hamzah** is written with the special sign ء, which is transliterated as /ʾ/.

7.2 The sound of **hamzah** exists in European languages in speech but is not represented in writing. In Arabic it is both heard and written. Phonetically it is a glottal stop, pronounced as a catch in the throat by holding one's breath and suddenly releasing it. This sound occurs as follows in some other languages:

In Cockney English 'little bottle' is pronounced as /liʾl boʾl/, i.e. with two glottal stops.

In German, **beobachten** 'to consider', is pronounced as /beʾobachten/. **Vereisen**, 'to freeze, be frozen', is pronounced as /ferʾaizen/, but the word **verreisen**, meaning 'to travel away' has no glottal stop. **Iss auch ein Ei!** 'Eat also an egg!', is pronounced as /ʾiss ʾauch ʾain ʾAi!/.

Note: **Hamzah** ء /ʾ/ should not be confused with the completely different letter ʿayn ع /ʿ/ in either pronunciation or transliteration.

7.3 **Hamzah** is used frequently, but the rules for writing it are quite complicated and are therefore dealt with in more detail in chapter 20.

7.4 Since **hamzah** does not have a regular independent form, it is mainly written on the letters أ, ؤ and ئ (without dots), and these three letters are called *seats* or *chairs* for the **hamzah**.

7.5 *Some basic rules for writing hamzah*

The initial glottal stop **hamzah** /ʾ/ is written above or below the letter **ʾalif** ا and is pronounced before the vowel, according to the following rules.

(a) **Hamzah** together with **fatḥah** are written above the **ʾalif**: أَ /ʾa/, e.g.

أَكْلٌ	أَصْلٌ	أَرْضٌ
ʾaklun, food	ʾaṣlun, origin	ʾarḍun, earth, ground

(b) **Hamzah** together with **ḍammah** are written above the **ʾalif**: أُ / ʾu/, e.g.

أُخْتٌ	أُمٌّ	أُفُقٌ
ʾuḫtun, sister	ʾummun, mother	ʾufuqun, horizon

(c) **Hamzah** together with **kasrah** are both written under the **ʾalif**: إِ /ʾi/, e.g.

إِصْبَعٌ	إِنَّ	إِذْ
ʾiṣbaʿun, finger	ʾinna, that, indeed	ʾiḏ, if, when

(d) **Hamzah** on **ʾalif** in the middle of the word, e.g.

سَأَلَ	رَأْيٌ	رَأْسٌ
saʾala, to ask	raʾyun, opinion	raʾsun, head

(e) **Hamzah** on **ʾalif** at the end of the word, e.g.

نَبَأٌ	قَرَأَ	بَدَأَ
nabaʾun, news	qaraʾa, to read	badaʾa, to start, to begin

7.6 *The maddah sign*

The **maddah** sign مَدَّةٌ is a long slanting or curved superscript line representing the ʾ**alif**, which is written above another ʾ**alif** to signify the lengthening of /ʾa/ as /ʾā/. It is used when an ʾ**alif** which has **hamzah** and **fatḥah** (أَ) is followed by another ʾ**alif** (أَا). The ʾ**alif**, **hamzah** and **fatḥah** are all omitted, and only one ʾ**alif** is written with the sign **maddah** above it as آ (for: أَا), which is pronounced as /ʾā/. This is to avoid having to write the ʾ**alif** twice, e.g.

أَلْقُرْآنُ (for: أَلْقُرْأَانُ)
ʾal-qurʾānu, the Quran

رَآهُ (for: رَأَاهُ)
raʾā-hu, he saw him/it

When an ʾ**alif** having **hamzah** and **fatḥah** أَ is followed by another ʾ**alif** with **hamzah** and **sukūn** (أْ), only one ʾ**alif** is written with **maddah** above it آ (for: أَأْ), which is also pronounced /ʾā/. In this way one avoids having to write two glottal stops in one syllable, e.g.

آمَنَ (for: أَأْمَنَ)
ʾāmana, to believe

آنَسَ (for: أَأْنَسَ)
ʾānasa, to be amused

Exercises

Read and practise your handwriting:

	ثَأْرٌ	إِمَامٌ	آخَرَ	أَخْبَارٌ	أُمَّهَاتٌ
(1)	ṯaʾrun	ʾimāmun	ʾāḫara	ʾaḫbārun	ʾummahātun
	revenge	prayer leader	another	news (pl.)	mothers
	أَنْتَ	مَبْدَأٌ	مَلْآنُ	أُذُنٌ	إِبْطٌ
(2)	ʾanta	mabdaʾun	malʾānu	ʾuḏunun	ʾibṭun
	you (m.)	principle	full	ear	armpit
	آبُ	إِنْتَاجٌ	آلَ	بَأْسًا	إِيجَارٌ
(3)	ʾābu	ʾintāǧun	ʾāla	baʾsan	ʾīǧārun
	August	production	to return	harm	rent

	إِبْلٌ	أَلَمٌ	إِمْشِ!	أَيْنَ	إِنْسَانٌ
(4)	ʾiblun	ʾalamun	ʾimši	ʾayna	ʾinsānun
	camels	pain	go!	where?	human being
	أَمِينٌ	إِثْمٌ	آبَادٌ	مُسْتَأْجِرٌ	إِبَّانَ
(5)	ʾamīnun	ʾiṯmun	ʾābādun	mustaʾǧirun	ʾibbāna
	faithful	sin	endless	renter	during
	إِبْدَاعٌ	أُورُوبِّيٌّ	أَكْبَرُ	أَجْنَبِيٌّ	أُسْبُوعٌ
(6)	ʾibdāʿun	ʾūrūbbiyyun	ʾakbaru	ʾaǧnabiyyun	ʾusbūʿun
	creation	European	bigger	foreigner	week
	مُتَأَسِّفٌ	أَسَرَ	أَمَّا	إِذْنٌ	فَأْرٌ
(7)	mutaʾassifun	ʾasara	ʾammā	ʾiḏnun	faʾrun
	sorry	to capture	but	permission	mouse
	إِيذَانٌ	أُنْبُوبٌ	زَأَرَ	أَلْمَانِيَا	إِرْثٌ
(8)	ʾīḏānun	ʾunbūbun	zaʾara	ʾalmāniyā	ʾirṯun
	proclamation	tube	to roar	Germany	heritage

Write in Arabic:

(9)	nabbaʾa to advise	taʾrīḫun dating	ʾabyaḍu white	ʾilzāmiyyun compulsory	malǧaʾun shelter
(10)	maḫbaʾun hiding place	ʾarǧaʾa to postpone	šaʾnun matter	ʾaṣarra to insist	ʾiḥmarra to turn red, blush
(11)	ʾarraḫa to date	ʾantum you (m.pl.)	ʾanā I	ʾislāmun Islam	wakaʾa to lean
(12)	ʾiʿlānun announcement	ṭaraʾa to happen	ʾābu August	ʾaʿraba to express	ʾazraqu blue
(13)	ʾiḍrābun strike	ʾaḫun brother	ʾibrīqun pot, jug	ʾabadan never	ʾufuqun horizon
(14)	ʾusṭūlun fleet	ʾilḥāḥun insistence	ʾarnabun rabbit	ʾimdādun help	ʾiǧbāriyyun compulsory

(15)	ʾayḍan also	ʾaswadu black	ʾusūdun lions	ʾīrānī Iranian	ʾustād̠un professor
(16)	ʾummiyyun illiterate	ʾaʿrağu lame	ʾaṣfaru yellow	ʾususun foundations	ʾaḥmaqu foolish
(17)	ʾiʿlāmun information	ʾaṣlaʿu bald	maʾmūrun official	mutaʾanniqun elegant	muttakiʾun leaning

Chapter 8

Definite article ...أَلْـ ʾal..., nominal sentences, verbal sentences, word order and adjectives

8.1 The definite article ...أَلْـ ʾal... is the only definite article in Arabic. It is used for all noun cases, genders and numbers by attaching it to the beginning of a noun or adjective. There is no indefinite article, but only an indefinite form, which has already been covered in chapter 5.

Note: Concerning writing **hamzah** over the ʾ**alif** (أ) in the definite article, see the final note in chapter 9.

8.2 When the indefinite form becomes definite, it loses its nunation /...n/, and only one vowel is written on or under the final consonant, e.g.

	Indefinite	***Definite***
Nominative:	بَيْتٌ bay**tun**, a house	أَلْبَيْتُ ʾal-bayt**u**, the house
Accusative:	بَيْتًا bayt**an**, a house	أَلْبَيْتَ ʾal-bayt**a**, the house
Genitive:	بَيْتٍ bayt**in**, of a house	أَلْبَيْتِ ʾal-bayt**i**, of the house

8.3 The basic functions of the three noun cases are as follows:

- The nominative case is used for the subject and predicate noun or adjective.
- The accusative case is used for the direct object, predicative complement in verbal sentences, and for most adverbs.

- The genitive case is used for expressing possession (explained in chapter 12) and after prepositions.

Note: Often the case endings are not pronounced, except for the indefinite accusative ending **-an** in adverbs, e.g. شُكْرًا šukran 'thank you!'.

8.4 The definite article أَلْـ... ᵓal... is used more frequently in Arabic than in English. One of the reasons for this is that nouns referring to abstract things, whole collectives and generic terms, generally take the definite article, e.g.

أَلْعِلْمُ ᵓal-ᶜilmu, science

أَلْكِلَابُ حَيَوَانَاتٌ ᵓal-kilābu ḥayawānātun. Dogs are animals.

8.5 *Nominal and verbal sentences*

There are two types of Arabic sentence: nominal sentences جُمْلَةٌ اِسْمِيَّةٌ ǧumlatun ismiyyatun, and verbal sentences جُمْلَةٌ فِعْلِيَّةٌ ǧumlatun fiᶜliyyatun.

8.6 A nominal sentence does not contain a verb and consists of two components: subject and predicate. The subject is usually a noun (phrase) or pronoun in the nominative case. The predicate may be a noun (phrase), pronoun, an indefinite adjective, or an adverb of place or time. A nominal sentence refers to the present tense and *does not require* the copula *to be*, e.g.

أَلْقِطُّ مَرِيضٌ ᵓal-qiṭṭu marīḍ**un**. The cat (is) ill.

أَنَا طَالِبٌ ᵓanā ṭālib**un**. I (am) a student.

أَلْوَلَدُ هُنَاكَ ᵓal-waladu hunāka. The boy (is) there.

هُمْ عُمَّالٌ hum ᶜummāl**un**. They (are) workers.

8.7 *Verbal sentence and word order*

A verbal sentence contains a verb, and has the following basic word order:

verb + subject + object or complement

The subject is normally in the nominative case. The direct object, which may occur only with transitive verbs, is in the accusative case.

خَرَجَ طَالِبٌ ḫaraǧa (verb) ṭālibun (subject).

A student went out.

أَكَلَ كَلْبٌ خُبْزًا ʾakala (verb) kalbun (subject) ḫubzan (object).

A dog ate bread.

Remember: If the subject or object is a personal pronoun, it is usually left out, because the verb is conjugated for the person, gender and number of the subject and pronominal object (see chapter 15).

8.8 *Adjectives*

An adjective normally follows the noun it qualifies and agrees with it in gender, number and case, except when the noun refers to non-humans, i.e. animals and things.

When the adjective functions as predicate in a nominal sentence (predicative construction), it is always indefinite, even when the subject is definite:

أَلْمَتْحَفُ جَمِيلٌ ʾal-matḥafu ǧamīlun. The museum (is) beautiful/nice.

أَلْبَيْتُ وَاسِعٌ ʾal-baytu wāsiʿun. The house (is) large.

When the adjective functions as a modifier of a noun (attributive construction), it also agrees with the head noun in terms of definiteness. In other words, if the head noun is definite, the adjective also takes the definite article, whereas if the head noun is indefinite, the adjective is also indefinite.

أَلْبَيْتُ ٱلْوَاسِعُ ʾal-baytu l-wāsiʿu, the large house

بَيْتٌ وَاسِعٌ baytun wāsiʿun, a large house OR A house is large.

Note a: The ʾ**alif** ا of the definite article in أَلْوَاسِعُ... ... l-wāsiʿu in the first of the two sentences above is elided in pronunciation after a vowel (discussed in chapter 9 dealing with **waṣlah**).

Note b: There is no formal difference between the predicative and attributive construction of an adjective when the head noun is indefinite (compare the translations of the second sentence in the above pair).

Note c: Again, when the combination of the letter ...ل /l/ followed by ʾ**alif** ا is written as لا, or ..ـلا /lā/, the same principle is applied as when ..ل /l/ is followed by ʾ**alif** with **hamzatu l-qaṭʿi** أ, i.e. لأ /l... ʾ/ (refer to chapter 6).

أَلْأُمُّ ʾal-ʾummu, the mother

أَلْأَمَلُ ʾal-ʾamalu, the hope

أَلْأَمِيرُ ʾal-ʾamīru, the commander, the prince

أَلْأُخْتُ ʾal-ʾuḫtu, the sister

Exercises

Practise your reading:

¹أَلْقَلَمُ ²طَوِيلٌ.

(1) ʾal-qalamu ṭawīlun.
¹The pen (is) ²long.

¹أَلْمَطْعَمُ ²وَاسِعٌ.

(2) ʾal-maṭʿamu wāsiʿun.
¹The restaurant (is) ²large.

أَنْتَ ¹طَالِبٌ ²عَاقِلٌ.

(3) ʾanta ṭālibun ʿāqilun.
You (m.) (are) ²a reasonable ¹student.

¹أَيْنَ هِيَ / هُوَ؟

(4) ʾayna hiya / huwa.
¹Where (is) she/he?

هِيَ [1]هُنَاكَ.

(5) hiya hunāka.
She (is) [1]there.

هُوَ كَاتِبٌ [1]مَشْهُورٌ.

(6) huwa kātibun mašhūrun.
He (is) [1]a famous writer.

[1]أَلْأَقَارِبُ فِي أَلْمَانْيَا.

(7) ʾal-ʾaqāribu fī ʾalmānyā.
[1]The relatives (are) in Germany.

هُوَ [1]طَبِيبٌ [2]شَاطِرٌ.

(8) huwa ṭabībun šāṭirun.
He (is) [2]a skilful [1]physician.

أَلْكَلْبُ [1]أَمِينٌ.

(9) ʾal-kalbu ʾamīnun.
The dog (is) [1]faithful.

أَلْأَكْلُ [1]طَيِّبٌ.

(10) ʾal-ʾaklu ṭayyibun.
The food (is) [1]delicious, good.

أَلْمُدِيرُ [1]مَكْرُوهٌ.

(11) ʾal-mudīru makrūhun.
The director (is) [1]hated.

[1]نَعَمْ، هُوَ [2]مَشْغُولٌ.

(12) naʿam, huwa mašġūlun.
[1]Yes, he (is) [2]busy.

[1]أَلْعُمْرُ [2]قَصِيرٌ.

(13) ʾal-ʿumru qaṣīrun.
[1](The) life (is) [2]short.

أَنَا [1]آسِفٌ.

(14) ʾanā ʾāsifun.
I (am)[1]sorry.

أَلْكَاتِبُ [1]مَحْبُوبٌ.

(15) ʾal-kātibu maḥbūbun.
The writer (is) [1]popular (beloved).

أَلأُسْتَاذُ [1]هُنَا.

(16) ʾal-ʾustāḏu hunā.
The professor (is) [1]here.

أَلْوَزِيرُ [1]مَرِيضٌ.

(17) ʾal-wazīru marīḍun.
The minister (is) [1]ill.

أَلْمَكْتَبُ [1]قَرِيبٌ.

(18) ʾal-maktabu qarībun.
The office (is) [1]nearby.

[1]أَلْمَطَارُ قَدِيمٌ.

(19) ʾal-maṭāru qadīmun.
[1]The airport (is) old.

[1]أَلْقَمِيصُ وَسِخٌ.

(20) ʾal-qamīṣu wasiḫun.
[1]The shirt (is) dirty.

أَلْفِنْجَانُ [1]نَظِيفٌ.

(21) ʾal-finğānu naḏīfun.
The cup (is) [1]clean.

[1]رَمَى تِلْمِيذٌ [2]قَلَماً [3]مَكْسُوراً.

(22) ramā tilmīḏun qalaman maksūran.
A pupil [1]threw (away) [3]a broken [2]pen.

[1]شَهْرٌ [2]حَارٌّ.

(23) šahrun ḥārrun
[2]a hot [1]month

[1]أَتَى طَالِبٌ [2]جَدِيدٌ.

(24) ʾatā ṭālibun ğadīdun.
[2]A new student [1]has come.

article,
nominal
and verbal
sentences,
adjectives

هٰذَا ¹أَمْرٌ ²صَعْبٌ.

(25) hāḏā ʾamrun ṣaʿbun.

This (is) ²a difficult ¹matter.

¹أَلْمَطَارُ بَعِيدٌ.

(26) ʾal-maṭāru baʿīdun.

¹The airport (is) far away.

هٰذَا ¹مَسْمُوحٌ ²لٰكِنْ ذٰلِكَ ³مَمْنُوعٌ.

(27) hāḏā masmūḥun lākin ḏālika mamnūʿun.

This (is) ¹allowed ²but that (is) ³forbidden/prohibited.

شَرِبَ ¹طِفْلٌ ²حَلِيبًا ³بَارِدًا.

(28) šariba ṭiflun ḥalīban bāridan.

¹A child drank ³cold ²milk.

¹بَنَى ²مُهَنْدِسٌ ³جِسْرًا جَمِيلاً.

(29) banā muhandisun ǧisran ǧamīlan.

²An engineer ¹built a beautiful ³bridge.

¹زَارَ طَبِيبٌ ²شَخْصًا ³مَرِيضًا.

(30) zāra ṭabībun šaḫṣan marīḍan.

A physician ¹visited a ³sick ²person (patient).

¹نَشَرَ ²صِحَافِيٌّ ³مَقَالاً طَوِيلاً.

(31) našara ṣiḥāfiyyun maqālan ṭawīlan.

²A journalist ¹published a long ³article.

أَنَا مِنْ سُورِيَّا.

(32) ʾanā min sūriyyā.

I (am) from Syria.

أَلْأَنْدَلُسُ فِي إِسْبَانْيَا.

(33) ʾal-ʾandalusu fī ʾisbānyā.

Andalusia (is) in Spain.

Translate into Arabic:

As mentioned in the Preface, the words used in the English exercises in all chapters are taken from the Arabic exercises of the same chapter.

(1) The airport (is) dirty.
(2) He (is) a busy engineer.
(3) He (is) popular.
(4) The director (is) busy.
(5) Yes, he (is) short.
(6) (The) life (is) long.
(7) This (is) forbidden.
(8) The shirt (is) beautiful.
(9) A new month
(10) The airport (is) nearby.
(11) This (is) allowed.
(12) The restaurant (is) famous.
(13) The relatives (are) in Syria.
(14) The food (is) here.
(15) The pen (is) there.
(16) Where (am) I?
(17) The professor (is) sorry.
(18) The journalist (is) busy.
(19) The dog (is) ill.
(20) The shirt (is) clean.
(21) The minister (is) from Syria.
(22) The office (is) old.
(23) He (is) new.

Chapter 9

Sun and moon letters, hamzatu l-waṣli (waṣlah)

9.1 Sun and moon letters

The Arabic consonants are phonetically divided into two major classes called:

sun letters, حُرُوفٌ شَمْسِيَّةٌ ḥurūfun šamsiyyatun, assimilating

moon letters, حُرُوفٌ قَمَرِيَّةٌ ḥurūfun qamariyyatun, non-assimilating

9.2 Sun letters

The sun letters have received their name from the Arabic word for 'sun', شَمْسٌ šamsun, whose first letter, ...شـ /š/, belongs to the class of assimilating letters.

There are fourteen sun letters. These letters are pronounced with the tongue touching the teeth or front part of the mouth:

ش	س	ز	ر	ذ	د	ث	ت	ن	ل	ظ	ط	ض	ص
š	s	z	r	ḏ	d	ṯ	t	n	l	ḏ̣	ṭ	ḍ	ṣ

9.3 When the definite article ...أَلْـ /ʾal.../ is attached to a word which begins with a sun letter, the sound ...لـ /l/ of the definite article is assimilated to the sound of the following sun letter. Although the ...لـ /l/ is not pronounced, it is written as such (without a **sukūn**), but in the transliteration it is omitted. Owing to the assimilation, the first consonant of the word is doubled, which is indicated by a **šaddah** ـّـ above it.

شَمْسٌ šamsun, a sun	أَلشَّمْسُ ʾaš-šamsu, the sun	(not: أَلْشَمْسُ ʾal-šamsu)
رَجُلٌ rağulun, a man	أَلرَّجُلُ ʾar-rağulu, the man	(not: أَلْرَجُلُ ʾal-rağulu)

9.4 *Moon letters*

The other fourteen letters are called moon letters, because the first letter, **قـ...** /q/, of the Arabic word for 'moon', **قَمَرٌ** **qamarun**, represents the class of non-assimilating letters:

ي	و	هـ	م	ك	ق	ف	غ	ع	خ	ح	ج	ب	أ
y	w	h	m	k	q	f	ġ	ʿ	ḫ	ḥ	ğ	b	ʾ

9.5 When the definite article **أَلْ...** /ʾal.../ is attached to a word beginning with a moon letter, the **lām** **...لـ** /l.../ of the article is not assimilated and retains its pronunciation, e.g.

قَمَرٌ qamarun, a moon	أَلْقَمَرُ ʾal-qamaru, the moon
كِتَابٌ kitābun, a book	أَلْكِتَابُ ʾal-kitābu, the book

Note: The letters ج /ğ/ and ي /y/ are counted as moon letters (non-assimilating), although they are pronounced with the tongue touching the front part of the mouth, e.g.

أَلْجَبَلُ ʾal-ğabalu, the mountain

9.6 *Hamzatu l-waṣli* (or *waṣlah*)

Hamzatu l-waṣli, **هَمْزَةُ ٱلْوَصْلِ**, also called **waṣlah,** **وَصْلَة**, means 'joining hamzah'. It is a small sign written above the **ʾalif** (ٱ), which is not pronounced and appears only at the beginning of a word.

The role of **hamzatu l-waṣli** (**waṣlah**) is to connect two words together in one pronunciation without an intervening glottal stop (**hamzatu l-qaṭʿi**). It may be compared to the French apostrophe in *l'homme* (instead of *le homme*).

9.7 When the article ...أَلْـ /ʾal.../ and the nouns in the table below, as well as certain verb forms (see chapter 18) with an initial **hamzatu l-qaṭʿi** such as أَ /ʾa/ and إِ /ʾi/, are preceded by another word or prefix, they lose their initial **hamzatu l-qaṭʿi** with its vowel. Instead the sign of **hamzatu l-waṣli (waṣlah)** ٱ is written in their place over the ʾ**alif**, as ٱ, e.g.

بَابُ ٱلْبَيْتِ	(not: بَابُ أَلْبَيْتِ
bābu **l**-bayti	bābu ʾal-bayti)
the door of the house	
شَرِبَ ٱلطِّفْلُ حَلِيبًا	(not: ... شَرِبَ أَلطِّفْلُ
šariba **ṭ-ṭ**iflu ḥalīban.	šariba ʾaṭ-ṭiflu ...)
The child drank milk.	

Note a: The above-mentioned word بَابُ /bābu/ does not take the definite article, according to a rule explained in chapter 12.

Note b: In the above word ..ٱلطِّفْلُ /..ṭ-ṭiflu/ (not: أَلْطِفْل– ʾal-ṭiflu) the definite article is not pronounced as such at all, because there is a **waṣlah** above the ʾ**alif** and the initial /ṭ/ is a sun letter.

Words with initial **hamzatu l-qaṭʿi** (إِ):

إِبْنٌ	إِمْرُؤٌ	إِمْرَأَةٌ	إِبْنَةٌ
ʾibnun	imruʾun	ʾimraʾatun	ʾibnatun
son	man	woman	daughter
إِثْنَانِ	إِثْنَتَانِ	إِسْمٌ	إِسْتٌ
ʾiṯnāni	ʾiṯnatāni	ʾismun	ʾistun
two (m.)	two (f.)	name	buttocks

Example:

هٰذَا ٱبْنُ ٱلْمَلِكِ	(not: . . . هٰذَا إِبْنُ
hāḏā bnu l-maliki	hāḏā ʾibnu . . .)
This is the son of the king.	

Note: The purist grammarians would be alarmed to see the definite article ...أَلْـ ʾal..., and other words mentioned in the table presented above, written with

hamzatu l-qaṭʿi. Grammarians recommend that only the **ʾalif** be written with a vowel over or under it and without **hamzatu l-qaṭʿi**, although it is fully pronounced at the beginning of a sentence or in isolation. However, most school textbooks throughout the Arab world do write **hamzatu l-qaṭʿi** initially over or under the **ʾalif** (أ , إ). In keeping with the principle of the phonetic rather than historical-etymological way of spelling, the **hamzatu l-qaṭʿi** initially over or under the **ʾalif** will be used in this book also.

Exercises

Practise your reading:

[1]فَهِمَ ٱلطَّالِبُ [2]ٱلدَّرْسَ.

(1) fahima ṭ-ṭālibu d-darsa.
The student [1]understood [2]the lesson.

قَرَأَ ٱلْإِمَامُ ٱلْقُرْآنَ.

(2) qaraʾa l-ʾimāmu l-qurʾāna.
The imam read the Quran.

[1]أَلطَّبِيبُ فِي ٱلْمُسْتَشْفَى.

(3) ʾaṭ-ṭabību fī l-mustašfā.
[1]The physician (is) at the hospital.

[1]كَسَرَ ٱلطَّالِبُ [2]ٱلْقَلَمَ.

(4) kasara ṭ-ṭālibu l-qalama.
The student [1]broke [2]the pen.

[1]شَرَحَ ٱلْأُسْتَاذُ [2]ٱلدَّرْسَ.

(5) šaraḥa l-ʾustāḏu d-darsa
The professor [1]explained [2]the lesson.

[1]رَسَمَ [2]ٱلْمُهَنْدِسُ [3]جِسْرًا [4]طَوِيلًا.

(6) rasama l-muhandisu ğisran ṭawīlan.
[2]The engineer [1]drew [4]a long [3]bridge.

[1]أَللَّوْحُ [2]ٱلْأَسْوَدُ قَدِيمٌ.

(7) ʾal-lawḥu l-ʾaswadu qadīmun.
[2]The black [1]board (is) old.

[1] أَلْاِبْنُ مَرِيضٌ.

(8) ʾal-ibnu marīḍun.
[1]The son (is) ill.

[1] أَلْفُنْدُقُ [2] ٱلْجَدِيدُ جَمِيلٌ.

(9) ʾal-funduqu l-ǧadīdu ǧamīlun.
[2]The new [1]hotel (is) beautiful.

[1] أَلْمَطْعَمُ ٱلصَّغِيرُ [2] قَدِيمٌ.

(10) ʾal-maṭʿamu ṣ-ṣaġīru qadīmun.
The small [1]restaurant (is) [2]old.

[1] أَلشَّارِعُ ٱلْقَدِيمُ [2] مُزْدَحِمٌ.

(11) ʾaš-šāriʿu l-qadīmu muzdaḥimun.
The old [1]street (is) [2]crowded.

[1] أَكَلَ ٱلْوَلَدُ [2] ٱلطَّعَامَ.

(12) ʾakala l-waladu ṭ-ṭaʿāma.
The boy [1]ate [2]the food.

[1] بَنَى [2] ٱلْعُمَّالُ ٱلْمَصْنَعَ.

(13) banā l-ʿummālu l-maṣnaʿa.
[2]The workers [1]built the factory.

[1] قَرَأَ ٱلطَّالِبُ [2] ٱلدَّرْسَ ٱلْجَدِيدَ.

(14) qaraʾa ṭ-ṭālibu d-darsa l-ǧadīda.
The student [1]read the new [2]lesson.

[1] كَتَبَ ٱلْأُسْتَاذُ [2] ٱلِاسْمَ.

(15) kataba l-ʾustāḏu l-isma.
The professor [1]wrote [2]the name.

[1] إِشْتَرَى [2] ٱلْوَزِيرُ ٱلْقَصْرَ.

(16) ʾištarā l-wazīru l-qaṣra.
[2]The minister [1]bought the palace.

[1] قَرَأَ [2] ٱلْمُوَظَّفُ ٱسْمًا [3] طَوِيلاً.

(17) qaraʾa l-muwaḏḏafu sman ṭawīlan.
[2]The employee [1]read [3]a long name.

[1]إِشْتَرَى ٱلْأَبُ [2]ٱللَّحْمَ.

(18) ʾištarā l-ʾabu l-laḥma.
The father [1]bought [2]the meat.

[1]صَعِدَ ٱلْمُسَافِرُ [2]ٱلْجَبَلَ.

(19) ṣaʿida l-musāfiru l-ğabala.
The traveller [1]climbed [2]the mountain.

دَخَلَ [1]ٱلزَّبُونُ [2]ٱلْمَطْعَمَ [3]ثُمَّ [4]طَلَبَ [5]ٱلْأَكْلَ.

(20) daḫala z-zabūnu l-maṭʿama ṯumma ṭalaba l-ʾakla.
[1]The customer entered [2]the restaurant, [3]then [4]he ordered [5]the food.

شَرِبَ [1]ٱلْمُسَافِرُ [2]شَايًا.

(21) šariba l-musāfiru šāyan.
[1]The traveller drank (some) [2]tea.

[1]نَامَ ٱلرَّجُلُ [2]ٱلْمَرِيضُ.

(22) nāma r-rağulu l-marīḍu.
The [2]sick man [1]slept.

أَلِابْنُ [1]ذَكِيٌّ.

(23) ʾal-ibnu ḏakiyyun.
The son is [1]intelligent.

Translate into Arabic:

(1) The pen (is) beautiful.

(2) The old restaurant (is) crowded.

(3) The workers ate the meat.

(4) The sick man entered the restaurant.

(5) The engineer built the palace.

(6) The student read the Quran.

(7) The engineer climbed the mountain.

(8) The employee (is) at the hospital.

(9) The workers entered the palace.

(10) The father read the Quran.

(11) The bridge (is) old.

(12) The sick traveller slept.

(13) The student wrote the name.

(14) The new customer slept.

(15) The new professor is intelligent.

(16) The student (is) ill.

Chapter 10

Gender

10.1 There are two genders in Arabic. The term used for gender is أَلْجِنْسُ ʾal-ǧinsu, which literally means 'sex, race, kind'.

(a) Masculine nouns, أَلْمُذَكَّرُ ʾal-mudakkaru, are without special form.

(b) Feminine nouns, أَلْمُؤَنَّثُ ʾal-muʾannaṯu, have several forms as explained below.

10.2 *Tāʾ marbūṭah*

When the letter **hāʾ** ه... ـه... /h/ (26) is written with two dots above (ة... ـة...), it is pronounced as /t/, exactly like the letter ت /t/ (3). It is then called **tāʾ marbūṭah** and occurs only at the end of a word, mostly to indicate the feminine gender of nouns or adjectives.

The most common way to derive feminine nouns and adjectives is by adding the ending ـَةٌ... ـَةٌ... /...atun/ to the masculine form, e.g.

Masculine	***Feminine***
هُوَ طَالِبٌ huwa ṭālib**un**.	هِيَ طَالِبَةٌ hiya ṭālib**atun**.
He is a student.	She is a student.
هُوَ وَالِدٌ huwa wālid**un**.	هِيَ وَالِدَةٌ hiya wālid**atun**.
He is a father.	She is a mother.

Note a: A few nouns with the feminine ending **tāʾ marbūṭah** are masculine, because they are used only in reference to males, e.g.

خَلِيفَةٌ ḫalīf**atun** Caliph | عَلَّامَةٌ ʿallām**atun** learned man | رَحَّالَةٌ raḥḥāl**atun** an explorer, traveller

Note b: Nouns ending in **tāʾ marbūṭah** ـَةٌ ... ـَةٌ ... /...atun/ do not take the extra final **ʾalif** ـا... in the indefinite accusative form. So the correct form is طَالِبَةً ṭālib**atan** (not: طَالِبَتًا).

Note c: At the end of a sentence the final vowel of a word is normally *not* pronounced. Even **tāʾ marbūṭah** is usually left unpronounced at the end of a sentence, as in طَالِبَةٌ /ṭāliba(**h**)/ for /ṭālib**atun**/ (cf. chapter 4).

10.3 Most parts or organs of the body which occur in pairs are feminine, e.g.

يَدٌ yadun, hand | عَيْنٌ ʿaynun, eye | رِجْلٌ riǧlun, foot, leg

10.4 There are words which are feminine by nature, e.g.

أُمٌّ ʾummun, mother | عَرُوسٌ ʿarūsun, bride | حَامِلٌ ḥāmilun pregnant

10.5 Most geographical proper names, i.e. names of countries, cities, towns, villages, etc. are treated as feminine. They are so-called diptotes, i.e. have only two case endings and no nunation (to be explained in chapter 22), e.g.

تُونِسُ tūnisu, Tunisia | دِمَشْقُ dimašqu, Damascus | بَارِيسُ bārīsu Paris

10.6 A few nouns are feminine by usage, e.g.

حَرْبٌ ḥarbun, war | أَرْضٌ ʾarḍun, earth, ground | شَمْسٌ šamsun sun

10.7 There are a number of words, which can be either masculine or feminine, e.g.

سُوقٌ sūqun, market | حَالٌ ḥālun, condition | سِكِّينٌ sikkīnun knife

10.8 There are also two other feminine endings. They form **diptotes** like the words in paragraph 10.5:

(a) **fatḥah + ʾalif + hamzah** (ـَاءُ... ...**āʾu**), e.g.

Feminine	***Masculine***
حَمْقَاءُ ḥamq**ā**ʾ**u**, stupid	أَحْمَقُ ʾaḥmaqu
حَمْرَاءُ ḥamr**ā**ʾ**u**, red	أَحْمَرُ ʾaḥmaru

Note: See the discussion of the independent **hamzah** after **ʾalif** in chapter 20.

(b) **fatḥah + ʾalif maqṣūrah** (ـَى... ...ā), e.g.

Feminine	***Masculine***
عَطْشَى ʿaṭšā, thirsty	عَطْشَانُ ʿaṭšānu
كُبْرَى kubrā, bigger	أَكْبَرُ ʾakbaru

Note: If a word ends in **sukūn** and is followed by another word beginning with **hamzatu al-waṣli** (**waṣlah**), the **sukūn** is changed to **kasrah**. This is to avoid three consonants occurring after each other. For example, the verb وَقَعَتْ /waqaʿat/ in number 1 in the exercise below is changed to وَقَعَتِ ٱلْـ... /waqaʿati l-.../.

Exercises

Practise your reading:

¹وَقَعَتِ ٱلْمَرْأَةُ ²ٱلْمَرِيضَةُ.

(1) waqaʿati l-marʾatu l-marīḍatu.
²The sick woman ¹fell over.

¹هَدَمَ ²ٱلْعَامِلُ ٱلسُّوقَ ³ٱلْقَدِيمَةَ / ³ٱلْقَدِيمَ.

(2) hadama l-ʿāmilu s-sūqa l-qadīmata / l-qadīma.
²The worker ¹pulled down ³the old market (m. or f.).

¹إِشْتَرَى ٱلْأَبُ ²دَجَاجَةً ³سَمِينَةً.

(3) ʾištarā l-ʾabu daǧāǧatan samīnatan.
The father ¹bought ³a fat ²chicken.

¹دَخَلَتْ ²كَلْبَةٌ ³بِنَايَةً ⁴وَاسِعَةً.

(4) daḫalat kalbatun bināyatan wāsiʿatan.
²A dog (f.) ¹entered ⁴a big ³building.

[1]أَعْطَتِ ٱلْمُمَرِّضَةُ [2]ٱلْمَرِيضَ [3]حَبَّةً [4]مُنَوِّمَةً.

(5) ʾaʿṭati l-mumarriḍatu l-marīḍa ḥabbatan munawwimatan.
The nurse [1]gave [2]the patient [4]a sleeping [3]pill.

[1]أَحَبَّ [2]ٱلْمُسَافِرُ ٱلْقَرْيَةَ.

(6) ʾaḥabba l-musāfiru l-qaryata.
[2]The traveller [1]liked the village.

[1]رَكِبَ ٱلْمُدِيرُ [2]سَيَّارَةً [3]خَاصَّةً.

(7) rakiba l-mudīru sayyāratan ḫāṣṣatan.
The director [1]rode (in) [3]a private [2]car.

[1]مَاتَتِ ٱلْأَمِيرَةُ [2]ٱلْمَرِيضَةُ.

(8) mātati l-ʾamīratu l-marīḍatu.
[2]The sick princess [1]died.

[1]وَقَعَتْ [2]صَخْرَةٌ كَبِيرَةٌ.

(9) waqaʿat ṣaḫratun kabīratun.
A big [2]rock [1]fell down.

[1]كَسَرَ ٱلْعَامِلُ [2]ٱلرِّجْلَ [3]ٱلْيُسْرَى.

(10) kasara l-ʿāmilu r-riǧla l-yusrā.
The worker [1]broke his ([3]the) left [2]leg.

[1]جَرَحَ [2]ٱلْخَيَّاطُ [3]ٱلْيَدَ [4]ٱلْيُمْنَى.

(11) ǧaraḥa l-ḫayyāṭu l-yada l-yumnā.
[2]The tailor [1]wounded his (the) [4]right [3]hand.

[1]أَطْفَأَ [2]ٱلطَّبَّاخُ [3]ٱلنَّارَ [4]ٱلْقَوِيَّةَ.

(12) ʾaṭfaʾa ṭ-ṭabbāḫu n-nāra l-qawiyyata.
[2]The cook [1]put out [4]the fierce (strong) [3]fire.

[1]أَلرَّحَّالَةُ عَطْشَانُ.

(13) ʾar-raḥḥālatu ʿaṭšānu.
[1]The explorer is thirsty.

أَلْخَلِيفَةُ [1]ٱلْمَرِيضُ فِي ٱلْمُسْتَشْفَى.

(14) ʾal-ḫalīfatu l-marīḍu fī l-mustašfā.
[1]The sick caliph is in the hospital.

أَلْمَرْأَةُ [1]ٱلْحَامِلُ [2]تَعْبَانَةٌ.

(15) ʾal-marʾatu l-ḥāmilu taʿbānatun.
[1]The pregnant woman is [2]tired.

بَغْدَادُ مَدِينَةٌ [1]قَدِيمَةٌ.

(16) baġdādu madīnatun qadīmatun.
Baghdad is [1]an old (ancient) city.

أَلشَّمْسُ [1]طَالِعَةٌ.

(17) ʾaš-šamsu ṭāliʿatun.
The sun [1]is rising.

[1]رِيحٌ شَدِيدَةٌ.

(18) rīḥun šadīdatun
a strong [1]wind

[1]أَلْعَرُوسُ [2]ٱلْجَالِسَةُ جَمِيلَةٌ.

(19) ʾal-ʿarūsu l-ǧālisatu ǧamīlatun.
[2]The sitting [1]bride is beautiful.

[1]أَلْعَرِيسُ [2]ٱلْوَاقِفُ [3]قَبِيحٌ.

(20) ʾal-ʿarīsu l-wāqifu qabīḥun.
[1]The bridegroom [2]standing up is [3]ugly.

[1]نَشَرَ [2]ٱلصِّحَافِيُّ [3]مَقَالَةً طَوِيلَةً.

(21) našara ṣ-ṣiḥāfiyyu maqālatan ṭawīlatan.
[2]The journalist [1]published a long [3]article.

[1]نَسِيَ [2]ٱلنَّاسُ [3]ٱلْحَرْبَ [4]ٱلعَالَمِيَّةَ ٱلْأُولَى وَٱلثَّانِيَةَ.

(22) nasiya n-nāsu l-ḥarba (f.) l-ʿālamiyyata l-ʾūlā wa-ṯ-ṯāniyata.
[2]The people [1]have forgotten the First and Second [4]World [3]Wars.

Translate into Arabic:

(1) The sick dog (f.) is thirsty.
(2) The father liked the old market.
(3) The sick cook (f.) died.
(4) The pregnant woman is in the hospital.
(5) The sick explorer is thirsty.
(6) The sitting bride is tired.
(7) The Caliph pulled down the old city.
(8) The father bought a big car.
(9) The engineer published an ugly article.
(10) The director liked the nurse.
(11) The tailor put out the strong fire.
(12) The worker wounded his (the) left hand.
(13) The cook broke his (the) right leg.
(14) The journalist has forgotten the First World War.

Chapter 11

Conjunctions, prepositions and the particle حَتَّى ḥattā

11.1 Some conjunctions and prepositions consist of only one consonant with a short vowel. They are joined to the following word.

11.2 Conjunctions حُرُوفُ ٱلْعَطْفِ ḥurūfu l-ʿaṭfi

The three conjunctions وَ wa, فَـ... fa and ثُمَّ ṯumma are the most commonly used coordinative conjunctions.

11.3 The conjunction وَ 'and' should be joined to the following word and repeated before every member (constituent) of a series of linked words, e.g.

[1]خَرَجَ ٱلْمُدِيرُ وَٱلْأُسْتَاذُ وَطَالِبٌ [2]مَعًا

ḫaraǧa l-mudīru **wa**-l-ʾustāḏu **wa**-ṭālibun **maʿan**.

The rector and the professor and a student [1]went out [2]together.

[1]أَكَلَ [2]ٱلزَّبُونُ [3]خُبْزًا [4]وَزُبْدَةً [5]وَجُبْنَةً [6]وَبَيْضًا

ʾakala z-zabūnu ḫubzan **wa**-zubdatan **wa**-ǧubnatan **wa**-bayḍan.

[2]The customer [1]ate [3]bread [4]and butter [5]and cheese [6]and eggs.

Note: In English it is customary to add the conjunction 'and' only before the last member of a series of coordinated words.

11.4 The conjunction فَـ... 'then, and then' is joined to the word which follows it. It indicates an order or succession between actions or states, e.g.

¹خَرَجَ ²اَلْمُدِيرُ فَٱلْأُسْتَاذُ فَطَالِبٌ

ḫarağa l-mudīru **fa**-lʾustādu **fa-**ṭālibun.

²The rector ¹went out **and then** the professor **and then** a student.

فَـ... is also used with a causal sense between two or more verbs or sentences. It can then be translated into English as 'so, therefore', e.g.

¹تَعِبَ ٱلطِّفْلُ ²فَنَامَ

taʿiba ṭ-ṭiflu **fa**-nāma. The child ¹became tired ²**and so** he slept.
OR The tiredness caused the child to sleep.

¹وَقَعَ فِي ٱلنَّهْرِ ²فَغَرِقَ

waqaʿa fī n-nahri **fa-**ġariqa.

¹He fell in the river ²**and so** he drowned.

11.5 ثُمَّ 'then, and', indicates succession with a break in time between the actions, e.g.

¹خَرَجَ ٱلْوَزِيرُ ²ثُمَّ ³ٱلسَّفِيرُ ثُمَّ ٱلشُّرْطِيُّ

ḫarağa l-wazīru **ṯumma** s-safīru **ṯumma** š-šurṭiyyu.

The minister ¹went out, ²**then** ³the ambassador **and then** the policeman.

Note: أَوْ ʾaw, 'or' is used as a disjunctive conjunction. There is also the expression: إِمَّا ʾimmā ... أَوْ ʾaw ... 'either ... or ...', e.g.

إِمَّا أَنَا أَوْ أَنْتَ

ʾimmā ʾanā ʾaw ʾantā
either me or you

11.6 حَتَّى ḥattā is a particle with many meanings and functions. In the meaning 'even', it is considered by Arab grammarians to be a conjunction, because in this function it can connect a clause or phrase with a following apposition. Modern Western linguists would, however, classify it then as a focus particle (or more generally, additive adjunct). When حَتَّى has this function, the following noun remains in the same case as the preceding one, e.g.

After a transitive verb:

أَكَلَ ٱلسَّمَكَةَ حَتَّى ٱلرَّأْسَ

ʾakala s-samakata ḥattā r-raʾsa.

He ate the fish, **even** the head.

After an intransitive verb:

مَاتَ ٱلنَّاسُ حَتَّى ٱلْمُلُوكُ.

māta n-nāsu **ḥattā** l-mulūku.

The people died, **even** the kings.

11.7 Prepositions حُرُوفُ ٱلْجَرِّ *ḥurūfu l-ğarri*

The Arabic prepositions can be formally divided into two basic groups: primary and secondary. The primary prepositions can moreover be divided into two subgroups: independent and bound (prefixed).

The noun governed by the preposition always follows it and is in the genitive case. If the preposition governs an adverb, the latter does not, of course, change its form.

As in many other languages, the Arabic prepositions have several different meanings. The primary prepositions with their basic meanings are:

مِنْ	إِلَى	عَنْ	عَلَى	فِي	مَعَ
min	ʾilā	ʿan	ʿalā	fī	maʿa
from, of, than	to, until	from, about	on, over, at	in, at	with
حَتَّى	مُنْذُ	...لِـ (...لَـ)	...بِـ	...كَـ	
ḥattā	munḏu	li... (la...)	bi...	ka...	
until, till, to, up to	since, ago, from	for, to because of	by, with, in	as, like	

Note a: The bound (prefixed) prepositions are: ...لِـ (...لَـ), ...بِـ and ...كَـ. They are written together with the following word.

Note b: When the prepositions مِنْ min 'from', and عَنْ ʿan, 'about', are followed by a word having an initial ʾalif with **hamzatu l-waṣli** (**waṣlah**), the **sukūn** is changed to **fatḥah** or **kasrah**, in order to avoid having three consonants following each other, thus smoothing the pronunciation, e.g.

مِنَ ٱلْمُدِيرِ	عَنِ ٱلْحَرْبِ
mina l-mudīri, from the director	ʿani l-ḥarbi, about the war

Note c: In certain idioms words such as those below with a suffixed personal pronoun have the preposition ...بِـ bi..., e.g.

بِأَجْمَعِهِمْ	بِأَسْرِهِمْ
bi-ʾağmaʿi-him, all together	**bi**-ʾasri-him, all together
أَلنَّاسُ بِأَجْمَعِهِمْ	أَلنَّاسُ بِأَسْرِهِمْ
ʾan-nāsu **bi**-ʾağmaʿi-**him**, all of the people	ʾan-nāsu **bi**-ʾasri-**him**, all of the people

(See more about ..بِـ bi... in chapter 37.)

Examples:

1 ذَهَبَ بِٱلسَّيَّارَةِ إِلَى 2 ٱلْمَسْبَحِ 3 مَعَ 4 صَدِيقٍ 5 لِي

ḏahaba bi-s-sayyārati ʾilā l-masbaḥi maʿa ṣadīqin l-ī.

[1]He went by car to [2]the swimming pool [3]with [4]a friend [5]of [5]mine.

(لِي l-ī is a combination of ...لِـ li... and ...ي ...ī, 'mine', see chapter 15.)

1 مَاتَ ٱلسَّفِيرُ فِي 2 ٱلْعَاصِمَةِ 3 مُنْذُ 4 شَهْرٍ

māta s-safīru **fī** l-ʿāṣimati **mundu** šahrin.

[4]One month [3]**ago** the ambassador [1]died **in** [2]the capital (city).

11.8 حَتَّى *ḥattā as a preposition*

When حَتَّى functions as a preposition with the meaning 'until, till, up to, as far as', the following noun *must* be in the genitive, e.g.

أَكَلَ 1 ٱلسَّمَكَةَ حَتَّى ٱلرَّأْسِ

ʾakala s-samakata ḥattā r-raʾs**i**. (*genitive*)

He ate [1]the fish as far as (i.e. except) the head.

Note: Because of the many uses of حَتَّى, the father of Arabic grammar, سِيبَوَيْهِ **Sībawayhi**, made the following immortal statement:

"أَمُوتُ وَفِي نَفْسِي شَيْءٌ مِنْ حَتَّى"

ʾamūtu wa-fī nafsī šayʾun min ḥattā

I shall die and still have some ḥattā left in my soul.

11.9 The secondary prepositions are formed from (verbal) nouns by means of the accusative ending -a. The following are the most common of them:

أَمَامَ	بَعْدَ	بَيْنَ	تَحْتَ	فَوْقَ
ʾamāma	baʿda	bayna	taḥta	fawqa
in front of	after	between, among	under	above, over
حَوْلَ	دُونَ	بِدُونِ	ضِدَّ	عِنْدَ
ḥawla	dūna	bi-dūni	ḍidda	ʿinda
around, about	without, under	without	against	by, with
قَبْلَ	قُدَّامَ	لَدَى	نَحْوَ	وَرَاءَ
qabla	quddāma	ladā	naḥwa	warāʾa
before	before, in front of	with, at, by	towards, approximately	behind

Examples:

قَبْلَ ٱلظُّهْرِ **qabla** ḏ-ḏuhri, before noon

بَعْدَ ٱلظُّهْرِ **baʿda** ḏ-ḏuhri, in the afternoon

Note: The above دُونَ dūna and بِدُونِ bi-dūni have the same function and may replace each other, e.g.

بَقِيَ[1] أُسْبُوعًا[2] دُونَ[3] / بِدُونِ[3] أَكْلٍ[4]

baqiya ʾusbūʿan dūna / bi-dūni ʾaklin.

[1]He stayed [3]without [4]food for [2]one week. (i.e. He didn't eat for a week.)

11.10 *Preposition used in the sense of 'to have'*

Arabic has no verb comparable to the English verb 'to have'. However, the same sense of owning or possessing can be expressed in nominal sentences by using any of the four prepositions مَعَ maʿa, عِنْدَ ʿinda, لَدَى ladā or ...لِـ (...لَـ) li... (la...) after the noun expressing the owner. The thing owned is expressed in the nominative case as the nominal predicate. The differences in the use of these prepositions often depend on nuances.

(a) The preposition مَعَ is more frequently used when referring to available possession at a given time, e.g.

مَعَ ٱلطَّالِبِ سَيَّارَةٌ maʿa ṭ-ṭālibi sayyāratun.

The student has a car (with him). (lit. With the student [now] a car.)

(b) The preposition عِنْدَ is the general way of expressing possession, both concrete and abstract, e.g.

عِنْدَ ٱلطَّالِبِ سَيَّارَةٌ

ʿinda ṭ-ṭālibi sayyāratun. The student has a car.

عِنْدَ ٱلْخَبِيرِ فِكْرَةٌ

ʿinda l-ḫabīri fikratun. The expert has an idea.

عِنْدَ can also be used for time, e.g.

عِنْدَ ٱلظُّهْرِ ʿinda ḏ-ḏuhri, at (by) noon

(c) The preposition لَدَى ladā is used in the elaborate literary style more or less in the same way as مَعَ maʿa and عِنْدَ ʿinda to express possession.

لَدَى ٱلتَّاجِرِ مَالٌ كَثِيرٌ

ladā t-tāǧiri mālun kaṯīrun. The merchant has a lot of money.

(d) The preposition ...لِـ (...لَـ) expresses both concrete and abstract possession and can also be used with inanimate possessors, as well as in the sense of 'for, to, because of', e.g.

لِلْبَيْتِ بَابٌ وَاحِدٌ

li-l-bayti bābun wāḥidun. The house has only one door.

أَلسَّيَّارَةُ لِلْمُعَلِّمِ

ʾas-sayyāratu **li**-l-muʿallimi, the car belonging to the teacher

لِهٰذَا / لِذٰلِكَ

li-hāḏā / **li**-ḏālika, for this reason, because of that, therefore

11.11 *Spelling rules for the preposition لِـ... li...*

(a) When لِـ... li... 'for, to' precedes a word with the definite article أَلْـ... ʾal..., the **hamzah** with its **ʾalif** أ is omitted in writing and pronunciation, and the two **lāms** are joined together, e.g.

أَلْعَامِلُ	لِلْعَامِلِ	(not: لِأَلْعَامِلِ **li**-ʾal-ʿāmili)
ʾal-ʿāmilu	**li**-l-ʿāmili	(Note: ع ʿ is a moon letter.)
the worker	for the worker	
أَلطَّبِيبُ	لِلطَّبِيبِ	(not: لِأَلطَّبِيبِ **li**-ʾaṭ-ṭabībi)
ʾaṭ-ṭabību	**li**-ṭ-ṭabībi	(Note: ط ṭ is a sun letter.)
the physician	for the physician	

(b) When the preposition لِـ... li... precedes a word which itself begins with the letter **lām** لـ... and which has a definite article, the **ʾalif** + **hamzah** of the definite article will again be elided, but because three **lāms** cannot be written in succession, the **lām** of the article and the initial **lām** of the following word are written as one with the sign **šaddah** (remember that **lām** is a sun letter), e.g.

لُغَةٌ	أَللُّغَةُ	لِلُّغَةِ	(not: لِأَللُّغَةِ
luġatun	ʾal-luġatu	li-l-luġati	li-ʾal-luġati)
a language	the language	for the language	
لَوْنٌ	أَللَّوْنُ	لِلَّوْنِ	(not: لِأَللَّوْنِ
lawnun	ʾal-lawnu	li-l-lawni	li-ʾal-lawni)
a colour	the colour	for the colour	

11.12 The adjective qualifying a noun preceded by a preposition is also in the genitive case, thus agreeing with the noun it qualifies, e.g.

سَكَنَ[1] فِي ٱلشَّارِعِ[2] ٱلْجَدِيدِ

sakana fī š-šāriʿ**i** l-ğadīd**i**. [1]He lived on the new [2]street.

جَلَسَ[1] تَحْتَ[2] ٱلشَّجَرَةِ[3] ٱلْكَبِيرَةِ

ğalasa taḥta š-šağarat**i** l-kabīrat**i**. [1]He sat [2]under the big [3]tree.

Exercises

Practise your reading:

[1]خَرَجَ ٱلْمَلِكُ وَٱلْوَزِيرُ [2]وَٱلسَّفِيرُ مَعًا مِنَ ٱلْقَصْرِ.

(1) ḫarağa l-maliku wa-l-wazīru wa-s-safīru maʿan mina l-qaṣri.

The king, the minister [2]and the ambassador [1]went out of the palace together.

كَتَبَ ٱلْأُسْتَاذُ [1]بِٱلطَّبْشُورَةِ عَلَى [2]ٱللَّوْحِ [3]ٱلْأَسْوَدِ.

(2) kataba l-ʾustāḏu bi-ṭ-ṭabšūrati ʿalā l-lawḥi l-ʾaswadi.

The professor wrote [1]with the chalk on the blackboard ([3]black [2]board).

[1]عَطِشَ [2]مُسَافِرٌ فَشَرِبَ [3]عَصِيرًا ثُمَّ شَرِبَ شَايًا.

(3) ʿaṭiša musāfirun fa-šariba ʿaṣīran ṯumma šariba šāyan.

[2]A traveller [1]got thirsty and (so) he drank [3]juice, then he drank tea.

[1]ضَرَبَ [2]ٱلْمُجْرِمُ [3]ٱلْحَارِسَ [4]بِٱلسِّكِّينِ [5]فَمَاتَ.

(4) ḍaraba l-muğrimu l-ḥārisa bi-s-sikkīni fa-māta.

[2]The criminal [1]stabbed (hit) [3]the guard [4]with a (the) knife, [5]and (so he) died.

[1]زَحَفَ [2]ٱلضَّابِطُ [3]بِٱلْجَيْشِ عَلَى ٱلْبِلَادِ [4]وَٱحْتَلَّ [5]ٱلْعَاصِمَةَ.

(5) zaḥafa ḍ-ḍābiṭu bi-l-ğayši ʿalā l-bilādi wa-ḥtalla l-ʿāṣimata.

[2]The officer [1]marched [3]with the army into the country [4]and occupied [5]the capital.

[1]وَقَعَ طِفْلٌ فِي [2]بِرْكَةٍ [3]فَسَبَحَ [4]وَخَرَجَ بِسَلَامَةٍ.

(6) waqaʿa ṭiflun fī birkatin fa-sabaḥa wa-ḫarağa bi-salāmatin.

A child [1]fell into [2]a pool [3]and swam and [4]came out safely.

[1]قَرَعَ [2]ٱلضَّيْفُ [3]ٱلْبَابَ ثُمَّ [4]دَخَلَ.

(7) qaraʿa ḍ-ḍayfu l-bāba ṯumma daḫala.

[2]The guest [1]knocked at [3]the door and (then) [4]went in.

[1]وَصَلَتْ [2]بَاخِرَةٌ / سَفِينَةٌ إِلَى ٱلْعَاصِمَةِ [3]مُحَمَّلَةٌ بِٱلنَّفْطِ

(8) waṣalat bāḫiratun / safīnatun ʾilā l-ʿāṣimati muḥammalatun bi-n-nafṭi.

[2]A ship (boat) [1]arrived at the capital [3]loaded with oil (petroleum).

[1]بَعَثَ ٱلْمَلِكُ [2]خَبَرًا [3]هَامًّا لِلْوَزِيرِ وَٱلسَّفِيرِ.

(9) baᶜaṯa l-maliku ḫabaran hāmman li-l-wazīri wa-s-safīri.

The king [1]sent an [3]important [2]message to the minister and to the ambassador.

[1]حَمَلَ [2]ٱلْبَوَّابُ [3]حَقِيبَةً / شَنْطَةً [4]لِلتَّاجِرِ.

(10) ḥamala l-bawwābu ḥaqībatan / šanṭatan li-t-tāğiri.

[2]The doorman [1]carried [3]a bag [4]belonging to the merchant.

أَكَلَ [1]ٱلزَّبُونُ [2]سَمَكًا [3]مَقْلِيًّا ثُمَّ شَرِبَ حَلِيبًا [4]بَارِدًا [5]فَمَرِضَ.

(11) ᵓakala z-zabūnu samakan maqliyyan ṯumma šariba ḥalīban bāridan fa-mariḍa.

The [1]guest (customer) ate [3]fried [2]fish, then he drank [4]cold milk [5]and (so he) got sick.

[1]عَمِلْتُ [2]ٱلْبَارِحَةَ / أَمْسِ فِي [3]ٱللَّيْلِ حَتَّى [4]ٱلصَّبَاحِ.

(12) ᶜamiltu l-bāriḥata / ᵓamsi fī l-layli ḥattā ṣ-ṣabāḥi.

[2]Yesterday [1]I worked through [3]the night **until** [4](the) morning.

قَرَأْتُ كِتَابًا [1]عَنِ [2]ٱلأَدَبِ ٱلْعَرَبِيِّ لِكَاتِبٍ [3]أَجْنَبِيٍّ.

(13) qaraᵓtu kitāban ᶜani l-ᵓadabi l-ᶜarabiyyi li-kātibin ᵓağnabiyyin.

I read a book [1]about Arabic [2]literature by [3]a foreign writer.

هٰذَا [1]ٱلطَّعَامُ لِلطِّفْلِ.

(14) hāḏā ṭ-ṭaᶜāmu li-ṭ-ṭifli.

This [1]food is for the child (or: the child's).

[1]وَعَدَ ٱلْمُوَظَّفُ [2]مُنْذُ [3]أُسْبُوعٍ [4]بِٱلْعَوْدَةِ إِلَى ٱلْعَمَلِ.

(15) waᶜada l-muwaḏḏafu munḏu ᵓusbūᶜin bi-l-ᶜawdati ᵓilā l-ᶜamali.

[3]A week [2]ago the employee [1]promised that he would [4]return to work.

أَلْمُهَنْدِسُ فِي ٱلْمَكْتَبِ [1]وَٱلْعَامِلُ فِي [2]ٱلْمَصْنَعِ.

(16) ᵓal-muhandisu fī l-maktabi wa-l-ᶜāmilu fī l-maṣnaᶜi.

The engineer is in the office [1]and the worker is in [2]the factory.

[1]سَمَحَتِ [2]ٱلْحُكُومَةُ [3]بِتَأْسِيسِ مَصْرِفٍ [4]لِلزِّرَاعَةِ.

(17) samaḥati l-ḥukūmatu bi-taᵓsīsi maṣrifin li-z-zirāᶜati.

[2]The government [1]permitted [3]the establishment of an [4]agricultural bank.

شَرِبَ [1]ٱلضَّيْفُ ٱلْقَهْوَةَ حَتَّى [2]ٱلثُّفْلَ.

(18) šariba ḍ-ḍayfu l-qahwata ḥattā ṯ-ṯufla.
The [1]guest drank the coffee, even [2]the grounds.

أَكَلَ ٱلْكَلْبُ [1]ٱللَّحْمَ حَتَّى [2]ٱلْعَظْمِ.

(19) ʾakala l-kalbu l-laḥma ḥattā l-ʿaḏmi.
The dog ate [1]the meat to [2]the bones.

أَكَلَ [1]ٱلْقِطُّ ٱللَّحْمَ حَتَّى ٱلْعَظْمَ.

(20) ʾakala l-qiṭṭu l-laḥma ḥattā l-ʿaḏma.
[1]The cat ate the meat, even the bones.

Translate into Arabic:

(1) The dog ate the fried fish and then he drank milk.

(2) The officer knocked at the door and (then) went into the office.

(3) The merchant wrote an important message to the government.

(4) The blackboard fell on the cat and (so) he died.

(5) The worker stabbed (hit) the engineer with a knife.

(6) The ambassador fell into the pool and (so) he died.

(7) The army occupied the factory.

(8) The child drank cold juice in the morning, (and) so he got sick.

(9) Yesterday I read an important book about the factory.

(10) The doorman carried the bag and the food to the palace.

(11) The minister promised to establish an agricultural bank in the country.

(12) The guest got thirsty and (so) drank cold juice and then he drank coffee.

(13) The employee knocked at the door and (then) he went in to the king.

Chapter 12

ʾIḍāfah construction (genitive attribute) and the five nouns

12.1 The meaning of the Arabic term **ʾiḍāfah** إِضَافَةٌ is 'addition', 'annexation', or 'attachment'. This kind of annexation occurs when two nouns (or an adjective and a noun) are linked together and immediately follow each other. It is comparable to a genitive or attributive construction, where the first noun (or adjective) is the head constituent and the second noun is the attribute.

The first noun (or adjective) of the **ʾiḍāfah** construction is called أَلْمُضَافُ ʾal-muḍāfu, meaning 'annexed' or 'attached'. The second noun is called أَلْمُضَافُ إِلَيْهِ ʾal-muḍāfu ʾilay-hi, meaning 'annexer' or 'attacher'. There are two variants of the **ʾiḍāfah** construction.

12.2 *The first variant: genitive construction*

The first variant is called أَلْإِضَافَةُ ٱلْحَقِيقِيَّةُ ʾal-ʾiḍāfatu l-ḥaqīqiyyatu, genuine annexation. It corresponds to the genitive construction and is similar to English 'of ...' or '...'s'. In the following examples, the annexer expresses the possessor and the annexed a possessed item:

Indefinite form		***Definite form***	
أَلْمُضَافُ إِلَيْهِ	أَلْمُضَافُ	أَلْمُضَافُ إِلَيْهِ	أَلْمُضَافُ
Annexer ***possessor***	**Annexed** ***possessed***	**Annexer** ***possessor***	**Annexed** ***possessed***
مُعَلِّمٍ	كِتَابُ	ٱلْمُعَلِّمِ	كِتَابُ

kitāb**u** muʿallim**in** (not: kitāb**un**...)
a book **of a** teacher
OR **a** teacher**'s** book

kitāb**u** l-muʿallim**i** (not: ʾ**al**-kitāb**u**...)
the book **of the** teacher
OR the teacher's book

12.3 The semantic relation between the two constituents of the **ʾiḍāfah** construction is not, however, always that of possessed/property + possessor or item + the entity to which the item belongs.

(a) In the following example the relation is that of item and material:

Indefinite form		*Definite form*	
أَلْمُضَافُ إِلَيْهِ	أَلْمُضَافُ	أَلْمُضَافُ إِلَيْهِ	أَلْمُضَافُ
Annexer	**Annexed**	**Annexer**	**Annexed**
material	***item***	***material***	***item***
خَشَبٍ	بَابُ	ٱلْخَشَبِ	بَابُ
bābu ḫašabin		bābu l-ḫašabi	
a wooden door		the wooden door	
a door of wood		the door of wood	

Note: You can also use the preposition مِنْ min to express the material, e.g.

بَابٌ مِنْ خَشَبٍ	أَلْبَابُ مِنْ خَشَبٍ
bābun min ḫašabin	ʾal-bābu min ḫašabin
a door (made) of wood	the door (made) of wood
A door is (made) of wood.	The door is (made) of wood.

(b) In the following example the relation is that between part and whole (partitive attribute):

Indefinite form		*Definite form*	
أَلْمُضَافُ إِلَيْهِ	أَلْمُضَافُ	أَلْمُضَافُ إِلَيْهِ	أَلْمُضَافُ
Annexer	**Annexed**	**Annexer**	**Annexed**
whole	***part***	***whole***	***part***
خُبْزٍ	قِطْعَةُ	ٱلْخُبْزِ	قِطْعَةُ
qiṭʿatu ḫubzin		qiṭʿatu l-ḫubzi	
a piece of bread		the piece of (the) bread	

(c) In the following cases, which are ambiguous, the relation is that of item and contents or item and purpose/material:

Indefinite form		*Definite form*	
أَلْمُضَافُ إِلَيْهِ	أَلْمُضَافُ	أَلْمُضَافُ إِلَيْهِ	أَلْمُضَافُ
Annexer	**Annexed**	**Annexer**	**Annexed**
contents/purpose	***item***	***contents/purpose***	***item***
قَهْوَةٍ	فِنْجَانُ	ٱلْقَهْوَةِ	فِنْجَانُ
finǧānu qahwatin		finǧānu l-qahwati	
a cup **of** coffee		the cup **of** coffee	
a coffee cup		the coffee cup	
عَسَلٍ	شَهْرُ	ٱلْعَسَلِ	شَهْرُ
šahru ʿasalin		šahru l-ʿasali	
a honey month (honeymoon)		the honey month (honeymoon)	
lit. a month **of** honey		lit. the month **of** honey	

(d) Sometimes the annexer can function either as genitive attribute or logical object, e.g.

Indefinite form		*Definite form*	
أَلْمُضَافُ إِلَيْهِ	أَلْمُضَافُ	أَلْمُضَافُ إِلَيْهِ	أَلْمُضَافُ
Annexer	**Annexed**	**Annexer**	**Annexed**
connection/object	***person***	***connection/object***	***person***
شَرِكَةٍ	مُدِيرُ	ٱلشَّرِكَةِ	مُدِيرُ
mudīru šarikatin		mudīru š-šarikati	
a director of a company		the director of the company	
a company director		the company director	

12.4 *Rules concerning the ʾiḍāfah construction*

(a) Whether or not the first noun (the annexed) refers to something definite or indefinite, it never takes the definite article **...أَلْـ** ʾal... or nunation.

(b) The second noun (the annexer) is always in the genitive case. It may take the article ...أَلْـ ʾal... or nunation according to its definiteness status.

(c) If the second noun (the annexer) is in the definite form, it causes the whole **ʾiḍāfah** construction to be definite. If the second noun is indefinite, then the entire **ʾiḍāfah** construction is indefinite.

12.5 The second variant: ʾiḍāfah adjective

The second variant of the **ʾiḍāfah** construction may also be called **ʾiḍāfah** adjective, because an adjective is construed with a definite noun in the genitive case. The noun then expresses something with regard or respect to which the quality of the adjective obtains (Latin: *genetivus respectus*). In Arabic this construction is called أَلْإِضَافَةُ غَيْرُ ٱلْحَقِيقِيَّةِ ʾal-ʾiḍāfatu ġayru l-ḥaqīqiyyati, which means improper annexation, e.g.

أَلْمُضَافُ إِلَيْهِ **Annexer** ***noun***	أَلْمُضَافُ **Annexed** ***adjective***
ٱلْمَنْظَرِ	قَبِيحُ qabīḥu l-manḏari, one of ugly appearance, bad-looking
ٱلْقَلْبِ	طَيِّبَةُ ṭayyibatu l-qalbi, one (f.) with a good heart
ٱلْمَالِ	كَثِيرُ kaṯīru l-māli, wealthy man (lit. abundant of wealth)
ٱلْوَجْهِ	جَمِيلَةُ ǧamīlatu l-waǧhi, one (f.) with a beautiful face, fair-faced
ٱلشُّكْرِ	جَزِيلُ ǧazīlu š-šukri, very thankful
ٱللَّوْنِ	غَامِقُ ġāmiqu l-lawni, dark- (deep-)coloured
ٱلْعَقْلِ	قَلِيلُ qalīlu l-ʿaqli, stupid, insane (lit. one with little intelligence)
ٱللِّسَانِ	طَوِيلَةُ ṭawīlatu l-lisāni, a gossip (f.), insolent (lit. one with a long tongue)

12.6 The first adjective in the above examples may take the definite article أَلْـ... ʾal... when a noun in the definite form precedes it, although this contradicts rule 12.4a mentioned above.

أَلْمُضَافُ إِلَيْهِ	أَلْمُضَافُ	
Annexer	**Annexed**	
noun	***adjective***	
أَلْوَجْهِ	أَلْبِنْتُ ٱلْجَمِيلَةُ	ʾal-bintu -l-ǧamīlatu l-waǧhi — the girl with a (the) beautiful face
أَلْقَلْبِ	أَلشَّيْخُ ٱلطَّيِّبُ	ʾaš-šayḫu ṭ-ṭayyibu l-qalbi — the sheikh with a kind heart
أَلْعَقْلِ	أَلرَّجُلُ ٱلْقَلِيلُ	ʾar-raǧulu l-qalīlu l-ʿaqli — the stupid man (lit. the man with little intelligence)

12.7 When the first noun (the annexed) in the genuine ʾ**iḍāfah** construction is qualified by an adjective, the adjective agrees with the noun in number, gender and case. But the adjective must be placed after the whole ʾ**iḍāfah** construction, e.g.

سَيَّارَةُ مُحَمَّدٍ ٱلْجَدِيدَةُ
sayyārat**u** Muḥammad**ini** l-ǧadīdat**u**
Muḥammad's new car

فِي سَيَّارَةِ مُحَمَّدٍ ٱلْجَدِيدَةِ
fī sayyārat**i** Muḥammad**ini** l-ǧadīdati
in Muḥammad's new car

12.8 In an unvocalized text it is difficult to know which noun (first or second) the adjective is referring to when it is placed after an ʾ**iḍāfah** construction. Vowelling/vocalization is the remedy for this, e.g.

مَدْخَلُ ٱلْبَيْتِ ٱلصَّغِيرِ
madḫalu **l-bayti** ṣ-ṣaǧīr**i**
the gate of the small **house**

مَدْخَلُ ٱلْبَيْتِ ٱلصَّغِيرُ
madḫalu l-bayti ṣ-ṣaǧīr**u**
the small **gate** of the house

12.9 A complex ʾ**iḍāfah** phrase may contain several nested annexers (مُضَافٌ إِلَيْهِ), but only the last annexer may take the definite article, e.g.

[1]مَدْخَلُ [2]حَدِيقَةِ [3]وَزِيرِ [4]ٱلْخَارِجِيَّةِ
madḫalu ḥadīqat**i** wazīr**i** l-ḫāriǧiyyati
[1]the gate to (of) [2]the garden of the [3]Minister of [4]Foreign Affairs

12.10 However, the noun to which the adjective refers may be ambiguous even in a vocalized text, e.g.

كَتَبَ بِقَلَمِ ٱلتِّلْمِيذِ ٱلْقَصِيرِ

kataba bi-qalami t-tilmīḏi l-qaṣīri. He wrote with the short pen of the student. OR He wrote with the pen of the short student.

12.11 The only element that can be placed between the annexed and the annexer is a demonstrative pronoun, e.g.

طَالِبُ هٰذِهِ ٱلْجَامِعَةِ

ṭālibu **hāḏihi** l-ǧāmiʿati, the student of **this** university

12.12 The five nouns أَلْأَسْمَاءُ ٱلْخَمْسَةُ ʾal-ʾasmāʾu l-ḫamsatu below take the three case endings, but they differ slightly from the usual ones. When these nouns enter an **ʾiḍāfah** construction, their case vowels become long: -ū, -ā, -ī (instead of -u, -a, -i).

أَبٌ	أَخٌ	حَمٌ	فُو	ذُو
ʾabun	ʾaḫun	ḥamun	fū	ḏū
father	brother	father-in-law	mouth	owner, possessor

Note: Instead of the nominative case form فُو fū, 'mouth', the alternative form فَمٌ famun is more frequently used.

Examples:

Nominative	***Accusative***	***Genitive***
أَبُو ٱلْوَلَدِ (not: أَبُ ʾab**u**)	أَبَا ٱلْوَلَدِ (not: أَبَ ʾab**a**)	أَبِي ٱلْوَلَدِ (not: أَبِ ʾab**i**)
ʾab**ū** l-waladi	ʾab**ā** l-waladi	ʾab**ī** l-waladi
the boy's father		
ذُو مَالٍ	ذَا مَالٍ	ذِي مَالٍ
ḏ**ū** mālin	ḏ**ā** mālin	ḏ**ī** mālin
rich, wealthy (lit. possessor of much wealth)		

Exercises

Practise your reading:

[1]صَلَّحَ ٱلْعَامِلُ [2]شُبَّاكَ ٱلسَّيَّارَةِ [3]ٱلْمُعَطَّلَ.

(1) ṣallaḥa l-ʿāmilu šubbāka s-sayyārati l-muʿaṭṭala.
The worker [1]repaired [3]the broken [2]window of the car.

أَكَلَ [1]ٱلنَّاسُ فِي قَصْرِ ٱلْمَلِكِ [2]ٱلْعَظِيمِ.

(2) ʾakala n-nāsu fī qaṣri l-maliki l-ʿaḏīmi.
[1]The people ate in [2]the great palace of the king. OR
The people ate in the palace of the great king.

[1]غَسَلَ ٱلطَّبِيبُ [2]بِٱلْمُطَهِّرِ [3]جُرْحَ ٱلطِّفْلِ [4]ٱلْمُلْتَهِبَ.

(3) ġasala ṭ-ṭabību bi-l-muṭahhiri ǧurḥa ṭ-ṭifli l-multahiba.
The physician [1]washed [4]the inflamed [3]wound of the child [2]with (the) antiseptic.

[1]صَدَمَتْ [2]شَاحِنَةٌ بَابَ ٱلْمَدْرَسَةِ [3]ٱلْغَرْبِيَّ [4]فَوَقَعَ ٱلْبَابُ عَلَى [5]ٱلْحَارِسِ.

(4) ṣadamat šāḥinatun bāba l-madrasati l-ġarbiyya, fa-waqaʿa l-bābu ʿalā l-ḥārisi.
[2]A truck [1]hit the school's [3]western door so the door [4]fell on [5]the watchman (guard).

[1]أَرْضُ [2]ٱلْمَصْنَعِ ٱلصَّغِيرِ [3]وَسِخَةٌ.

(5) ʾarḍu l-maṣnaʿi ṣ-ṣaġīri wasiḫatun.
[1]The floor (f.) of the small [2]factory is [3]dirty.

[1]بِنَايَةُ [2]ٱلْبَلَدِيَّةِ [3]ٱلْجَدِيدَةُ [4]بَعِيدَةٌ [5]وَبَشِعَةٌ.

(6) bināyatu l-baladiyyati l-ǧadīdatu baʿīdatun wa-bašiʿatun.
[3]The new [2]municipality [1]building is [4]far away [5]and ugly.

[1]مَتْحَفُ [2]ٱلْمَدِينَةِ ٱلْقَدِيمُ [3]عَصْرِيٌّ وَجَمِيلٌ.

(7) matḥafu l-madīnati l-qadīmu ʿaṣriyyun wa-ǧamīlun.
The old [1]museum of the [2]city is [3]modern and beautiful.

[1]شُبَّاكُ / نَافِذَةُ ٱلْجَامِعَةِ [2]ٱلشَّرْقِيُّ [3]مُغْلَقٌ / مُغْلَقَةٌ.

(8) šubbāku / nāfiḏatu l-ǧāmiʿati š-šarqiyyu muġlaqatun.
The university's [2]eastern [1]window is [3]closed.

^{1}مَدْخَلُ ^{2}حَدِيقَةِ ^{3}ٱلْحَيَوَانَاتِ ٱلْجَدِيدُ ^{4}مَفْتُوحٌ.

(9) madḫalu ḥadīqati l-ḥayawānāti l-ǧadīdu maftūḥun.

The new ^{1}gate (entrance) of the ^{2,3}zoo (lit. ^{2}garden of the ^{3}animals) is ^{4}open.

^{1}وَافَقَ ^{2}مَجْلِسُ ^{3}ٱلنُّوَّابِ ^{4}أَمْسِ عَلَى ^{5}مَشْرُوعٍ ^{6}عَاجِلٍ لِوَزِيرِ ^{7}ٱلْمَالِيَّةِ.

(10) wāfaqa maǧlisu n-nuwwābi ʾamsi ʿalā mašrūʿin ʿāǧilin li-wazīri l-māliyyati.

The ^{2,3}parliament (^{2}council of ^{3}deputies) ^{1}agreed ^{4}yesterday on ^{6}an urgent ^{5}project for the Minister of ^{7}Finance.

^{1}غَضِبَ ٱلطَّبِيبُ عَلَى ^{2}ٱلْمُمَرِّضَةِ ^{3}ٱلطَّوِيلَةِ ^{4}ٱللِّسَانِ / ^{4,3}ٱلثَّرْثَارَةِ.

(11) ġaḍiba ṭ-ṭabību ʿalā l-mumarriḍati ṭ-ṭawīlati l-lisāni /ṯ-ṯarṯārati.

The physician ^{1}became angry with the ^{4,3}gossiping (insolent) ^{2}nurse (lit. with the ^{3}long-^{4}tongued ^{2}nurse).

^{1}غَسَلَ ^{2}ٱلْجَارُ ^{3}يَدَ ٱلْكَلْبِ ٱلصَّغِيرِ ^{4}ٱلْوَسِخَةَ.

(12) ġasala l-ǧāru yada l-kalbi ṣ-ṣaġīri l-wasiḫata.

^{2}The neighbour ^{1}washed the small dog's ^{4}dirty ^{3}paw (^{3}hand).

^{1}حَمَلَ ٱلْبَوَّابُ ^{2}حَقِيبَةَ /شَنْطَةَ ٱلْمُدِيرِ ^{3}ٱلثَّقِيلَةَ.

(13) ḥamala l-bawwābu ḥaqībata / šanṭata l-mudīri ṯ-ṯaqīlata.

The doorman ^{1}carried the director's ^{3}heavy ^{2}suitcase.

^{1}لَوْنُ ٱلْبَابِ ^{2}ٱلشَّمَالِيِّ ^{3}لِلْمَتْحَفِ ^{4}قَبِيحٌ.

(14) lawnu l-bābi š-šamāliyyi li-l-matḥafi qabīḥun.

^{1}The colour of the ^{3}museum's ^{2}northern door is ^{4}ugly.

^{1}دَرَجُ ^{2}ٱلْمَدْخَلِ ^{3}ٱلْجَنُوبِيِّ ^{4}لِلْفُنْدُقِ ضَيِّقٌ.

(15) daraǧu l-madḫali l-ǧanūbiyyi li-l-funduqi ḍayyiqun.

^{1}The stairs ^{4}of the hotel's ^{3}southern ^{2}entrance are narrow.

^{1}وَصَلَ إِلَى ^{2}مَطَارِ ٱلْكُوَيْتِ ^{3}ٱلدَّوْلِيِّ ^{4}مَنْدُوبُ ^{5}ٱلْأَمِينِ ^{6}ٱلْعَامِّ ^{7}لِلْأُمَمِ ^{8}ٱلْمُتَّحِدَةِ.

(16) waṣala ʾilā maṭāri l-kuwayti d-dawliyyi mandūbu l-ʾamīni l-ʿāmmi li-l-ʾumami l-muttaḥidati.

^{4}The representative of ^{5}the Secretary- ^{6}General of the ^{8}United ^{7}Nations ^{1}has arrived at Kuwait's ^{3}International ^{2}Airport.

[1]خَدَمَ [2]ضَابِطُ [3]ٱلشُّرْطَةِ فِي قَصْرِ [4]ٱلْمَلِكِ ٱلْجَدِيدِ.

(17) ẖadama ḍābiṭu š-šurṭati fī qaṣri l-maliki l-ǧadīdi.

The [3,2]police officer [1]served in the new palace of [4]the king. OR:
The police officer served in the palace of the new king.

فِي [1]حَفْلَةِ [2]ٱلْعُرْسِ [3]جَلَسَ أَبُو [4]ٱلْعَرُوسِ عَلَى [5]كُرْسِيٍّ [6]بِٱلْقُرْبِ مِنْ أَبِي [7]ٱلْعَرِيسِ.

(18) fī ḥaflati l-ʿursi ǧalasa ʾabū l-ʿarūsi ʿalā kursiyyin bi-l-qurbi min ʾabī l-ʿarīsi.

At [2]the wedding [1]party [4]the bride's father [3]sat on [5]a chair [6]near the [7]bridegroom's father.

Translate into Arabic:

(1) The doorman repaired the gate of the new king's palace.
(2) The physician ate in the palace of the minister.
(3) The worker washed the stairs of the museum.
(4) A truck hit the school's western gate (entrance).
(5) The colour of the building of the new hotel is ugly.
(6) The floor (f.) of the old zoo is dirty (f.).
(7) The watchman (guard) washed the small dog's wound.
(8) The director's heavy suitcase is open.
(9) The physician served in the United Nations.
(10) The new building of the parliament is modern and beautiful.
(11) At the party the child sat on a chair near the nurse.
(12) The university's eastern door is closed.
(13) The neighbour sat on the stairs of the entrance.
(14) The king's representative arrived at the International Airport.
(15) The police officer served in the old building of the municipality.
(16) At the wedding the bridegroom's father became angry with the bride's father.

Chapter 13

Number

Dual and plural

13.1 Arabic nouns and adjectives are inflected for three numbers:

singular مُفْرَدٌ mufradun   dual مُثَنًّى muṯannan   plural جَمْعٌ ǧamʿun

13.2 *Dual*

The dual is used for pairs, namely for two individuals or things of the same kind or class, e.g. two boys, two girls, two hands, two books, etc.

The dual is formed by replacing the case endings of the singular form with the following suffixes:

...ـَانِ /...āni/ for nominative

...ـَيْنِ /...ayni/ for accusative and genitive

Singular (nom.)	*Dual (nom.)*	*Dual (acc. and gen.)*
رَجُلٌ	رَجُلاَنِ	رَجُلَيْنِ
raǧulun, a man	raǧul**āni**, two men	raǧul**ayni**, two men
بِنْتٌ	بِنْتَانِ	بِنْتَيْنِ
bintun, a girl	bint**āni**, two girls	bint**ayni**, two girls

13.3 The final **tāʾ marbūṭah** ـَةٌ...، ـَةٌ... in a singular noun becomes a regular ...ـتـ.../...t.../ before dual endings, e.g.

Singular	*Dual (nom.)*	*Dual (acc. and gen.)*
مَلِكَةٌ	مَلِكَتَانِ	مَلِكَتَيْنِ
malikatun, a queen	malikat**āni**	malikat**ayni**

13.4 The final syllable نِ.../...ni/ of the dual masculine and feminine is elided when the word is in the ʾ**iḍāfah** construction, e.g.

(a) Dual (nom. masc.)

كِتَابَا ٱلطَّالِبِ (not كِتَابَانِ ٱلطَّ...

kitāb**ā** ṭ-ṭālibi kitāb**āni** ṭ-ṭa...)

the (two) books of the student

(b) Dual (acc. and gen. masc.)

كِتَابَيِ ٱلطَّالِبِ (not كِتَابَيْنِ ٱلطَّ...

kitāb**ayi** ṭ-ṭālibi kitāba**yni** ṭ-ṭa...)

the (two) books of the student

(c) Dual (nom. fem.)

مُعَلِّمَتَا ٱلْمَدْرَسَةِ (مُعَلِّمَةٌ sing.) (not: مُعَلِّمَتَانِ ٱلْـ...

muʿallimat**ā** l-madrasati (muʿallimatun) muʿallimat**āni** l-...)

the (two) teachers (f.) of the school

(d) Dual (acc. and gen. fem.)

مُعَلِّمَتَيِ ٱلْمَدْرَسَةِ (not: مُعَلِّمَتَيْنِ ٱلْـ...

muʿallimat**ayi** l-madrasati muʿallimata**yni** l-...)

the (two) teachers (f.) of the school

13.5 When a singular feminine noun ends with ـَاءٌ..., /...āʾ/, the final hamzah ء /ʾ/ is replaced by **wāw** و before dual endings, e.g.

Singular	***Dual (nom.)***	
حَمْرَاءُ	حَمْرَاوَانِ	(not: حَمْرَاءَانِ
ḥamrāʾ**u**, red	ḥamrā**w**āni	ḥamrāʾāni)
	Dual (acc. and gen.)	
	حَمْرَاوَيْنِ	(not: حَمْرَاءَيْنِ
	ḥamrā**w**ayni	ḥamrāʾayni)

(There is more about **hamzah** as a final radical ـَاءٌ... in chapter 20.)

13.6 The final ʾ**alif maqṣūrah** ـَى... of a singular noun becomes yāʾ ...ـيـ... /...y.../ before dual endings, e.g.

Singular	*Dual (nom.)*	*Dual (acc. and gen.)*
مُسْتَشْفًى	مُسْتَشْفَيَانِ	مُسْتَشْفَيَيْنِ
mustaš**fan**, hospital	mustašfay**āni**	mustašfay**ayni**

13.7 In the dual, adjectives always agree with the nouns they qualify in gender and case, e.g.

أَلْمُعَلِّمَانِ مَرِيضَانِ
ʾal-muʿallim**āni** marīḍ**āni**.
The two teachers (m.) are sick.

أَلْمُعَلِّمَتَانِ مَرِيضَتَانِ
ʾal-muʿallimatāni marīḍat**āni**.
The two teachers (f.) are sick.

أَلْكَلْبَانِ صَغِيرَانِ
ʾal-kalbāni ṣaġīr**āni**.
The two dogs (m.) are small.

أَلْكَلْبَتَانِ صَغِيرَتَانِ
ʾal-kalbatāni ṣaġīrat**āni**.
The two dogs (f.) are small.

13.8 *The plural*

There are two plural types in Arabic:

(a) The sound plural أَلْجَمْعُ ٱلسَّالِمُ may be compared to the English external plural or regular plural.

(b) The broken plural جَمْعُ ٱلتَّكْسِيرِ may be compared to the English internal or irregular plural. (Broken plurals are explained in chapter 21.)

13.9 The sound masculine plural جَمْعُ ٱلْمُذَكَّرِ ٱلسَّالِمُ of nouns and adjectives is formed by replacing the case endings of the singular with the following two suffixes:

...ـُونَ /...ūna/ in the nominative

...ـِينَ /...īna/ in the accusative and genitive

Sing. (masc.)	*Plur. nom. (masc.)*	*Plur. acc. and gen. (masc.)*
مُعَلِّمٌ	مُعَلِّمُونَ	مُعَلِّمِينَ
muʿallim**un**, teacher	muʿallim**ūna**, teacher	muʿallim**īna**, (of) teachers

13.10 As in the dual, the final syllable ...نَ /...na/ of the sound plural masculine disappears, if the word enters the ʾiḍāfah construction, e.g.

(a) Sound masculine plural nominative:

مُعَلِّمُو ٱلْمَدْرَسَةِ	(not: مُعَلِّمُونَ ٱلْـ...)
muʿallimū l-madrasati	muʿallimūna l-..)
the teachers of the school	

(b) Sound masculine plural accusative and genitive:

مُعَلِّمِي ٱلْمَدْرَسَةِ	(not: مُعَلِّمِينَ ٱلْـ..)
muʿallimī l-madrasati	muʿallimīna.l-..)
the teachers of the school	

13.11 The sound feminine plural جَمْعُ ٱلْمُؤَنَّثِ ٱلسَّالِمُ is formed by adding the following two suffixes to the singular word stem:

...ـَاتٌ /...ātun/ in the nominative

...ـَاتٍ /...ātin/ in the accusative and genitive

13.12 It should be noted that the sound feminine plural has only two vowel endings for the three cases, whether they are in the definite or indefinite form, e.g.

Sing. (fem.)	***Plur. nom. (fem.)***	***Plur. acc. and gen. (fem.)***
مَلِكَةٌ	مَلِكَاتٌ	مَلِكَاتٍ
malik**atun**, a queen	malik**ātun**, queens	malik**ātin**, (of) queens
أَلْمَلِكَةُ	أَلْمَلِكَاتُ	أَلْمَلِكَاتِ
ʾal-malik**atu**, the queen	ʾal-malik**ātu**, the queens	ʾal-malik**āti**, (of) the queens

13.13 The sound feminine plural mostly refers to human beings. However, some masculine nouns indicating non-human beings also take the sound feminine plural endings, e.g.

Masc. sing.	***Plur. nom. (fem.)***	***Plur. acc. and gen. (fem.)***
حَمَّامٌ	حَمَّامَاتٌ	حَمَّامَاتٍ
ḥammām**un**, bath (m.)	ḥammām**ātun**, baths (f.)	ḥammām**ātin**, (of) baths (f.)

13.14 As in the dual, any feminine noun which has a final **hamzah** ...ـَاءُ /...āʾu/ replaces it in the plural with **wāw** و /w/, e.g.

Sing. (fem.)	***Plur. nom. (fem.)***	***Plur. acc. and gen. (fem.)***
صَحْرَاءُ	صَحَرَاوَاتٌ	صَحْرَاوَاتٍ
ṣaḥrāʾu, a desert	ṣaḥrā**w**ātun, deserts	ṣaḥrā**w**ātin, (of) deserts

13.15 As in the dual, an adjective always agrees in gender and case with the noun it qualifies, e.g.

أَلطَّالِبَاتُ مَرِيضَاتٌ
ʾaṭ-ṭālibātu marīḍātun.
The students (f.) are ill.

أَلْمُمَرِّضَاتُ مَاهِرَاتٌ
ʾal-mumarriḍātu māhirātun.
The nurses (f.) are skilled.

13.16 An adjective qualifying a sound feminine plural referring to non-human beings or things is in the feminine singular, e.g.

إِمْتِحَانَاتٌ سَهْلَةٌ
ʾimtiḥānātun sahlatun
easy examinations

أَلسَّنَوَاتُ صَعْبَةٌ
ʾa-sanawātu ṣaʿbatun.
The years are difficult.

Note a: The general principle is that plural non-human nouns are grammatically feminine singular, which is why the adjective and any other element (including the verb) that qualifies such a noun will also be in the feminine singular. This is called agreement or concord.

Note b: If two nouns of different gender are qualified by the same element, that element will be in the masculine dual.

Exercises

Practise your reading:

[1]سَكَنَ [2]ٱلتَّاجِرَانِ [3]ٱلْغَنِيَّانِ فِي قَصْرَيْنِ كَبِيرَيْنِ [4]بَيْنَ نَهْرَيِ ٱلْمَدِينَةِ.

(1) sakana t-tāǧirāni l-ġaniyyāni fī qaṣrayni kabīrayni bayna nahrayi l-madīnati.
[3]The two rich [2]merchants [1]lived in two big palaces [4]between the two rivers of the city.

[1]ذَبَحَ [2]صَاحِبُ ٱلْمَطْعَمِ دَجَاجَتَيْنِ (s. دَجَاجَةٌ) [3]سَوْدَاوَيْنِ (s. سَوْدَاءُ).

(2) ḏabaḥa ṣāḥibu l-maṭʿami daǧāǧatayni sawdāwayni.
[2]The owner of the restaurant [1]slaughtered [3]two black hens.

[1]سَيَّارَتَا (s. سَيَّارَةٌ) ٱلطَّبِيبَيْنِ ٱلْجَدِيدَيْنِ [2]حَمْرَاوَانِ (s. حَمْرَاءُ).

(3) sayyāratā ṭ-ṭabībayni l-ǧadīdayni ḥamrāwāni.
[1]The two cars of the two new physicians are [2]red.

فِي [1]جُنَيْنَتَيْ (s. جُنَيْنَةٌ) حَدِيقَتَيْ [2]صَاحِبِ [3]ٱلشَّرِكَةِ [4]شَجَرَتَانِ
كَبِيرَتَانِ [5]وَمَوْقِفَانِ [6]لِسَيَّارَتَيْنِ.

(4) fī ǧunaynatay / ḥadīqatay ṣāḥibi š-šarikati šaǧaratāni kabīratāni wa-mawqifāni li-sayyāratayni.
In [1]the two gardens of [2]the owner of [3]the company there are two big [4]trees [5]and two car parks [6]for two cars.

فِي [1]ٱلْعَالَمِ ٱلْعَرَبِيِّ [2]عَدَدٌ كَبِيرٌ مِنَ ٱلْإِمَارَاتِ (s. إِمَارَةٌ)
وَٱلْجُمْهُورِيَّاتِ (s. جُمْهُورِيَّةٌ).

(5) fī l-ʿālami l-ʿarabiyyi ʿadadun kabīrun mina l-ʾimārāti wa-l-ǧumhūriyyāti.
In the Arab [1]world there is a large [2]number of emirates and republics.

[1]ذَهَبَ [2]مُصَوِّرُو [3]وَصِحَافِيُّو [4]ٱلْجَرِيدَةِ إِلَى [5]مَكَانَيِ [6]ٱلْإِضْرَابِ
[7]وَٱلْمُظَاهَرَاتِ (s. مُظَاهَرَةٌ).

(6) ḏahaba muṣawwirū wa-ṣiḥāfiyyū l-ǧarīdati ʾilā makānayi l-ʾiḍrābi wa-l-muḏāharāti.
[2]The photographers [3]and the journalists of [4]the newspaper [1]went to [5]both [5]the location (place) of [6]the strike(s) and [5]the location of [7]the demonstration.

[1]زَعِلَ / [1]غَضِبَ [2]بَعْضُ ٱلْمُعَلِّمِينَ وَٱلْمُعَلِّمَاتِ مِنْ مُدِيرِ [3]ٱلدَّوْرَةِ [4]ٱلتَّدْرِيبِيَّةِ.

(7) zaᶜila / ġaḍiba baᶜḍu l-muᶜallimīna wa-l-muᶜallimāti min mudīri d-dawrati t-tadrībiyyati.

[2]Some of the male and the female teachers [1]became angry with the director of [4]the training [3]course / [3]session.

[1]مُهَنْدِسُو ٱلشَّرِكَةِ ٱلْمِصْرِيُّونَ [2]مُسَافِرُونَ [3]غَدًا فِي [4]عُطْلَةٍ [5]قَصِيرَةٍ.

(8) muhandisū š-šarikati l-miṣriyyūna musāfirūna ġadan fī ᶜuṭlatin qaṣīratin.

The company's Egyptian [1]engineers are [2]travelling [3]tomorrow on [5]a short [4]holiday.

[1]فَرِحَ ٱلْمُعَلِّمُونَ وَٱلْمُعَلِّمَاتُ [2]بِخَبَرِ [3]نَجَاحِ ٱلطَّالِبَاتِ فِي [4]مَعْهَدِ [5]ٱلتَّمْرِيضِ.

(9) fariḥa l-muᶜallimūna wa-l-muᶜallimātu bi-ḫabari naǧāḥi ṭ-ṭālibāti fī maᶜhadi t-tamrīḍi.

The male and female teachers [1]were happy [2]at the news of the female students' [3]success in [5]the nursing [4]institute.

[1]رَبِحَ [2]ٱلزَّوْجَانِ ٱلسَّعِيدَانِ [3]بِطَاقَتَيْ (s. بِطَاقَةٌ) [4]سَفَرٍ إِلَى [5]عَاصِمَتَيْنِ فِي أُورُوبَّا.

(10) rabiḥa z-zawǧāni s-saᶜīdāni biṭāqatay safarin ʾilā ᶜāṣimatayni fī ʾūrūbbā.

The happily [2]married couple [1]won two [4]travel [3]tickets to [5]two capital cities in Europe.

[1]أَلشُّرْطِيَّانِ ٱلْجَدِيدَانِ [2]غَيْرُ [3]مُخْلِصَيْنِ [4]لِلْقَانُونِ.

(11) ʾaš-šurṭiyyāni l-ǧadīdāni ġayru muḫliṣayni li-l-qānūni.

The two new [1]policemen are [2]not [3]faithful [4]to the law.

إِبْنَتَا (s. إِبْنَةٌ) [1]ٱلسَّفِيرِ ٱلْجَدِيدِ [2]مُهَذَّبَتَانِ (s. مُهَذَّبَةٌ) وَجَمِيلَتَانِ.

(12) ʾibnatā s-safīri l-ǧadīdi muhaḏḏabatāni wa-ǧamīlatāni.

The two daughters of the new [1]ambassador are [2]polite (well mannered) and beautiful.

[1]زَارَ ٱلْمُعَلِّمُونَ وَٱلْمُعَلِّمَاتُ [2]مَتْحَفَيْنِ جَدِيدَيْنِ فِي [3]وَسَطِ ٱلْمَدِينَةِ.

(13) zāra l-muᶜallimūna wa-l-muᶜallimātu matḥafayni ǧadīdayni fī wasaṭi l-madīnati.

The male and female teachers [1]visited two new [2]museums in [3]the centre of the city.

[1]بَدَأَ [2]مُصَوِّرُو [3]ٱلْجَرِيدَةِ [4]ٱلْإِضْرَابَ [5]لِمُدَّةِ [6]سَاعَتَيْنِ (s. سَاعَةٌ).

(14) badaʾa muṣawwirū l-ğarīdati l-ʾiḍrāba li-muddati sāʿatayni.
[2]The photographers of [3]the newspaper [1]began the [6]two-hour ([5]time) [4]strike.

[1]مُهَنْدِسُو [2]شَرِكَةِ [3]ٱلنَّفْطِ [4]مَدْعُوُّونَ إِلَى [5]حَفْلَةٍ [6]عِنْدَ ٱلْوَزِيرِ.

(15) muhandisū šarikati n-nafṭi madʿuwwūna ʾilā ḥaflatin ʿinda l-wazīri.
[1]The engineers of the [3]oil [2]company are [4]invited to [5]a party [6]at the minister's (house).

Translate into Arabic:

(1) The (two) merchants' car is black.

(2) The owner of the restaurant slaughtered two red hens.

(3) A large number of journalists went to two capitals (cities) in the Arab world.

(4) The male and female teachers are travelling tomorrow on a short holiday.

(5) The two rich owners of the restaurant lived in two big palaces in the centre of the city.

(6) The two new engineers are not faithful to the company.

(7) The married couple visited two new gardens in the centre of the city.

(8) The two new policemen won two travel tickets to Europe.

(9) The photographers of the newspaper are travelling to some of the emirates and republics in the Arab world.

(10) The two new physicians were (became) angry with the director of the training course.

(11) The two engineers were angry with the ambassador at the party (given) by the minister.

(12) The director of the nursing institute was happy at the news of the (female) students' success.

Chapter 14

Perfect tense verbs, root and radicals, triliteral verbs and word order

14.1 There are two main verb tenses in Arabic:

(a) Perfect tense: corresponds usually to the English past or perfect tense.

(b) Imperfect tense: corresponds usually to the English present or future tense (see chapter 17).

Note: The tenses in Arabic do *not* express the time of an event in the same precise way as the primary tenses in Indo-European languages. The Arabic tenses can be better understood as different aspects of viewing the action in terms of an opposition between a stated or proposed fact and an action or state in progress or preparation. That is why the terms perfect and imperfect tense do not correspond to the meaning of these terms in, for example, English (in fact, the literal Latin meanings of the terms perfect and imperfect are more helpful in this regard). In spite of this, we will keep to the traditional terms, since they are widely employed in Western Arabic textbooks.

14.2 *Perfect tense*

The perfect tense, أَلْفِعْلُ ٱلْمَاضِي, indicates mostly a past state, completed action or established fact. In the third and second persons the perfect may also express a wish or benediction. In conditional sentences the perfect expresses a hypothesis (to be explained in chapter 39).

Note: Because there is no infinitive in Arabic in the same sense as in English, the third person masculine singular of the perfect tense is given as the corresponding basic or reference form of the verb. Thus, for example, the basic verb form كَتَبَ kataba means 'he wrote' or 'he has written'. But when used as a general reference form for the said verb with all its various forms, كَتَبَ kataba is conventionally translated by the English infinitive 'to write'.

14.3 *Root and radicals*

Most of the Arabic basic verb forms consist of three consonants (radicals) and three vowels (CVCVCV). The three consonants constitute the root of the verb, which is why they are called radicals (i.e. 'root-makers'). (*Vowels cannot function as radicals.*) It is important to know and recognize the root of every verb, because the root is the absolute (invariable) basis of all the different forms of the verb as well as of most nouns, adjectives and adverbs and even many prepositions. In Arabic dictionaries most words and word forms are therefore entered alphabetically under the respective root.

Note: The abbreviation 'C' above denotes 'consonant' and 'V' denotes 'vowel'.

14.4 *Triliteral verbs*

(a) Roots with three radicals are called triliteral verbs (singular: أَلْفِعْلُ ٱلثُّلَاثِي ʾal-fiʿlu ṯ-ṯulāṯī). Thus the root of the triliteral verb **kataba** 'to write' is ***k-t-b***. This is the form under which you will find the verb **kataba** (and other forms of this verb) in Arabic dictionaries.

(b) The triliteral verbs have three patterns of vowelling. In the basic form the first and last consonants (radicals) are always vowelled with **fatḥah** /a/. But the middle consonant (radical) may be vowelled with any of the three short vowels:

CaCaCa	CaCiCa	CaCuCa
كَتَبَ	شَرِبَ	كَبُرَ
kataba	šariba	kabura
he wrote	he drank	he grew up

14.5 Separate personal pronouns for the subject and object are usually not used in Arabic verbal sentences. Verbs are conjugated for the person, gender and number of the subject and pronominal object by means of suffixes (and in the imperfect also prefixes). Suffixes which refer to the subject are called personal endings. These endings are written in bold type in the transliteration of the conjugation table below.

Note: There are various ways to read the order of the Arabic verb conjugation. The order used in this book is not the Arabic way, but rather an old tradition still employed in most of the European Arabic textbooks.

Conjugation of the verb كَتَبَ kataba 'to write' in the perfect tense in all persons, genders and numbers (of the subject):

	singular	dual	plural
3. m.	كَتَبَ katab+**a** he wrote	كَتَبَا katab+**ā** they (2) wrote	كَتَبُوا katab+**ū** they wrote
3. f.	كَتَبَتْ katab+**at** she wrote	كَتَبَتَا katab+**atā** they (2) wrote	كَتَبْنَ katab+**na** they wrote
2. m.	كَتَبْتَ katab+**ta** you wrote	كَتَبْتُمَا katab+**tumā** you (2) wrote	كَتَبْتُمْ katab+**tum** you wrote
2. f.	كَتَبْتِ katab+**ti** you wrote	كَتَبْتُمَا katab+**tumā** you (2) wrote	كَتَبْتُنَّ katab+**tunna** you wrote
1. m. and f.	كَتَبْتُ katab+**tu** I wrote	——	كَتَبْنَا katab+**nā** we wrote

Note: The extra ʾ**alif** ا at the end of the third person masc. plural is not pronounced, and it is elided when a suffix denoting the object is added.

14.6 The normal word order in sentences with a perfect tense verb is:

verb + subject + object / complement + adverbial(s)

(a) When a verb in the third person is placed first in the sentence, the verb must be in the singular, even though the subject may be in the plural or dual. The verb always agrees with the gender of the subject, however, e.g.

شَرِبَ ٱلْمُعَلِّمُونَ عَصِيراً

šariba l-muᶜallimūna ᶜaṣīran.

The teachers (m. pl.) drank juice.

شَرِبَتِ ٱلْبِنْتَانِ عَصِيراً

šaribati l-bintāni ᶜaṣīran.

The two girls (dual) drank juice.

Remember: When a verb in the third person feminine singular is followed by a word beginning with **hamzatu l-waṣli** (**waṣlah**), the **sukūn** on the final /...t/ **...ـتْ** is replaced by **kasrah** **...ـتِ** to avoid having three consonants in succession, e.g.

...شَرِبَتِ ٱلْبِنْتُ šaribat**i** l-bintu... (not: .شَرِبَتْ ٱلْبِنْتُ šariba**t** l-bintu...)

(b) If the subject refers to a human being and the verb is placed after the subject, the verb must agree with the subject in number and gender, e.g.

أَلْمُعَلِّمُونَ شَرِبُوا عَصِيراً

ʾal-muᶜallimūna šaribū ᶜaṣīran.

The teachers (m. pl.) drank juice.

أَلْمُعَلِّمَتَانِ شَرِبَتَا عَصِيراً

ʾal-muᶜallimatāni šaribatā ᶜaṣīran.

The (two) teachers (f.) drank juice.

14.7 If the subject is not expressed by a noun or separate pronoun, the verb alone expresses its number, whether it be singular, dual or plural, e.g.

شَرِبُوا عَصِيراً

šaribū ᶜaṣīran.

They (m. pl.) drank juice.

شَرِبَتَا عَصِيراً

šaribatā ᶜaṣīran.

They (f. dual) drank juice.

14.8 If the subject is in the plural and refers to non-humans, the verb is in the feminine singular, e.g.

شَرِبَتِ ٱلْكِلَابُ حَلِيبًا
šaribati (sing.) l-kilābu ḥalīban.
The dogs drank milk.

أَلْكِلَابُ شَرِبَتْ حَلِيبًا
ʾal-kilābu **šaribat** ḥalīban.
The dogs drank milk.

14.9 If the subject is in the dual and refers to non-humans, the verb is in the dual (if following the subject) and agrees with the gender of the subject, just as with dual human beings, e.g.

شَرِبَ ٱلْكَلْبَانِ حَلِيبًا

šariba l-kalbāni ḥalīban. The (two) dogs (m.) drank (m. sing.) milk.

أَلْكَلْبَانِ شَرِبَا حَلِيبًا

ʾal-kalbāni **šaribā** ḥalīban. The (two) dogs (m.) drank (m. dual) milk.

شَرِبَتِ ٱلْكَلْبَتَانِ حَلِيبًا

šaribati l-kalbatāni ḥalīban. The (two) dogs (f.) drank (f. sing.) milk.

أَلْكَلْبَتَانِ شَرِبَتَا حَلِيبًا

ʾal-kalbatāni **šaribatā** ḥalīban. The (two) dogs (f.) drank (f. dual) milk.

14.10 The verb in the perfect tense is sometimes preceded by the particle قَدْ qad, or لَقَدْ la-qad, which is usually not translated. The purpose of these particles is merely a matter of style or to emphasize the completion or realization of the action of the verb, like adding the corroborating auxiliary 'do', the adverb 'really' or 'already', e.g.

قَدْ شَرِبَ ٱلْحَلِيبَ **qad** šariba l-ḥalība.

He **did** drink the milk. OR He has **already** drunk the milk.

14.11 *Negative of the perfect tense*

The negative particle مَا mā 'not' is used to negate the perfect tense and is placed before the verb, e.g.

مَا شَرِبَ ٱلْحَلِيبَ **mā** šariba l-ḥalība. He did not drink the milk.

Note: A more common way of negating the perfect in modern literary Arabic is introduced in chapter 28.

Exercises

Practise your reading:

أَكَلَ ٱلسَّبَّاحُونَ [1]طَعَامًا [2]فَاسِدًا [3]فَمَرِضُوا.

(1) ʾakala s-sabbāḥūna ṭaʿāman fāsidan fa-mariḍū.

The swimmers ate [2]rotten (spoiled) [1]food [3]and (so) became ill.

[1]طَلَبَ [2]ٱلْقَاضِي مِنَ ٱلْكَاتِبِ [3]تَقْرِيرًا عَنِ [4]ٱلْحَادِثِ.

(2) ṭalaba l-qāḍī mina l-kātibi taqrīran ʿani l-ḥādiṯi.

[2]The judge [1]asked the clerk (secretary) for [3]a report about [4]the accident.

[1]جَلَسَتِ ٱلْمَرْأَةُ [2]ٱلتَّعِبَةُ عَلَى [3]كُرْسِيٍّ [4]مَكْسُورٍ أَمَامَ [5]مَدْخَلِ [6]ٱلدُّكَّانِ.

(3) ǧalasati l-marʾatu t-taʿibatu ʿalā kursiyyin maksūrin ʾamāma madḫali d-dukkāni.

[2]The tired woman [1]sat on [4]a broken [3]chair in front of [5]the entrance of [6]the shop.

[1]نَجَحَتِ ٱلطَّالِبَتَانِ ٱلْأَجْنَبِيَّتَانِ فِي [2]ٱمْتِحَانِ [3]ٱلْقُبُولِ لِكُلِّيَّةِ [4]ٱلطِّبِّ.

(4) naǧaḥati ṭ-ṭālibatāni l-ʾaǧnabiyyatāni fī mtiḥāni l-qubūli li-kulliyati ṭ-ṭibbi.

The two foreign students (f.) [1]passed the [3]entrance [2]exam to the faculty of [4]medicine (medical college).

أَكَلَ [1]ٱلْقِطُّ [2]ٱلْجُبْنَةَ عَنِ ٱلطَّاوِلَةِ [3]وَخَطَفَ [4]قِطْعَةَ ٱللَّحْمِ مِنَ [5]ٱلْبَرَّادِ [6]وَهَرَبَ [7]بِهَا إِلَى [8]ٱلْحَدِيقَةِ.

(5) ʾakala l-qiṭṭu l-ǧubnata ʿani ṭ-ṭāwilati wa-ḫaṭafa qiṭʿata l-laḥmi mina l-barrādi wa-haraba bi-hā ʾilā l-ḥadīqati.

[1]The cat ate [2]the cheese from the table, [3]then snatched [4]the piece of meat from [5]the refrigerator [6]and ran away [7]with it to [8]the garden.

[1]حَمَلَ [2]ٱلْعَامِلَانِ [3]ٱلْكِيسَ [4]ٱلثَّقِيلَ [5]وَطَلَعَا بِهِ عَلَى [6]ٱلدَّرَجِ إِلَى [7]ٱلطَّابِقِ [8]ٱلْخَامِسِ.

(6) ḥamala l-ʿāmilāni l-kīsa ṯ-ṯaqīla wa-ṭalaʿā bi-hi ʿalā d-daraǧi ʾilā ṭ-ṭābiqi l-ḫāmisi.

[2]The two workers [1]carried the [4]heavy [3]sack [5]and climbed with it up [6]the stairs to [8]the fifth [7]floor.

[1]ذَكَرَتْ [2]جَرِيدَةُ [3]ٱلْيَوْمِ أَنَّ ٱلْوَزِيرَيْنِ قَدْ [4]رَفَضَا [5]ٱلْمَشْرُوعَ.

(7) d̲akarat ğarīdatu l-yawmi ʾanna l-wazīrayni qad rafaḍā l-mašrūʿa.
[3]Today's [2]newspaper [1]mentioned that the two ministers had [4]rejected [5]the project.

[1]رَجَعَ ٱلْمُعَلِّمُونَ مِنَ [2]ٱلْوِزَارَةِ بَعْدَ أَنْ [3]حَضَرُوا [4]ٱجْتِمَاعًا مَعَ [5]ٱلْوَزِيرِ.

(8) rağaʿa l-muʿallimūna mina l-wizārati baʿda ʾan ḥaḍarū ğtimāʿan maʿa l-wazīri.
The teachers (m.) [1]returned from [2]the ministry after they [3]attended [4]a meeting with [5]the minister.

[1]كَسَرَ [2]بَعْضُ [3]ٱلْمُتَظَاهِرِينَ بَابَ [4]ٱلْمَصْنَعِ [5]وَدَخَلُوا [6]مَكْتَبَ [7]ٱلْمُدِيرِ.

(9) kasara baʿḍu l-mutaẓāhirīna bāba l-maṣnaʿi wa-daḫalū maktaba l-mudīri.
[2]Some of [3]the demonstrators [1]broke down the door of [4]the factory [5]and entered the [7]director's [6]office.

[1]شَرَحَ [2]ٱلْمُحَاضِرُ ٱلدَّرْسَ [3]بِصَوْتٍ [4]مُنْخَفِضٍ [5]فَمَا [6]سَمِعَ ٱلطُّلَّابُ وَمَا [7]فَهِمُوا ٱلدَّرْسَ.

(10) šaraḥa l-muḥāḍiru d-darsa bi-ṣawtin munḫafiḍin fa-mā samiʿa ṭ-ṭullābu wa-mā fahimū d-darsa.
[2]The lecturer [1]explained the lesson in [4]a low [3]voice, and the students [5]neither [6]heard nor [7]understood the lesson.

[1]نَشَرَتِ [2]ٱلْجَرِيدَةُ [3]مَقَالًا طَوِيلًا عَنِ [4]ٱلْأَزْمَةِ [5]ٱلِاقْتِصَادِيَّةِ فِي ٱلْبِلَادِ.

(11) našarati l-ğarīdatu maqālan ṭawīlan ʿani l-ʾazmati l-ʾiqtiṣādiyyati fī l-bilādi.
[2]The newspaper [1]published a long [3]article on [5]the economic [4]crisis in the country.

[1]دَفَعَتِ [2]ٱلشَّرِكَةُ [3]أَجْرًا حَسَنًا [4]لِلْمُهَنْدِسِ ٱلْجَدِيدِ [5]وَرَفَعَتْ [6]أُجُورَ [7]بَاقِي ٱلْمُوَظَّفِينَ.

(12) dafaʿati š-šarikatu ʾağran ḥasanan li-l-muhandisi l-ğadīdi wa-rafaʿat ʾuğūra bāqī l-muwaẓẓafīna.
[2]The company [1]paid a good [3]salary to the new [4]engineer [5]and raised the [6]wages of the [7]rest of the employees.

[1]مَنَعَ [2]ٱلْحَارِسُ [3]دُخُولَ ٱلنَّاسِ إِلَى [4]ٱلْمَلْعَبِ [5]دُونَ [6]بِطَاقَاتٍ [7]فَقَفَزُوا
مِنْ [8]فَوْقِ [9]ٱلْجِدَارِ [10]وَشَاهَدُوا [11]ٱلْمُبَارَاةَ.

(13) manaʿa l-ḥārisu duḫūla n-nāsi ʾilā l-malʿabi dūna biṭāqātin fa-qafazū min fawqa l-ǧidāri wa-šāhadū l-mubārāta.
[2]The guard [1]prevented the people [5]without [6]tickets [3]from entering [4]the stadium (lit. playground) [7]so they jumped [8]over the [9]wall and [10]watched [11]the match.

[1]ذَهَبَتِ ٱلطَّالِبَاتُ فِي [2]رِحْلَةٍ إِلَى [3]ٱلْقَلْعَةِ [4]وَبَعَثْنَ لِمُعَلِّمَاتِهِنَّ [5]بِطَاقَاتٍ
[6]بَرِيدِيَّةً.

(14) ḏahabati ṭ-ṭālibātu fī riḥlatin ʾilā l-qalʿati wa-baʿaṯna li-muʿallimāti-hinna biṭāqātin barīdiyyatan.
The students (f.) [1]went on [2]a trip to [3]the fortress [4]and sent [6]post[5]cards to their teachers (f.).

[1]رَفَضَتِ [2]ٱلطِّفْلَةُ [3]ٱلْمَرِيضَةُ [4]ٱلطَّعَامَ وَٱلشَّرَابَ.

(15) rafaḍati ṭ-ṭiflatu l-marīḍatu ṭ-ṭaʿāma wa-š-šarāba.
[3]The sick [2]child (f.) [1]rejected (the) [4]food and (the) drink.

Translate into Arabic:

(1) The judge ate rotten meat and he became ill.
(2) The tired swimmer sat on a broken table.
(3) The sick woman carried the heavy sack from the shop.
(4) The company raised the salary of the new employee.
(5) The workers attended a meeting with the minister.
(6) The engineer published a long article in the newspaper.
(7) The two ministers asked for a report about the project.
(8) The engineer carried the heavy sack and took it up the stairs to the fifth floor.
(9) The foreign student (m.) did not understand the lesson.
(10) The ministry asked (مِنْ) the clerk for a report on the economic crisis.
(11) The newspaper rejected a long article on the crisis in the factory.
(12) The teacher (m.) returned from the fortress.

(13) The guard prevented the demonstrators from entering the fortress.

(14) The cat snatched the piece of cheese from the refrigerator and ran away (with it) to the director's office.

Chapter 15

Separate personal pronouns and suffix pronouns

15.1 The separate personal pronouns أَلضَّمَائِرُ الْمُنْفَصِلَةُ are:

	singular	dual	plural
1. m. f.	أَنَا		نَحْنُ
	ʾanā, I	(as in the plural)	naḥnu, we
2. m.	أَنْتَ	أَنْتُمَا	أَنْتُمْ
	ʾanta, you	ʾantumā, you two	ʾantum, you
2. f.	أَنْتِ	أَنْتُمَا	أَنْتُنَّ
	ʾanti, you	ʾantumā, you two	ʾantunna, you
3. m.	هُوَ	هُمَا	هُمْ
	huwa, he, it	humā, they two	hum, they
3. f.	هِيَ	هُمَا	هُنَّ
	hiya, she, it	humā, they two	hunna, they

Note: When dual or plural pronouns refer to mixed gender, the masculine predominates.

15.2 The separate personal pronouns have no case forms other than the nominative. Hence they replace nominative nouns, e.g.

أَلرَّجُلُ طَوِيلٌ

ʾar-rağulu ṭawīlun. The man is tall.

هُوَ طَوِيلٌ

huwa ṭawīlun. He is tall.

أَلْبِنْتُ لَطِيفَةٌ

ʾal-bintu laṭīfatun. The girl is kind.

هِيَ لَطِيفَةٌ

hiya laṭīfatun. She is kind.

Note: A separate pronoun can be added as an apposition to a word containing a suffix pronoun to give special emphasis, e.g.

مَرَرْتُ بِكَ أَنْتَ

marartu bi-ka ʾanta.

I passed by **you**. (**You** are the one I passed by.)

15.3 Sometimes the verb is preceded by a separate personal pronoun referring to the subject to put stress on the statement or subject, or to make the expression clear and to avoid misunderstandings in an unvocalized text, e.g.

أَنَا شَكَرْتُ ٱلطَّبِيبَ ʾ**anā** šakartu ṭ-ṭabība. **I** thanked the doctor.

أَنْتَ سَمِعْتَ ٱلْخَبَرَ ʾ**anta** samiʿta l-ḫabara. **You** heard the piece of news.

أَنَا أُحِبُّكِ/ أُحِبُّكَ ʾ**anā** ʾuḥibbu-**ki** (f.) / ʾuḥibbu-**ka** (m.). **I** (certainly) love you.

15.4 The suffix pronouns أَلضَّمَائِرُ ٱلْمُتَّصِلَةُ function as accusative and genitive forms of the personal pronouns. They can be attached to nouns, prepositions or verbs:

	singular	dual	plural
1.	..ـي /..ī/ my; ..ـنِي /..nī/ me	(as in the plural)	..ـنَا /..nā/ our, us
2. m.	..ـكَ /..ka/ your, you	..ـكُمَا /..kumā/ your, you (two)	..ـكُمْ /..kum/ your, you
2. f.	..ـكِ /..ki/ your, you	..ـكُمَا /..kumā/ your, you (two)	..ـكُنَّ /..kunna/ your, you
3. m.	..ـهُ /..hu/ his, him, its, it	..ـهُمَا /...humā/ their, them (two)	..ـهُمْ /..hum/ their, them
3. f.	..ـهَا /..hā/ her, its, it	..ـهُمَا /...humā/ their, them (two)	..ـهُنَّ /..hunna/ their, them

Note: The suffix pronoun for the first person singular ـنِي... /..nī/ 'me', is attached only to a verb, indicating the direct object (verbal object).

15.5 When suffix pronouns are attached to nouns, they function as possessive pronouns, i.e. as the genitive case of the separate personal pronouns. The noun and the suffixed pronoun form together a type of ʾiḍāfah construction, e.g.

قَلَمِي qalam-**ī**, my pen بَيْتُهُ baytu-**hu**, his house

15.6 The final syllable **nūn** ن... /...n/ + **fatḥah/kasrah** of the dual and sound masculine plural endings is dropped before a suffix pronoun, e.g.

		dual	
Nom.	كِتَابَانِ kitāb**āni** two books	كِتَابَاكَ kitābā-**ka** your (m.) (two) books	(not: كِتَابَانِكَ kitāb**āni**-ka)
Acc. and gen.	كِتَابَيْنِ kitābay**ni** two books	كِتَابَيْكَ kitābay-**ka** your (m.) (two) books	(not: كِتَابَيْنِكَ kitābay**ni**-ka)
		plural	
Nom.	مُعَلِّمُونَ muʿallimū**na** teachers (m.)	مُعَلِّمُوكَ muʿallimū-**ka** your (m.) teachers	(not: مُعَلِّمُونَكَ muʿallimū**na**-ka)
Acc. and gen.	مُعَلِّمِينَ muʿallimīna teachers (m.)	مُعَلِّمِيكَ muʿallimī-**ka** your (m.) teachers	(not: مُعَلِّمِينَكَ muʿallimī**na**-ka)

15.7 The first person singular suffix ي ... /...ī/ 'my' becomes يَ... /...ya/ when it is preceded by a long vowel or a diphthong, e.g.

dual		
Nom. عَيْنَانِ ʿaynān-**i** two eyes	عَيْنَايَ ʿaynā-**ya** my (two) eyes	(not: عَيْنَانِيَ ʿaynāni-**ya**)
Acc. and gen. عَيْنَيْنِ ʿaynayn-**i** two eyes	عَيْنَيَّ ʿaynay-**ya** my (two) eyes	(not: عَيْنَيْنِيَ ʿaynayni-**ya**)

15.8 When the suffix pronoun for the first person singular is attached to a sound masculine plural, the final ...ُو /...ū/ is changed to ...ِيَّ /...iyya/ in all three cases, e.g.

plural		
مُعَلِّمُونَ	مُعَلِّمِيَّ	(not: مُعَلِّمُونِيَ
muʿallim-**ūna**, teachers	muʿallim-**iyya**, my teachers	muʿallimūna-**ya**)

15.9 The ʾ**iḍāfah** construction may contain more than one annexed noun أَلْمُضَافُ. In this case only one annexed noun is placed before the annexer أَلْمُضَافُ إِلَيْهِ. The other annexed nouns are placed after the annexer, each preceded by the conjunction وَ /**wa...**/ 'and' and followed by a (possessive) suffix pronoun referring to the annexer and agreeing with it in number and gender, e.g.

قَلَمُ ٱلطَّالِبِ وَكِتَابُهُ وَدَفْتَرُهُ وَحَقِيبَتُهُ

qalam**u** ṭ-ṭālibi **wa**-kitāb**u-hu** **wa**-daftaru-**hu** **wa**-ḥaqībatu-**hu**

the student's pen, book, notebook and bag

(lit. the student's pen **and his** book **and his** notebook **and his** bag)

مَدْرَسَةُ ٱلْقَرْيَةِ وَجَامِعُهَا وَدُكَّانُهَا وَمَكْتَبَتُهَا

madrasat**u** **l-qaryati** **wa**-ǧāmiʿ**u-hā** **wa**-dukkān**u-hā** **wa**-maktabat**u-hā**

the school, mosque, store and library of the village

(lit. the school of the village **and its** mosque **and its** store **and its** library)

15.10 In contradiction to the above grammatical rule, in modern literary Arabic two coordinated annexed nouns are often placed before the annexer, e.g.

According to the rule	*In modern literary Arabic*
بَابُ ٱلسَّيَّارَةِ وَمِفْتَاحُهَا	بَابُ وَمِفْتَاحُ ٱلسَّيَّارَةِ
bābu s-sayyārati **wa-miftāḥu-hā**	**bābu wa-miftāḥu** s-sayyārati
the door and the key of the car	
إِسْمُ ٱلرَّجُلِ وَعُمْرُهُ	إِسْمُ وَعُمْرُ ٱلرَّجُلِ
ʾismu r-rağuli **wa-ʿumru-hu**	**ʾismu wa-ʿumru** r-rağuli
the name and age of the man	

15.11 Remember that when a suffix pronoun is attached to any of the four prepositions مَعَ maʿa, عِنْدَ ʿinda, لَدَى ladā or ...لِـ (...لَـ) li- (la-), the expression may be equivalent to the English verb to have (see chapter 11.10), e.g.

عِنْدَهُ سَيَّارَةٌ	مَعَهُمْ كِتَابٌ	لَهُ بَيْتٌ كَبِيرٌ
ʿinda-**hu** sayyāratun.	maʿa-**hum** kitābun.	la-**hu** baytun kabīrun.
He has a car.	They have a book.	He has a big house.

15.12 When the alternative form ...يَ /...ya/ (see paragraph 15.7) of the suffix pronoun for the first person singular is attached to a preposition ending in **ʾalif maqṣūrah** ...ى, they combine into ...يَّ /...yya/, e.g.

إِلَى ʾilā, to	*becomes:*	إِلَيَّ ʾila-**yya**, to me
عَلَى ʿalā, on	*becomes:*	عَلَيَّ ʿala-**yya**, on me

15.13 When the suffix pronoun for the first person singular ـِي.../...ī/ is attached to the two prepositions below, the final ...نْ /n/ of the prepositions is doubled:

مِنْ min, from	*becomes:*	مِنِّي minn-**ī**, from me
عَنْ ʿan, about	*becomes:*	عَنِّي ʿann-**ī**, about me

15.14 The preposition ...لِ /li.../ 'for, to, belonging to' takes the form ...لَ /la.../ before all suffix pronouns, except before the suffix pronoun of the first person singular, e.g.

لَكَ **la**-ka	لَهُمْ **la**-hum
for you, belonging to you	for them, belonging to them

BUT:

لِي **l**-ī,

for me, belonging to me

15.15 The **ḍammah** of the suffix pronouns is changed to **kasrah** when the suffix is preceded by **kasrah** or **yā'**:

...هُ /...hu/ ...هُمَا /...humā/ ...هُمْ /...hum/ ...هُنَّ /...hunna/

These suffixes become:

...هِ /...hi/ ...هِمَا /...himā/ ...هِمْ /...him/ ...هِنَّ /...hinna/

Examples:

فِي بَيْتِهِ	مِنْ مُعَلِّمَيْهِمَا	إِلَيْهِمْ
fī bayti-**hi**	min muʿallimay-**himā**	ʾilay-**him**
in his house	from their (two) teachers	to them

15.16 When the suffix pronouns are attached to verbs, they function as the direct (or indirect) object of transitive verbs, e.g.

شَتَمَنِي	سَمِعَهُ	حَمَلَهُمْ
šatama-**nī**.	samiʿa-**hu**.	ḥamala-**hum**.
He insulted me.	He heard him.	He carried them.

Remember: The suffix pronoun for the first person singular ...نِي /...nī/ 'me' is attached only to a verb (see 15.4 note).

15.17 When a suffix pronoun is attached to the second person masculine plural of a verb in the perfect tense, the personal ending ...تُمْ /...tum/ becomes ...تُمُو /...tum-ū/, e.g.

سَمِعْتُمْ samiᶜtum	*becomes:*	سَمِعْتُمُوهُ samiᶜtum-**ū-hu**
you (pl.) heard		you (pl.) heard him

15.18 Please recall that when the suffix pronouns are attached to the third person masculine plural of a verb in the perfect tense, the final ᵓ**alif** (ا) is elided, e.g.

سَمِعُوا samiᶜū, they heard — سَمِعُوهُ samiᶜū-**hu**, they heard him

15.19 The suffix : ...كُمْ /...kum/ *becomes:* ...كُمُ /...kum-**u**/ and
...هُمْ /...hum/ *becomes:* ...هُمُ /...hum-**u**/

The **sukūn** is replaced by **ḍammah** when it is followed by a word beginning with **waṣlah**, e.g.

شَكَرَكُمْ	شَكَرَكُمُ ٱلْمُعَلِّمُ
šakarakum.	šakarakum**u** l-muᶜallimu.
He thanked you (masc. plur.).	The teacher thanked you.

15.20 The preposition بَيْنَ is used with the meaning 'between'. It must be repeated before each coordinated member, if any of these members is expressed by a suffix pronoun, e.g.

بَيْنَ ٱلْمُدِيرِ وَبَيْنَكَ	بَيْنَهُ وَبَيْنَكَ
bayna l-mudīri wa-**bayna-ka**	**bayna-hu** wa-**bayna-ka**
between the director and you	between him and you

Compare:

بَيْنَ ٱلْمُدِيرِ وَٱلْمُوَظَّفِ

bayna l-mudīri wa-l-muwaḏḏafi

between the director and the employee

15.21 The suffix pronouns may be attached to the bound particle إِيَّا ʾiyyā, which functions as supporter for the direct object when it is placed first or when the verb takes a suffix pronoun that denotes the indirect object.

إِيَّاكَ نَعْبُدُ وَإِيَّاكَ نَسْتَعِينُ

ʾiyyā-ka naʿbudu wa-**ʾiyyā-ka** nastaʿīnu.

Thee (alone) do we worship; **Thee** (alone) we do ask for help. (Quran)

بَاعَنِي إِيَّاهُ bāʿa-**nī** ʾiyyā-**hu**. He sold **it** to **me**.

In the above sentence the suffix pronoun after the verb is the indirect object. Therefore the particle إِيَّا ʾiyyā is needed to carry the suffix pronoun that functions as direct object.

(a) The particle إِيَّا ʾiyyā can also be used in the meaning '(together) with' in combination with the prefixed conjunction وَ wa in phrases coordinating a separate pronoun with a suffix pronoun, e.g.

أَنَا وَإِيَّاهُمْ ʾanā wa-ʾiyyā-**hum**, I together with **them**

(b) The particle إِيَّا ʾiyyā may be used as a warning when it is attached to a suffix pronoun in the second person singular and plural, e.g.

إِيَّاكَ ٱلْكَذِبَ ʾiyyā-**ka** l-kaḏiba. OR إِيَّاكَ وَٱلْكَذِبَ ʾiyyā-**ka wa**-l-kaḏiba.
Beware of lies!

15.22 The ʾ**alif maqṣūrah** ...ى /ā/ changes to the regular form of ...ا /ā/ when a suffix pronoun is attached to the word, e.g.

رَمَى ramā, he threw

رَمَاهُ ramā-hu, he threw it

Exercises

Practise your reading:

[1]غَسَلَ [2]ٱلْخَادِمُ [3]دَرَجَ بَيْتِ ٱلْمُدِيرِ [4]وَسَيَّارَتَهُ [5]وَأَرْضَ مَكْتَبِهِ.

(1) ġasala l-ḫādimu daraǧa bayti l-mudīri wa-sayyārata-hu wa-ʾarḍa maktabi-hi.

[2]The servant [1]washed [3]the stairs of the director's house, [4]and his car [5]and the floor of his office.

[1]زَارَ ٱلطَّبِيبُ [2]ٱلْمَرِيضَةَ فِي بَيْتِهَا [3]وَفَحَصَهَا فِي [4]سَرِيرِهَا.

(2) zāra ṭ-ṭabību l-marīḍata fī bayti-hā wa-faḥaṣa-hā fī sarīri-hā.

The physician [1]visited [2]the patient ([2]the sick person, f.) in her house [3]and examined her [4]in her bed.

كَتَبْتُ [1]لَهُ رِسَالَةً [2]وَسَأَلْتُهُ [3]عَنْكُمْ وَعَنْ [4]مَوْضُوعِ [5]سَكَنِكُمْ [6]وَمِنْحَتِكُمْ.

(3) katabtu la-hu risālatan wa-saʾaltu-hu ʿan-kum wa-ʿan mawḍūʿi sakani-kum wa-minḥati-kum.

I wrote a letter [1]to him [2]and I asked him [3]about you and about [4]the subject (question, issue) of [5]your housing [6]and scholarship.

[1]وَجَدْتُ [2]قِطْعَةَ [3]لَحْمٍ فِي [4]ٱلْبَرَّادِ [5]فَطَبَخْتُهَا وَأَكَلْتُهَا.

(4) waǧadtu qiṭʿata laḥmin fī l-barrādi fa-ṭabaḫtu-hā wa-ʾakaltu-hā.

[1]I found [2]a piece [3]of meat in [4]the refrigerator, [5]I (then) cooked (it) and ate it.

ذَهَبْتُ [1]وَإِيَّاهَا إِلَى [2]حَدِيقَةِ [3]ٱلْحَيَوَانَاتِ وَمِنْ [4]هُنَاكَ ذَهَبْتُ
[5]مَعَهَا إِلَى مَنْزِلِهَا [6]وَسَهِرْتُ [7]عِنْدَهَا [8]بَعْضَ ٱلْوَقْتِ.

(5) ḏahabtu wa-ʾiyyā-hā ʾilā ḥadīqati l-ḥaywānāti wa-min hunāka ḏahabtu maʿa-hā ʾilā manzili-hā wa-sahirtu ʿinda-hā baʿḍa l-waqti.

I went [1](together) [1]with her to [2,3]the zoo (lit. [2]the garden of [3]animals), and from [4]there I went [5]with her to her home and [6]I spent [8]some time (in [6]the evening) [7]at her place.

[1]أَنْتُمْ [2]لَكُمْ [3]رَأْيُكُمْ وَأَنَا [4]لِي رَأْيِي.

(6) ʾantum la-kum raʾyu-kum wa-ʾanā l-ī raʾyī.

[1]You [2]have [3]your (own) opinion and [4]I have my (own) opinion.

أَبُوكَ وَأَخُوكَ [1]رَكِبَا [2]مَعِي فِي [3]نَفْسِ [4]ٱلْحَافِلَةِ إِلَى [5]وَسَطِ ٱلْمَدِينَةِ.

(7) ʾabū-ka wa-ʾaḫū-ka rakibā maʿ-ī fī nafsi l-ḥāfilati ʾilā wasaṭi madīnati.
Your father and brother [1]travelled ([1]rode) [2]with me in [3]the same [4]bus to the [5]centre of the city.

[1]أَخَذْتُ أَبَاكَ وَأَخَاكَ [2]مَعِي فِي [3]سَيَّارَتِي إِلَى ٱلسُّوقِ.

(8) ʾaḫaḏtu ʾabā-ka wa-ʾaḫā-ka maʿ-ī fī sayyāratī ʾilā s-sūqi.
[1]I took your father and brother [2]with me in [3]my car to the market.

[1]فَرِحْتُ [2]بِمُشَاهَدَةِ أَبِيكَ وَأَخِيكَ.

(9) fariḥtu bi-mušāhadati ʾabī-ka wa-ʾaḫī-ka.
[1]I was pleased [2]at seeing your father and brother.

[1]فَتَحَ [2]ٱلْعُصْفُورُ [3]مِنْقَارَهُ ([3]فَمَهُ) [4]فَسَقَطَتِ [5]ٱلْجُبْنَةُ عَلَى [6]ٱلْأَرْضِ فَأَكَلَهَا [7]ٱلْقِطُّ.

(10) fataḥa l-ʿuṣfūru minqāra-hu (fama-hu) fa-saqaṭati l-ğubnatu ʿalā l-ʾarḍi fa-ʾakala-hā l-qiṭṭu.
[2]The bird [1]opened [3]its beak (mouth) and so [5]the cheese [4]fell [6]to the ground so [7]the cat ate it.

كَتَبَتْ طَالِبَةٌ [1]رِسَالَةً إِلَى [2]صَدِيقَتِهَا، [3]ذَكَرَتْ [4]فِيهَا:

(11) (a) katabat ṭālibatun risālatan ʾilā ṣadīqati-hā ḏakarat fī-hā:
A student wrote [1]a letter to [2]her girlfriend [3]saying ([4]in it):

[5]شُكْرًا عَلَى رِسَالَتِكِ لَقَدْ [6]وَصَلَتْنِي [7]أَمْسِ [8]وَعَلِمْتُ [9]مِنْهَا،

(b) šukran ʿalā risālati-ki la-qad waṣalat-nī ʾamsi wa-ʿalimtu min-hā.
[5]Thank you for your letter (which) [6]I received (lit. [6]has arrived to me)[7]yesterday, and [8]I learned [9]from it ...

أَنَّكِ فِي [10]عِيدِ [11]مِيلَادِكِ ذَهَبْتِ فِي [12]رِحْلَةٍ مَعَ صَدِيقَتِكِ،

(c) ʾanna-ki fī ʿīdi mīlādi-ki ḏahabti fī riḥlatin maʿa ṣadīqati-ki,
that on your [10,11]birthday you went with your girlfriend [12]on a trip,

وَأَنَا [13]أَيْضًا قَدْ [14]بَعَثْتُ إِلَيْكِ [15]ٱلْيَوْمَ [16]هَدِيَّةَ [17]عِيدِ [18]مِيلَادِكِ.

(d) wa-ʾanā ʾayḍan qad baʿaṯtu ʾilay-ki l-yawma hadiyyata ʿīdi mīlādi-ki.
and [15]today [13]I also [14]sent (to) you a [17]birthday (lit. [17]anniversary, festival of [18]your birth) [16]present.

[1] أَنْتُمَا كَتَبْتُمَا ٱلْكِتَابَ [2] وَنَحْنُ [3] قَرَأْنَاهُ.

(12) ʾantumā katabtumā l-kitāba [2]wa-naḥnu qaraʾnā-hu.
[1]You (dual) wrote the book [2]and we [3]read it.

[1] مَعِي [2] قِصَّةٌ بِٱلْعَرَبِيَّةِ كَتَبَهَا [3] عَالِمٌ [4] مَشْهُورٌ.

(13) maʿī qiṣṣatun bi-l-ʿarabiyyati kataba-hā ʿālimun mašhūrun.
[1]I have (with me) [2]a novel in Arabic written by (wrote it) [4]a famous [3]scholar.

[1] أَمَامَ بَيْتِي [2] جُنَيْنَةٌ [3] فِيهَا [4] بِرْكَةٌ [5] وَاسِعَةٌ.

(14) ʾamāma bayt-ī ǧunaynatun fī-hā birkatun wāsiʿatun.
[1]In front of my house there is [2]a garden in which [3]there is ([3]in it) [5]a large [4]pond.

Translate into Arabic:

(1) Your father washed his car in front of our garden.
(2) His office is in front of the large pond.
(3) The physician visited me at my home and examined me in my bed.
(4) I wrote to her and I asked her about her birthday and about her trip to her father and brother.
(5) I found your (f.) book and the novel in my girlfriend's office.
(6) I spent some time with her at the zoo, and from there we went to the market.
(7) I was pleased at seeing your father and brother in the centre of the city.
(8) The servant opened the director's refrigerator and he found a piece of meat, which he cooked and ate (lit. and he cooked it and ate it).
(9) Thank you for your letter and birthday present.
(10) The scholar has written (wrote) his novel in Arabic.
(11) Yesterday I read her letter about her trip with her girlfriend.
(12) The sick bird fell on the ground and the cat ate it.
(13) The servant travelled (rode) with his girlfriend in the same bus.

Chapter 16

Demonstrative, reflexive and reciprocal pronouns

16.1 As in English, there are in Arabic two series of demonstrative pronouns أَسْمَاءُ ٱلْإِشَارَةِ ʾasmāʾu l-ʾišārati. Both of them have separate masculine and feminine forms in the singular and dual (in the plural there is no distinction between masculine and feminine forms). In the singular and plural each series has only one form for all three cases, but in the dual they are declined for two cases: nominative and accusative-genitive:

	this, this one				
	singular		dual		plural
	masc.	fem.	masc.	fem.	masc. and fem.
Nom.	هٰذَا	هٰذِهِ	هٰذَانِ	هَاتَانِ	هٰؤُلَاءِ
	hāḏā	hāḏihi	hāḏāni	hātāni	hāʾulāʾi
	this (one)		these two		these (ones)
Acc.	هٰذَا	هٰذِهِ	هٰذَيْنِ	هَاتَيْنِ	هٰؤُلَاءِ
and	hāḏā	hāḏihi	hāḏayni	hātayni	hāʾulāʾi
gen.	this (one)		these two		these (ones)

	that, that one				
	singular		dual		plural
	masc.	fem.	masc.	fem.	masc. and fem.
Nom.	ذٰلِكَ ذَاكَ	تِلْكَ	ذَانِكَ	تَانِكَ	أُولٰئِكَ
	ḏālika **or** ḏāka	tilka	ḏānika	tānika	ʾūlāʾika
	that (one)		those two		those (ones)
Acc.	ذٰلِكَ ذَاكَ	تِلْكَ	ذَيْنِكَ	تَيْنِكَ	أُولٰئِكَ
and	ḏālika **or** ḏāka	tilka	ḏaynika	taynika	ʾūlāʾika
gen.	that (one)		those two		those (ones)

Note: Regarding the spelling rules for the **hamzah** in هٰؤُلَاءِ and أُولَائِكَ, see chapter 20.

16.2 The demonstrative pronouns can be used both independently (as nouns) and adjectivally in Arabic:

Independently	***Adjectively***
هٰذَا قَلَمٌ	هٰذَا ٱلْقَلَمُ قَصِيرٌ
hāḏā qalamun.	hāḏā l-qalamu qaṣīrun.
This (is) a pen.	This pen (is) short (small).
ذٰلِكَ حِصَانٌ	ذٰلِكَ ٱلْحِصَانُ سَرِيعٌ
ḏālika ḥiṣānun.	ḏālika l-ḥiṣānu sarīʿun.
That (is) a horse (stallion).	That horse (is) fast.

Note: In the adjectival construction the noun must be preceded by the definite article.

16.3 When a demonstrative pronoun is used as the subject in a nominal sentence where the predicate is a noun made definite by the article أَلْـ... ʾal-, a third-person personal pronoun must be inserted between the subject and predicate to serve as a copula 'is, are', e.g.

هٰذَا هُوَ ٱلْقَلَمُ	هٰذِهِ هِيَ ٱلْبِنْتُ	هٰؤُلَاءِ هُمُ ٱلْمُعَلِّمُونَ
hāḏā **huwa** l-qalamu.	hāḏi-hi **hiya** l-bintu.	hāʾulāʾi **humu** l-muʿallimūna.
This **is** the pen.	This **is** the girl.	These **are** the teachers.

16.4 When the predicate noun is in the ʾiḍāfah construction, or followed by a suffixed pronoun, or when it is a proper name, the insertion of the personal pronoun between the demonstrative pronoun and predicate is optional, e.g.

هٰذَا (هُوَ) مُعَلِّمُ ٱلْوَلَدِ
hāḏā (**huwa**) **muʿallimu** l-waladi.
This (**is**) the boy's **teacher**.

هٰذِهِ (هِيَ) سَيَّارَةُ ٱلْمُدِيرِ
hāḏihi (**hiya**) **sayyāratu** l-mudīri.
This (**is**) the manager's **car**.

ذٰلِكَ (هُوَ) بَيْتِي
ḏālika (**huwa**) **baytī**.
That (**is**) **my house**.

هٰذَا (هُوَ) مُحَمَّدٌ
hāḏā (**huwa**) **Muḥammadun**.
This (**is**) **Muhammad**.

16.5 When the predicate is a noun in the indefinite form, no personal pronoun is needed between the demonstrative pronoun and predicate to act as copula, e.g.

هٰذَا قَلَمٌ
hāḏā qalamun.
This (**is**) a pen.

هٰذِهِ بِنْتٌ
hāḏihi bintun.
This (**is**) a girl.

هٰؤُلَاءِ مُعَلِّمُونَ
hāʾulāʾi muʿallimūna.
These (**are**) teachers.

ذٰلِكَ حِصَانٌ
ḏālika ḥiṣānun.
That (**is**) a horse (stallion).

16.6 Demonstrative pronouns qualifying plural nouns referring to non-human beings take the feminine singular forms, viz. هٰذِهِ 'this' and تِلْكَ 'that', e.g.

هٰذِهِ ٱلْحَيَوَانَاتُ مَرِيضَةٌ
hāḏihi l-ḥayawānātu marīḍatun.
These animals (are) ill.

تِلْكَ ٱلْكَرَاسِي مَكْسُورَةٌ
tilka l-karāsī maksūratun.
Those chairs (are) broken.

Note: The adjectives مَكْسُورَةٌ and مَرِيضَةٌ are in the singular because they refer to non-human beings.

16.7 When a demonstrative pronoun qualifies the first noun (the annexed) in the ʾiḍāfah construction, the demonstrative pronoun is placed after the whole phrase, e.g.

مُعَلِّمُ ٱلْبِنْتِ هٰذَا جَيِّدٌ	سَيَّارَةُ ٱلْمُدِيرِ هٰذِهِ قَدِيمَةٌ
muʿallimu l-binti **hāḏā** ǧayyidun.	sayyāratu l-mudīri **hāḏihi** qadīmatun.
This teacher of the girl is good.	***This*** car of the director is old.

16.8 *Reflexive and emphasizing (corroborative) pronouns*

(a) Arabic uses the noun نَفْسٌ nafsun (pl. أَنْفُسٌ ʾanfusun), 'soul, self, same', as a reflexive pronoun: '-self, -selves'. Then it must be followed by a suffix pronoun, e.g.

قَتَلَ نَفْسَهُ	شَاهَدْتُ نَفْسِي فِي ٱلْمِرْآةِ
qatala nafsa-**hu**.	šāhadtu nafs-**ī** fī l-mirʾāti.
He killed **himself**.	I saw **myself** in the mirror.

(b) Another use of نَفْسٌ nafsun is to emphasize or corroborate a following noun in the ʾ**iḍāfah** construction. It then has the meaning 'same' or '-self, -selves', e.g.

فِي نَفْسِ ٱلْيَوْمِ
fī nafsi l-yawmi
on the **same** day

(c) Alternatively, نَفْسٌ nafsun can follow the noun or (implicit) pronoun it emphasises, but then it must take a suffix pronoun, e.g.

فِي ٱلْيَوْمِ نَفْسِهِ	هُوَ نَفْسُهُ ذَهَبَ	ذَهَبَ بِنَفْسِهِ
fī l-yawmi nafsi-**hi**	huwa nafsu-**hu** ḏahaba.	ḏahaba bi-nafsi-**hi**.
on the **same** day	He went **himself**.	He went **himself**.

(d) The noun ذَاتٌ ḏātun (pl. ذَوَاتٌ ḏawātun) 'essence, identity, same, self' can be used just like نَفْسٌ nafsun, though less commonly in the reflexive meaning. For example:

فِي ذَاتِ ٱلْيَوْمِ
fī ḏāti l-yawmi
on the **same** day

(e) The adjective form (**nisbah**, introduced in chapter 25) of ذَاتٌ ḏātun is ذَاتِي ḏātī, 'self-', e.g.

أَلْحُكْمُ ٱلذَّاتِي

ʾal-ḥukmu ḏ-ḏātī

self-rule (autonomy)

Note a: رُوحٌ rūḥun (pl. أَرْوَاحٌ ʿarwāḥun), 'spirit', is used in some Arabic-speaking countries in the same way as نَفْس nafsun.

Note b: The word عَيْنٌ ʿynun 'eye, essence' is also sometimes used to emphasize a noun, just like نَفْس nafsun.

Note c: Reflexive action is often expressed by special derived verb forms, which will be introduced in chapter 18.

16.9 *Reciprocal pronoun*

Arabic uses the noun بَعْضٌ baʿḍun 'some, a few', as the reciprocal pronoun, 'each other, one another'. Then بَعْضٌ baʿḍun is often repeated. The first بَعْضٌ baʿḍun takes a suffix pronoun, e.g.

لَعِبَ ٱلْأَوْلَادُ بَعْضُهُمْ مَعَ بَعْضٍ

laʿiba l-ʾawlādu baʿḍu-hum maʿa baʿḍin.

The children played with each other.

ضَرَبَ بَعْضُهُمْ بَعْضاً

ḍaraba baʿḍu-hum baʿḍan.

They hit each other.

Note: A reciprocal action is often conveyed in Arabic by a special derived verb form to be introduced in chapter 18.

Exercises

Practise your reading:

[1]جَلَسَ هٰذَا [2]ٱلْعَجُوزُ [3]أَمَامَ ذٰلِكَ ٱلْبَابِ.

(1) ǧalasa hāḏā l-ʿaǧūzu ʾamāma ḏālika l-bābi.

This [2]old man [1]sat [3]in front of that door.

هٰذَا [1]مَسْمُوحٌ وَذٰلِكَ [2]مَمْنُوعٌ.

(2) hāḏā masmūḥun wa-ḏālika mamnūʿun.

This is [1]permitted and that is [2]forbidden.

بَابُ هٰذِهِ [1]ٱلسَّيَّارَةِ [2]مَقْفُولٌ [3]وَٱلْمِفْتَاحُ [4]لَيْسَ [5]مَعِي.

(3) bābu hāḏihi s-sayyārati maqfūlun wa-l-miftāḥu laysa maʿ-ī.
The door of this [1]car is [2]locked and I [4]do not [5]have [3]the key ([3]the key [4]is not [5]with me).

هٰذِهِ [1]هِيَ ٱلْكُتُبُ [2]ٱلْقَدِيمَةُ وَذٰلِكَ ٱلْكِتَابُ عَلَى [3]ٱلرَّفِّ ([4]هُوَ) جَدِيدٌ.

(4) hāḏihi hiya l-kutubu l-qadīmatu wa-ḏālika l-kitābu ʿalā r-raffi (huwa) ǧadīdun.
These [1]are [2]the old books (*broken plur.*), and that book on the [3]shelf [4]is new.

[1]قَبِلَ مُدِيرُ [2]ٱلشَّرِكَةِ [3]عُذْرَ هٰذَا ٱلْمُوَظَّفِ.

(5) qabila mudīru š-šarikati ʿuḏra hāḏā l-muwaḍḍafi.
The manager of [2]the company [1]accepted this employee's [3]excuse (alibi).

[1]كَثْرَةُ [2]ٱلْخَوْفِ هٰذِهِ مِنَ [3]ٱلسَّفَرِ [4]بِٱلْجَوِّ لَيْسَتْ [5]طَبِيعِيَّةً.

(6) kaṯratu l-ḫawfi hāḏi-hi mina s-safari bi-l-ǧawwi laysat ṭabīʿiyyatan.
This [1]much [2]fear [4]of air [3]travel is not [5]normal.

كَاتِبُ [1]ٱلْقِصَّةِ هٰذَا [2]هُوَ أُسْتَاذُ [3]ٱلْأَدَبِ ٱلْعَرَبِيِّ فِي جَامِعَتِنَا.

(7) kātibu l-qiṣṣati hāḏā huwa ʾustāḏu l-ʾadabi l-ʿarabiyyi fī ǧāmiʿati-nā.
This writer of [1]the novel [2]is a professor of Arabic [3]literature at our university.

[1]مَكْتَبَةُ ٱلْمَدِينَةِ هٰذِهِ (هِيَ) [2]قَدِيمَةٌ [3]وَلَيْسَ [4]فِيهَا كُتُبٌ [5]حَدِيثَةٌ.

(8) maktabatu l-madīnati hāḏi-hi (hiya) qadīmatun wa-laysa fī-hā kutubun ḥadīṯatun.
This city [1]library ([1]bookshop) is [2]old [3]and contains no (lit. there are not [4]in it) [5]contemporary books.

كَتَبَتْ تِلْكَ [1]ٱلصِّحَافِيَّةُ [2]ٱلْأَجْنَبِيَّةُ تِلْكَ [3]ٱلْمَقَالَاتِ ٱلطَّوِيلَةَ فِي هٰذِهِ [4]ٱلْمَجَلَّاتِ [5]ٱلشَّهْرِيَّةِ.

(9) katabat tilka ṣ-ṣiḥāfiyyatu l-ʾaǧnabiyyatu tilka l-maqālāti ṭ-ṭawīlata fī hāḏi-hi l-maǧallāti š-šahriyyati.
That [2]foreign [1]journalist (f.) wrote those long [3]articles in these [5]monthly [4]magazines.

مَا (هُوَ) [1]سَبَبُ هٰذِهِ [2]ٱلْمُشْكِلَةِ؟ سَبَبُ مُشْكِلَتِنَا هٰذِهِ [3]مُعَقَّدٌ وَلَيْسَ لَهُ [4]تَفْسِيرٌ.

(10) mā (huwa) sababu hāḏihi l-muškilati? sababu muškilati-nā hāḏihi muʿaqqadun wa-laysa la-hu tafsīrun.
What is [1]the reason for this [2]problem? The reason for this problem of ours is [3]complicated and has no [4]explanation.

هٰؤُلَاءِ [1]ٱلْمُتَقَاعِدُونَ وَأُولٰئِكَ [2]ٱلشَّبَابُ (s. شَابٌّ) [3]مُسَافِرُونَ [4]مَعًا فِي [5]نَفْسِ [6]ٱلْقِطَارِ.

(11) hāʾulāʾi l-mutaqāʿidūna wa-ʾūlāʾika š-šabābu (šābbun) musāfirūna maʿan fī nafsi l-qiṭāri.
These [1]retired persons and those [2]youths are [3]travelling [4]together on [5]the same [6]train.

أَكَلْتُ [1]أَمْسِ فِي [2]مَطْعَمٍ عَلَى تِلْكَ [3]ٱلتَّلَّةِ ثُمَّ [4]نَزَلْتُ إِلَى ذٰلِكَ [5]ٱلْوَادِي [6]ٱلْبَعِيدِ.

(12) ʾakaltu ʾamsi fī maṭʿamin ʿalā tilka t-tallati ṯumma nazaltu ʾilā ḏālika l-wādī l-baʿīdi.
[1]Yesterday I ate in [2]a restaurant on that [3]hill, then [4]I went down to that [6]distant [5]valley.

هٰذَا [1]ٱلْقَامُوسُ [2]قَدِيمٌ جِدًّا [3]وَمُمَزَّقٌ [4]وَلِهٰذَا [5]فَهُوَ [6]صَعْبُ [7]ٱلِاسْتِعْمَالِ.

(13) hāḏā l-qāmūsu qadīmun ğiddan wa-mumazzaqun wa-li-hāḏā fa-huwa ṣaʿbu l-istiʿmāli.
This [1]dictionary is very [2]old [3]and torn, [4]and therefore [5]it is [6]difficult [7]to use.

[1]جَلَسْتُ مَعَ هَاتَيْنِ ٱلْبِنْتَيْنِ فِي ذٰلِكَ [2]ٱلْمَقْهَى [3]ٱلْغَالِي.

(14) ğalastu maʿa hātayni l-bintayni fī ḏālika l-maqhā l-ġālī.
[1]I sat in that [3]expensive [2]coffee shop with these two girls.

أَلرَّجُلُ [1]ٱلْقَبِيحُ [2]ٱلْجَالِسُ عَلَى ذٰلِكَ [3]ٱلْكُرْسِيِّ هُوَ [4]كَذَّابٌ [5]وَطَوِيلُ [6]ٱللِّسَانِ.

(15) ʾar-rağulu l-qabīḥu l-ğālisu ʿalā ḏālika l-kursiyyi huwa kaḏḏābun wa-ṭawīlu l-lisāni.
[1]The ugly man [2]sitting on that [3]chair is [4]a liar and [5,6]talks too much (lit. has [5]a long [6]tongue).

Translate into Arabic:

(1) The manager accepted the excuse of these two girls.

(2) This is forbidden and that is permitted.

(3) This door of the university is new.

(4) Those youths are travelling together on this train to that distant city.

(5) This professor accepted the excuse of that foreign journalist (m.).

(6) This much fear of that problem has no explanation.

(7) I sat yesterday on that chair with this old man.

(8) The girl's dictionary is from that bookshop (library).

(9) This ugly man is the cause of this problem.

(10) The writer sat on a chair in front of this library.

(11) These retired persons are travelling in this car.

(12) I sat with this old man in that expensive coffee shop.

(13) This professor's book is old and torn.

(14) The door of this library is locked and the key is with that employee.

(15) The writer (f.) of those articles in these monthly magazines is a foreign journalist (f.).

Chapter 17

Imperfect tense verb in the indicative and word order

17.1 The Arabic imperfect tense أَلْمُضَارِعُ expresses an incomplete, continuous or habitual action or on-going state. It refers usually to the present, in which case it is translated by the English (simple or progressive) present tense, for example يَشْرَبُ yašrabu, 'he drinks' OR 'he is drinking'. In certain appropriate contexts, which will be explained later, it may, however, refer to the past or future, in which case it is translated by the English (simple or progressive) imperfect or future (sometimes present), respectively. It is thus to be emphasized that the Arabic imperfect tense is not like the English imperfect, which almost always refers to the past. (See also chapter 14 on the perfect tense.)

17.2 There are three moods in Arabic for the imperfect tense: indicative, subjunctive and jussive. The indicative mood is the basic mood of the verb and it is mostly used in forming statements and questions. In this chapter we will deal only with the indicative mood of the imperfect tense, أَلْمُضَارِعُ ٱلْمَرْفُوعُ. (See chapter 28 regarding the other moods.)

17.3 *'Vowelling' of the middle radical in the imperfect tense*

It was mentioned in chapter 14 that the triliteral verb in the perfect tense has three patterns of vowelling for the middle radical. The following are the rules of corresponding vowelling for the middle radical in the imperfect tense:

If the middle radical in the perfect tense has:

(a) **fatḥah,** then the middle vowel of the imperfect tense can be **fatḥah, kasrah** or **ḍammah,** e.g.

Perfect tense	***Imperfect tense***
ذَهَبَ da̱haba, he went	يَذْهَبُ yad̲habu /**a**/, he goes
كَتَبَ kataba, he wrote	يَكْتُبُ yaktubu /**u**/, he writes
غَسَلَ ġasala, he washed	يَغْسِلُ yaġsilu /**i**/, he washes

(b) **kasrah,** then the middle vowel of the imperfect is in almost all cases **fatḥah,** e.g.

Perfect tense	***Imperfect tense***
شَرِبَ šariba, he drank	يَشْرَبُ yašrabu /**a**/, he drinks, he is drinking

(c) **ḍammah,** then the middle vowel of the imperfect is also **ḍammah,** e.g.

Perfect tense	***Imperfect tense***
كَرُمَ karuma, he was generous	يَكْرُمُ yakrumu /**u**/, he is generous

17.4 Here is the conjugation of the imperfect indicative as exemplified by the verb كَتَبَ kataba, 'to write'. The third person masculine singular of this verb is يَكْتُبُ yaktubu, which can be translated as 'he writes', 'he is writing', or 'he will write'. In the conjugation table below, the prefixes and endings referring to the person, gender and number of the subject are written in bold type and small letters, and the roots in capitals. (See also conjugation A2.1 in Appendix 2.)

	singular	dual	plural
	يَكْتُبُ	يَكْتُبَانِ	يَكْتُبُونَ
3. m.	**ya**+KTUB+**u**	**ya**+KTUB+**āni**	**ya**+KTUB+**ūna**
	he writes	they (2) write	they write
	he is writing	they (2) are writing	they are writing

	singular	dual	plural
	تَكْتُبُ	تَكْتُبَانِ	يَكْتُبْنَ
3. f.	**ta**+KTUB+**u**	**ta**+KTUB+**āni**	**ya**+KTUB+**na**
	she writes	they (2) write	they write
	she is writing	they (2) are writing	they are writing
	تَكْتُبُ	تَكْتُبَانِ	تَكْتُبُونَ
2. m.	**ta**+KTUB+**u**	**ta**+KTUB+**āni**	**ta**+KTUB+**ūna**
	you write	you (2)write	you write
	you are writing	you (2) are writing	you are writing
	تَكْتُبِينَ	تَكْتُبَانِ	تَكْتُبْنَ
2. f.	**ta**+KTUB+**īna**	**ta**+KTUB+**āni**	**ta**+KTUB+**na**
	you write	you (2)write	you write
	you are writing	you (2) are writing	you are writing
	أَكْتُبُ		نَكْتُبُ
1. m. f.	**ʾa**+KTUB+**u**		**na**+KTUB+**u**
	I write		we write
	I am writing		we are writing

Note: If the subject refers to non-human beings in the plural, the verb is in the feminine singular.

17.5 *Word order in sentences with an imperfect tense verb*

The imperfect verb either precedes or follows its subject. The verb agrees with its subject in the same way as for the perfect tense, e.g.

Sing. أَلْعَامِلُ يَذْهَبُ كُلَّ يَوْمٍ إِلَى عَمَلِهِ

ʾal-ʿāmilu **yad͟habu** kulla yawmin ʾilā ʿamali-hi.

The worker **goes** to his work every day.

Plur. أَلْعُمَّالُ يَذْهَبُونَ كُلَّ يَوْمٍ إِلَى عَمَلِهِمْ

ʾal-ʿummālu **yad͟habūna** kulla yawmin ʾilā ʿamali-him.

The workers **go** to their work every day.

OR

Sing. يَذْهَبُ ٱلْعَامِلُ كُلَّ يَوْمٍ إِلَى عَمَلِهِ

yadhabu l-ʿāmilu kulla yawmin ʾilā ʿamali-hi.

Plur. يَذْهَبُ ٱلْعُمَّالُ كُلَّ يَوْمٍ إِلَى عَمَلِهِمْ

yadhabu l-ʿummālu kulla yawmin ʾilā ʿamali-him.

17.6 *Future*

The imperfect tense indicates the future when the context clearly refers to the future, e.g.

يَذْهَبُ ٱلْوَزِيرُ بَعْدَ أُسْبُوعٍ إِلَى بَيْرُوتَ (ذَهَبَ .v)

yadhabu l-wazīru baʿda ʾusbūʿin ʾilā bayrūta.
The minister **will go** (OR is going) to Beirut after one week (in a week's time).

أَبْعَثُ هٰذِهِ ٱلرِّسَالَةَ غَدًا (بَعَثَ .v)

ʾ**abʿaṯu** hāḏihi r-risālata ġadan.
I **will send** (OR I am going to send) this letter tomorrow.

17.7 When the context does not refer specifically to the future, it is necessary to specify it by adding the particle ...سَـ sa... or سَوْفَ sawfa 'will, shall' before the imperfect verb, e.g.

سَوْفَ / سَيَسْكُنُ مَعِي (سَكَنَ .v)

sawfa/sa-yaskunu maʿī. He will live with me.

Note: Even when the context refers to the future, very often the particles ...سَـ sa... or سَوْفَ sawfa are added before the imperfect verb anyway, e.g.

سَوْفَ / سَيَذْهَبُ ٱلْوَزِيرُ بَعْدَ أُسْبُوعٍ إِلَى بَيْرُوتَ

sawfa/sa-yadhabu l-wazīru baʿda ʾusbūʿin ʾilā bayrūta.
The minister **will go** to Beirut after one week (in a week's time).

17.8 *The particle* قَدْ *qad with the imperfect*

The particle قَدْ has already been mentioned in chapter 14 in connection with the perfect tense in order to emphasize the completion of an action or state. But the particle قَدْ is used with the imperfect tense to denote the uncertainty of an action or state, and is translated as 'may', 'might' or 'perhaps', e.g.

قَدْ نَكْتُبُ إِلَيْهِمْ **qad** naktubu ʾilay-him.

We **may** write to them. OR **Perhaps** we will write to them.

قَدْ يَحْضُرُ ٱلْأُسْتَاذُ غَدًا **qad** yaḥḍuru l-ʾustāḏu ġadan.

The teacher **might** come tomorrow.

17.9 *Negative of the imperfect tense*

The following three negative particles precede the verb in the imperfect:

لَا lā, not, neither   وَلَا wa-lā, nor
مَا mā, not (rarely used in the imperfect)

Example:

مَا / لَا يَشْرَبُ قَهْوَةً فِي ٱلْمَسَاءِ

mā / **lā** yašrabu qahwatan fī l-masāʾl.

He does **not** drink coffee in the evening.

سَوْفَ لَا يَذْهَبُ وَلَا يَكْتُبُ إِلَى أُمِّهِ

sawfa lā yaḏhabu **wa-lā** yaktubu ʾilā ʾummi-hi.

He **will** neither go **nor** write to his mother.

Exercises

Practise your reading:

فِي [1]أَيِّ [2]شَارِعٍ [3]تَسْكُنُ وَأَيْنَ تَسْكُنُ [4]عَائِلَتُكَ؟

(1) fī ʾayyi šāriʿin taskunu wa-ʾayna taskunu ʿāʾilatu-ka?

On [1]which [2]street do [3]you live and where does [4]your family live?

[1]قَدْ [2]لاَ يَأْكُلُ [3]ٱلطِّفْلُ [4]وَلاَ يَشْرَبُ [5]لِأَنَّ [6]أَسْنَانَهُ (.s سِنٌّ) [7]بَدَأَتْ [8]تَنْبُتُ.

(2) qad lā yaʾkulu ṭ-ṭiflu wa-lā yašrabu li-ʾanna ʾasnāna-hu badaʾat tanbutu.
[3]The child (baby) [1]may [2]neither eat [4]nor drink [5]because [6]his teeth [7]have begun [8]to grow.

[1]أَشْعُرُ [2]بِأَلَمٍ فِي [3]مَعِدَتِي [4]وَلِهٰذَا سَوْفَ لاَ [5]أَدْرُسُ [6]ٱلْيَوْمَ وَلاَ [7]أَذْهَبُ إِلَى [8]ٱلْمُحَاضَرَةِ.

(3) ʾašʿuru bi-ʾalamin fī maʿidat-ī wa-li-hāḏā sawfa lā ʾadrusu l-yawma wa-lā ʾaḏhabu ʾilā l-muḥāḍarati.
[1]I feel [2]pain in [3]my stomach [4]and therefore [6]today I will not [5]study nor [7]go to [8]the lecture.

سَوْفَ لاَ [1]يَنْدَمُونَ عَلَى [2]عَمَلِهِمْ فِي [3]ٱلْمُسْتَقْبَلِ

(4) sawfa lā yandamūna ʿalā ʿamali-him fī l-mustaqbali.
They will not [1]regret [2]their action (what they have done) in [3]the future.

[1]أَلْكِلاَبُ (.s كَلْبٌ) [2]عَادَةً تَشْرَبُ [3]حَلِيباً وَلاَ تَشْرَبُ [4]عَصِيراً [5]وَكَثِيراً مَا [6]لاَ تَأْكُلُ [7]عُشْباً.

(5) ʾal-kilābu ʿādatan tašrabu ḥalīban wa-lā tašrabu ʿaṣīran wa-kaṯīran-mā lā taʾkulu ʿušban.
[1]Dogs [2]normally drink [3]milk but they neither drink [4]juice [6]nor do they [5]often eat [7]grass.

[1]قَدْ [2]أَبْعَثُ هٰذَا [3]ٱلطَّلَبَ إِلَى مُدِيرِ [4]ٱلْمَصْنَعِ [5]شَخْصِيًّا.

(6) qad ʾabʿaṯu hāḏā ṭ-ṭalaba ʾilā mudīri l-maṣnaʿi šaḫṣiyyan.
I [1]may [2]send this [3]application to the director of [4]the factory [5]personally.

[1]أَيْنَ [2]سَتَذْهَبُونَ فِي [3]عِيدِ [4]رَأْسِ [5]ٱلسَّنَةِ [6]ٱلْجَدِيدَةِ؟

(7) ʾayna sa-taḏhabūna fī ʿīdi raʾsi s-sanati l-ǧadīdati?
[1]Where [2]will you go (masc. pl.) for [6]the New [5]Year [3]celebration? (lit. [3]feast of [4]the head/start of [6]the New [5]Year)

[1]سَأَجْلِسُ هُنَا مَعَ [2]صَدِيقَاتِي وَسَوْفَ لاَ [3]أَذْهَبُ إِلَى [4]ٱلْحَفْلَةِ.

(8) sa-ʾaǧlisu hunā maʿa ṣadīqātī wa-sawfa lā ʾaḏhabu ʾilā l-ḥaflati.
[1]I will [1]stay (sit) here with my [2]girlfriends and I will not [3]go to [4]the party.

لاَ [1]نَعْرِفُ [2]أَحَدًا [3]يَعْمَلُ فِي [4]شَرِكَةِ [5]ٱلنَّفْطِ.

(9) lā naᶜrifu ᵓaḥadan yaᶜmalu fī šarikati n-nafṭi.
We don't [1]know [2]anyone (who) [3]works for [5]the oil [4]company.

[1]بِسَبَبِ [2]ٱلضَّجَّةِ لاَ [3]نَسْمَعُ [4]مَاذَا [5]يَشْرَحُ [6]ٱلْخَبِيرُ.

(10) bi-sababi ḍ-ḍağğati lā nasmaᶜu māḏā yašraḥu l-ḫabīru.
[1]Because of [2]the noise we can't [3]hear [4]what [6]the expert [5]is explaining.

لاَ [1]يَسْمَحُ ٱلْإِمَامُ [2]بِدُخُولِ [3]ٱلنِّسَاءِ [4]لِلْجَامِعِ [5]بِدُونِ [6]حِجَابٍ.

(11) lā yasmaḥu l-ᵓimāmu bi-duḫūli n-nisāᵓi li-l-ğāmiᶜi bi-dūni ḥiğābin.
The imām does not [1]allow [3]women [2]to enter (lit. [2]the entering of women into) [4]the mosque [5]without [6]a veil.

[1]يَزْرَعُ [2]ٱلْمُزَارِعُونَ [3]أَرْضَهُمْ [4]قَمْحًا [5]ثُمَّ [6]يَحْصُدُونَهُ [7]وَيَطْحَنُونَهُ [8]وَيَعْجِنُونَ [9]ٱلطَّحِينَ ثُمَّ [10]يَخْبِزُونَهُ وَنَأْكُلُهُ [11]خُبْزًا.

(12) yazraᶜu l-muzāriᶜūna ᵓarḍa-hum qamḥan ṯumma yaḥṣudūna-hu wa-yaṭḥanūna-hu wa-yaᶜğinūna ṭ-ṭaḥīna ṯumma yaḫbizūna-hu wa-naᵓkulu-hu ḫubzan.
[2]The farmers [1]sow [3]their fields (lit. land) with [4](the) wheat, [5]then they [6]harvest [7]and grind it and they [8]knead [9]the dough (lit. flour), then they [10]bake it and we eat it as [11]bread.

[1]تَسْبَحُ ٱلْبِنْتُ ٱلصَّغِيرَةُ كُلَّ [2]يَوْمٍ فِي [3]ٱلْبِرْكَةِ [4]وَتَجْلِسُ أُمُّهَا عَلَى [5]كُرْسِيٍّ [6]تَحْتَ [7]ٱلْمِظَلَّةِ / [7]ٱلشَّمْسِيَّةِ [8]وَتَنْظُرُ إِلَيْهَا.

(13) tasbaḥu l-bintu ṣ-ṣağīratu kulla yawmin fī l-birkati wa-tağlisu ᵓummu-hā ᶜalā kursiyyin taḥta l-miḏallati / š-šamsiyyati wa-tanḏuru ᵓilay-hā.
The small girl [1]swims every [2]day in [3]the pool, and her mother [4]sits on [5]a chair [6]under [7]the umbrella [8]and watches her.

[1]يَذْهَبُ [2]غَدًا إِلَى عَمَّانَ [3]وَفْدٌ لُبْنَانِيٌّ [4]تِجَارِيٌّ [5]وَيَمْكُثُ [6]أُسْبُوعًا فِي ٱلْعَاصِمَةِ ٱلْأُرْدُنِّيَّةِ [7]وَيَبْحَثُ [8]مَسْأَلَةَ [9]ٱلاِسْتِيرَادِ [10]وَٱلتَّصْدِيرِ بَيْنَ ٱلْبَلَدَيْنِ.

(14) yaḏhabu ġadan ᵓilā ᶜammāna wafdun lubnāniyyun tiğāriyyun wa-yamkuṯu ᵓusbūᶜan fī l-ᶜāṣimati l-ᵓurdunniyyati, wa-yabḥaṯu masᵓalata l-istīrādi wa-t-taṣdīri bayna l-baladayni.

A Lebanese [4]commercial [3]delegation [1]will go to Amman [2]tomorrow [5]and will stay for [6]one week in the Jordanian capital [7]and discuss [8]the question of [9]imports [10]and exports between the two countries.

[1]أَلْمُمَرِّضَاتُ [2]يَجْلِسْنَ [3]كُلَّ يَوْمٍ فِي هٰذَا [4]ٱلْمَقْهَى وَيَشْرَبْنَ
[5]قَهْوَةً أَوْ [6]شَايًا.

(15) ᵓal mumarriḍātu yaǧlisna kulla yawmin fī hāḏā l-maqhā wa-yašrabna qahwatan ᵓaw šāyan.
[1]The nurses [2]sit [3]every day in this [4]cafe and drink [5]coffee or [6]tea.

[1]سَمِعْتُ أَنَّكُمَا [2]سَتَتْرُكَانِ [3]عَمَلَكُمَا وَتَعْمَلَانِ فِي شَرِكَةٍ [4]أُخْرَى.
[5]نَعَمْ! سَوْفَ [6]نَتْرُكُ عَمَلَنَا فِي [7]ٱلشَّهْرِ [8]ٱلْقَادِمِ وَلٰكِنْ
[9]سَنُسَافِرُ إِلَى أَمْرِيكَا وَنَدْرُسُ [10]ٱللُّغَةَ ٱلْإِنْجِلِيزِيَّةَ هُنَاكَ.

(16) samiᶜtu ᵓanna-kumā sa-tatrukāni ᶜamala-kumā wa-taᶜmalāni fī šarikatin ᵓuḫrā. naᶜam! sawfa natruku ᶜamala-nā fī š-šahri l-qādimi, wa-lākin sa-nusāfiru ᵓilā ᵓamrīkā wa-nadrusu l-luġata l-ᵓinǧlīziyyata hunāka.
[1]I have heard that [2]you (dual) will leave [3]your jobs and work for [4]another company! [5]Yes! We will [6]leave (our) jobs [8]next [7]month, but we [9]will travel to America and study the English [10]language there.

Translate into Arabic:

(1) On which street does the imām live and in which mosque is he working?

(2) I have heard that the director of the factory may go to Amman tomorrow.

(3) The small girl feels pain in her stomach and therefore she neither drinks nor eats bread.

(4) My friends (f.) will regret entering the mosque without a veil.

(5) Because of the noise of the dogs I will not stay (sit) in this cafe.

(6) The director of the oil company will travel on the New Year holiday to the Jordanian capital and will stay there for one week.

(7) Next month the director will not allow the farmers to enter the factory (lit. the entering of the farmers into the factory).

(8) The women will leave their jobs in the factory and work in their own fields.

(9) The mother swims every day in the pool and sits on a chair under the umbrella and drinks coffee.

(10) The commercial delegation will leave the capital next month and go to the Jordanian capital and discuss the question of imports and exports.

Chapter 18

Derived verb forms (stems), roots and radicals, transitive and intransitive verbs

18.1 Until now we have dealt with the basic verb form of triliteral verbs (أَلْفِعْلُ ٱلثُّلَاثِيُّ ʾal-fiʿlu t̲-t̲ulāt̲ī). The basic verb form has the pattern CVCVCV, as for example كَتَبَ kataba 'to write' (lit. 'he wrote', perfect tense). The basic verb form is called in Arabic أَلْمُجَرَّدُ ʾal-muǧarradu, meaning 'peeled' or 'stripped', because it lacks prefixes and infixes.

18.2 At this point it is important to explain more about the terms (verbal) root and radical, which are very special features in Arabic grammar. The root is the absolute basis for forming all verb forms as well as most nouns, adjectives, adverbs and even prepositions (see chapter 14). The root usually consists of three consonants. These consonants are called radicals, because together they make up the root, e.g. كتب /ktb/ 'to write', كِتَابٌ kitābun 'book', قول /qwl/ 'to speak' (basic verb form قَالَ qāla 'he spoke', imperfect يَقُولُ yaqūlu 'he speaks'), verbal noun قَوْلٌ qawlun 'speech'.

18.3 Some grammarians call the radicals simply letters, but the term radical is more appropriate, because letters refer to units of writing, whereas radicals refer to more theoretical units, which may sometimes be dropped or transformed in the actual verb forms and derivations (see chapters 31–33 on weak radicals). Roots with three radicals are called triliteral. There are no roots with fewer than three radicals. Some roots have four radicals. They are called quadriliteral. This type of verb will be dealt with in chapter 29.

18.4 The derived verb forms are called أَلْمَزِيد, ʾal-mazīdu, which means 'increased' or 'added'. They are formed from the root by means of consonant doubling, prefixes or infixes, according to certain patterns (mentioned below, and in table A1.1, the ten forms of فَعَلَ faʿala, in Appendix 1).

18.5 The meanings of the derived verb forms are generally derived from the basic verb form according to a system explained below. As a rule, grammarians prefer to call the derived verb forms derived verb stems, because each derived verb form has a complete set of conjugated forms (tenses, verbal noun, participles, etc.). (See table A1.1 **faʿala** in Appendix 1.)

18.6 There are 14 derived verb forms (stems). Western Arabists traditionally number these forms with Roman numerals starting from the basic form, which is numbered as I, and the derived verb forms as II, III, IV, etc. Forms I to X are the most frequent and only these will be explained in this book.

18.7 There is no verb which is used in all ten forms; normally the verb is used in five or six of the derived forms, and sometimes even the basic verb form itself is not used. For example, the verb form I عَلِمَ ʿalima 'to know' occurs in forms II, IV, V, and X, but another verb might occur only in forms III, VI, X, and so on.

18.8 As mentioned in chapter 14, there is no infinitive in Arabic in the same sense as in Indo-European languages. The derived verb forms are listed in the dictionary under the root, which is mostly the same as the basic verb form (I) without vowels.

18.9 It is crucially important to learn by heart these ten verb forms and their derivations from table A1.1 of the verb فَعَلَ faʿala in Appendix 1; otherwise it is almost impossible to find a word in a dictionary.

18.10 Arab grammarians chose the basic verb فَعَلَ /fʿl/ faʿala 'to do, to act' as a pattern or model for describing other verb forms and nouns which are derived from it.

18.11 Although the vowelling of the middle consonant (radical) of the basic verb form (I) in the perfect tense varies: كَتَبَ kataba 'to write',

شَرِبَ šariba 'to drink' or كَبُرَ kabura 'to grow up', the vowelling of the derived verb forms remains the same for all verbs.

18.12 *Transitive and intransitive verbs*

A transitive verb is called مُتَعَدٍّ mutaʿaddin, and an intransitive verb غَيْرُ مُتَعَدٍّ ġayru mutaʿaddin or لَازِمٌ lāzimun. Transitive verbs can take a direct object in the accusative case, whereas intransitive cannot do so (some of them can, however, take an accusative predicative complement). The basic verb form may be transitive or intransitive, depending on its meaning and construction. Some derived verb forms are typically transitive, while others are generally intransitive, but there are no absolute rules for determining their meaning.

In the following examples, the basic form (I) is transitive and the corresponding form VII is intransitive.

Transitive sentence	***Intransitive sentence***
كَسَرَ ٱلطَّالِبُ ٱلنَّظَّارَاتِ	إِنْكَسَرَتِ ٱلنَّظَّارَاتُ
kasara (I) ṭ-ṭālibu n-naḏḏārāti.	ʾ**inkasarati (VII)** n-naḏḏārātu.
The student **broke** the spectacles.	The spectacles **were/got broken.**

18.13 In addition to the nouns mentioned in chapter 9, with the initial **hamzatu l-qaṭʿi** إِ /ʾi/ or أُ /ʾu/, the verb forms VII–X (perfect, imperative and verbal noun) also follow the rule of **hamzatu l-waṣli** (**waṣlah**). However, the verb form IV follows the rule of **hamzatu l-qaṭʿi**.

18.14 *Formation of the ten verb forms I–X*

The table presents the ten verb forms I–X in the perfect and the imperfect (third person sing. masc.), as exemplified by the verb فَعَلَ faʿala 'to do, to act'.

		perfect		
I	II	III	IV	V
فَعَلَ	فَعَّلَ	فَاعَلَ	أَفْعَلَ	تَفَعَّلَ
faʿala	faʿʿala	fāʿala	ʾafʿala	tafaʿʿala
		imperfect		
يَفْعَلُ	يُفَعِّلُ	يُفَاعِلُ	يُفْعِلُ	يَتَفَعَّلُ
yafʿalu	yufaʿʿilu	yufāʿilu	yufʿilu	yatafaʿʿalu
		perfect		
VI	VII	VIII	IX	X
تَفَاعَلَ	إِنْفَعَلَ	إِفْتَعَلَ	إِفْعَلَّ	إِسْتَفْعَلَ
tafāʿala	ʾinfaʿala	ʾiftaʿala	ʾifʿalla	ʾistafʿala
		imperfect		
يَتَفَاعَلُ	يَنْفَعِلُ	يَفْتَعِلُ	يَفْعَلُّ	يَسْتَفْعِلُ
yatafāʿalu	yanfaʿilu	yaftaʿilu	yafʿallu	yastafʿilu

18.15 *The meanings of the ten verb forms I–X*

The basic meanings of the ten verb forms **I–X** are outlined below with some examples. Observe that many derived verb forms can have several different meanings and that some verbs have quite idiomatic or specialized meanings in some of their derived verb forms. Therefore it is recommended that the student learn the specific meaning of each derived verb form of each verb separately, rather than relying upon the general rules given below.

Form I

The basic form (I) can be transitive or intransitive.

I كَتَبَ kataba (transitive) imperf. يَكْتُبُ yaktubu
to write

I جَلَسَ ǧalasa (intransitive) imperf. يَجْلِسُ yaǧlisu
to sit

Form II

(a) II is causative: to cause someone to do something (transitive).

I عَلِمَ ʿalima	II عَلَّمَ ʿallama	imperf. يُعَلِّمُ yuʿallimu
to know	to teach (lit. cause someone to learn)	

(b) II is intensifying or iterative: repeating the action (transitive).

I كَسَرَ kasara	II كَسَّرَ kassara	imperf. يُكَسِّرُ yukassiru
to break	to smash, to break into pieces	

(c) II is declarative: to consider someone or something to be something, (transitive).

I كَذَبَ kaḏaba	II كَذَّبَ kaḏḏaba	imperf. يُكَذِّبُ yukaḏḏibu
to lie	to consider someone a liar, to disbelieve someone else	

(d) II is denominative (forming verb from noun).

سِلاَحٌ silāḥun (noun)	II سَلَّحَ sallaḥa	imperf. يُسَلِّحُ yusalliḥu
weapon	to arm	

Form III

III denotes an effort to do or achieve that which is expressed by the basic form. Often it expresses an action directed at (or done together with) someone else. Form III is mostly *transitive*.

I كَتَبَ kataba	III كَاتَبَ kātaba	imperf. يُكَاتِبُ yukātibu
to write	to correspond with somebody	
I سَبَقَ sabaqa	III سَابَقَ sābaqa	imperf. يُسَابِقُ yusābiqu
to precede	to compete with, to race	
I بَلَغَ balaġa	III بَالَغَ bālaġa	imperf. يُبَالِغُ yubāliġu
to reach	to exaggerate	

Form IV

IV is prefixed with أَ /ʾa.../ which is elided in the imperfect tense.

(a) IV is causative: to cause someone to do the action (transitive).

I عَلِمَ ʿalima — to know
IV أَعْلَمَ ʾaʿlama — to inform (to cause someone to know) — imperf. يُعْلِمُ yuʿlimu

(b) IV is declarative of I: to declare that someone has a certain quality (transitive).

I حَمِدَ ḥamida — to praise
IV أَحْمَدَ ʾaḥmada — to consider praiseworthy — imperf. يُحْمِدُ yuḥmidu

(c) IV is denominative (intransitive verb derived from a noun).

ذَنْبٌ ḏanbun (noun) — sin
IV أَذْنَبَ ʾaḏnaba — to commit a sin, to do wrong — imperf. يُذْنِبُ yuḏnibu

e.g. أَذْنَبَ تِجَاهَ... ʾaḏnaba tiǧāha ..., he committed a sin against ....

Form V

V is generally reflexive of form II (transitive or intransitive).

II عَلَّمَ ʿallama — to teach
V تَعَلَّمَ taʿallama — to learn (lit. he taught himself) — imperf. يَتَعَلَّمُ yataʿallamu

II شَرَّفَ šarrafa — to honour
V تَشَرَّفَ tašarrafa — to have the honour — imperf. يَتَشَرَّفُ yatašrrafu

II كَلَّمَ kallama — to talk to somebody
V تَكَلَّمَ takallama — to speak, utter — imperf. يَتَكَلَّمُ yatakallamu

---

Form VI

(a) VI is reflexive or reciprocal of form III (mostly transitive). In this form both or all partners are involved in action, therefore the subject is in the dual or plural.

III قَاسَمَ qāsama — to share
VI تَقَاسَمَ taqāsama — to divide or distribute among themselves — imperf. يَتَقَاسَمُ yataqāsamu

III كَاتَبَ kātaba — to correspond with a person
VI تَكَاتَبَ takātaba — to correspond with each other — imperf. يَتَكَاتَبُ yatakātabu

(b) VI can also be a kind of pretence form of (I), denoting pretending to be in a certain condition or trying to be something (intransitive).

I مَرِضَ mariḍa — to be ill
VI تَمَارَضَ tamāraḍa — to pretend to be ill — imperf. يَتَمَارَضُ yatamāraḍu

(c) VI can also denote a successive or uninterrupted sequence (intransitive).

I سَقَطَ saqaṭa   VI تَسَاقَطَ tasāqaṭa   imperf. يَتَسَاقَطُ yatasāqaṭu
    to fall   to fall consecutively, one after the other

Form VII

VII this form is prefixed with ...اِنْ /ʾin.../, and /ʾi.../ is elided in the imperfect tense. It is reflexive-passive or anticausative of form I (intransitive).

I كَسَرَ kasara   VII إِنْكَسَرَ ʾinkasara   imperf. يَنْكَسِرُ yankasiru
    to break   to break (by itself), get broken

Form VIII

VIII has an infix ...ت... /...t.../ in the middle and is prefixed with اِ /ʾi.../, which is elided in the imperfect tense.

(a) VIII is reflexive-intransitive of form I.

I جَمَعَ ğamaʿa   VIII إِجْتَمَعَ ʾiğtamaʿa   imperf. يَجْتَمِعُ yağtamiʿu
    to collect (trans.)   to gather, come together (intr.)

(b) VIII has the passive meaning of form I.

I حَرَقَ ḥaraqa   VIII إِحْتَرَقَ iḥtaraqa   imperf. يَحْتَرِقُ yaḥtariqu
    to burn (trans.)   to be burned, burn (intr.)

(c) VIII sometimes has the same meaning as form I (transitive).

I شَرَى šarā   VIII إِشْتَرَى ʾištarā   imperf. يَشْتَرِي yaštarī
    to buy   to buy

I بَاعَ bāʿa   VIII إِبْتَاعَ ʾibtāʿa   imperf. يَبْتَاعُ yabtāʿu
    to sell   to buy

Form IX

IX has its last consonant doubled and is prefixed with اِ /ʾi.../, which is elided in the imperfect tense. It refers to colours or defects and has the meaning 'to become or turn...'. It is intransitive and can be formed from the first or second form or directly from adjectives.

I عَوَجَ ʿawağa	IX إِعْوَجَّ ʾiʿwağğa	imperf. يَعْوَجُّ yaʿwağğu
to bend	to be twisted, bent

I not used II حَمَّرَ ḥammara IX إِحْمَرَّ ʾiḥmarra imperf. يَحْمَرُّ yaḥmarru
to redden, colour red	to turn red, blush

Form X

X is formed by adding the prefix ...إِسْتَ /ʾista.../ to form I, and إِ /ʾi.../ is elided in the imperfect tense.

(a) X is reflexive of form IV (transitive).

IV أَعْلَمَ ʾaʿlama	X إِسْتَعْلَمَ ʾistaʿlama	imperf. يَسْتَعْلِمُ yastaʿlimu
to inform, to let know	to enquire, seek information

(b) X is transitive of form I (often denoting attempt, request or desire to obtain something)

I خَرَجَ ḫarağa	X إِسْتَخْرَجَ ʾistaḫrağa	imperf. يَسْتَخْرِجُ yastaḫriğu
to come out	to take out, extract, deduce

(c) X is declarative of form I or IV (transitive or intransitive).

I حَسُنَ ḥasuna	X إِسْتَحْسَنَ ʾistaḥsana	imperf. يَسْتَحْسِنُ yastaḥsinu
to be nice, good	to consider nice, good

18.16 *Pronunciation and spelling rules*

The following modifications are made for certain derived verbs of form VIII in order to smooth the pronunciation:

(a) If the first consonant of the basic verb form is one of the following four emphatic letters: ص /ṣ/, ض /ḍ/, ط /ṭ/, ظ /ḏ̣/, the infix ..تـ.. /-t-/ of form VIII as in the pattern verb إِفْتَعَلَ /ʾiftaʿala/ is changed into ..ـطـ.. /-ṭ-/, e.g. ضَرَبَ ḍaraba 'to hit', whose form VIII is إِضْطَرَبَ ʾiḍṭaraba 'to be troubled', (not: إِضْتَرَبَ). And طَلَعَ ṭalaʿa 'to rise' has as its form VIII إِطَّلَعَ ʾiṭṭalaʿa 'to become aware' (not: إِطْتَلَعَ).

(b) If the first consonant of the basic verb form is ز /z/, as in زَهَرَ zahara ‘to shine’, the infix ..تـ.. /-t-/ of form VIII is changed into د /-d-/, thus yielding the form إِزْدَهَرَ ʾizdahara ‘to flourish’ (not: إِزْتَهَرَ ʾiztahara).

Note: If the first consonant of the basic verb form is ..تـ /t/, as in تَبِعَ tabiʿa ‘to follow’, the infix ..تـ.. /-t-/ of form VIII is written as doubled: إِتَّبَعَ ʾittabaʿa, ‘to follow, succeed’ (not: إِتْتَبَعَ).

Exercises

Analyse the following verbs according to:

(a) form number
(b) basic verb form
(c) imperfect tense.

	أَبْعَدَ	تَفَرَّقَ	جَمَّعَ	أَنْتَجَ	حَرَّرَ
(1)	to send away	to be split	to gather	to produce	to liberate
	إِسْتَخْرَجَ	عَلَّمَ	سَامَحَ	إِسْوَدَّ	كَاتَبَ
(2)	to take out	to teach	to forgive	to become black	to correspond with
	إِسْتَمْتَعَ	تَحَسَّنَ	سَهَّلَ	أَعْلَمَ	هَاجَرَ
(3)	to enjoy	to improve	to make easy	to inform	to emigrate
	تَكَاتَبَ	تَجَنَّبَ	تَسَلَّحَ	إِنْتَقَلَ	تَكَلَّمَ
(4)	to correspond	to avoid	to arm oneself	to move	to speak
	إِنْقَسَمَ	إِنْسَرَقَ	تَسَابَقَ	شَارَكَ	تَقَاتَلَ
(5)	to be divided	to be stolen	to compete	to share	to fight
	سَلَّمَ	إِنْتَصَرَ	تَعَلَّمَ	تَكَبَّرَ	إِنْفَجَرَ
(6)	to greet	to gain	to learn	to be proud	to explode

	دَافَعَ	إِنْتَبَهَ	إِسْتَهْلَكَ	أَجْبَرَ	إِسْتَصْعَبَ
(7)	to defend	to notice	to consume	to force	to find difficult
	جَرَّبَ	إِسْمَرَّ	تَقَدَّمَ	أَهْمَلَ	إِمْتَنَعَ
(8)	to try	to become brown	to progress	to neglect	to reject
	قَارَنَ	إِحْتَرَمَ	تَبَاحَثَ	إِقْتَنَعَ	إِسْتَعْمَلَ
(9)	to compare	to respect	to discuss	to be convinced	to use

Practise your reading:

[1]تُدَرِّسُ زَوْجَتِي فِي [2]ذَاتِ / [2]نَفْسِ ٱلْجَامِعَةِ [3]ٱلَّتِي [4]تَخَرَّجَتْ [5]مِنْهَا.

(1) tudarrisu zawǧat-ī fī ḏāti / nafsi l-ǧāmiʿati llatī taḫarraǧat min-hā.

My wife [1]teaches at [2]the same university from [3]which [4]she graduated ([5]from it).

[1]يَتَقَاسَمُ ٱلتَّاجِرَانِ [2]رِبْحَ ٱلشَّرِكَةِ فِي [3]آخِرِ [4]كُلِّ [5]سَنَةٍ.

(2) yataqāsamu t-tāǧirāni ribḥa š-šarikati fī ʾāḫiri kulli sanatin.

The two merchants [1]share [2]the profits of the company at [3]the end of [4]every [5]year.

[1]بِسَبَبِ [2]كَثْرَةِ [3]ٱلْمَطَرِ [4]ٱنْهَدَمَ [5]ٱلْجِسْرُ [6]وَٱنْقَطَعَ [7]ٱلطَّرِيقُ [8]بَيْنَ ٱلْقَرْيَتَيْنِ.

(3) bi-sababi kaṯrati l-maṭari n-hadama l-ǧisru wa-nqaṭaʿa ṭ-ṭarīqu bayna l-qaryatayni.

[1]Because of [2]the heavy (abundance of) [3]rain, [5]the bridge [4]collapsed and [7]the road [8]between the two villages [6]was cut off.

سَوْفَ لَا [1]تُمْطِرُ [2]غَدًا وَلِهٰذَا [3]سَيُشَارِكُ كَثِيرٌ مِنَ ٱلنَّاسِ فِي [4]حَفْلَةِ [5]ٱلْعُرْسِ.

(4) sawfa lā tumṭiru ġadan wa-li-hāḏā sa-yušāriku kaṯīrun mina n-nāsi fī ḥaflati l-ʿursi.

It will not [1]rain [2]tomorrow and therefore many people [3]will attend [5]the wedding [4]party.

¹هَاجَمَتِ ²ٱلشُّرْطَةُ ³مَكَانَ ⁴ٱلْإِرْهَابِيِّينَ ⁵وَتَبَادَلُوا ⁶ٱلنَّارَ مَعَهُمْ ⁷وَبَعْدَ ⁸سَاعَةٍ مِنَ ⁹ٱلْقِتَالِ ¹⁰سَلَّمَ ¹¹ٱلْإِرْهَابِيُّونَ ¹²أَنْفُسَهُمْ (s. نَفْسٌ).

(5) hāğamati š-šurṭatu makāna l-ʾirhābiyyīna wa-tabādalū n-nāra maʿa-hum, wa-baʿda sāʿatin mina l-qitāli sallama l-ʾirhābiyyūna ʾanfusa-hum.

²The police ¹attacked ⁴the terrorists' ³location (place) ⁵and exchanged ⁶fire with them ⁷and after ⁸one hour of ⁹fighting ¹¹the terrorists ¹⁰gave ¹²themselves up.

¹تَضَارَبَ ²فَرِيقَا ³كُرَةِ ⁴ٱلْقَدَمِ فِي ⁵ٱلْمَلْعَبِ ⁶قَبْلَ ⁷ٱلْمُبَارَاةِ ⁸وَتَصَالَحَا ⁹بَعْدَهَا.

(6) taḍāraba farīqā kurati l-qadami fī l-malʿabi qabla l-mubārāti wa-taṣālaḥā baʿda-hā.

The two ^{4,3}football ²teams ¹fought each other in ⁵the stadium ⁶before ⁷the match ⁸and made up (reconciled) ⁹after (it).

¹صَرَّحَ ²زَعِيمُ أَحَدِ ³ٱلْأَحْزَابِ (s. حِزْبٌ) ⁴ٱلسِّيَاسِيَّةِ بِأَنَّهُ ⁵يُعَارِضُ ⁶فِكْرَةَ ⁷قُبُولِ ٱلْعُمَّالِ (s. عَامِلٌ) ⁸ٱلْأَجَانِبِ فِي ٱلْبِلَادِ.

(7) ṣarraḥa zaʿīmu ʾaḥadi l-ʾaḥzābi s-siyāsiyyati bi-ʾanna-hu yuʿāriḍu fikrata qubūli l-ʿummāli l-ʾağānibi fī l-bilādi.

²The leader of one of the ⁴political ³parties ¹declared that he ⁵is against ⁶the idea ⁷of accepting ⁸foreign workers in the country.

فِي ¹فَصْلِ ²ٱلرَّبِيعِ ³يَخْضَرُّ ⁴ٱلشَّجَرُ (s. شَجَرَةٌ) ⁵وَتَتَفَتَّحُ ⁶ٱلْأَزْهَارُ (s. زَهْرَةٌ)، أَمَّا فِي فَصْلِ ⁷ٱلْخَرِيفِ ⁸فَتَصْفَرُّ ⁹أَوْرَاقُ (s. وَرَقَةٌ) ٱلشَّجَرِ ¹⁰وَتَتَسَاقَطُ.

(8) fī faṣli r-rabīʿi yaḫḍarru š-šağaru wa-tatafattaḥu l-ʾazhāru, ʾammā fī faṣli l-ḫarīfi fa-taṣfarru ʾawrāqu š-šağari wa-tatasāqaṭu.

In the ²spring (¹season) ⁴the trees ³become green and ⁶the flowers ⁵open, but in ⁷the autumn (season) ⁹the leaves of the trees ⁸become yellow ¹⁰and fall.

[1]إِجْتَمَعَ [2]أَمْسِ/ [2]ٱلْبَارِحَةَ [3]مُمَثِّلُو [4]ٱلنِّقَابَاتِ [5]وَتَكَلَّمُوا عَنْ [6]رَفْعِ [7]أُجُورِ (أَجْرٌ) [8]ٱلْعُمَّالِ [9]وَٱلْمُوَظَّفِينَ.

(9) ʾiǧtamaʿa ʾamsi / ʾal-bāriḥata mumaṯṯilū n-niqābāti wa-takallamū ʿan rafʿi ʾuǧūri l-ʿummāli wa-l-muwaḏḏafīna.

[3]The representatives of [4]the trade unions [1]met [2]yesterday [5]and talked about [6]increasing the [7]wages of [8]workers and [9]civil servants (employees).

مُوَظَّفُو [1]ٱلشَّرِكَةِ [2]يَسْتَعْمِلُونَ [3]عَادَةً [4]سَيَّارَاتِهِمِ [5]ٱلْخَاصَّةَ عِنْدَمَا [6]يُسَافِرُونَ فِي [7]رِحْلَاتٍ [8]طَوِيلَةٍ.

(10) muwaḏḏafū š-šarikati yastaʿmilūna ʿādatan sayyārāti-himi l-ḫāṣṣata ʿindamā yusāfirūna fī riḥlātin ṭawīlatin.

The employees of [1]the company [3]usually [2]use [4]their [5]own cars when [6]they travel on [8]long [7]trips.

[1]تَبَادَلَ [2]ٱلْجَيْشَانِ [3]ٱلنَّارَ [4]بِٱلْقُرْبِ مِنَ [5]ٱلْحُدُودِ (.s حَدٌّ) ثُمَّ [6]تَرَاجَعَا عِنْدَمَا [7]تَدَخَّلَتْ [8]قُوَّاتُ [9]ٱلْأُمَمِ (.s أُمَّةٌ) [10]ٱلْمُتَّحِدَةِ.

(11) tabādala l-ǧayšāni n-nāra bi-l-qurbi mina l-ḥudūdi ṯumma tarāǧaʿā ʿindamā tadaḫḫalat quwwātu l-ʾumami l-muttaḥidati.

[2]The two armies [1]exchanged [3]fire [4]near [5]the border, then [6]they withdrew when [10]the United [9]Nations [8]forces [7]intervened.

[1]دَفَعَ [2]ٱلطِّفْلُ [3]ٱلْكَأْسَ عَنِ ٱلطَّاوِلَةِ [4]فَسَقَطَ عَلَى [5]ٱلْأَرْضِ [6]فَٱنْكَسَرَ [7]وَٱنْتَشَرَتْ [8]كَسَرَاتُهُ (.s كَسْرَةٌ) فِي [9]كُلِّ [10]مَكَانٍ.

(12) dafaʿa ṭ-ṭiflu l-kaʾsa ʿani ṭ-ṭāwilati fa-saqaṭa ʿalā l-ʾarḍi fa-nkasara wa-ntašarat kasarātu-hu fī kulli makānin.

[2]The child [1]pushed [3]the glass off the table [4]so it fell on [5]the floor and [6]broke and [8]the pieces [7]went [9,10]everywhere (lit. [8]the pieces [7]spread into [9]every [10]place).

[1]إِنْطَلَقَتْ سَيَّارَاتُ [2]ٱلسِّبَاقِ عَلَى [3]ٱلطَّرِيقِ [4]حَيْثُ [5]ٱجْتَمَعَ [6]ٱلْمُشَاهِدُونَ [7]يَتَحَمَّسُونَ [8]لَهُمْ.

(13) ʾinṭalaqat sayyārātu s-sibāqi ʿalā ṭ-ṭarīqi ḥayṯu ǧtamaʿa l-mušāhidūna yataḥammasūna la-hum.

[2]The racing cars [1]started off along [3]the road, [4]where [6]the spectators had [5]gathered [7]to cheer them on (lit. [7]be enthusiastic [8]towards them).

[1]هَلْ [2]تَتَكَلَّمُ [3]ٱللُّغَةَ ٱلْعَرَبِيَّةَ؟ [4]نَعَمْ، [5]أَتَكَلَّمُهَا [6]قَلِيلاً.

(14) hal tatakallamu l-luġata l-ʿarabiyyata? naʿam ʾatakallamu-hā qalīlan.
[1]Do [2]you speak (the) Arabic ([3]language)? [4]Yes, [5]I speak (it) [6]a little.

Translate into Arabic:

(1) At the end of every season the two merchants share the profit.

(2) The spectators gathered on the road between the two villages in order to see the racing cars.

(3) After the football match the spectators fought with (مَعَ) the police forces in the stadium.

(4) The civil servants usually speak (the) Arabic (language) in the company.

(5) I graduated from the same university from which you (m.) graduated.

(6) At the wedding party the child pushed the flowers off the table and they fell and scattered on the floor.

(7) It will rain tomorrow and therefore many of the workers and civil servants (employees) will use their own cars.

8) The workers met yesterday and talked about increasing their wages at the end of each year.

Chapter 19

Passive verbs

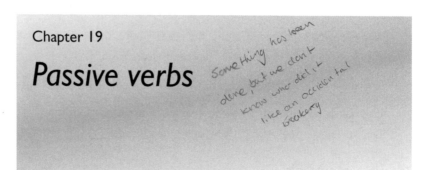

19.1 The passive verb, أَلْفِعْلُ الْمَجْهُولُ, is used in Arabic when the performer of the action is not named.

The active verb, أَلْفِعْلُ اَلْمَعْلُومُ, is used in Arabic when the performer of the action is named and expressed as the grammatical subject. So far we have only dealt with active verb forms in the perfect and imperfect tense.

The passive forms of the perfect and imperfect tenses differ from their active counterparts by having different vocalization. A characteristic sign of all passive tense forms is that they have the vowel **ḍammah** /u/ on the first radical.

The passive of the perfect tense has only one pattern of vowelling for all verbs and forms (stems I–X). The first radical has **ḍammah** /u/ (as mentioned) and the second radical has **kasrah** /i/. The pattern of the passive perfect in the third person masculine singular is thus: فُعِلَ fuʿila, e.g.

Perfect

Active		***Passive***
CaC**a**Ca, CaC**i**Ca, CaC**u**Ca	⇒	C**u**C**i**Ca
كَتَبَ kat**a**ba, he wrote		كُتِبَ k**u**t**i**ba, it was written
شَرِبَ šar**i**ba, he drank		شُرِبَ š**u**r**i**ba, it was drunk
بَعُدَ baʿ**u**da, he/it was distant		بُعِدَ b**u**ʿ**i**da, he was expelled

(See conjugation A2.1 in Appendix 2.)

19.2 The passive of the basic form (I) of the verb in the imperfect tense has also only one pattern of vowelling for all verbs. The first radical still has **ḍammah**, but the middle radical has **faṭḥah** /a/, the basic pattern being: يُفْعَلُ yufʿalu, e.g.

Imperfect

Active	***Passive***
يَكْتُبُ **ya**k**tu**bu, he writes	يُكْتَبُ **yu**k**ta**bu, it is (being) written
يَشْتُمُ **ya**š**tu**mu, he insults	يُشْتَمُ **yu**š**ta**mu, he is (being) insulted

19.3 The passive forms of the derived verb forms (stems) II, III, IV, VIII and X are conjugated regularly in the perfect and the imperfect like the active verbs, except for the internal vowel changes mentioned above, e.g.

	perfect		imperfect	
	active	passive	active	passive
Form II	دَرَّسَ darrasa he taught	دُرِّسَ durrisa he was taught	يُدَرِّسُ yudarrisu he teaches	يُدَرَّسُ yudarrasu he is taught
Form III	شَاهَدَ šāhada he saw	شُوهِدَ šūhida he was seen	يُشَاهِدُ yušāhidu he sees	يُشَاهَدُ yušāhadu he is seen
Form IV	أَرْسَلَ ʾarsala he sent	أُرْسِلَ ʾursila he was sent	يُرْسِلُ yursilu he sends	يُرْسَلُ yursalu he is sent
Form VIII	إِنْتَخَبَ ʾintaḫaba he elected	أُنْتُخِبَ ʾuntuḫiba he was elected	يَنْتَخِبُ yantaḫibu he elects	يُنْتَخَبُ yuntaḫabu he is elected
Form X	إِسْتَقْبَلَ ʾistaqbala he received	أُسْتُقْبِلَ ʾustuqbila he was received	يَسْتَقْبِلُ yastaqbilu he receives	يُسْتَقْبَلُ yustaqbalu he is received

Note: In the passive of the eighth and tenth forms, the initial vowel in modern Arabic is commonly **kasrah**, e.g. إِنْتُخِبَ and إِسْتُقْبِلَ.

See the conjugations of the derived verb forms in Appendix 2.

19.4 The derived verb forms V, VI and VII have no passive because their active forms often have a passive or intransitive meaning, e.g.

Form V تَغَيَّرَ taġayyara, to be changed (he/it changed)

Form VI تَبَارَكَ tabāraka, to be blessed (he/it got blessed)

Form VII إِنْكَسَرَ ʾinkasara, to be broken (he/it broke)

19.5 The grammatical subject of the passive verb is called in Arabic grammar نَائِبُ ٱلْفَاعِلِ, which means 'the deputy of the doer'. Like any subject, it takes the ending of the nominative case and the verb agrees with it in person, gender and number. But logically it represents the object (or goal) of the action; compare in English: 'I (subject) saw **him** (object)' ⇒ '**He** (subject) was seen [by me (agent)].' Arabic passive sentences are considered to be impersonal, because they do not express the performer of the action.

Passive

Perfect	***Imperfect***
كُتِبَ كِتَابٌ	يُكْتَبُ كِتَابٌ
k**u**t**i**ba kitāb**un**.	y**u**kt**a**bu kitāb**un**.
A book **was** written.	A book **is** (being) written.
كُتِبَ ٱلْكِتَابُ	يُكْتَبُ ٱلْكِتَابُ
k**u**t**i**ba l-kitāb**u**.	y**u**kt**a**bu l-kitāb**u**.
The book **was** written.	The book **is** (being) written.

19.6 When the performer of the action is mentioned, one cannot use a passive verb in traditional Arabic. This means that the English sentence 'The book was written by the teacher' should in Arabic be rendered by an active sentence, where the performer (semantic agent) is expressed by the grammatical subject: 'The teacher wrote the book': كَتَبَ ٱلْمُعَلِّمُ ٱلْكِتَابَ kataba l-muʿallimu l-kitāba.

19.7 In modern literary Arabic, it is, however, increasingly common to use certain compound prepositions to express the semantic agent in passive sentences, in the same way as in many European languages. The following are the most common prepositions used to express the passive agent:

مِنْ طَرَفِ	مِنْ قِبَلِ	مِنْ جَانِبِ
min ṭarafi	min qibali	min ğānibi

from the side of, on behalf of = **by**

Examples:

كُتِبَ ٱلْكِتَابُ مِنْ قِبَلِ ٱلْمُعَلِّمِ

kutiba l-kitābu **min qibali** l-muᶜallimi.
The book was written by the teacher.
(lit. The book was written from the side of the teacher.)

كُتِبَ مِنْ طَرَفِهِ

kutiba **min ṭarafi-hi.** It was written by him. (lit. It was written from his side.)

Exercises

Practise your reading:

[1]قُتِلَ [2]ثَلَاثَةُ [3]أَشْخَاصٍ (.s شَخْصٌ) [4]وَجُرِحَ [5]أَرْبَعَةٌ فِي [6]حَادِثِ [7]سَيْرٍ
[8]أَمْسِ [9]وَنُقِلُوا [10]جَمِيعًا إِلَى ٱلْمُسْتَشْفَى.

(1) qutila ṯalāṯatu ᵓašḫāṣin (s. šaḫṣun) wa-ğuriḥa ᵓarbaᶜatun fī ḥādiṯi sayrin ᵓamsi wa-nuqilū ğamīᶜan ᵓilā l-mustašfā.
[2]Three [3]people [1]were killed and [5]four [4]injured in [7]a traffic [6]accident [8]yesterday and [10]all [9]were taken (transported) to (the) hospital.

[1]بُعِثَ [2]وَفْدٌ [3]رَسْمِيٌّ [4]مِنْ قِبَلِ [5]سُمُوِّ ٱلْأَمِيرِ [6]فَٱسْتُقْبِلَ فِي [7]ٱلْمَطَارِ
[8]وَأُخِذُوا [9]جَمِيعًا [10]لِمُقَابَلَةِ [11]جَلَالَةِ ٱلْمَلِكِ.

(2) buᶜiṯa wafdun rasmiyyun min qibali sumuwwi l-ᵓamīri fa-stuqbila fī l-maṭāri wa-ᵓuḫiḏū ğamīᶜan li-muqābalati ğalālati l-maliki.
[3]An official [2]delegation [1]was sent [4]by [5]His Highness the Emir. [6]They were received at [7]the airport, and [9]all of them [8]were taken [10]to meet [11]His Majesty the King.

[1]بَعْدَ أَنْ [2]قُفِلَ بَابُ [3]ٱلدُّكَّانِ [4]عُلِّقَ [5]ٱلْمِفْتَاحُ إِلَى [6]جَانِبِ ٱلْبَابِ
[7]فَسُرِقَ مِنْ هُنَاكَ [8]وَفُتِحَ ٱلْبَابُ وَسُرِقَتْ [9]أَغْرَاضٌ (s. غَرَضٌ) [10]كَثِيرَةٌ.

(3) baᶜda ᵓan qufila bābu d-dukkāni ᶜulliqa l-miftāḥu ᵓilā ǧānibi l-bābi fa-suriqa min hunāka wa-futiḥa l-bābu wa-suriqat ᵓaġrāḍun (s. ġaraḍun) kaṯīratun.

[1]After the door of [3]the shop was [2]locked, [5]the key [4]was hung [6]beside the door. [7]It was stolen from there, the door [8]was opened and [10]many [9]things were stolen.

[1]نُبِّهَ [2]ٱلْعُمَّالُ (s. عَامِلٌ) [3]مِنْ قِبَلِ [4]ٱلنِّقَابَةِ [5]بِعَدَمِ [6]ٱلْقِيَامِ [7]بِٱلْإِضْرَابِ.

(4) nubbiha l-ᶜummālu (s. ᶜāmilun) min qibali n-niqābati bi-ᶜadami l-qiyāmi bi-l-ᵓiḍrābi.

[2]The workers [1]were warned [3]by the [4]trade union [5]not [6]to go on [7]strike.

[1]سَيُعْقَدُ [2]غَدًا [3]ٱجْتِمَاعٌ فِي [4]وِزَارَةِ [5]ٱلدَّاخِلِيَّةِ [6]وَتُبْحَثُ [7]فِيهِ [8]قَضِيَّةُ
[9]تَأْجِيلِ [10]ٱلِٱنْتِخَابَاتِ ٱلْبَرْلَمَانِيَّةِ.

(5) sa-yuᶜqadu ġadan ᵓiǧtimāᶜun fī wizārati d-dāḫiliyyati wa-tubḥaṯu fī-hi qaḍiyyatu taᵓǧīli l-intiḫābāti l-barlamāniyyati.

[3]A meeting [1]will be held [2]tomorrow at the [4]Ministry of the [5]Interior, and ([7]at it) [8]the issue [9]of postponing parliamentary [10]elections [6]will be discussed.

[1]عُرِضَ [2]مَأْتَمُ [3]ٱلْأَمِيرَةِ عَلَى [4]شَاشَةِ ٱلتِّلْفِزْيُونِ [5]وَقُدِّرَ [6]عَدَدُ
[7]ٱلْمُشَاهِدِينَ [8]بِأَكْثَرَ مِنْ [9]مِئَةِ مِلْيُونِ [10]مُشَاهِدٍ.

(6) ᶜuriḍa maᵓtamu l-ᵓamīrati ᶜalā šāšati t-tilifizyūni wa-quddira ᶜadadu l-mušāhidīna bi-ᵓakṯara min miᵓati milyūni mušāhidin.

[2]The funeral of [3]the princess [1]was shown on (the) television ([4]screen). [6]The number of [7](the) viewers [5]was estimated to be [8]more than one [9]hundred million ([10]viewers).

[1]نُقِلَ ٱلْمَصْنَعُ إِلَى [2]خَارِجِ ٱلْمَدِينَةِ [3]وَسُرِّحَ مِنَ [4]ٱلْعَمَلِ [5]أَكْثَرُ مِنْ
[6]نِصْفِ [7]ٱلْعُمَّالِ (s. عَامِلٌ).

(7) nuqila l-maṣnaᶜu ᵓilā ḫāriǧi l-madīnati wa-surriḥa mina l-ᶜamali ᵓakṯaru min niṣfi l-ᶜummāli.

The factory [1]was moved [2]outside the city and [5]more than [6]half of [7]the workers [3]were released (fired) from [4]work.

[1]أُنْتُخِبَ مُدِيرُ ٱلْجَامِعَةِ ٱلْجَدِيدُ [2]بِأَغْلَبِيَّةٍ [3]سَاحِقَةٍ.

(8) ʾuntuḫiba mudīru l-ğāmiʿati l-ğadīdu bi-ʾaġlabiyyatin sāḥiqatin.
The new director of the university [1]was elected by an [3]overwhelming [2]majority.

سَوْفَ لَا [1]يُسْمَحُ [2]بِتَقْدِيمِ [3]ٱلْمَشْرُوبَاتِ ٱلْكُحُولِيَّةِ فِي ٱلْمَطَاعِمِ
(s. مَطْعَمٌ) [4]وَسَيُمْنَعُ [5]بَيْعُهَا فِي [6]ٱلْأَسْوَاقِ (s. سُوقٌ).

(9) sawfa lā yusmaḥu bi-taqdīmi l-mašrūbāti l-kuḥūliyyati fī l-maṭāʿimi (s. maṭʿamun) wa-sa-yumnaʿu bayʿu-hā fī l-ʾaswāqi (s.sūqun).
Alcoholic [3]drinks (liquors) will not [1]be allowed [2]to be served in restaurants [4]and their [5]sale in [6]the markets [4]will be prohibited.

[1]ذُكِرَ فِي [2]جَرِيدَةِ ٱلْيَوْمِ أَنَّ [3]مُؤْتَمَرَ [4]ٱلْكُتَّابِ (s. كَاتِبٌ) ٱلْعَرَبِ [5]سَيُعْقَدُ
[6]ٱلْيَوْمَ فِي [7]ٱلْعَاصِمَةِ ٱلْمَغْرِبِيَّةِ ٱلرِّبَاطِ.

(10) ḏukira fī ğarīdati l-yawmi ʾanna muʾtamara l-kuttābi (kātibun) l-ʿarabi sa-yuʿqadu l-yawma fī l-ʿāṣimati l-maġribiyyati r-Ribāṭi.
In today's [2]newspaper it was [1]mentioned that the Arab [4]writers' [3]congress [5]will be held [6]today in Rabat, the Moroccan [7]capital.

Translate into Arabic:

(1) The funeral of His Majesty the King was shown today on (the) television (screen).

(2) The door of the shop was opened and many things were stolen.

(3) More than half of the workers were moved to the factory outside the city.

(4) After the door of the restaurant was locked with the key, the door was opened and the alcoholic drinks were stolen.

(5) In today's newspaper it is mentioned that the Arab writers' congress will be held tomorrow at (in) the airport restaurant.

(6) Four workers were killed and three injured in an accident in the factory and all were taken (transported) to (the) hospital.

(7) Alcoholic drinks will be prohibited from sale in the market and at the airport.

(8) A delegation was sent by the Ministry of the Interior. They were received at the airport and all of them were taken to meet His Highness the Prince.

Chapter 20

Rules for writing the hamzah (hamzatu l-qaṭʿi)

20.1 With regard to the discussion in chapter 7 of the **hamzah** and the difficulties with its orthography, the following rules can contribute to the student's understanding of the biggest part of this problem.

It is not necessary to learn all these rules by heart now. The idea is to become acquainted with them, and to use them for reference.

20.2 As mentioned in chapter 7, the **hamzah** can be written on any of the three letters **ʾalif** أ, **wāw** ؤ and **yāʾ** ئ .. ـئـ .. .. ئـ without dots. When they have the **hamzah**, these three letters are not pronounced as vowels, but function merely as bearers (seats) of the **hamzah.** In some cases the **hamzah** is left without a bearer, however.

It is important to remember that each of these three letters is related to one of the three vowels as follows:

(a) The related letter of **fatḥah** ـَ /a/ is **ʾalif** ا.

(b) The related letter of **ḍammah** ـُ /u/ is **wāw** و.

(c) The related letter of **kasrah** ـِ /i/ is **yāʾ** ى (without dots).

The three vowels have different strengths, as explained in the list below. The letter bearing the **hamzah** in a word is decided by the relative strength of the vowels, when one compares the vowel of the **hamzah** itself and the vowel of the preceding letter. The stronger vowel (usually) decides which related letter becomes the bearer of the **hamzah.**

(a) The strongest vowel is **kasrah** ـِ /i/. (The **yāʾ** with the **sukūn** يْ ..ـيْـ.. ..يْـ /y/ is considered to be as strong as the **kasrah.**)

(b) The second strongest vowel is **ḍammah** ـُ /u/.

(c) The weakest vowel is **fatḥah** ـَ /a/.

(d) The **sukūn** ـْ is not a vowel and has no related letter. It is considered as the weakest of all, except when it is written with **yāʾ**, as mentioned above.

Note: **Hamzah** at the beginning of a word has already been discussed in chapter 7.

20.3 *Hamzah in the middle of a word*

When the **hamzah** appears with a **sukūn** in the middle of a word, the bearer of the **hamzah** is the related letter of the preceding vowel, e.g.

بَأْسٌ	بُؤْسٌ	بِئْسٌ
b**a**ʾsun, harm	b**u**ʾsun, misery	b**i**ʾsun, misfortune

(The bearer of the **hamzah** is the related letter of the preceding vowel, because the preceding vowel is stronger than its own **sukūn**.)

20.4 When the **hamzah** appears with a vowel of its own after a **sukūn** in the middle of a word, the bearer of the **hamzah** is the related letter of its own vowel, e.g.

يَسْأَلُ	مَسْؤُولٌ	أَسْئِلَةٌ
yasʾ**a**lu, he asks	masʾ**ū**lun, responsible	ʾasʾ**i**latun, questions

(The bearer of the **hamzah** is the related letter of its own vowel, because its own vowel is stronger than the preceding **sukūn**.)

20.5 When the **hamzah** appears with a vowel of its own after another vowel in the middle of a word, the bearer of the **hamzah** is the related letter of the stronger one of these two vowels, e.g.

(a) سُئِلَ suʾ**i**la, he was asked (The **kasrah** of the **hamzah** is stronger than the preceding **ḍammah**.)

مِئَةٌ m**i**ʾatun, hundred (The preceding **kasrah** is stronger than the **fatḥah** of the **hamzah**.)

(b) لَؤُمَ la'uma, he was wicked (The **ḍammah** of the **hamzah** is stronger than the preceding **fatḥah**.)

سُؤَالٌ su'ālun, question (The preceding **ḍammah** is stronger than the **fatḥah** of the **hamzah**).

(c) سَأَلَ sa'ala, he asked
(Here the **bearer** of the **hamzah** is 'alif أ, because both its own vowel and the **preceding** vowel are **fatḥahs**.)

20.6 When the **hamzah** appears with a vowel of its own after **yā'** with **sukūn** ...ـيْـ... /...y.../, the bearer of the **hamzah** is **yā'** without dots ...ـئـ..., e.g.

هَيْئَةٌ hay'atun, organization

شَيْئَانِ šay'āni, two things

(The preceding **yā'** with **sukūn** ...ـيْـ... is stronger than the **fatḥah** of the **hamzah** and therefore the bearer of the **hamzah** is ...ـئـ... /y/ without dots.)

20.7 When the **hamzah** appears with **fatḥah** between one of the long vowels ـَا ... /ā/ or ـُو... /ū/ and **tā' marbūṭah** ة, ـة.., the **hamzah** will stand alone without a bearer:

(a) alone after **'alif**: اء /...ā'.../, e.g. قِرَاءَةٌ qir**ā**'atun, reading

(b) alone after **wāw**: وء /...ū'.../, e.g. مُرُوءَةٌ mur**ū**'atun, valour

BUT: If the **hamzah** appears with **fatḥah** between the long vowel ...ـيـ... /ī/ and **tā' marbūṭah** ة, ـة.., the bearer of the **hamzah** is ...ـئـ... /y/, e.g. خَطِيئَةٌ ḫaṭī'atun 'sin'.

20.8 When the **hamzah** in the middle of a word is preceded by **'alif** ا, the bearer of the **hamzah** is the related letter of its own vowel. However, if the vowel of the **hamzah** is **fatḥah**, the **hamzah** remains without a bearer:

Nominative	***Accusative***	***Genitive***
أَصْدِقَاؤُهُ	أَصْدِقَاءَهُ	أَصْدِقَائِهِ
'aṣdiq**ā**'u-hu, his friends	'aṣdiq**ā**'a-hu	'aṣdiq**ā**'i-hi

20.9 When the **hamzah** occurs between two long ᵓ**alifs** اءا /āᵓā/, it is again written without a bearer, e.g. قِرَاءَاتٌ qirāᵓātun 'readings' (not: قِرَاأَاتٌ).

20.10 *Hamzah at the end of a word (or word stem)*

When **hamzah** with a vowel occurs at the end of a word (or word stem) after a vowel, the bearer of the **hamzah** is the related letter of the preceding vowel, regardless of the vowel of the **hamzah**, e.g.

(a) بَدَأَ bada**ᵓ**a, he started (ᵓ**alif** ا is the related letter of the preceding vowel /**a**/)

(b) جَرُؤَ ğar**u**ᵓa, he dared (**wāw** و is the related letter of the preceding vowel /**u**/)

(c) قُرِئَ qur**i**ᵓa, it was read (**yā**ᵓ ى is the related letter of the preceding vowel /**i**/)

Nominative	***Accusative***	***Genitive***
نَبَأٌ nabaᵓun, news	نَبَأً nabaᵓan	نَبَإٍ nabaᵓin
تَنَبُّؤٌ tanabbuᵓun, prophecy	تَنَبُّؤًا tanabbuᵓan	تَنَبُّؤٍ tanabbuᵓin

Note: If a word ending in **hamzah** has the accusative ending with nunation /...an/, an extra final ᵓ**alif** ا is added (as in the above example: تَنَبُّؤًا tanabbuᵓan 'prophecy'), except when the bearer of the **hamzah** itself is ᵓ**alif** ا (owing to a preceding **fatḥah** or ᵓ**alif**), e.g. نَبَأً nabaᵓan (not: نَبَأًا), مَسَاءً masāᵓan 'evening' (not: مَسَاءًا); see the following paragraph.

20.11 When **hamzah** with a vowel occurs at the end of a word (or word stem) following a long vowel or **sukūn**, the **hamzah** will have no bearer:

Nominative	***Accusative***	***Genitive***
مَسَاءٌ masāᵓun, evening	مَسَاءً masāᵓan	مَسَاءٍ masāᵓin
سُوءٌ sūᵓun, offence	سُوءً sūᵓan	سُوءٍ sūᵓin
رَدِيءٌ radīᵓun, evil	رَدِيئًا radīᵓan	رَدِيءٍ radīᵓin

جُزْءٌ ǧuzʾun, a part	جُزْءًا ǧuzʾan	جُزْءٍ ǧuzʾin
أَلْجُزْءُ ʾal-ǧuzʾu, the part	أَلْجُزْءَ ʾal-ǧuzʾa	أَلْجُزْءِ ʾal-ǧuzʾi

20.12 When **hamzah** is followed by the extra **ʾalif** (ـًا..), mentioned in chapter 5, or by a suffix pronoun, and preceded by a letter which can be connected in writing from both sides (such as: ..ـبـ.. ..ـتـ.. ..ـجـ.. etc.) and which has a **sukūn** ـْ, the bearer of the **hamzah** is always **yāʾ** /y/ ..ـئـ.. (without dots), e.g.

(a) Followed by an extra **ʾalif**:

(عِبْءٌ) ʿibʾun, a burden (nom.)	عِبْئًا ʿibʾan, a burden (acc.)
دِفْئًا difʾan, warmth (acc.)	بُطْئًا buṭʾan, slowness (acc.)

(b) Followed by a suffix pronoun:

Nominative	*Accusative*	*Genitive*
عِبْئُهُ ʿibʾu-hu, his burden	عِبْئَهُ ʿibʾa-hu	عِبْئِهِ ʿibʾi-hi

20.13 When the **hamzah** occurs at the end of a word (or word stem) preceded by one of the five letters ..ـد.. ..ـذ.. ..ـر.. ..ـز.. ..ـو.., which can be connected only from the right and which have a **sukūn** ـْ , there will be two alternatives for writing the **hamzah**:

(a) The **hamzah** will stand alone, inasmuch as the following letter is considered as part of a suffix pronoun, e.g.

	Nominative	*Accusative*	*Genitive*
(ضَوْءٌ) ḍawʾun, a light	ضَوْءُكَ ḍawʾu-ka, your light	ضَوْءَكَ ḍawʾa-ka	ضَوْءِكَ ḍawʾi-ka
(جُزْءٌ) ǧuzʾun, a part	جُزْءُكَ ǧuzʾu-ka, your part	جُزْءَكَ ǧuzʾa-ka	جُزْءِكَ ǧuzʾi-ka

Rules for writing the hamzah (hamzatu l-qaṭʿi)

(b) The bearer of the **hamzah** is decided by its own vowel, inasmuch as it is considered as being in the middle of a word preceded by a **sukūn**, and the suffix pronoun is considered to be a part of the word, e.g.

Nominative	***Accusative***	***Genitive***
ضَوْؤُكَ	ضَوْأَكَ	ضَوْئِكَ
ḍawʾu-ka, your light	ḍawʾa-ka	ḍawʾi-ka
جُزْؤُكَ	جُزْأَكَ	جُزْئِكَ
ǧuzʾu-ka, your part	ǧuzʾa-ka	ǧuzʾi-ka

20.14 If a prefix (or prefixed conjunction or preposition) is attached to a word beginning with **hamzah,** the prefix will not interfere with the spelling of the **hamzah**, e.g.

لِأَنَّ **li**-ʾanna, because (not: لِئَنَّ)   فَإِنَّ **fa**-ʾinna, that (not: فَئِنَّ)

(An exception is لِئَلَّا li-ʾallā 'in order not to'.)

20.15 In contradiction to the above rules, some exceptional variations can be found in the writing of well-known authors, even in common words, e.g.

Exceptional variations	***According to the above rules***
مَسْئَلَةٌ masʾalatun, a question	مَسْأَلَةٌ
مَسْئُولٌ masʾūlun, responsible	مَسْؤُولٌ
يَقْرَأُونَ yaqraʾūna, they are reading	يَقْرَؤُونَ
شُئُونٌ šuʾūnun, matters	شُؤُونٌ
تَقْرَإِينَ taqraʾīna, you (f.) are reading	تَقْرَئِينَ
مَسَاءًا masāʾan, evening (acc.)	مَسَاءً

Exercises

Practise your reading:

[1]سَاءَنِي أَنَّكَ [2]جِئْتَ [3]مُتَأَخِّرًا إِلَى [4]ٱلْمُؤْتَمَرِ.

(1) sāʾa-nī ʾanna-ka ǧiʾta mutaʾaẖẖiran ʾilā l-muʾtamari.

[1]I was offended that you [2]came [3]late to [4]the conference (congress).

[1]أَلْأَلَمُ يُعَلِّمُ [2]ٱلْمَرْءَ [3]كُلَّ [4]شَيْءٍ عَنْ [5]أُمُورِ (s. أَمْر) [6]ٱلْحَيَاةِ.

(2) ʾal-ʾalamu yuʿallimu l-marʾa kulla šayʾin ʿan ʾumūri l-ḥayāti.

[1]Pain teaches [2]a (the) man [3,4]everything about [5]the matters of [6]life.

[1]مَا [2]قَرَؤُوا [3]شَيْئًا عَنْ [4]تَارِيخِ [5]حَيَاةِ [6]ٱلشَّاعِرِ [7]ٱلْمَعْرُوفِ ٱمْرِئِ ٱلْقَيْسِ.

(3) mā qaraʾū šayʾan ʿan tārīẖi ḥayāti š-šāʿiri l-maʿrūfi mriʾi l-Qaysi.

They have [1]not [2]read [3]anything about [5,4]the biography ([5]life [4]history) of [7]the well-known [6]poet Imruʾ l-Qays.

[1]هَنِيئًا [2]لِلزَّهْرَةِ [3]ٱلذَّابِلَةِ؛ إِنَّ [4]ٱلسَّمَاءَ [5]سَتُمْطِرُ [6]غَدًا.

(4) hanīʾan li-z-zahrati ḏ-ḏābilati; ʾinna s-samāʾa sa-tumṭiru ġadan.

[1]Salute ([2]to) [3]the withered [2]flower. [6]Tomorrow there [4,5]will be rain (lit. [4]the sky [5]will rain).

[1]يُؤْمِنُ ٱلْمُسْلِمُ بِٱللّٰهِ وَلَا [2]يَأْذَنُ ٱلْإِسْلَامُ [3]بِٱلْقَتْلِ.

(5) yuʾminu l-muslimu bi-llāhi wa-lā yaʾḏanu l-ʾislāmu bi-l-qatli.

A Muslim [1]believes in God and Islam does not [2]allow [3]killing.

[1]جِئْتُ [2]لِأُهَنِّئَكَ عَلَى [3]مُكَافَأَةِ [4]قَائِدِ [5]ٱلْجَيْشِ.

(6) ǧiʾtu li-ʾuhanniʾa-ka ʿalā mukāfaʾati qāʾidi l-ǧayši.

[1]I came [2]to congratulate you on [3]the reward of the [5]army [4]commander.

[1]مَتَى [2]تُهَنِّئُ ٱلطُّلَّابَ [3]ٱلْفَائِزِينَ فِي [4]ٱلْاِمْتِحَانِ [5]ٱلنِّهَائِيِّ؟

(7) matā tuhanniʾu ṭ-ṭullāba l-fāʾizīna fī l-ʾimtiḥāni n-nihāʾiyyi?

[1]When [2]will you congratulate the students who were [3]successful in [5]the final [4]exam?

مَا [1]جَرُؤَ [2]ٱلْمَسْؤُولُ فِي [3]وِزَارَةِ [4]ٱلْبِيئَةِ [5]ٱلْإِدْلَاءَ [6]بِرَأْيِهِ [7]حَوْلَ [8]مَسْأَلَةِ [9]تَلَوُّثِ [10]ٱلشَّاطِئِ.

(8) mā ǧaruʾa l-masʾūlu fī wizārati l-bīʾati l-ʾidlāʾi bi-raʾyi-hi ḥawla masʾalati talawwuṯi š-šāṭiʾi.

[2]The (official) responsible at [3]the Ministry of the [4]Environment did not [1]dare [5]to express [6]his opinion [7]about [8]the matter of [10]the coastal [9]pollution.

[1]أَلْمَرْءُ [2]مُعَرَّضٌ [3]لِأَفْرَاحٍ (s. فَرَحٌ) [4]وَأَحْزَانٍ (s. حُزْنٌ) وَكُلُّ شَيْءٍ [5]لَهُ [6]نِهَايَةٌ [7]إِلَّا [8]شَيْئًا [9]وَاحِدًا [10]وَهُوَ [11]ٱلرُّوحُ.

(9) ʾal-marʾu muʿarraḍun li-ʾafrāḥin wa-ʾaḥzānin, wa-kullu šayʾin la-hu nihāyatun ʾillā šayʾan wāḥidan wa-huwa r-rūḥu.
[1]A (the) human being [2]is exposed [3]to happiness [4]and sadness, and everything [5]has [6]an end [7]except for [9]one [8]thing, [10]and that is [11]the soul (spirit).

[1]أَلْإِنْسَانُ [2]ٱلْجَرِيءُ [3]يَعْتَرِفُ [4]بِخَطِيئَتِهِ.

(10) ʾal-insānu l-ǧarīʾu yaʿtarifu bi-ḫaṭīʾati-hi.
[2]A (the) brave [1]person [3]admits [4]his fault.

[1]مِنْ [2]حُبِّي [3]لَهَا [4]مَا [5]هَدَأَتْ [6]دَقَّاتُ [7]فُؤَادِي [8]ٱلْبَرِيءِ.

(11) min ḥubbī la-hā mā hadaʾat daqqātu fuʾādī l-barīʾi.
[1]Because of [2]my love [3]for her, [6]the beats of my [8]innocent [7]heart [4]did not [5]slow down ([5]calm).

[1]سَئِمَ [2]ٱلْمُؤَلِّفُ مِنْ [3]قِرَاءَةِ [4]مُسَاعِدِهِ [5]ٱلْبَطِيئَةِ [6]لِلْمَخْطُوطَةِ [7]ٱلْقَدِيمَةِ.

(12) saʾima l-muʾallifu min qirāʾati musāʿidi-hi l-baṭīʾati li-l-maḫṭūṭati l-qadīmati.
[2]The author [1]was bored with [4]his assistant's [5]slow [3]reading of [7]the old [6]manuscript.

[1]شَارَكَتْ فِي [2]ٱلْمُؤْتَمَرِ ٱلَّذِي [3]ٱنْعَقَدَ [4]مُؤَخَّرًا كُلُّ [5]ٱلْفِئَاتِ [6]ٱلْمُتَنَازِعَةِ عَلَى [7]مَسْأَلَةِ [8]تَوْزِيعِ [9]مِيَاهِ [10]ٱلرَّيِّ.

(13) šārakat fī l-muʾtamari llaḏī-nʿaqada muʾaḫḫaran kullu l-fiʾāti l-mutanāziʿati ʿalā masʾalati tawzīʿi miyāhi r-rayyi.
All of [6]the conflicting [5]parties on [7]the matter of [8]distributing [10]irrigation [9]water [1]participated in [2]the conference which [3]was held [4]recently.

شَرِبَ [1]ٱلسَّائِحُ [2]ٱلْعَطْشَانُ [3]مَاءً [4]عَكِرًا مِنْ [5]بِئْرٍ [6]عَمِيقَةٍ فِي [7]ٱلصَّحْرَاءِ.

(14) šariba s-sāʾiḥu l-ʿaṭšānu māʾan ʿakiran min biʾrin ʿamīqatin fī ṣ-ṣaḥrāʾi.
[2]The thirsty [1]tourist drank [4]muddy [3]water from [6]a deep [5]well in [7]the desert.

Translate into Arabic:

(1) Pain teaches everything about (the) happiness and (the) sadness.

(2) Everything has an end except one thing, and that is love.

(3) The beats of the thirsty tourist's heart won't slow down.

(4) A Muslim does not believe in, nor allow, killing.

(5) The author took part in the conference (congress) which was held recently in the Ministry of Environment.

(6) I came to congratulate the students on the army commander's reward.

(7) The well-known poet Imruʾ l-Qays drank muddy water from a deep well in the desert.

(8) Salute (to) the thirsty tourist in the desert, tomorrow there will be rain.

(9) They have not read anything about the history of the brave commander.

(10) I was offended that you came late to the Ministry of the Environment and you did not dare to express your opinion about the coastal pollution.

Chapter 21

Broken plurals and collective nouns

21.1 A very large number of nouns and adjectives have a plural called the broken plural, جَمْعُ ٱلتَّكْسِيرِ. It may be compared to the English irregular plural, e.g., 'man – men', 'mouse – mice', 'foot – feet', etc.

Broken plurals are formed from the singular by internal changes and/or specific increments according to some thirty different patterns. There are hardly any rules about how to form the broken plural from the singular. The broken plural occurs more frequently than the sound plural (regular plural).

Some singular nouns may have more than one form of the broken plural, and some may have both a sound plural and a broken plural.

21.2 The list below contains some of the most common patterns of the broken plural.

singular	broken plural	singular	broken plural
(a) بَابٌ bābun door	أَبْوَابٌ ʾabwābun	(b) مَلِكٌ malikun king	مُلُوكٌ mulūkun
(c) كَبِيرٌ kabīrun big	كِبَارٌ kibārun	(d) شَهْرٌ šahrun month	أَشْهُرٌ ʾašhurun
(e) أَخٌ ʾaḫun brother	إِخْوَانٌ ʾiḫwānun	(f) مَبْنًى mabnan building	مَبَانٍ mabānin
(g) سُؤَالٌ suʾālun question	أَسْئِلَةٌ ʾasʾilatun	(h) طَرِيقٌ ṭarīqun road	طُرُقٌ ṭuruqun

(i) عَامِلٌ ʿāmilun worker	عُمَّالٌ ʿummālun	(j) نَبِيٌّ nabiyyun prophet	أَنْبِيَاءُ ʾanbiyāʾu (dipt.)
(k) رِسَالَةٌ risālatun letter	رَسَائِلُ rasāʾilu	(l) قِصَّةٌ qiṣṣatun story	قِصَصٌ qiṣaṣun

Note: It is recommended that the plural form be learnt along with the singular.

21.3 *Agreement of adjectives with plural nouns*

(a) Broken plurals referring to masculine or feminine human beings may take the adjective both in the broken plural and sound plural, e.g.

Masc. sing.	***Adjective broken plur.***	***Adjective sound plur.***
وَلَدٌ سَعِيدٌ	أَوْلَادٌ سُعَدَاءُ	أَوْلَادٌ سَعِيدُونَ
waladun saʿīdun	ʾawlādun suʿadāʾu	ʾawlādun saʿīdūna
a happy boy	happy boys	
Fem. sing.		
عَرُوسٌ سَعِيدَةٌ	عَرَائِسُ سُعَدَاءُ	عَرَائِسُ سَعِيدَاتٌ
ʿarūsun saʿīdatun	ʿarāʾisu suʿadāʾu	ʿarāʾisu saʿīdātun
a happy bride	happy brides	

(b) Even sound plurals referring to masculine human beings may take the adjective in both broken plural and sound plural, e.g.

Masc. sing.	***Adjective broken plur.***	***Adjective sound plur.***
مُعَلِّمٌ سَعِيدٌ	مُعَلِّمُونَ سُعَدَاءُ	مُعَلِّمُونَ سَعِيدُونَ
muʿallimun saʿīdun	muʿallimūna suʿadāʾu	muʿallimūna saʿīdūna
a happy teacher	happy teachers	

(c) Broken plurals or sound plurals referring to non-human beings take the adjective in the feminine singular, e.g.

Masc. sing.	***Sound plur.***
بَيْتٌ صَغِيرٌ	بُيُوتٌ صَغِيرَةٌ
baytun **ṣaġīrun**, a small house	buyūtun **ṣaġīratun**

Fem. sing.	
طَاوِلَةٌ صَغِيرَةٌ	طَاوِلاتٌ صَغِيرَةٌ
ṭāwilatun **ṣaġīratun**, a small table	ṭāwilātun **ṣaġīratun**

21.4 Collective nouns, إِسْمُ ٱلْجَمْعِ, indicate a gathering in one unit or group, and they can refer to both humans and non-humans. They may form either the sound or the broken plural or sometimes both.

Collective noun	*Broken plur.*	*Singular*	*Sound plur.*
Masc.	*Fem.*	*Fem.*	*Fem.*
شَجَرٌ šağarun	أَشْجَارٌ ʾašğārun	شَجَرَةٌ šağaratun	شَجَرَاتٌ šağarātun
trees	(some) trees	a tree	trees (specified)
لَيْلٌ laylun	لَيَالٍ layālin	لَيْلَةٌ laylatun	لَيْلاَتٌ laylātun
night, night-time	(some) nights	a night	nights (specified)
سَمَكٌ samakun	أَسْمَاكٌ ʾasmākun	سَمَكَةٌ samakatun	سَمَكَاتٌ samakātun
fish	(some) fish	a fish	fish (specified)

Some collective nouns do not have a corresponding singular:

Collective noun	*Broken plur.*	*Singular*	*Sound plur.*
Masc.	*Fem.*	*Fem.*	*Fem.*
جَيْشٌ ğayšun	جُيُوشٌ ğuyūšun	———	———
army	armies		
شَعْبٌ šaʿbun	شُعُوبٌ šuʿūbun	———	———
people, folk	peoples, folk		
خَيْلٌ ḫaylun	خُيُولٌ ḫuyūlun	———	———
horses	horses		

21.5 ***Agreement of verbs and adjectives with collective nouns***

Collective nouns, إِسْمُ ٱلْجَمْعِ , referring either to humans or non-human beings, are treated mostly as masculine singular. They thus take the preceding verb or the following adjective in the masculine singular.

Collective noun	***Broken plural***
(Treated as masc. sing.)	*(Treated as fem. sing.)*
ذَهَبَ شَعْبٌ عَظِيمٌ	ذَهَبَتْ شُعُوبٌ عَظِيمَةٌ
ḏahaba šaʿbun ʿaḏīmun.	ḏahabat šuʿūbun ʿaḏīmatun.
A great nation (lit. people) has vanished (gone).	Great nations (lit. peoples) have vanished (gone).
إِحْتَرَقَ شَجَرٌ كَثِيرٌ	إِحْتَرَقَتْ أَشْجَارٌ كَثِيرَةٌ
ʾiḥtaraqa šaǧarun kaṯīrun.	ʾiḥtaraqat ʾašǧārun kaṯīratun.
Many trees burned.	Many (individual) trees burned.

Note: Some collective nouns may also take the predicate verb in the feminine singular, e.g.

With masc. verb	***With fem. verb***
نَشَرَ ٱلْعَرَبُ ٱلْحَضَارَةَ	نَشَرَتِ ٱلْعَرَبُ ٱلْحَضَارَةَ
našara l-ʿarabu l-ḥaḍārata.	**našarati** l-ʿarabu l-ḥaḍārata.
The Arabs spread civilization.	

Exercises

Practise your reading:

[1]آبَاءُ (s. أَبٌ) ٱلتَّلَامِيذِ (s. تِلْمِيذٌ) [2]وَأُمَّهَاتُهُمْ [3]مَشْغُولُونَ فِي [4]تَحْضِيرِ [5]حَفْلَةٍ لِأَطْفَالِهِمْ (s. طِفْلٌ).

(1) ʾābāʾu t-talāmīḏi wa-ʾummahātu-hum mašġūlūna fī taḥḍīri ḥaflatin li-ʾaṭfāli-him

The pupils' [1]fathers [2]and mothers [3]are busy (with) [4]preparing [5]a party for their children.

كَثِيرٌ مِنْ [1]سُكَّانِ (s. سَاكِنٌ) [2]مَبَانِي (s. مَبْنًى) [3]ٱلْحَيِّ مِنْ رِجَالٍ [4]وَنِسَاءٍ (s. إِمْرَأَةٌ) هُمْ [5]عَجَائِزُ (s. عَجُوزٌ) [6]وَضُعَفَاءُ (s. ضَعِيفٌ) وَلَيْسَتْ عِنْدَهُمْ [7]مَصَاعِدُ (s. مِصْعَدٌ).

(2) kaṯīrun min sukkāni mabānī l-ḥayyi min riǧālin wa-nisāʾin hum ʿaǧāʾizu wa-ḍuʿafāʾu wa-laysat ʿinda-hum maṣāʿidu.

Many of [1]the inhabitants of [2]the buildings in [3]the area, men [4]and women, are [5]old [6]and weak and have no [7]lifts (elevators).

[1]سَمَكُ (s. سَمَكَةٌ) [2]ٱلْأَنْهُرِ (s. نَهْرٌ) [3]وَٱلْبُحَيْرَاتِ [4]أَطْيَبُ مِنْ سَمَكِ
[5]ٱلْبِحَارِ (s. بَحْرٌ).

(3) samaku l-ʾanhuri wa-l-buḥayrāti ʾaṭyabu min samaki l-biḥāri.
[2,3]Freshwater [1]fish are [4]tastier than [5]sea fish (lit. [1]the fish of [2]rivers [3]and lakes are [4]tastier than the fish of [5]the seas).

[1]إِنْقَلَبَتْ [2]شَاحِنَةٌ [3]بِحَادِثِ [4]سَيْرٍ [5]فَسَقَطَتْ مِنْهَا [6]صَنَادِيقُ
(s. صُنْدُوقٌ) [7]ٱلْفَاكِهَةِ [8]وَأَكْيَاسٌ (s. كِيسٌ) [9]مَمْلُوءَةٌ [10]بِٱلزَّيْتُونِ.

(4) ʾinqalabat šāḥinatun bi-ḥādiṯi sayrin fa-saqaṭat min-hā ṣanādīqu l-fākihati wa-ʾakyāsun mamlūʾatun bi-z-zaytūni.
In a [4]traffic [3]accident [2]a truck [1]turned upside down and [6]boxes (cases) of [7]fruit [8]and sacks [9]filled with [10]olives [5]fell out.

[1]خَسِرَ [2]ٱلْجَيْشُ ٱلْأَلْمَانِيُّ [3]ٱلْقَوِيُّ [4]ٱلْحَرْبَ [5]ضِدَّ [6]ٱلْجُيُوشِ (s. جَيْشٌ)
[7]ٱلتَّابِعَةِ [8]لِدُوَلِ (s. دَوْلَةٌ) [9]ٱلْحُلَفَاءِ (s. حَلِيفٌ).

(5) ḫasira l-ǧayšu l-ʾalmāniyyu l-qawiyyu l-ḥarba ḍidda l-ǧuyūši t-tābiʿati li-duwali l-ḥulafāʾi.
[3]The strong German [2]army [1]lost [4]the war [5]against [6]the armies [7]belonging to [9]the allied [8]countries.

[1]أَلْمَصَارِفُ (s. مَصْرِفٌ) ٱلْكَبِيرَةُ [2]وَٱلتُّجَّارُ (s. تَاجِرٌ) ٱلْكِبَارُ
[3]مَسْؤُولُونَ عَنِ [4]ٱرْتِفَاعِ [5]أَسْعَارِ (s. سِعْرٌ) [6]ٱلْمَوَادِّ (s. مَادَّةٌ)
[7]ٱلْغِذَائِيَّةِ فِي ٱلْبِلَادِ.

(6) ʾal-maṣārifu l-kabīratu wa-t-tuǧǧāru l-kibāru masʾūlūna ʿani rtifāʿi ʾasʿāri l-mawāddi l-ġiḏāʾiyyati fī l-bilādi.
The big [1]banks and big [2]merchants are [3]responsible for [4]the rise in [5]the price(s) of [7,6]foodstuffs in the country.

[1]إِجْتَمَعَ مُدَرَاءُ (s. مُدِيرٌ) ٱلشَّرِكَاتِ مَعَ [2]مَنْدُوبِي [3]ٱلنِّقَابَاتِ [4]وَتَبَاحَثُوا
[5]بِمَوَاضِيعَ (s. مَوْضُوعٌ) [6]عَدِيدَةٍ مِنْهَا: [7]رَفْعُ [8]أُجُورِ (s. أَجْرٌ) ٱلْعُمَّالِ
وَٱلْمُوَظَّفِينَ [9]وَتَخْفِيضُ [10]سَاعَاتِ ٱلْعَمَلِ.

(7) ʾiǧtamaʿa mudarāʾu š-šarikāti maʿa mandūbī n-niqābāti wa-tabāḥaṯū

bi-mawāḍīʿa ʿadīdatin min-hā: rafʿu ʾuǧūri l-ʿummāli wa-l-muwaḏḏafīna wa-taḫfīḍu sāʿāti l-ʿamali.

The company managers (the managers of the companies) had [1]a meeting with [3]the trade union [2]representatives [4]and discussed [6]many [5]issues, among them [7]raising the [8]wages of workers and employees [9]and reducing their working [10]hours.

[1]قَدَّمَتْ [2]مَجْمُوعَةٌ مِنْ [3]عُلَمَاءِ (s. عَالِمٌ) ٱلْكِيمْيَاءِ [4]تَقْرِيرًا عَنِ
[5]ٱكْتِشَافِهِمْ [6]أَدْوِيَةً (s. دَوَاءٌ) جَدِيدَةً [7]ضِدَّ [8]أَمْرَاضِ (s. مَرَضٌ) [9]ٱلْجِلْدِ.

(8) qaddamat maǧmūʿatun min ʿulamāʾi l-kīmyāʾi taqrīran ʿani-ktišāfi-him ʾadwiyatan ǧadīdatan ḍidda ʾamrāḍi l-ǧildi.

[2]A group of chemical [3]scientists [1]presented [4]a report on [5]its (their) discovery of new [6]medicines [7]against [9]skin [8]diseases.

[1]بِسَبَبِ [2]كَثْرَةِ [3]ٱلْأَمْطَارِ (s. مَطَرٌ) فِي هٰذِهِ [4]ٱلْأَشْهُرِ (s. شَهْرٌ)
[5]طَافَتِ / فَاضَتِ [6]ٱلْأَنْهُرُ (s. نَهْرٌ) [7]وَجَرَفَتْ مَعَهَا [8]مَنَازِلَ (s. مَنْزِلٌ)
[9]عَدِيدَةً [10]قَرِيبَةً مِنَ [11]ٱلضِّفَافِ (s. ضَفَّةٌ).

(9) bi-sababi kaṯrati l-ʾamṭāri fī hāḏi-hi l-ʾašhuri ṭāfati / fāḍati l-ʾanhuru wa-ǧarafat maʿa-hā manāzila ʿadīdatan qarībatan mina ḍ-ḍifāfi.

[1]Because of the [2]heavy [3]rain (lit. [2]lot of [3]rain) during these [4]months, [6]the rivers have [5]flooded [7]and swept away [9]many [8]houses [10]near [11]the banks.

[1]نَسِيَ [2]ٱلْحَارِسُ أَبْوَابَ (s. بَابٌ) ٱلْمَكْتَبِ [3]وَشَبَابِيكَهُ (s. شُبَّاكٌ)
[4]مَفْتُوحَةً [5]فَدَخَلَ [6]لُصُوصٌ (s. لِصٌّ) [7]وَسَرَقُوا [8]أَشْيَاءَ (s. شَيْءٌ) [9]ثَمِينَةً.

(10) nasiya l-ḥārisu ʾabwāba l-maktabi wa-šabābīka-hu maftūḥatan, fa-daḫala luṣūṣun wa-saraqū ʾašyāʾa ṯamīnatan.

[2]The guard [1]left (lit. [1]forgot) the doors [3]and windows of the office [4]open, so [6]thieves [5]went in [7]and stole [9]valuable [8]things.

[1]نَشَرَتْ [2]دُورُ (s. دَارٌ) [3]ٱلنَّشْرِ [4]أَعْمَالَ (s. عَمَلٌ) [5]ٱلْكُتَّابِ (s. كَاتِبٌ)
[6]وَٱلشُّعَرَاءِ (s. شَاعِرٌ) [7]وَرَفَضَتْ بَعْضَهَا [8]مَعَ أَنَّهَا كَانَتْ [9]جَيِّدَةً.

(11) našarat dūru n-našri ʾaʿmāla l-kuttābi wa-š-šuʿarāʾi wa-rafaḍat baʿḍa-hā maʿa ʾanna-hā kānat ǧayyidatan.

[3]The publishing [2]houses [1]published [4]the works of [5]the writers [6]and poets [7]and rejected some of them [8]although they were [9]good.

[1]بِسَبَبِ [2]قِلَّةِ [3]ٱلْأَمْطَارِ (.s مَطَرٌ) فِي [4]ٱلْأَعْوَامِ (.s عَامٌ) [5]ٱلْأَخِيرَةِ
[6]تَضَرَّرَتْ [7]مَوَاسِمُ (.s مَوْسِمٌ) [8]ٱلْخُضَارِ [9]وَٱلْفَاكِهَةِ فِي
[10]ٱلْمَزَارِعِ (.s مَزْرَعَةٌ).

(12) bi-sababi qillati l-ʾamṭāri fī l-ʾaʿwāmi l-ʾaḫīrati taḍarrarat mawāsimu l-ḫuḍāri wa-l-fākihati fī l-mazāriʿi.
[1]Because of [2]lack ([2]scarcity) of [3]rain in [5]recent [4]years, [8]the vegetable [9]and fruit [7]harvests on [10]the farms have been [6]damaged.

[1]أَلشَّعْبُ ٱلْعَرَبِيُّ [2]مِنْ بَيْنِ ٱلشُّعُوبِ [3]ٱلْعَظِيمَةِ فِي [4]ٱلْعَالَمِ ٱلَّتِي [5]نَشَرَتِ
[6]ٱلْحَضَارَةَ.

(13) ʾaš-šaʿbu l-ʿarabiyyu min bayni š-šuʿūbi l-ʿaḏīmati fī l-ʿālami llatī našarati l-ḥaḍārata.
The Arabs (Arab [1]people) are [2]among the [3]great peoples (of [4]the world) who have [5]spread [6]civilization.

Translate into Arabic:

(1) The inhabitants of the area are busy (in) preparing a party for their poets and writers.

(2) Because of the heavy rain, a truck turned upside down and the boxes and sacks filled with fruit and vegetables fell out.

(3) The merchants discussed the wages of the workers and employees and the reduction of working hours.

(4) The sea fish is tastier than the freshwater fish.

(5) The thieves went into the company through (from) the window and stole medicines and valuable things.

(6) The guard left the door of the publishing house open, so thieves went in and stole some of the works of the writers and poets.

(7) Some of the Arab scientists published works on their discovery of new medicines.

Chapter 22

Triptotes and diptotes

22.1 Nouns, adjectives and proper names are classified according to their inflection into two major inflectional types: triptotes and diptotes.

(a) Triptotes

All definite as well as most other nouns and adjectives and some proper names are triptotes. This means that they take all three different vocalic case endings (-u, -a, -i) and nunation (-un, -an, -in) in the indefinite form (see chapters 5 and 8). In Arabic a triptotic noun or adjective is called أَلْمُنْصَرِفُ, i.e. *fully declined.*

(b) Diptotes

Certain indefinite nouns and adjectives as well as many proper nouns are called diptotes. They have only two vocalic case endings: -u for the nominative, and -a for the accusative and genitive jointly. Another important feature is that they do not take nunation (-un, -an, -in). Diptotes are therefore called in Arabic غَيْرُ ٱلْمُنْصَرِفِ or أَلْمَمْنُوعُ مِنَ ٱلصَّرْفِ, i.e. *not fully declined.*

	Diptote indefinite
Nominative: one **ḍammah**	ــُ /-u/
Accusative and genitive: one **fatḥah**	ــَ /-a/

22.2 When a diptote is made definite by the definite article أَلْـ.., a suffix possessive pronoun, or by being the first noun (أَلْمُضَافُ ʾal-muḍāfu) of an ʾ**iḍāfah** construction, it takes the usual three case endings, i.e. it becomes a triptote, e.g.

	Indefinite form, sing. *Diptote (not fully declined)*		***Definite form, sing.*** *Triptote (fully declined)*
Nom.:	أَحْمَرُ ʾaḥmar**u**, red	(not: أَحْمَرٌ ʾaḥmar**un**)	أَلْأَحْمَرُ ʾal-ʾaḥmar**u**
Acc.:	أَحْمَرَ ʾaḥmar**a**	(not: أَحْمَرًا ʾaḥmar**an**)	أَلْأَحْمَرَ ʾal-ʾaḥmar**a**
Gen.:	أَحْمَرَ ʾaḥmar**a**	(not: أَحْمَرٍ ʾaḥmar**in**)	أَلْأَحْمَرِ ʾal-ʾaḥmar**i**

	Indefinite form, plur. *Diptote (not fully declined)*	***Definite form, plur.*** *Triptote (fully declined, with suffix pronoun)*
Nom.:	رَسَائِلُ rasāʾil**u**, letters, messages	رَسَائِلُكَ rasāʾil**u**-ka, your (m.) letters
Acc.:	رَسَائِلَ rasāʾil**a**	رَسَائِلَكَ rasāʾil**a**-ka
Gen.:	رَسَائِلَ rasāʾil**a**	رَسَائِلِكَ rasāʾil**i**-ka

The most common classes of diptotes are:

22.3 *Proper names*

(a) Feminine proper names, with or without **tāʾ marbūṭah** ـَةُ.. ةُ.. /..atu/, e.g.

مَرْيَمُ Maryamu زَيْنَبُ Zaynabu سُعَادُ Suʿādu

عَائِشَةُ ʿĀʾišatu فَاطِمَةُ Fāṭimatu مَاجِدَةُ Māğidatu

Note: Even masculine proper names ending in ـَـةُ.. ـَةُ... /...atu/ are diptotes, e.g.

نَخْلَةُ Naḫlatu   مُعَاوِيَةُ Muᶜāwiyatu

(b) Feminine proper names containing three consonants and **sukūn** ـْ on the middle consonant are treated either as triptotes or diptotes, e.g.

Triptote				***Diptote*** (more common)		
هِنْدٌ	رَغْدٌ	مِصْرٌ	OR	هِنْدُ	رَغْدُ	مِصْرُ
Hindun	Raġdun	Miṣrun	OR	Hindu	Raġdu	Miṣru
		Egypt				Egypt

Note: Most commonly in modern Arabic, مِصْرُ miṣ**ru** is used as a diptote and هِنْدٌ hind**un** as a triptote.

(c) Masculine proper names which contain more than three consonants, e.g.

إِسْحَاقُ	إِبْرَاهِيمُ	يُوسُفُ	يَعْقُوبُ
ʾIsḥāqu, Isaac	ʾIbrāhīmu, Abraham	Yūsufu, Joseph	Yaᶜqūbu, Jacob

(d) All geographical names which do not have the definite article أَلْـ.., e.g.

بَارِيسُ	مَكَّةُ	دِمَشْقُ	لُبْنَانُ
Bārīsu	Makkatu	Dimašqu	Lubnānu
Paris	Mecca	Damascus	Lebanon

Note: The name of Cairo has the definite article أَلْـ../ʾal../. It is therefore a triptote and takes all three cases endings: أَلْقَاهِرَةُ أَلْقَاهِرَةَ أَلْقَاهِرَةِ.

(e) Compound geographical names:

بُورْ سَعِيدُ	بَعْلَبَكُّ	بَيْتَ لَحْمَ	نِيُورْكُ
Būr Saᶜī**du**	Baᶜla-bakk**u**	Bayt**a** Laḥm**a**	Niyūrk**u**
Port Said	Baalbek	Bethlehem	New York

(f) Masculine and feminine proper names which simulate verbal forms and do not have the ending ـَـةُ.. ـَةُ.. /..atu/ in the feminine singular, e.g.

أَحْمَدُ	يَزِيدُ	تَغْلِبُ
ʾAḥmadu	Yazīdu	Taġlibu

Note: The noun below has the same structure as the proper names above, but it is not a diptote, because its feminine singular is formed by adding the ending ةٌ... ـَةٌ.. /...atun/ e.g.

أَرْمَلٌ	أَرْمَلاً	أَرْمَلٍ	(fem. أَرْمَلَةٌ
ʾarmal**un**, widower	ʾarmal**an**	ʾarmal**in**	ʾarmala**tun**)

(g) Masculine proper names ending in ـَانُ.. /...ānu/, e.g.

عُثْمَانُ	سُلَيْمَانُ	زَيْدَانُ
ʿUṯmānu	Sulaymānu	Zaydānu

(h) Proper names (masculine and feminine) which have the pattern of فُعَلُ fuʿalu, e.g.

عُمَرُ	زُحَلُ	قُزَحُ
ʿUmaru	Zuḥalu	Quzaḥu

22.4 *Adjectives*

(a) Most of the classical grammarians consider the masculine adjectives ending in ـَانُ.. /...ān**u**/ (pattern: فَعْلَانُ faʿlān**u**) and having the feminine ending ـَى.. /...ā/ (pattern: فَعْلَى faʿlā) to be diptotes, but some other grammarians consider the feminine ending of the above ـَانُ.. /...ānu/ to be ـَةٌ.. /...atun/ (pattern: فَعْلَانَةٌ faʿlāna**tun**, not فَعْلَى faʿlā). In this case they have to be triptotes (as pattern: فَعْلَانٌ faʿlān**un**), according to the rule mentioned in note (b) below, and this type of feminine is more frequently used in modern Arabic, e.g.

Masc. sing.	***Fem. sing.***	
	Classical usage	***Modern usage***
كَسْلَانُ OR كَسْلَانٌ kaslānu/un, lazy	كَسْلَى kaslā OR	كَسْلَانَةٌ kaslānatun
سَكْرَانُ OR سَكْرَانٌ sakrānu/un, drunk	سَكْرَى sakrā OR	سَكْرَانَةٌ sakrānatun

عَطْشَانُ OR عَطْشَانٌ ʿaṭšānu/un, thirsty — عَطْشَى ʿaṭšā OR عَطْشَانَةٌ ʿaṭšānatun

غَضْبَانُ OR غَضْبَانٌ ġaḍbānu/un, angry — غَضْبَى ġaḍbā OR غَضْبَانَةٌ ġaḍbānatun

Note a: When the above adjectives occur as proper names then they are treated as diptotes, following rule 3 (g) above, e.g. غَضْبَانُ ġaḍbān**u** (as proper name).

Note b: The adjective below is not a diptote, because its feminine singular does not end in ـَى /...ā/ (pattern: فَعْلَى faʿlā):

Nom.	***Acc.***	***Gen.***	***Fem. sing.***
نَدْمَانٌ	نَدْمَانًا	نَدْمَانٍ	(نَدْمَانَةٌ)
nadmān**un**, regretful	nadmān**an**	nadmā**nin**	(nadmān**atun**)

Note c: Adjectives of the pattern فُعْلَانٌ fuʿlān**un** are all triptotes, e.g.

عُرْيَانٌ	عُرْيَانًا	عُرْيَانٍ	(عُرْيَانَةٌ)
ʿuryān**un**, naked	ʿuryān**an**	ʿuryā**nin**	(ʿuryāna**tun**)
فُلَانٌ	فُلَانًا	فُلَانٍ	(فُلَانَةٌ)
fulānun, somebody	fulānan	fulānin	(fulānatun)

(b) Masculine adjectives of the pattern أَفْعَلُ ʾafʿalu, e.g.

أَحْمَرُ	أَصْغَرُ	آخَرُ	أَعْرَجُ
ʾaḥmaru	ʾaṣġaru	ʾāẖaru	ʾaʿrağu
red	smaller	other, another	lame

(c) Nouns and adjectives ending in ـَاءُ /...āʾu/ which is not part of the verb root, e.g.

عَذْرَاءُ (v. عَذَرَ)	سَوْدَاءُ (v. سَوَدَ)	رُؤَسَاءُ (v. رَأَسَ)
ʿaḏrāʾu (ʿaḏara)	sawdāʾu (sawada)	ruʾasāʾu (raʾasa)
virgin	black (f.)	presidents

Note a: The triptote nouns ending in ـَاءٌ /...āʾun/ below do not belong to the above group, because they are derived from verbs ending in a weak radical (chapter 33), e.g.

قُرَّاءٌ	(v. قَرَأَ	سَمَاءٌ	(v. سَمَوَ	شِرَاءٌ	(v. شَرَيَ
qurrāʾ**un**	qaraʾa)	samāʾ**un**	samawa)	širāʾ**un**	šaraya)
readers		heaven		purchase, buy(ing)	

Note b: The word أَشْيَاءُ ʾašyāʾ**u** 'things' (sing. شَيْءٌ šayʾun) is an exception because it is a diptote in the Quran.

(d) A few nouns and adjectives ending in ـَى.. are indeclinable (they have the same form in all cases) in both the definite and indefinite form, e.g.

Indefinite	***Definite***
مَقْهًى maqhan, a coffee house	أَلْمَقْهَى ʾal-maqhā
سُكْنَى suknā, housing, dwelling	أَلسُّكْنَى ʾas-suknā

22.5 *Broken plurals as diptotes*

Broken plurals having the pattern of مَفَاعِلُ mafāʿilu or مَفَاعِيلُ mafāʿīlu are diptotes, e.g.

مَوَادُّ	أَصَابِعُ	أَكَارِمُ	مَسَاجِدُ
mawāddu	ʾaṣābiʿu	ʾakārim**u**	masāǧid**u**
materials	fingers	nobles	mosques
عَصَافِيرُ	قَنَادِيلُ	شَبَابِيكُ	أَنَاشِيدُ
ʿaṣāfīru	qanādīlu	šabābīku	ʾanāšīdu
birds	lamps	windows	songs, hymns

Exercises

Practise your reading:

[1]إِسْتَمَعْتُ [2]لِمُؤَذِّنِينَ (s. مُؤَذِّنٌ) [3]مُمْتَازِينَ فِي [4]مَسَاجِدَ (s. مَسْجِدٌ) [5]عَدِيدَةٍ فِي مَكَّةَ [6]ٱلْمُكَرَّمَةِ.

(1) ʾistamaʿtu li-muʾaḏḏinīna mumtāzīna fī masāǧida ʿadīdatin fī Makkata l-mukarramati.

[1]I listened to [3]excellent [2]muezzins ([2]reciters of the Holy Quran) in [5]many [4]mosques in the [6]Honored (Holy) city of Mecca.

[1]سَكَنْتُ / [1]أَقَمْتُ (IV) [2]نِصْفَ [3]سَنَةٍ فِي [4]صَحْرَاءِ سِينَا [5]قَرِيبًا مِنَ [6]ٱلْبَحْرِ [7]ٱلْمُتَوَسِّطِ.

(2) sakantu niṣfa sanatin fī ṣaḥrāʾi Sīnā qarīban mina l-baḥri l-mutawassiṭi.

[1]I lived/stayed for [2]half a [3]year in [4]the Sinai Desert [5]near the [7]Mediterranean [6]Sea.

[1]جَلَسْتُ [2]لِمُدَّةٍ [3]طَوِيلَةٍ مَعَ [4]عُلَمَاءَ (s. عَالِمٌ) [5]عُظَمَاءَ (s. عظيمٌ) فِي [6]مَقْهًى عَلَى [7]ٱلْبَحْرِ.

(3) ǧalastu li-muddatin ṭawīlatin maʿa ʿulamāʾa ʿuḏamāʾa fī maqhan ʿalā l-baḥri.

[1]I sat for a [3]long [2]time with [5]great [4]scholars in [6]a coffee shop by the [7]sea.

[1]سَكَنْتُ / [1]أَقَمْتُ (IV) [2]سَنَةً فِي بَيْرُوتَ [3]وَشَهْرًا فِي عَمَّانَ [4]وَأُسْبُوعًا [5]وَنِصْفَ [6]ٱلْأُسْبُوعِ فِي ٱلْقَاهِرَةِ.

(4) sakantu / ʾaqamtu sanatan fī Bayrūta wa-šahran fī ʿAmmāna wa-ʾusbūʿan wa-niṣfa l-ʾusbūʿi fī l-Qāhirati.

[1]I lived / [1]I stayed [2]for a year in Beirut, [3]a month in Amman and [4]one and [5]a half [6]weeks in Cairo.

ذَهَبْتُ [1]أَمْسِ [2]بِرِحْلَةٍ مَعَ يُوسُفَ وَسُعَادَ وَهِنْدٍ إِلَى بَيْتَ لَحْمَ.

(5) ḏahabtu ʾamsi bi-riḥlatin maʿa Yūsufa wa-Suʿāda wa-Hindin ʾilā bayta laḥma.

I went [2]on a trip to Bethlehem [1]yesterday with Josef, Suad and Hind.

[1]شَاهَدْتُ [2]تَمَاثِيلَ (s. تِمْثَالٌ) [3]ضَخْمَةً فِي [4]مَعَابِدَ (s. مَعْبَدٌ) كَثِيرَةٍ فِي مِصْرَ [5]وَبِخَاصَّةٍ فِي ٱلْقَاهِرَةِ.

(6) šāhadtu tamāṯīla ḍaḫmatan fī maʿābida kaṯīratin fī miṣra wa-bi-ḫāṣṣatin fī l-Qāhirati.

[1]I saw [3]huge [2]statues in many [4]temples in Egypt, [5]especially in Cairo.

[1]تَكَلَّمْتُ مَعَ أَكْرَمَ وَمُحَمَّدٍ وَأَحْمَدَ وَجُورْجَ، [2]وَكَتَبْتُ إِلَى عَلِيٍّ وَعُمَرَ وَسُلَيْمَانَ وَعُثْمَانَ وَإِبْرَاهِيمَ وَيَزِيدَ.

(7) takallamtu maʿa ʾAkrama wa-Muḥammadin wa-ʾAḥmada wa-Ǧūrǧa, wa-katabtu ʾilā ʿAliyyin wa-ʿUmara wa-Sulaymāna wa-ʿUṯmāna wa-ʾIbrāhīma wa-Yazīda.

[1]I spoke to (with) ᵓAkram, Mohammad, ᵓAhmad and George, [2]and I wrote to Ali, Omar, Solomon, Othman, Abraham and Yazid.

[1]تَنَزَّهْتُ فِي [2]جُنَيْنَةٍ [3]خَضْرَاءَ (.m أَخْضَرُ) فِي [4]ضَاحِيَةِ دِمَشْقَ [5]وَقَطَفْتُ [6]مِنْهَا [7]زَهْرَةً [8]حَمْرَاءَ (.m أَحْمَرُ).

(8) tanazzahtu fī ǧunaynatin ḫaḍrāᵓa fī ḍāḥiyati Dimašqa wa-qaṭaftu min-hā zahratan ḥamrāᵓa.
[1]I took a walk ([1]I went for a walk) in [3]a green [2]garden in [4]a suburb of Damascus [5]and I picked ([6]from it) [8]a red [7]flower.

[1]تَكَلَّمَ رَجُلٌ [2]أَعْرَجُ فِي [3]مُؤْتَمَرٍ [4]لِلْمُعَاقِينَ عَنْ [5]مَشَاكِلِهِمْ (.s مُشْكِلٌ) [6]وَمَوَاضِيعَ (.s مَوْضُوعٌ) [7]أُخْرَى [8]تَخُصُّهُمْ.

(9) takallama rağulun ᵓaᶜrağu fī muᵓtamarin li-l-muᶜāqīna ᶜan mašākili-him wa-mawāḍīᶜa ᵓuḫrā taḫuṣṣu-hum.
[2]A lame man [1]spoke at [3]a conference (congress) [4]for the disabled (handicapped) about [5]their [5]problems and [7]other [6]subjects [8]concerning them.

[1]قَدَّمَتِ [2]ٱلْمُمَرِّضَةُ [3]لِلْمَرِيضِ [4]دَوَاءً [5]أَصْفَرَ فِي [6]صَحْنٍ [7]أَزْرَقَ.

(10) qaddamati l-mumarriḍatu li-l-marīḍi dawāᵓan ᵓaṣfara fī ṣaḥnin ᵓazraqa.
[2]The nurse [1]gave [3]the patient some [5]yellow [4]medicine on a [7]blue [6]plate.

[1]طَلَبَ [2]طِفْلٌ [3]عَطْشَانُ [4]شَرَابًا [5]وَطَلَبَتْ بِنْتٌ [6]جَوْعَانَةٌ [7]طَعَامًا / أَكْلًا.

(11) ṭalaba ṭiflun ᶜaṭšānu šarāban wa-ṭalabat bintun ğawᶜānatun ṭaᶜāman / ᵓaklan.
[3]A thirsty [2]child (m.) [1]requested [4]a drink and [6]a hungry girl [5]requested [7]food.

كَتَبَ [1]مُفَتِّشٌ [2]غَضْبَانُ [3]تَقْرِيرًا [4]ضِدَّ مُوَظَّفٍ [5]مَسْؤُولٍ عَنْ [6]مَسَائِلَ (.s مَسْأَلَةٌ) [7]سِرِّيَّةٍ فِي [8]ٱلْحُكُومَةِ.

(12) kataba mufattišun ġaḍbānu taqrīran ḍidda muwaḏḏafin masᵓūlin ᶜan masāᵓila sirriyyatin fī l-ḥukūmati.
[2]An angry [1]inspector wrote [3]a report [4]condemning (lit. [4]against) an employee [5]responsible for [7]confidential (secret) [6]matters in [8]the government.

[1]رَسَبَ طَالِبٌ [2]كَسْلَانُ فِي [3]ٱمْتِحَانِ [4]قَوَاعِدِ (.s قَاعِدَةٌ) [5]ٱللُّغَةِ ٱلْعَرَبِيَّةِ.

(13) rasaba ṭālibun kaslānu fī-mtiḥāni qawāʿidi l-luġati l-ʿarabiyyati.
[2]A lazy student [1]failed (in) the Arabic [4]grammar [3]exam (lit. [4]the grammar of the Arabic [5]language).

[1]تَنَزَّهْتُ مَعَ [2]شُعَرَاءَ (.s شَاعِرٌ) [3]أَجَانِبَ (.s أَجْنَبِيٌّ) [4]مَشْهُورِينَ فِي [5]حَدَائِقَ (.s حَدِيقَةٌ) جَمِيلَةٍ [6]بِٱلْقُرْبِ مِنْ دِمَشْقَ.

(14) tanazzahtu maʿa šuʿarāʾa ʾaǧāniba mašhūrīna fī ḥadāʾiqa ǧamīlatin bi-l-qurbi min dimašqa.
[1]I took a walk with (some) [4]famous [3]foreign [2]poets in beautiful [5]gardens (parks) [6]near Damascus.

Translate into Arabic:

(1) I sat for a long time in a coffee shop by the sea with a famous poet.

(2) I took a walk in the suburb(s) of Cairo and saw many statues and a huge temple.

(3) I listened for a long time to an angry inspector who spoke about (the) confidential matters concerning (the) foreigners.

(4) I lived for a year in Cairo, half a year in Bethlehem, one month in Amman and one and a half weeks in Beirut near the sea.

(5) I went yesterday to the mosque and I listened to an excellent reciter (of the Quran) in (the) Honoured (Holy) city of Mecca.

(6) I sat yesterday with a lame man in a garden and he spoke about his problem and the problems of the disabled.

(7) The hungry and thirsty patient asked the nurse for medicine, food and drink.

(8) The nurse gave the ill child the medicine on a green plate and the food on a blue plate.

(9) The employee responsible wrote a report condemning (lit. against) the Arabic grammar exam.

Chapter 23

Participles, verbal nouns (maṣdar), nouns of place, time and instrument

23.1 *Active participle*

The active participle, إِسْمُ ٱلْفَاعِل, is a deverbal adjective or noun indicating the doer of an action or doing the action. The pattern of the active participle of the triliteral verb (form I) is فَاعِلٌ (fem. فَاعِلَةٌ), from the verb فَعَلَ, e.g.

كَاتِبٌ kātibun, one who writes, writer, clerk (from the verb كَتَبَ kataba, to write)

قَاتِلٌ qātilun, one who kills, killer, murderer (from the verb قَتَلَ qatala, to kill)

23.2 Some active participles are often used to indicate an on-going, simultaneous or imminent action or state, having a meaning close to the verb in the imperfect tense. They may then correspond to the English present participle, progressive present or future, e.g.

مُسَافِرٌ (III) travell**ing, going** to travel جَالِسٌ sitt**ing** ذَاهِبٌ go**ing**

Hence it is sometimes difficult to know whether to use the active participle or the imperfect tense. It is a question of practice, e.g.

Active participle	***Imperfect verb***
أَنَا مُسَافِرٌ غَدًا	أُسَافِرُ غَدًا
ʾanā musāfirun ġadan.	ʾusāfiru ġadan.
I am travelling tomorrow.	I will travel tomorrow.

خَرَجَ ضَاحِكًا	خَرَجَ (وَهُوَ) يَضْحَكُ
ḫaraǧa ḍāḥikan.	ḫaraǧa (wa-huwa) yaḍḥaku.
He went out laughing.	He went out (while) laughing. He was laughing as he went out.

Note: The above words غَدًا and ضَاحِكًا are in the accusative case, because they function as adverbs (see chapter 38).

23.3 In the case of a habitual action or something which happens regularly, the imperfect tense should replace the active participle as follows:

With the active participle	***With the imperfect (a habitual action)***
أَلْحَارِسُ جَالِسٌ هُنَا	أَلْحَارِسُ يَجْلِسُ (دَائِمًا) هُنَا
ʾal-ḥārisu **ǧālisun** hunā.	ʾal-ḥārisu **yaǧlisu** (dāʾiman) hunā.
The guard **is sitting** here.	The guard **(always) sits** here.
أَلْعَامِلُ ذَاهِبٌ إِلَى عَمَلِهِ	يَذْهَبُ ٱلْعَامِلُ إِلَى عَمَلِهِ فِي ٱلصَّبَاحِ
ʾal-ʿāmilu **ḏāhibun** ʾilā ʿamali-hi.	**yaḏhabu** l-ʿāmilu ʾilā ʿamali-hi fī ṣ-ṣabāḥi.
The worker **is going** (or: **is on his way**) to (his) work.	The worker **(always) goes** to (his) work in the morning.
أَنَا رَاكِبٌ حِصَانًا	أَرْكَبُ حِصَانًا كُلَّ يَوْمٍ
ʾanā **rākibun** ḥiṣānan.	ʾ**arkabu** ḥiṣānan kulla yawmin.
I am **riding** a horse (just now).	I **ride** a horse every day.

23.4 ***Passive participle***

The passive participle, إِسْمُ ٱلْمَفْعُول , is a deverbal adjective or noun which indicates (the result or effect of) a completed action. In English it corresponds to the past participle. The passive participle of the triliteral verb (form I) is formed according to the pattern of مَفْعُولٌ mafʿūlun, e.g.

مَكْتُوبٌ written, a letter   مَقْتُولٌ (is) killed, murdered

23.5 Active participles and passive participles of the derived verb forms II–X are formed according to the pattern below with the prefix ...مُـ :

(a) Active participle

(I)	II	III	IV	V	VI	VII	VIII
(فَاعِلٌ)	مُفَعِّلٌ	مُفَاعِلٌ	مُفْعِلٌ	مُتَفَعِّلٌ	مُتَفَاعِلٌ	مُنْفَعِلٌ	مُفْتَعِلٌ
						IX	**X**
						مُفْعَلٌّ	مُسْتَفْعِلٌ

(b) Passive participle

(I)	II	III	IV	V	VI	VII	VIII
(مَفْعُولٌ)	مُفَعَّلٌ	مُفَاعَلٌ	مُفْعَلٌ	مُتَفَعَّلٌ	مُتَفَاعَلٌ	مُنْفَعَلٌ	مُفْتَعَلٌ
						IX	**X**
							مُسْتَفْعَلٌ

(See also table A1.1 of the verb **faᶜala** in Appendix 1.)

Examples of verb forms II and III:

	verb	active participle	passive participle
II	عَلَّمَ ᶜallama to teach	مُعَلِّمٌ muᶜallimun teacher	مُعَلَّمٌ muᶜallamun taught, educated
III	سَاعَدَ sāᶜada to help	مُسَاعِدٌ musāᶜidun helper, assistant	مُسَاعَدٌ musāᶜadun one who has received help, been assisted

23.6 ***Verbal noun (maṣdar)***

(a) The verbal noun is called مَصْدَرٌ maṣdar, which means 'source'. It is a noun derived from the verb and denotes the action, quality or state expressed by the verb. For example, the verbal noun

قَتْلٌ qatlun, 'killing, murder' is derived from the verb قَتَلَ qatala, 'to kill'; similarly, حُسْنٌ ḥusnun 'beauty', is derived from حَسُنَ ḥasuna 'to be handsome'. The Arabic verbal noun corresponds to the English gerund ending in '-ing' (e.g. 'playing, going'), or to action nouns like 'departure', 'arrival', 'treatment', etc.

The patterns for forming verbal nouns from the different verb forms (I–X) are given below:

(I)	II	III	IV	V	VI	VII	VIII
(فَعْلٌ)	تَفْعِيلٌ	فِعَالٌ	إِفْعَالٌ	تَفَعُّلٌ	تَفَاعُلٌ	إِنْفِعَالٌ	إِفْتِعَالٌ
	تَفْعِلَةٌ	مُفَاعَلَةٌ					

IX	X
إِفْعِلاَلٌ	إِسْتِفْعَالٌ

(See also table A1.1 (**faʿala**) in Appendix 1.)

Note a: The verbal nouns of forms IV–X have only one pattern, but forms II and III may have two.

Note b: The initial **hamzatu l-qaṭʿi** إِ and أُ in the verbal nouns of verb forms VII–X is subject to the rule of **hamzatu l-waṣli** (**waṣlah**), in the same way as the corresponding **hamzah** in the perfect and imperative forms.

b) There are dozens of patterns for the verbal noun of a triliteral verb in form I. They can only be learned from more advanced Arabic grammar books or by consulting the dictionary. The following are some examples:

Verbal noun (maṣdar)	***Verb form I***
قَتْلٌ qatlun, killing	قَتَلَ qatala, to kill
دُخُولٌ duḫūlun, entering	دَخَلَ daḫala, to enter
شُرْبٌ šurbun, drinking	شَرِبَ šariba, to drink
سَمْعٌ samʿun, hearing	سَمِعَ samiʿa, to hear
حُسْنٌ ḥusnun, beauty	حَسُنَ ḥasuna, to be handsome
سَهَرٌ saharun, sleeplessness	سَهِرَ sahira, to stay awake (at night)

(c) The Arabic verbal noun can often be translated by an English infinitive or gerund, e.g.

قَصَدَ ٱلْقَتْلَ qaṣada l-**qatla**. He intended **to kill**.

عَلَّمَ ٱلسِّبَاحَةَ ʿallama **s-sibāḥata**. He taught **swimming (how to swim)**.

23.7 Nouns of place and time, إِسْمُ ٱلْمَكَانِ وَٱلزَّمَانِ, express the place or time of the verbal action or state. They are formed by prefixing مـ... /ma.../ to the root according to the patterns: مَفْعَلٌ, مَفْعِلٌ or مَفْعَلَةٌ. Their broken plural is formed according to the pattern مَفَاعِلُ or مَفَاعِيلُ and is a **diptote**, e.g.

Noun of place/time	*Broken plural*	*Triliteral verb (form I)*
مَخْزَنٌ **ma**ḫzanun store, warehouse	مَخَازِنُ **ma**ḫāzinu	خَزَنَ ḫazana to store
مَوْعِدٌ **maw**ʿidun appointment	مَوَاعِيدُ **mawā**ʿīdu	وَعَدَ waʿada to promise
مَنْزِلٌ **man**zilun stopping place, house	مَنَازِلُ **ma**nāzilu	نَزَلَ nazala to go down
مَسْجِدٌ **mas**ğidun mosque	مَسَاجِدُ **ma**sāğidu	سَجَدَ sağada to bow down

23.8 The nouns of place and time of the derived verb forms from II–X are the same as the corresponding passive participles, e.g.

مُنْتَزَهٌ muntazahun, park (form VIII)

مُسْتَقْبَلٌ mustaqbalun, future (form X)

23.9 *Nouns of instrument*

Nouns of instrument إِسْمُ ٱلْآلَةِ express the instrument or tool by which the action is performed. They are prefixed with مـ... /mi.../ and formed only from verb form I, according to the following patterns:

Noun of instrument	***Verb form I***
(a) Pattern مِفْعَالٌ , e.g.	
مِنْشَارٌ **mi**nšārun, saw	نَشَرَ našara, to saw
مِفْتَاحٌ **mi**ftāḥun, key	فَتَحَ fataḥa, to open
(b) Pattern مِفْعَلٌ, e.g.	
مِبْرَدٌ **mi**bradun, file	بَرَدَ barada, to file
مِقَصٌّ **mi**qaṣṣun, scissors	قَصَّ qaṣṣa, to cut
(c) Pattern مِفْعَلَةٌ, e.g.	
مِكْنَسَةٌ **mi**knasatun, broom	كَنَسَ kanasa, to sweep
مِنْشَفَةٌ **mi**nšafatun, towel	نَشِفَ našifa, to dry

Exercises

(The transliterations will be omitted from the exercises from this point on, as the student should now be familiar enough with the Arabic script not to need to rely on transliteration.)

Analyse each of the following nouns according to: a) the verb form number, b) the first (basic) verb form, c) the grammatical form, i.e. whether it is an active participle, passive participle, or verbal noun (**maṣdar**).

مُعَلَّمٌ educated	مُعَلِّمٌ teacher	إِسْتِعْلَامٌ information	مَقْتُولٌ killed	مَفْهُومٌ understood
مَخْطُوفٌ kidnapped	إِسْتِعْمَارٌ colonizing	مُسْتَعْمِرٌ colonial	مَسْمُوعٌ heard	مَغْلُوبٌ defeated
مُسَاعِدٌ assistant	مُشَاهِدٌ spectator	مُسَامَحٌ excused	مُرَاسِلٌ news correspondent	مُبَالِغٌ exaggerator
مُتَحَمِّسٌ enthusiastic	مُحْتَرَمٌ respected	مُسْتَعْمَلٌ used	مُهَاجِرٌ emigrant, immigrant	مُسْتَقْبَلٌ future
مَشْهُورٌ famous	إِمْتِحَانٌ exam	إِضْرَابٌ strike	إِحْتِرَامٌ respect	إِنْفِجَارٌ explosion

إِحْمِرَارٌ	تَقْدِمَةٌ	تَسْلِيحٌ	مُخْتَرِعٌ	مُسَابَقَةٌ
reddening blushing	gift	armament arming	inventor	competition
إِنْفِرَادٌ	مُشْرِفٌ	مُقَدَّسٌ	مُسْتَعْجِلٌ	مُعَاهَدَةٌ
loneliness isolation	supervisor	holy	speedy	treaty

Practise your reading:

فِي كُلِّ [1]صَبَاحٍ [2]يُكَنِّسُ [3]ٱلْمُنَظِّفُ [4]أَرْضَ [5]ٱلْجَامِعِ [6]وَسَجَّادَهُ (s. سَجَّادَةٌ) [7]بِٱلْمِكْنَسَةِ [8]ٱلْكَهْرَبَائِيَّةِ [9]وَيَغْسِلُ [10]ٱلْمَدْخَلَ [11]وَٱلدَّرَجَ (s. دَرَجَةٌ) [12]بِٱلْمَاءِ [13]ٱلسَّاخِنِ [14]وَٱلصَّابُونِ (s. صَابُونَةٌ).

(1) Every [1]morning [3]the cleaner [2]sweeps [4]the floor and [6]the carpets of [5]the mosque with [8]the [7,8]vacuum cleaner (lit. [8]electric [7]broom) [9]and washes [10]the entrance [11]and the stairs with [13]warm [12]water [14]and soap.

[1]أَعْجَبَتْنِي [2]طَرِيقَةُ [3]تَعْلِيمِ ٱلْأُسْتَاذِ [4]ٱلْمَبْعُوثِ مِنْ جَامِعَةِ ٱلرِّبَاطِ [5]لِتَدْرِيسِ [6]ٱللُّغَةِ ٱلْعَرَبِيَّةِ.

(2) [1]I liked the [3]teaching [2]method (way) of the professor [4]sent over from the University of Rabat [5]to teach the Arabic [6]language.

[1]بَدَأَ [2]ٱلنَّاسُ فِي [3]ٱلشَّرْقِ [4]ٱلْأَوْسَطِ [5]يَعْرِفُونَ [6]قَدْرَ [7]ٱلْعِلْمِ [8]بَعْدَ [9]ٱنْقِطَاعٍ [10]طَوِيلٍ.

(3) [2]The people in [4]the Middle [3]East [1]began [5]to realize [6]the value of [7]science (knowledge), [8]after [10]a long [9]halt (break).

[1]سَمِعْتُ فِي هٰذَا [2]ٱلصَّبَاحِ مِنَ [3]ٱلْإِذَاعَةِ أَنَّ [4]رَئِيسَ [5]ٱلْجُمْهُورِيَّةِ ٱلتُّونِسِيَّةِ [6]سَيَتَبَاحَثُ [7]غَدًا مَعَ [8]نَائِبِ مُدِيرِ ٱلْبَنْكِ [9]ٱلدَّوْلِيِّ [10]بِخُصُوصِ [11]مُسَاعَدَاتٍ [12]مَالِيَّةٍ.

(4) [1]I heard this [2]morning on [3]the radio that [4]the president of [5]the Republic of Tunisia [6]will [7]tomorrow [6]discuss ([10]concerning) [12]financial [11]assistance (support) with the [8]vice-director of [9]the International Bank.

[1]عُيِّنَ [2]زَوْجِي [3]مَنْدُوبَ لُبْنَانَ فِي [4]ٱلْأُمَمِ (أُمَّةٌ) [5]ٱلْمُتَّحِدَةِ [6]وَسَيُبَاشِرُ [7]عَمَلَهُ فِي [8]وَسَطِ [9]ٱلْعَامِ [10]ٱلْمُقْبِلِ.

(5) [2]My husband [1]has been appointed as the Lebanese [3]representative at the [5]United [4]Nations and [6]he will start [7]his post (work) by [8]the middle of [10]the next [9]year.

[1]تَسَلَّمَ ٱلْأُسْتَاذُ [2]ٱلْيَوْمَ [3]رِسَالَةً مِنْ رَئِيسِ [4]مَعْهَدِ [5]تَدْرِيسِ [6]ٱللُّغَةِ ٱلْعَرَبِيَّةِ [7]لِلْأَجَانِبِ (.s أَجْنَبِيٌّ) [8]يَسْأَلُهُ [9]فِيهَا [10]عَنْ [11]تَقَدُّمِ ٱلطُّلَّابِ (.s طَالِبٌ) فِي [12]دِرَاسَاتِهِمْ.

(6) The professor [1]received [2]today [3]a letter from the director of the Arabic [6]Language [5]Teaching [4]Institute [7]for Foreigners, [8]asking him ([9]in it) [10]about [11]the progress of the students in [12]their studies.

[1]حَادِثُ [2]ٱلصِّدَامِ [3]بَيْنَ [4]ٱلشُّرْطَةِ [5]وَٱلْمُتَظَاهِرِينَ [6]أَمْسِ [7]مَنْشُورٌ [8]عَنْهُ فِي [9]جَرِيدَةِ ٱلْيَوْمِ.

(7) The [1]incident of [6]yesterday's [2]clash [3]between [4]police [5]and demonstrators is [7]reported ([7]published [8]about it) in today's [9]newspaper.

[1]بَعْدَمَا [2]تَخَرَّجَ ٱبْنِي مِنَ ٱلْجَامِعَةِ بِدَرَجَةٍ فِي [3]ٱلْعُلُومِ [4]ٱلسِّيَاسِيَّةِ، [5]إِنْتَقَلَ إِلَى جَامِعَةِ لُنْدُنَ [6]حَيْثُ كَتَبَ [7]أُطْرُوحَتَهُ [8]ثُمَّ رَجَعَ إِلَى [9]وَطَنِهِ [10]بَعْدَ [11]حُصُولِهِ عَلَى [12]ٱلدُّكْتُورَاةِ.

(8) [1]After my son [2]graduated from university with a degree in [4]Political [3]Science, [5]he moved to the University of London, [6]where he wrote [7]his thesis, [8]and then returned to his [9]homeland [10]after [11]obtaining his [12]doctorate.

[1]مُنِعَ [2]مُرَاسِلُ [3]لِوَكَالَةِ [4]أَنْبَاءٍ (.s نَبَأٌ) [5]أَجْنَبِيَّةٍ مِنَ [6]ٱلدُّخُولِ إِلَى قَصْرِ رَئِيسِ ٱلْجُمْهُورِيَّةِ [7]لِحُضُورِ [8]ٱحْتِفَالِ [9]عِيدِ [10]ٱلْاِسْتِقْلَالِ، [11]لِأَنَّهُ كَانَ لَا [12]يَحْمِلُ [13]بِطَاقَةَ [14]دَعْوَةٍ [15]مَعَ [16]ٱلْعِلْمِ أَنَّهُ قَدْ [17]سُمِحَ [18]لِغَيْرِهِ مِنَ [19]ٱلصِّحَافِيِّينَ [20]بِٱلدُّخُولِ [21]مِنْ [22]دُونِ [23]بِطَاقَاتٍ.

(9) [5]A foreign [4]news [3]agency [2]correspondent [1]was prevented from [6]entering the presidential palace (lit. the palace of the President of the Republic)

[7]to attend the [10]Independence [9]Day [8]festivities, [11]because he was not [12]carrying an [14]invitation [13]card, [15,16]although [18]other (lit. [18]for other than he) [19]journalists [17]were permitted [20]to enter [21,22]without [23]cards.

Translate into Arabic:

(1) In the middle of next year my husband will start his post at the radio (station).

(2) The cleaner began sweeping the stairs and the floor of the Institute of Arabic Language with warm water and soap.

(3) At the Independence Day celebration I asked the professor about the progress of Arab students' studies at the university.

(4) Tomorrow the vice-director of the International Bank will discuss the financial assistance with the representative of Tunisia at the UN (with the UN representative of Tunisia).

(5) Today my son received an invitation card from the President of the Republic to attend the Independence Day festivities.

(6) After I graduated from the university, I was appointed as a correspondent for a foreign news agency.

(7) I heard on the radio about the clash between the demonstrators and the police.

(8) After a long halt (break) the people in the Middle East began to realize the value of teaching Arabic (language) to foreigners.

(9) The professor sent over from the University of Rabat was prevented from entering the Institute of Arabic Language to take part in a celebration, because he was not carrying an invitation card.

Chapter 24

Interrogative particles and pronouns, vocative particles

24.1 Interrogative particles حُرُوفُ ٱلاِسْتِفْهَامِ

(a) A sentence is made interrogative by introducing it with the interrogative particle هَلْ hal, or by prefixing the first word of the sentence with the interrogative particle .. أَ ʾa.

هَلْ فَتَحْتَ ٱلشُّبَّاكَ؟ OR أَفَتَحْتَ ٱلشُّبَّاكَ؟

hal fataḥta š-šubbāka? ʾ**a**-fataḥta š-šubbāka?

Did you open the window?

(b) The particle أَ cannot be used before a word having the definite article ..أَلْ. It can, however, be joined to another word which begins with ... أَ, e.g.

هَلْ أَنْتَ تَاجِرٌ؟ OR أَأَنْتَ تَاجِرٌ؟

hal ʾanta tāǧirun? Are you a merchant? ʾ**a**-ʾanta tāǧirun?

Remember: هَلْ becomes هَلِ before **hamzatu l-waṣli** (**waṣlah**). This form is used to avoid three consecutive consonants, e.g.

هَلِ ٱلْوَلَدُ فِي ٱلْمَدْرَسَةِ؟

hal**i** l-waladu fī l-madrasati? Is the boy at school?

24.2 Interrogative pronouns ضَمَائِرُ ٱلاِسْتِفْهَامِ

In addition to the above interrogative particles, there are several interrogative pronouns, the following being the most common:

(a) مَنْ؟ man, 'who? whom? whose?'

This pronoun may occur as subject, object or in any other nominal function in the sentence. In a nominal sentence مَنْ is placed before or after a pronominal subject. In an ʾiḍāfah construction it is, of course, placed after the first noun, e.g.

هُوَ مَنْ؟ huwa man?	مَنْ هُوَ؟ man huwa?	بَيْتُ مَنْ؟ baytu man?
Who is he?	Who is he?	whose house?

Note: Like the following interrogative pronoun مَا؟ mā 'what?', مَنْ is indeclinable, i.e. it has the same form for all genders, numbers and cases.

(b) When the prefixed preposition لِـ... precedes مَنْ, it has the meaning 'whose?', 'for/to whom?', e.g.

لِمَنِ ٱلْبَيْتُ li-mani l-baytu? Whose house is it? (lit. For whom is the house?)

Note: In the above sentence مَنْ gets the **kasrah** and becomes مَنِ, because it is followed by **hamzatu al-waṣli** (**waṣlah**).

(c) مَا؟ mā 'what?' may be preceded by the preposition لِـ and is then written as لِمَ؟ (لِـ..+...مَا), meaning 'why? for what?'.

(d) The above-mentioned pronoun has a longer synonym مَاذَا؟ māḏā 'what?'. It can also be preceded by the bound preposition لِـ..., giving: لِمَاذَا؟ (لِـ..+...مَاذَا), which means 'why? for what?'.

(e) أَيٌّ ʾayyun, masc., أَيَّةٌ ayyatun, fem., are adjectival interrogative pronouns meaning 'which...?, what...?'. They precede the noun they qualify, which is always in the indefinite singular genitive, e.g.

Masc: أَيُّ مُعَلِّمٍ؟ ʾayyu muʿallimin, which/what teacher?

Fem: أَيَّةُ مُعَلِّمَةٍ؟ ayyatu muʿallimatin, which/what teacher?

Note: أَيٌّ and أَيَّةٌ can also be used as (adjectival) indefinite pronouns in the meaning 'any', e.g.

مِنْ أَيِّ مَكَانٍ min ʾayyi makānin, from **any** place

فِي / عَلَى أَيَّةِ حَالٍ fī / ʿalā ʾayyati ḥālin, in **any** case

(f) كَمْ 'how many?, how much?'

كَمْ takes the following noun, which it qualifies, in the indefinite accusative singular, e.g.

كَمْ سَيَّارَةً عِنْدَكَ؟ kam sayyāratan ʿinda-ka? How many cars do you have?

كَمْ كِتَابًا قَرَأْتَ؟ kam kitāban qaraʾta? How many books did you read?

24.3 *Vocative particles* حُرُوفُ ٱلنِّدَاءِ

(a) The vocative particles are يَا yā for both genders, أَيُّهَا ʾayyuhā for the masculine, and أَيَّتُهَا ʾayyatuhā for the feminine. They can be rendered as 'O(h)...!', 'Hey (you)...!', 'I say...!' Often they need not be translated at all, the final exclamation mark after the noun or sentence being sufficient.

(b) يَا 'O...!' is followed by a noun (in any number) or proper name in the nominative case without the definite article or nunation, e.g.

يَا رَبُّ **yā** rabbu! **O** Lord!

يَا أَللّٰهُ **yā** ʾallāhu! **O** God!

يَا رَجُلُ **yā** rağulu! **O** man!

يَا رِجَالُ **yā** riğālu! **O** men!

يَا سَيِّدَةُ **yā** sayyidatu! **O** lady!

يَا سَيِّدَاتُ **yā** sayyidātu! **O** ladies!

يَا يُوسُفُ **yā** yūsufu! **O** Joseph!

يَا سُعَادُ **yā** suʿādu! **O** Suaad!

(c) In complex titles and compound names, the noun after the vocative particle is followed by another noun and this last noun must be in the genitive case. However, the noun after the vocative particle must be in the accusative instead of the nominative case, e.g.

سَعَادَةُ ٱلسَّفِيرِ saʿādatu s-safīri, His Excellency the Ambassador

becomes in the vocative:

يَا سَعَادَةَ ٱلسَّفِيرِ yā saʿādata s-safīri! (O) Your Excellency Mr. Ambassador!

عَبْدُ ٱللّٰهِ ʿabdu-llāhi, Abdullah (a name), slave/worshipper of God

becomes in the vocative:

يَا عَبْدَ ٱللّٰهِ **yā** ʿabda-llāhi! (O) Abdullah!

(d) The vocative particles أَيُّهَا ʾayyuhā, masc., and أَيَّتُهَا ʾayyatuhā, fem., are also used for all numbers. As usual, the following noun is in the nominative case, but it takes the definite article أَلْـ ... . These longer vocative particles are often used at the beginning of a speech or by the announcers of radio and television programmes. They may be preceded by the shorter vocative particle يَا, e.g.

أَيُّهَا / يَا أَيُّهَا ٱلْمُعَلِّمُ

ʾayyuhā OR **yā ʾayyuhā** l-muʿallimu! O teacher!

أَيُّهَا / يَا أَيُّهَا ٱلْمُعَلِّمُونَ

ʾayyuhā OR **yā ʾayyuhā** l-muʿallimūna! O teachers!

أَيَّتُهَا / يَا أَيَّتُهَا ٱلْمُعَلِّمَةُ

ʾayyatuhā OR **yā ʾayyatuhā** l-muʿallimatu! O teacher! (fem.)

أَيَّتُهَا / يَا أَيَّتُهَا ٱلْمُعَلِّمَاتُ

ʾayyatuhā OR **yā ʾayyatuhā** l-muʿallimātu! O teachers! (fem.)

أَيُّهَا ٱلسَّيِّدَاتُ وَٱلسَّادَةُ

ʾayyuhā s-sayyidātu wa-s-sādatu! Ladies and gentlemen!

Note: In the last mentioned phrase the masculine vocative particle أَيُّهَا is used, because in phrases with mixed gender, the masculine determines agreement.

24.4 *Negation with* غَيْرُ *ġayru*

(a) The noun غَيْرٌ ġayrun, 'other (than)', can be used before an indefinite adjective or noun in the genitive case to express negation or contradiction. It is thus translated as 'not..., non-, un-, in-, dis-', etc. Note that غَيْرُ then appears without article or nunation (i.e. in the form called construct state), e.g.

غَيْرُ قَادِرٍ ġayru qādirin, **un**able (other than able)

غَيْرُ مُهِمٍّ ġayru muhimmin, **un**important

غَيْرُ مُمْكِنٍ ġayru mumkinin, **im**possible

غَيْرُ عَرَبِيٍّ ġayru ʿarabiyyin, **not** an Arab, **non**-Arab

غَيْرُ مَوْجُودٍ ġayru mawǧūdin, **un**available, **not** present, **ab**sent, **non**-existent

(b) When غَيْرُ ġayru has a suffixed pronoun, it means 'other(s) (than)', e.g.

أَلْمُدِيرُ وَغَيْرُهُ	ʾal-mudīru wa-ġayru-hu the director (masc.) and others (than him)
أَلْمُدِيرَةُ وَغَيْرُهَا	ʾal-mudīratu wa-ġayru-hā the director (fem.) and others (than her)

(c) When غَيْرُ is preceded by a negative predicate or negative particle like لاَ, it is translated as 'only', e.g.

لاَ يَعْلَمُ هٰذَا غَيْرُ ٱلْمُدِيرِ **lā** yaʿlamu hāḏā **ġayru** l-mudīri.
Only the director knows this. (lit. No one knows this **other** than the director).

أَلْفُ دِينَارٍ لاَ غَيْرُ ʾalfu dīnārin lā ġayru, **only** a thousand dinars

(d) When غَيْرُ precedes أَنَّ, as in غَيْرَ أَنَّ, it means 'except that, nevertheless, however, but'.

24.5 *Negation with عَدَمُ ʿadamu*

The noun عَدَم ʿadamun 'non-being, lack, absence' or the adjective عَدِيمُ ʿadīmun 'lacking', can be followed by a noun in the genitive, meaning 'non-, in-, un-, dis-, -less, lack of...', etc. The noun عَدَمُ appears without article or nunation, e.g.

عَدَمُ ٱلْوُجُودِ ʿadamu l-wuǧūdi, **non-**existence

عَدَمُ ٱلْخِبْرَةِ ʿadamu l-ḫibrati, **in**experience, **lack** of experience, ignorance

عَدَمُ ٱلْأَخْلَاقِ ʿadamu l-ʾaḫlāqi, **im**morality, **lack** of manners, **bad** manners

عَدِيمُ ٱلْحَيَاةِ ʿadīmu l-ḥayāti, life**less**, dead

عَدَمُ حُضُورِ أَحَدٍ ʿadamu ḥuḍūri ʾaḥadin, **without** anyone being present

24.6 *Negation of nominal sentences with* لَا *lā*

The negative particles لَا 'no, not' and وَلَا 'neither, nor' have already been discussed as negative particles for the verb of the imperfect tense. The negative particle لَا can also be placed before a noun that functions as the subject of a nominal sentence. The noun must be in the accusative case without article or nunation. The negative particle functions then as an existential or locative negative copula: 'There is no X' OR 'X is not (there)', e.g.

لَا أَحَدَ فِي ٱلْبَيْتِ lā ʾaḥada fī l-bayti. (There is) no one (nobody) at home.

لَا سَلَامَ وَلَا حَرْبَ lā salāma wa-lā ḥarba. (There is) neither peace nor war.

24.7 كُلٌّ *kullun*

The noun كُلٌّ kullun means basically 'totality, entirety, whole, all, everything'. It is fully declined (inflected for all cases) and can be employed as a universal indefinite pronoun modifying a following noun, or standing alone. The following are its uses:

(a) When كُلّ without an article or nunation is followed by an indefinite noun in the genitive singular, it means 'each, every', e.g.

كُلُّ طَالِبٍ kullu ṭālibin, each student

كُلُّ يَوْمٍ kullu yawmin, every day

(b) When كُلّ without an article or nunation is followed by a definite noun in the genitive singular, it means 'all, the whole', e.g.

كُلَّ ٱلْيَوْمِ kullu l-yawmi, the whole day, all day long

كُلَّ ٱلْوَقْتِ kullu l-waqti, the whole time, all the time

(c) When كُلّ without an article or nunation is followed by a definite noun in the genitive plural, it means 'all', e.g.

كُلَّ ٱلْحَيَوَانَاتِ kullu l-ḥayawānāti, all the animals

كُلَّ الْبُيُوتِ kullu l-buyūti, all the houses

(d) When كُلّ is indefinite (having nunation) and followed by the preposition مِنْ min 'from', i.e. كُلٌّ مِنْ, it has the meaning 'each (one) of (a group)', e.g.

كُلٌّ مِنَ ٱلطُّلَّابِ kullun mina ṭ-ṭullābi, each (one) of the students

(e) When the definite article أَلْـ.. is attached to كُلّ as أَلْكُلّ, it becomes an independent (pro)noun which means 'everyone, everything, the whole thing', e.g.

شَاهَدْتُ ٱلْكُلَّ šāhadtu l-kulla. I saw everything (the whole thing).

24.8 كِلاَ *kilā (masc.)*, كِلْتَا *kiltā (fem.)*

These two words mean 'both, both of them, each one of the two'. They are used in the **ʾiḍāfah** construction preceding a dual noun which is definite and in the genitive case, or preceding a dual suffix pronoun. The following predicative adjective or verb is, nevertheless, in the singular. Both كِلاَ kilā and كِلْتَا kiltā are indeclinable before nouns, but declinable before a suffix pronoun.

Note: كِلاَ kilā is likely to be from كِلاَنِ kilā-ni, and كِلْتَا kiltā from كِلْتَانِ kiltā-ni (see chapter 13 on the elision of the final ـنِ... of the dual).

Masculine	***Feminine***
كِلاَ ٱلْخَبِيرَيْنِ أَجْنَبِيٌّ	كِلْتَا ٱلْخَبِيرَتَيْنِ أَجْنَبِيَّةٌ
kilā l-ḫabīrayni ʾağnabiyyun. (sing.)	kiltā l-ḫabīrtayni ʾağnabiyyatun. (sing.)

Both experts are foreigners.
(lit. Each one of the two experts is a foreigner.)

Interroga-
tive
particles
and
pronouns,
vocative
particles

رَأَيْتُ كِلاَ ٱلْخَبِيرَيْنِ

raʾaytu kilā l-ḫabīrayni.

I saw both experts.

(lit. I saw each one of the two experts.)

رَأَيْتُ كِلْتَا ٱلْخَبِيرَتَيْنِ

raʾaytu kiltā l-ḫabīrtayni.

مَرَرْتُ بِكِلاَ ٱلْخَبِيرَيْنِ

marartu bi-kilā l-ḫabīrayni.

I passed by both the experts.

(lit. I passed by each one of the two experts.)

مَرَرْتُ بِكِلْتَا ٱلْخَبِيرَتَيْنِ

marartu bi-kiltā l-ḫabīratayni.

(a) The accusative and genitive forms are كِلَيْ kilay (masc.) and كِلْتَيْ kiltay (fem.). These forms are used only when they are followed by a suffix pronoun, e.g.

Masculine

كِلاَهُمَا أَجْنَبِيٌّ

kilā-humā ʾaǧnabiyyun. (nom.)

Both of them are foreigners.

Feminine

كِلْتَاهُمَا أَجْنَبِيَّةٌ

kiltā-humā ʾaǧnabiyyatun. (nom.)

رَأَيْتُ كِلَيْهِمَا

raʾaytu **kilay**-himā. (acc.)

I saw both of them.

رَأَيْتُ كِلْتَيْهِمَا

raʾaytu **kiltay**-himā. (acc.)

مَعَ كِلَيْهِمَا

maʿa **kilay**-himā (gen.)

with both of them

(lit. with each one of the two)

مَعَ كِلْتَيْهِمَا

maʿa **kiltay**-himā (gen.)

(b) The verb with كِلاَ kilā is in the singular

كِلاَ ٱلْخَبِيرَيْنِ سَافَرَ جَوًّا

kilā l-ḫabīrayni sāfara (sing.) ǧawwan.

Both experts flew by air.

(lit. Each one of the two experts flew by air.)

كِلْتَا ٱلْخَبِيرَتَيْنِ سَافَرَتْ جَوًّا

kiltā l-ḫabīratayni sāfarat (sing.) ǧawwan.

كِلَاهُمَا يَعْرِفُ	كِلْتَاهُمَا تَعْرِفُ
kilā-humā yaʿrifu. (sing.)	kiltā-humā taʿrifu. (sing.)
Both of them know.	
(lit. Each one of the two knows.)	

24.9 هُنَاكَ *hunāka*

The adverb هُنَاكَ means 'there', but, like its English equivalent, it is also used in nominal sentences in the meaning 'there is, there are', e.g.

هُنَاكَ ٱحْتِمَالٌ بِٱلنَّجَاحِ

hunāka-ḥtimālun bi-n-naǧāḥi. There is a possibility of success.

هَلْ هُنَاكَ كَثِيرٌ مِنَ ٱلنَّاسِ؟

hal hunāka kaṯīrun mina n-nāsi? Are there many people?

24.10 فُلَانٌ *fulānun (masc.)*, فُلَانَةٌ *fulānatun (fem.)*

The above nouns are frequently used in Arabic in the sense 'so and so, such and such, somebody, a certain (person or thing)'. The idea is to substitute an unknown or unnamed, person, thing or source for a more general or less precise expression, e.g.

Masculine	***Feminine***
قَالَ فُلَانٌ	جَاءَتْ فُلَانَةٌ
qāla fulānun.	ǧāʾat fulānatun.
Somebody (OR: a certain person) said.	Somebody (a certain person) came.
So and so said.	So and so came.
فِي ٱلْيَوْمِ ٱلْفُلَانِيِّ	فِي ٱللَّيْلَةِ ٱلْفُلَانِيَّةِ
fī l-yawmi l-fulāniyyi	fī l-laylati l-fulāniyyati
on such and such a day	on such and such a night
on a certain day	on a certain night
on that and that day	on that and that night

Exercises

Practise your reading:

[1]يَا [2]حَضْرَةَ ٱلْأُسْتَاذِ! فِي [3]أَيَّةِ جَامِعَةٍ أَنْتَ؟ [4]وَأَيَّةَ [5]مَادَّةٍ [6]تُدَرِّسُ؟ وَفِي أَيَّةِ مَدِينَةٍ [7]تَسْكُنُ، [8]وَأَيْنَ تَسْكُنُ [9]عَائِلَتُكَ؟

(1) [1]O [2]respected (O [2]sir) Professor! [3]Which university are you at? [4]What [5]subject do you [6]teach? In which city [7]do you live? [8]Where does [9]your family live?

[1]هَلْ [2]تُسَافِرُ [3]كُلَّ [4]يَوْمٍ [5]بَيْنَ ٱلْمَدِينَتَيْنِ؟ [6]أُسَافِرُ [7]فَقَطْ [8]خَمْسَ [9]مَرَّاتٍ (s. مَرَّةٌ) فِي [10]ٱلْأُسْبُوعِ [11]وَكَيْفَ تُسَافِرُ؟ [12]أَرْكَبُ [13]ٱلْقِطَارَ فِي [14]بَعْضِ [15]ٱلْأَحْيَانِ [16]وَأَحْيَانًا [17]آخُذُ سَيَّارَتِي. [18]كَمِ [19]ٱلْمَسَافَةُ [20]وَكَمْ [21]ثَمَنُ [22]بِطَاقَةِ [23]ٱلْقِطَارِ؟

(2) [1]Do you [2]travel [3]every [4]day [5]between the two cities? [6]I travel [7]only [8]five [9]times a [10]week. [11]And how do you travel? [14,15]Sometimes [12]I take (lit. I ride) [13]the train [16]and sometimes [17]I take my car. [18]What is [19]the distance [20]and how much does [23]the train [22]ticket [21]cost?

[1]هَرَبَ [2]ٱلسَّارِقُ مِنَ [3]ٱلسِّجْنِ وَلَا [4]أَحَدٌ [5]غَيْرَ [6]زَوْجَتِهِ [7]يَعْرِفُ [8]أَيْنَ يَخْتَبِئُ.

(3) [2]The thief [1]escaped from [3]prison and no [4]one [5]except [6]his wife [7]knows [8]where he is hiding.

[1]عَلَى [2]أَيَّةِ [3]طَائِرَةٍ [4]سَيُسَافِرُ [5]ٱلْوَفْدُ؟ [6]وَهَلْ [7]أَعْلَمْتُمْ [8]ٱلطَّاقَمَ أَنَّ [9]بَيْنَ [10]ٱلْمُسَافِرِينَ [11]شَخْصًا [12]مُعَاقًا [13]وَهُوَ [14]غَيْرُ [15]قَادِرٍ عَلَى [16]صُعُودِ [17]ٱلسُّلَّمِ [18]دُونَ [19]مُسَاعَدَةٍ؟

(4) [1]On [2]which [3]aeroplane will [5]the delegation [4]travel ? [6]Did [7]you (pl.) inform [8]the crew that [9]among [10]the travellers there is [12]a disabled [11]person [13]who is [14,15]unable [16]to go up [17]the steps (ladder) [18]without [19]help?

[1]تَحَدَّثَ مُدِيرُ ٱلشَّرِكَةِ إِلَى [2]كُلِّ ٱلْمُوَظَّفِينَ عَنْ [3]عَدَمِ [4]قُبُولِ ٱلشَّرِكَةِ
[5]رَفْعَ [6]أُجُورِهِمْ (.s أَجْرٌ).

(5) The company director [1]talked to [2]all the employees about the company's [3,4]refusal ([3]not [4]accepting) [5]to raise [6]their wages.

[1]قَفَزَ [2]ٱلْقِطُّ عَلَى [3]ٱلْمَائِدَةِ / ٱلطَّاوِلَةِ [4]وَأَكَلَ كُلَّ [5]ٱللَّحْمِ [6]وَبَعْضَ [7]قِطَعِ
(.s قِطْعَةٌ) [8]ٱلْجُبْنَةِ [9]فَلَحِقَهُ [10]ٱلْكَلْبُ [11]غَيْرَ أَنَّهُ [12]لَمْ [13]يَتَمَكَّنْ مِنْ أَنْ
[14]يُمْسِكَ بِهِ.

(6) [2]The cat [1]jumped onto [3]the table [4]and ate all [5]the meat [6]and some [7]pieces of [8]cheese. [10]The dog [9]chased it, [11]although [13]he was [12]unable to [14]catch it.

[1]هُنَاكَ [2]ٱحْتِمَالٌ [3]بِعَدَمِ [4]مُشَارَكَةِ [5]ٱلسَّفِيرِ فِي [6]مُؤْتَمَرِ [7]حِلْفِ [8]شَمَالِ
[9]ٱلْأَطْلَسِي، [10]نَظَرًا [11]لِعَدَمِ [12]خِبْرَتِهِ [13]ٱلْعَسْكَرِيَّةِ.
[14]غَيْرَ أَنَّ [15]ٱلْحُكُومَةَ [16]تُفَكِّرُ [17]بِإِرْسَالِ [18]وَفْدٍ [19]بَعْضُ [20]أَعْضَائِهِ
(.s عُضْوٌ) مِنَ [21]ٱلْعَسْكَرِيِّينَ [22]وَٱلْبَعْضُ [23]ٱلآخَرُ مِنْ [24]غَيْرِ ٱلْعَسْكَرِيِّينَ.

(7) [1]There is [2]a possibility that [5]the ambassador [3]will not [4]take part in the NATO ([8]North [9]Atlantic [7]Treaty Organization) [6]conference [10]because of (regarding) his [11]lack of [13]military [12]experience.
[14]However, [15]the government is [16]thinking [17]of sending [18]a delegation, of which [19]some (of its) [20]members are [21]military personnel [22]and the [23]others [24]non-military.

[1]يَا [2]حَضْرَةَ [3]ٱلْوَزِيرِ! [4]هَلْ [5]تَعْرِفُ [6]كَمْ [7]حَادِثَ [8]سَيْرٍ [9]وَقَعَ عَلَى
[10]ٱلطُّرُقِ (.s طَرِيقٌ) فِي [11]ٱلصَّيْفِ [12]ٱلْمَاضِي؟ [13]وَهَلْ هُنَاكَ
[14]تَدَابِيرُ (.s تَدْبِيرٌ) [15]لِحَلِّ هٰذِهِ [16]ٱلْمُشْكِلَةِ؟

(8) [1]O! (Your [2]Excellency), [3]Minister, [4]do you [5]know [6]how many [8]road traffic [7]accidents [9]happened on [10]the roads [12]last [11]summer? [13]Have any [14]measures been taken [15]to solve this [16]problem?

مَعَ [1]كَمْ [2]صَدِيقٍ ذَهَبْتَ وَكَمْ [3]فِنْجَانَ قَهْوَةٍ شَرِبْتَ؟ [4]مَنْ [5]دَفَعَ؟ [6]وَكَمْ؟

(9) [1]How many [2]friends did you go with and how many [3]cups of coffee did you drink? [4]Who [5]paid and [6]how much?

[1]هَلْ [2]تَسْكُنِينَ [3]وَحْدَكِ فِي هٰذِهِ [4]ٱلشَّقَّةِ [5]ٱلْوَاسِعَةِ؟

(10) [1]Are you (f.) [2]living [3]alone in this [5]large [4]apartment?

Translate into Arabic:

(1) Is the disabled person living alone in this large apartment?

(2) How many cups of coffee? Who paid? How much?

(3) Do you know how many traffic accidents happened in the city last summer?

(4) The director of the prison talked to all the employees about raising their wages.

(5) Where are you living (m.s.)? And are you living with your family?

(6) I travel every week between the city and the university. Sometimes I travel by train and sometimes I take my car.

(7) The cat ate the piece of cheese and some of the meat from the table and then it escaped.

(8) The thief jumped from the apartment to the road and escaped. The dog chased him but could not catch him.

(9) There is a possibility that the minister will take part in the NATO (North Atlantic Treaty Organization) conference.

(10) Do you know how many ministers there are in the government?

(11) Is the government intending to send military personnel to the conference?

(12) The thief escaped by car and no one knows where he is hiding.

(13) O! Your excellency, Ambassador! On which aeroplane will the delegation travel? And did you inform the crew that among the passengers there is a person who is unable to climb the steps to (go up the ladder of) the aeroplane without help?

Chapter 25

Adjectival patterns, relative adjectives (nisbah), comparatives and superlatives, diminutives

25.1 Adjectives أَلصِّفَةُ

There are several adjectival forms in Arabic and the following patterns for forming adjectives from verbs are the most common:

pattern	singular	plural
(a) فَاعِلٌ fāʿilun	عَالِمٌ ʿālimun, learned	عُلَمَاءُ ʿulamāʾu
(b) فَعِيلٌ faʿīlun	كَبِيرٌ kabīrun, big	كِبَارٌ kibārun
(c) فَعَلٌ faʿalun	حَسَنٌ ḥasanun, beautiful, fine	حِسَانٌ ḥisānun
(d) فَعْلَانُ faʿlānu	كَسْلَانُ kaslānu, lazy	كَسَالَى kasālā
(e) فَعُولٌ faʿūlun	حَسُودٌ ḥasūdun, envious	حُسُدٌ ḥusudun
(f) مَفْعُولٌ mafʿūlun	مَجْرُوحٌ mağrūḥun, injured	مَجَارِيحُ mağārīḥu

25.2 Adjectives denoting colours or (bodily) defects are formed according to the patterns أَفْعَلُ ʾafʿalu, masc. sing., and فَعْلَاءُ faʿlāʾu, fem. sing. Both of these patterns are diptotes and the corresponding broken plural pattern (for both genders) is: فُعْلٌ fuʿlun (triptote), e.g.

Masc. sing. (diptote)	***Fem. sing. (diptote)***	***Masc. and fem. plur.***
أَسْوَدُ ʾaswadu, black	سَوْدَاءُ sawdāʾu	سُودٌ sūdun
أَحْمَرُ ʾaḥmaru, red	حَمْرَاءُ ḥamrāʾu	حُمْرٌ ḥumrun

أَزْرَقُ ʾazraqu, blue	زَرْقَاءُ zarqāʾu	زُرْقٌ zurqun
أَخْضَرُ ʾaḫḍaru, green	خَضْرَاءُ ḫaḍrāʾu	خُضْرٌ ḫuḍrun
أَصْفَرُ ʾaṣfaru, yellow	صَفْرَاءُ ṣafrāʾu	صُفْرٌ ṣufrun
أَبْيَضُ ʾabyaḍu, white	بَيْضَاءُ bayḍāʾu	بِيضٌ bīḍun
أَطْرَشُ ʾaṭrašu, deaf	طَرْشَاءُ ṭaršāʾu	طُرْشٌ ṭuršun
أَعْرَجُ ʾaʿrağu, lame	عَرْجَاءُ ʿarğāʾu	عُرْجٌ ʿurğun
أَعْمَى ʾaʿmā, blind	عَمْيَاءُ ʿamyāʾu	عُمْيَانُ ʿumyānu

25.3 *Relative adjectives,* نِسْبَةٌ *nisbah*

The relative adjective is called in Arabic نِسْبَةٌ nisbah, which means 'relation'. Relative adjectives are derived from nouns by adding the so-called **nisbah** suffix, which is ...ـِيٌّ /..iyyun/ in the masculine and ...ـِيَّةٌ /...iyyatun/ in the feminine. The **nisbah** suffix thus makes a noun into an adjective (which often can be employed as a noun as well), expressing the meaning: 'related or pertaining to (the entity or thing denoted by the noun)'. It may be compared to English derivational morphemes like '-ish, -(i)an, -ese, -i, -ic(al), -al, -ly,' e.g. 'Engl**ish**, Americ**an**, Egypt**ian**, Leban**ese**, Iraq**i**, Arab**ic**, form**al**, period**ical**, month**ly**', etc. The relative adjective often refers to geographical, national or ethnic names or names of occupations (as in English, these kinds of derived adjectives may often be reused as independent nouns), e.g.

Relative adjective (nisbah)

Noun	***Masc.***	***Fem.***
لُبْنَانُ lubnānu, Lebanon	لُبْنَانِيٌّ lubnāniyyun, Lebanese	لُبْنَانِيَّةٌ lubnāniyyatun
عَرَبٌ ʿarabun, Arabs	عَرَبِيٌّ ʿarabiyyun, Arab, Arabic	عَرَبِيَّةٌ ʿarabiyyatun
كُحُولٌ kuḥūlun, alcohol	كُحُولِيٌّ kuḥūliyyun, alcoholic	كُحُولِيَّةٌ kuḥūliyyatun

شَهْرٌ	شَهْرِيٌّ	شَهْرِيَّةٌ
šahrun, month	šahriyyun, monthly	šahriyyatun

25.4 The feminine ending **tāʾ marbūṭah** ـة... is elided with the noun when adding the **nisbah** suffix ـِيٌّ... /...iyyun/ or ـِيَّةٌ... /...iyyatun/, e.g.

Relative adjective (nisbah)

Noun	***Masc.***	***Fem.***
ثَقَافَةٌ	ثَقَافِيٌّ	ثَقَافِيَّةٌ
t̲aqāfatun, culture	t̲aqāfiyyun, cultural	t̲aqāfiyyatun
مِهْنَةٌ	مِهَنِيٌّ	مِهَنِيَّةٌ
mihnatun, profession	mihaniyyun, professional	mihaniyyatun

25.5 If the noun ends in the long vowel ـَا... /...ā/, this is elided with the noun when adding the **nisbah** suffix ـِيٌّ... /...iyyun/ or ـِيَّةٌ... /...iyyatun/, e.g.

Relative adjective (nisbah)

Noun	***Masc.***	***Fem.***
أَمْرِيكَا	أَمْرِيكِيٌّ	أَمْرِيكِيَّةٌ
ʾamrīkā, America	ʾamrīkiyyun, American	ʾamrīkiyyatun
فِنْلَنْدَا	فِنْلَنْدِيٌّ	فِنْلَنْدِيَّةٌ
finlandā, Finland	finlandiyyun, Finnish	finlandiyyatun

25.6 The feminine singular form of the relative adjective (**nisbah**) is often used as a noun with abstract meaning, e.g.

Relative adjective (nisbah)

Noun	***Masc.***	***Fem.*** *(abstract noun)*
إِنْسَانٌ	إِنْسَانِيٌّ	إِنْسَانِيَّةٌ
ʾinsānun, man	ʾinsāniyyun, human	ʾinsāniyyatun, humanity, humaneness

إِشْتِرَاكٌ ʾištirākun, co-operation	إِشْتِرَاكِيٌّ ʾištirākiyyun, socialist	إِشْتِرَاكِيَّةٌ ʾištirākiyyatun, socialism
قَوْمٌ qawmun, people, nation	قَوْمِيٌّ qawmiyyun, nationalist	قَوْمِيَّةٌ qawmiyyatun, nationalism

Note: Plural **nisbah** forms often have a collective meaning, e.g. أَللِّسَانِيَّاتُ ʾal-lisāniyyātu 'linguistics', from the noun لِسَانٌ 'tongue, language'.

25.7 In pausal form (at the end of a sentence) the above **nisbah** suffix ...ـِيٌّ /...iyyun/ is pronounced as a long vowel: ...ـِي /...ī/, which does not take nunation. In pausa the final **tāʾ marbūṭah** (ة ـة...) /...t/ is pronounced as /...h/, e.g.

لُبْنَانِيٌّ lubnān**ī**, Lebanese (m.)	لُبْنَانِيَّةٌ lubnāniyya**h**, (f.)
قَوْمِيٌّ qawm**ī**, nationalist	قَوْمِيَّةٌ qawmiyya**h**, nationalism

25.8 The above relative adjective (**nisbah**) usually takes the sound plural, e.g.

Masculine plural	***Feminine plural***
أَلْمُعَلِّمُونَ ٱلْمِصْرِيُّونَ ʾal-muʿallimūna l-miṣriyyūna the Egyptian teachers	أَلْمُعَلِّمَاتُ ٱلْمِصْرِيَّاتُ ʾal-muʿallimātu l-miṣriyyātu the Egyptian teachers

Note: The adjective عَرَبِيٌّ ʿarabiyyun 'Arab, Arabic' does *not* form the sound plural, but uses the collective noun عَرَبٌ ʿarabun 'the Arabs, Arab' as the plural form, e.g.

Masculine plural

أَلْمُعَلِّمُونَ ٱلْعَرَبُ ʾal-muʿallimūna l-ʿarabu the Arab teachers	(not: أَلْمُعَلِّمُونَ ٱلْعَرَبِيُّونَ ʾal-muʿallimūna l-ʿarabiyyūna)

25.9 Comparative and superlative أَفْعَلُ ٱلتَّفْضِيلِ

As mentioned in 25.2, the pattern أَفْعَلُ ʾafʿalu (diptote) is characteristic of adjectives denoting colours and bodily defects. But the same pattern is also used to form the comparative and superlative degree of adjectives, and participles of the first form in all genders and numbers. This form of the adjective is also called the elative, e.g.

Adjective	**Comparative/superlative** (according to the pattern أَفْعَلُ ʾafʿalu)
صَغِيرٌ ṣaġīrun, small	أَصْغَرُ ʾaṣġaru, smaller, smallest
جَمِيلٌ ǧamīlun, beautiful	أَجْمَلُ ʾaǧmalu, more beautiful, most beautiful
وَاسِعٌ wāsiʿun, wide	أَوْسَعُ ʾawsaʿu, wider, widest
حَسَنٌ ḥasanun, good	أَحْسَنُ ʾaḥsanu, better, best
مَشْهُورٌ mašhūrun, famous	أَشْهَرُ ʾašharu, more famous, most famous

25.10 Comparative sentences

The preposition مِنْ min 'from' is used like the English preposition 'than' as a link between the two parts (item compared and object of comparison) of the comparative sentence. The comparative sentence thus has the following structure: item compared + comparative (elative) form of the adjective + مِنْ min + object of comparison, e.g.

أَلْوَلَدُ أَصْغَرُ مِنْ أُخْتِهِ ʾal-waladu ʾaṣġaru min ʾuḫti-hi.
The boy is younger than his sister.

أَلْأُمُّ أَجْمَلُ مِنْ بِنْتِهَا ʾal-ʾummu ʾaǧmalu min binti-hā.
The mother is more beautiful than her daughter.

أَلْبَنَاتُ أَحْسَنُ مِنَ ٱلْأَوْلَادِ ʾal-banātu ʾaḥsanu mina l-ʾawlādi.
(The) girls are better than (the) boys.

25.11 The pattern أَفْعَلُ ʾafʿalu cannot be used to form the comparative of the participles of the derived forms, nor of adjectives with more than three consonants. In these cases, the comparative is formed by using أَكْثَرُ ʾakṯaru ‘more’, أَشَدُّ ʾašaddu ‘stronger, more’ or أَقَلُّ ʾaqallu ‘less’, followed by an accusative abstract noun related to the participle or adjective, e.g.

أَكْثَرُ إِخْلاَصًا ʾakṯaru ʾiḫlāṣan, more faithful (lit. more as regards faithfulness)

أَشَدُّ سَوَادًا ʾašaddu sawādan, blacker (lit. stronger as regards blackness)

أَقَلُّ جَمَالاً ʾaqallu ǧamālan, less beautiful (lit. less as regards beauty)

25.12 The two nouns/adjectives خَيْرٌ ḫayrun ‘good(ness)’ and شَرٌّ šarrun ‘evil’ are used as comparatives and superlatives with the meanings ‘better’ and ‘worst’, respectively, e.g.

أَلصَّلَاةُ خَيْرٌ مِنَ ٱلنَّوْمِ
ʾaṣ-ṣalātu ḫayrun mina n-nawmi.
Prayer is **better** than sleep. (The Quran)

هُوَ مِنْ شَرِّ ٱلْأَوْلَادِ
huwa min šarri l-ʾawlādi.
He is one of the **worst** boys.

25.13 *Superlative sentences*

The superlative is formed by making the comparative pattern أَفْعَلُ ʾafʿalu definite, either with the definite article أَلْـ... or with the **ʾiḍāfah** construction. This form is used for both genders and all numbers, e.g.

ʾIḍāfah construction

هُوَ أَطْوَلُ وَلَدٍ
huwa ʾaṭwalu waladin. He is the tallest boy.

هِيَ أَقْصَرُ بِنْتٍ
hiya ʾaqṣaru bintin. She is the shortest girl.

هُمْ أَطْوَلُ ٱلْأَوْلَادِ
hum ʾaṭwalu l-ʾawlādi. They are the tallest boys.

Definite article

هُوَ ٱلْأَطْوَلُ
huwa l-ʾaṭwalu. He is the tallest.

هِيَ ٱلْأَقْصَرُ
hiya l-ʾaqṣaru. She is the shortest.

هُمُ ٱلْأَطْوَلُ
humu l-ʾaṭwalu. They are the tallest.

هُنَّ أَطْوَلُ ٱلْبَنَات	هُنَّ ٱلْأَطْوَلُ
hunna ᵓaṭwalu l-ᵓbanāti. They are the tallest girls.	hunna l-ᵓaṭwalu. They are the tallest.

25.14 Some adjectives having the superlative pattern أَلْأَفْعَلُ ᵓal-ᵓafᶜalu can also have a feminine superlative form أَلْفُعْلَى ᵓal-fuᶜlā, e.g.

Superlative masculine	*Superlative feminine*
أَلْأَكْبَرُ	أَلدُّوَلُ ٱلْكُبْرَى
ᵓal-ᵓakbaru, the biggest, the greatest	ᵓad-duwalu l-kubrā, the great(est) countries
أَلْأَعْظَمُ	بَرِيطَانْيَا ٱلْعُظْمَى
ᵓal-ᵓaᶜḏamu, the greatest	barīṭānyā l-ᶜuḏmā, Great Britain
أَلْوَلَدُ ٱلْأَصْغَرُ	أَلْبِنْتُ ٱلصُّغْرَى
ᵓal-waladu l-ᵓaṣġaru, the smallest boy	ᵓal-bintu ṣ-ṣuġrā, the smallest girl

25.15 The dual and plural of the above superlatives take their number and gender according to the preceding noun, e.g.

Singular	*Dual*	*Plural*
أَلْوَلَدُ ٱلْأَصْغَرُ	أَلْوَلَدَانِ ٱلْأَصْغَرَانِ	أَلْأَوْلَادُ ٱلْأَصْغَرُونَ
ᵓal-waladu l-ᵓaṣġaru	ᵓal-waladāni l-ᵓaṣġarāni	ᵓal-ᵓawlādu l-ᵓaṣġarūna
the smallest boy	the two smallest boys	the smallest boys
أَلْبِنْتُ ٱلصُّغْرَى	أَلْبِنْتَانِ ٱلصُّغْرَيَانِ	أَلْبَنَاتُ ٱلصُّغْرَيَاتُ
ᵓal-bintu ṣ-ṣuġrā	ᵓal-bintāni ṣ-ṣuġrayāni	ᵓal-banātu ṣ-ṣuġrayātu
the smallest girl	the two smallest girls	the smallest girls
أَلدَّوْلَةُ ٱلْعُظْمَى	أَلدَّوْلَتَانِ ٱلْعُظْمَيَانِ	أَلدُّوَلُ ٱلْعُظْمَى
ᵓad-dawlatu l-ᶜuḏmā	ᵓad-dawlatāni l-ᶜuḏmayāni	ᵓad-duwalu l-ᶜuḏmā
the greatest country	the two greatest countries	the greatest countries
أَلْحَرْبُ ٱلْكُبْرَى	أَلْحَرْبَانِ ٱلْكُبْرَيَانِ	أَلْحُرُوبُ ٱلْكُبْرَى
ᵓal-ḥarbu l-kubrā	ᵓal-ḥarbāni l-kubrayāni	ᵓal-ḥurūbu l-kubrā
the greatest war	the two greatest wars	the greatest wars

Remember: Both أَلدُّوَلُ and أَلْحُرُوبُ refer to non-human entities and therefore take the superlative adjective in the feminine singular (see chapter 14).

25.16 *The diminutive*

The diminutive إِسْمُ ٱلتَّصْغِيرِ can be formed according to the pattern فُعَيْلٌ fuʿaylun. It is restricted to certain nouns and adjectives and indicates diminishing or reducing. As in many other languages, the diminutive may, in addition, often be employed with a positive or negative feeling or tone. With a positive feeling it expresses flirtation, coquetry or endearment. With a negative feeling it conveys contempt or downgrading.

The diminutive form can be learned with practice or from the dictionary. Some diminutives are common as proper names, e.g.

	Diminutive فُعَيْلٌ ***fuʿaylun***
حَسَنٌ Ḥasanun, good (a name)	حُسَيْنٌ Ḥus**ay**nun, little good one (a name)
عَبْدٌ ʿAbdun, slave (a name)	عُبَيْدٌ ʿUb**ay**dun, little slave (a name)
كَلْبٌ kalbun, dog	كُلَيْبٌ kul**ay**bun, small dog
بَحْرٌ baḥrun, sea	بُحَيْرَةٌ buḥ**ay**ratun, lake (fem. ending)

25.17 Some prepositions can sometimes be used in diminutive form, e.g.

قَبْلَ ٱلظُّهْرِ qabla ḍ-ḍuhri before noon	قُبَيْلَ ٱلظُّهْرِ qub**ay**la ḍ-ḍuhri a little before noon

In words where the second consonant is followed by a long vowel, the vowel changes to ..ـَيِّـ.. /...ayyi.../ in the diminutive, e.g.

كِتَابٌ kitābun, book	كُتَيِّبٌ kut**ayyi**bun, little book, booklet, pamphlet
صَغِيرٌ ṣaġīrun, small	صُغَيِّرٌ ṣuġ**ayyi**run, very small

Exercises

Practise your reading:

[1]إِبْنَةُ [2]عَمِّي وَٱبْنَةُ [3]خَالِي [4]هُمَا [5]أَكْثَرُ طَالِبَاتِ ٱلْجَامِعَةِ [6]جَمَالاً [7]وَأَقَلُّهُنَّ [8]ٱجْتِهَاداً.

(1) [1,2]My cousin ([1]the daughter of [2]my paternal uncle) and my other cousin (the daughter of [3]my maternal uncle) [4]are [5]the most [6]beautiful (prettiest) female students in the university [7]and the least [8]diligent.

[1]تَزَوَّجَتِ ٱلْبِنْتُ [2]ٱلْكُبْرَى مِنْ بَنَاتِ [3]جَارِنَا [4]لٰكِنْ [5]مَعَ [6]ٱلْأَسَفِ [7]وُلِدَ [8]لَهَا طِفْلٌ [9]أَعْمَى.

(2) [2]The oldest daughter of [3]our neighbour [1]got married, [4]but [5,6]unfortunately [7]she gave birth to ([7]born [8]to her) [9]a blind baby.

طُلاَّبُ (s. طَالِب) [1]ٱللُّغَةِ ٱلْعَرَبِيَّةِ [2]مِنْ [3]أَحْسَنِ ٱلطُّلاَّبِ فِي ٱلْجَامِعَةِ، [4]وَأَكْثَرِهِمْ [5]خِبْرَةً.

(3) The students of Arabic ([1]language) are [2]among the [3]best [4]and most [5]experienced students in the university.

[1]ٱلْعَجُوزُ [2]ٱلْأَشَدُّ / [2]ٱلْأَكْثَرُ [3]طَرَشاً [4]هُوَ [5]أَجْنَبِيٌّ.

(4) [3,2]The deafest (lit. [2]the most [3]deaf) [1]old man [4]is [5]a foreigner.

أَلْقُرْآنُ [1]ٱلْكَرِيمُ [2]أَحْسَنُ كِتَابٍ وَكَثِيرٌ مِنَ ٱلْمُسْلِمِينَ [3]يَعْرِفُونَهُ [4]غَيْباً.

(5) [1]The Holy Quran is [2]the best book, and many Muslims [3]know it [4]by heart.

[1]سَتَنْشُرُ [2]دُورُ (s. دَار) [3]ٱلنَّشْرِ [4]أَعْمَالَ (s. عَمَل) [5]ٱلشَّاعِرِ ٱللُّبْنَانِيِّ [6]ٱلْمَشْهُورِ [7]وَسَتُتَرْجِمُ [8]أَغْلَبَ كُتُبِهِ إِلَى [9]لُغَاتٍ [10]أَجْنَبِيَّةٍ [11]عَدِيدَةٍ.

(6) [3]The publishing [2]houses [1]will publish [4]the works of [6]the famous Lebanese [5]poet [7]and will translate [8]most of his books into [11]many [10]foreign [9]languages.

[1]نَشَرَتْ [2]جَرِيدَةٌ [3]مَسَائِيَّةٌ [4]مَقَالاً مَعَ [5]صُوَرٍ (.s صُورَةٌ) [6]لِلْغَارَةِ [7]ٱلْجَوِّيَّةِ
[8]أَمْسِ [9]ٱلَّتِي [10]قَتَلَتْ [11]وَجَرَحَتْ [12]عَدَدًا كَبِيرًا مِنَ [13]ٱلْمَدَنِيِّينَ،
[14]وَتُعْتَبَرُ [15]أَعْنَفَ [16]غَارَةٍ [17]خِلَالَ [18]عَامٍ.

(7) [3]An evening [2]newspaper [1]published [4]an article with [5]pictures of [7]the air [6]raid [8]yesterday, [9]which [10]killed and [11]injured (wounded) a large [12]number of [13]civilians, and [14]is regarded as [15]the worst ([15]most violent) [16]raid [17]for [18]a year.

[1]نَقَلَ [2]ٱلْهِلَالُ [3]ٱلْأَحْمَرُ [4]وَٱلصَّلِيبُ ٱلْأَحْمَرُ [5]ٱلْمَجَارِيحَ / ٱلْجَرْحَى
(.s مَجْرُوحٌ) [6]وَٱلْمَنْكُوبِينَ إِلَى ٱلْمُسْتَشْفَى [7]ٱلْقَرِيبِ.

(8) The [3]Red [2]Crescent and the Red [4]Cross [1]transported [5]the injured (wounded) [6]and the victims to the [7]nearby hospital.

[1]سَمَكُ (.s سَمَكَةٌ) [2]ٱلْبُحَيْرَاتِ فِي [3]شَمَالِيِّ أُورُوبَّا [4]أَطْيَبُ مِنْ سَمَكِ [5]ٱلْبَحْرِ.

(9) [1]The fish from (lit. of) the [2]lakes in [3]northern Europe is [4]tastier (better) than [5]sea fish.

[1]ذَهَبَ [2]وَفْدٌ [3]صِحَافِيٌّ [4]أَجْنَبِيٌّ إِلَى رَئِيسِ [5]دَوْلَةٍ إِفْرِيقِيَّةٍ [6]وَسَأَلَهُ عَنِ
[7]ٱلْأَزْمَةِ [8]ٱلِاقْتِصَادِيَّةِ [9]وَٱلسِّيَاسِيَّةِ فِي إِفْرِيقْيَا [10]ٱلسَّوْدَاءِ.

(10) [4]A foreign [3]press [2]delegation [1]went to the president of an African [5]state [6]and asked him about [8]the economic [9]and political [7]crisis in [10]Black Africa.

[1]ذَكَرَتِ [2]ٱلْإِذَاعَةُ ٱلْيَوْمَ أَنَّ [3]ٱجْتِمَاعَ [4]رُؤَسَاءِ (.s رَئِيسٌ) [5]ٱلدُّوَلِ (.s دَوْلَةٌ)
[6]ٱلْكُبْرَى [7]ٱلْمَعْقُودَ فِي بَارِيسَ كَانَ مِنْ [8]أَطْوَلِ [9]ٱلِاجْتِمَاعَاتِ [10]وَأَكْثَرِهَا
[11]تَعْقِيدًا.

(11) [2]The radio (broadcast) [1]mentioned today that [3]the meeting of [4]the presidents of [6]the great [5]countries which was [7]held in Paris was one of the [8]longest [10]and most [11]complicated [9]meetings.

[1]أَوْرَاقُ (.s وَرَقَةٌ) [2]ٱلشَّجَرِ (.s شَجَرَةٌ) [3]صَفْرَاءُ فِي [4]ٱلْخَرِيفِ
[5]وَخَضْرَاءُ فِي [6]ٱلرَّبِيعِ.

(12) [1]The leaves of the [2]trees are [3]yellow in [4]autumn [5]and green in [6]spring.

[1]أَلْجُنْدِيُّ [2]ٱلْمَجْرُوحُ فِي [3]حَادِثِ [4]أَمْسِ هُوَ [5]تَعْبَانُ ٱلْيَوْمَ [6]وَنَائِمٌ فِي [7]سَرِيرِهِ.

(13) [1]The soldier [2]injured (wounded) in [4]yesterday's [3]incident is [5]tired today [6]and asleep in (his) [7]bed.

[1]مَنْ [2]هُوَ [3]أَكْبَرُ [4]مِنْكَ [5]بِيَوْمٍ هُوَ [6]أَخْبَرُ مِنْكَ [7]بِسَنَةٍ.

(14) He [1]who [2]is [5]a day [3]older [4]than you is [7]a year [6]more experienced than you. (Proverb)

[1]نَشَرَ ثَلَاثَةُ [2]ضُبَّاطٍ (ضَابِطٌ) [3]مُتَقَاعِدُونَ مِنَ [4]ٱلْجَيْشِ ٱلْأَلْمَانِيِّ [5]مُذَكِّرَاتِهِمْ [6]عَنِ [7]ٱلْحَرْبِ [8]ٱلْعَالَمِيَّةِ [9]ٱلْأُولَى.

(15) Three [3]retired [2]officers from the German [4]army [1]published [5]their memoirs [6]of [9]the First [8]World [7]War.

Translate into Arabic:

(1) My paternal cousin married (prep.: مِنْ) a foreign journalist.

(2) Sea fish is tastier than fish from (of) the lakes.

(3) The leaves of the trees are green in spring and yellow in autumn.

(4) Many students know the works of the famous Lebanese poet by heart.

(5) The president of an African state published his memoirs yesterday and the publishing house will translate them into many foreign languages.

(6) The newspaper published an article about (عَنْ) yesterday's incident.

(7) The German officer is one of the most experienced officers in warfare.

(8) The army officer injured in the air raid yesterday is tired today and asleep in (his) bed.

(9) The publishing house will translate and publish the book about the First World War.

(10) The radio mentioned today that the Red Crescent and the Red Cross transported the injured (victims) to the nearby hospital.

(11) My eldest maternal cousin got married but, unfortunately, she gave birth to a blind baby.

(12) The radio mentioned the air raid yesterday which killed (in it) one soldier and injured (wounded) a large number of civilians.

(13) A journalist published an article in an evening newspaper about the economic and political crisis in north Africa.

Chapter 26

ʾInna إِنَّ and its sisters, kāna كَانَ and its sisters

26.1 إِنَّ ʾinna is an assertive particle, which can be translated as 'indeed, certainly', or by the biblical word 'verily, (and) lo'. Mostly it is not, however, translated at all, as it is basically used as a matter of style or a simple syntactic device. It is placed at the beginning of a nominal sentence before the (logical) subject, which takes the accusative case or is expressed by a suffixed pronoun.

There are a number of other particles (and conjunctions) that are construed in the same way as إِنَّ ʾinna. The Arab grammarians refer to them as إِنَّ وَأَخَوَاتُهَا 'ʾinna and its sisters'. After all these particles the (logical) subject is in the accusative case. The nominal predicate remains in the nominative case.

The following are the particles إِنَّ ʾinna and its sisters:

إِنَّ ʾinna, indeed, that	أَنَّ ʾanna, that	كَأَنَّ kaʾanna, as if
لٰكِنَّ lākinna, but	لَيْتَ layta, would, if only, wish	لَعَلَّ laʿalla, perhaps

Note: لٰكِنَّ lākinna is very often prefixed with وَ wa. لَيْتَ layta is very often prefixed with يَا yā.

Examples:

إِنَّ ٱلْمُدِيرَ مَشْغُولٌ
ʾinna l-mudīra mašġūlun.
The director is (indeed) busy.

إِنَّهُ مَشْغُولٌ
ʾinna-hu mašġūlun.
He is (indeed) busy.

26.2 After إِنَّ ʾinna, the nominal predicate can be emphasized by prefixing ... لَـ /la.../. (This is optional.) This particle has no influence on the case of the predicate, e.g.

إِنَّ ٱللَّهَ لَعَظِيمٌ	إِنَّ ٱلْبَاخِرَةَ لَكَبِيرَةٌ
ʾinna llāha **la-**ʿaḏīmun.	**ʾinna** l-bāḫirata **la**-kabīratun.
God is **indeed** great. (The Quran)	The ship is **indeed** big.

26.3 إِنَّ ʾinna and its sisters can also occur before the (logical) subject in a verbal sentence, but then the subject must be in the accusative case, e.g.

إِنَّ ٱلسَّفَرَ أَتْعَبَهُ	لَعَلَّ ٱلصِّيَاحَ أَزْعَجَهَا
ʾinna s-safara ʾatʿaba-hu.	laʿalla ṣ-ṣiyāḥa ʾazʿağa-hā.
The travel made him tired.	Perhaps the shouting bothered her.

26.4 إِنَّ ʾinna, takes the form أَنَّ ʾanna 'that' (complementizer), when it introduces indirect speech or a complement clause after the main clause, e.g.

سَمِعَ أَنَّ ٱلرَّئِيسَ مَرِيضٌ	سَمِعَ أَنَّهُ مَرِيضٌ
samiʿa **ʾa**nna r- raʾīsa marīḍun.	samiʿa **ʾa**nna-hu marīḍun.
He heard ***that*** the president is ill.	He heard ***that*** he is ill.

Note: إِنَّ ʾinna, nevertheless, remains unchanged after the verb قَالَ qāla 'to say', e.g.

قَالَ إِنَّ ٱلْمُوَظَّفَ مَرِيضٌ	قَالَ إِنَّهُ مَرِيضٌ
qāla ʾ**inna** l-muwaḏḏafa marīḍun.	**qāla** ʾ**inna**-hu marīḍun.
He said **that** the employee is ill.	He said **that** he is ill.

26.5 أَنَّ ʾanna can be combined with prepositions and then gets various other meanings:

لِأَنَّ li-ʾanna, because   مَعَ أَنَّ maʿa ʾanna, although, in spite of the fact that

سَأَذْهَبُ إِلَى ٱلشَّاطِئِ لِأَنَّ ٱلطَّقْسَ حَارٌّ

sa-ʾaḏhabu ʾilā š-šāṭiʾi **li-ʾanna** ṭ-ṭaqsa ḥārrun.

I will go to the beach, ***because*** the weather is hot.

سَبَحَ مَعَ أَنَّ ٱلْمَاءَ وَسِخٌ

sabaḥa **maʿa ʾanna** l-māʾa wasiḫun.

He swam, ***although*** the water was dirty.

26.6 When إِنَّ ʾinna or أَنَّ ʾanna takes a suffixed pronoun in the first person singular or plural, there are two alternative forms:

Singular	***Plural***
إِنِّي ʾinn-ī OR إِنَّنِي ʾinna-nī	إِنَّا ʾinn-ā OR إِنَّنَا ʾinna-nā

26.7 When إِنَّ ʾinna or أَنَّ ʾanna is not immediately followed by the subject in a verbal sentence, it takes the suffixed pronoun of the third person masculine singular: ـهُ... /...hu/, i.e. إِنَّهُ ʾinna-**hu**, أَنَّهُ ʾanna-**hu**, for all genders and numbers, e.g.

سَمِعْتُ أَنَّ ٱلْبِنْتَ تُسَافِرُ غَدًا OR سَمِعْتُ أَنَّهُ تُسَافِرُ ٱلْبِنْتُ غَدًا

samiʿtu **ʾanna** l-binta tusāfiru ġadan. samiʿtu **ʾanna-hu** tusāfiru **l-bintu** ġadan.

I heard **that** the **girl** will travel tomorrow.

26.8 *Kāna* كَانَ *and its sisters*

There are dozens of verbs which behave like the verb كَانَ kāna 'to be' (lit. 'he was'), referred to as كَانَ وَأَخَوَاتُهَا 'kāna and its sisters'. All these verbs take the predicative complement in the accusative case. Hence they are construed in the opposite way to إِنَّ 'ʾinna and its sisters'.

26.9 The following are the most common verbs known as sisters of كَانَ kāna:

أَصْبَحَ ʾaṣbaḥa, to become (to be/become in the morning) (form IV)

أَضْحَى ʾaḍḥā, to become

ظَلَّ ḏalla, to continue, to keep on, to remain

بَاتَ bāta, to become, to spend the night

أَمْسَى ʾamsā, to become (to be/become in the evening)

مَا زَالَ mā-zāla, to keep on, not to cease, (to be/do) still

مَا بَرِحَ mā-bariḥa, to continue, (to be/do) still

مَا دَامَ mā-dāma, to continue, as long as (... lasts)

صَارَ ṣāra, to become

لَيْسَ laysa, is not (see chapters 32 and 37)

Examples:

كَانَ ٱلْكِتَابُ جَدِيداً	أَصْبَحَ ٱلطَّالِبُ مُهَنْدِساً
kāna l-kitābu ǧadīdan.	ʾaṣbaḥa ṭ-ṭālibu muhandisan.
The book was new.	The student became an engineer.
لَيسَ ٱلْرَّجُلُ قَصِيراً	ظَلُّوا جَالِسِينَ
laysa r-raǧulu qaṣīran.	ḏallū ǧālisīna.
The man is not short.	They remained sitting.

26.10 The above-mentioned verb زَالَ zāla (imperfect: يَزَالُ yazālu) means literally 'to cease, to disappear, to go away'. It is frequently used as an auxiliary when preceded by the negative particle مَا /mā/ in the perfect tense, or لَا /lā/ in the imperfect tense. It is then translated as 'is still (doing)' or 'continues to (do)', with the main action expressed by a participle. Both tenses have the same meaning (see also chapter 36), e.g.

مَا ***mā + perfect***		لَا ***lā + imperfect***
مَا زَالَ جَالِساً	OR	لَا يَزَالُ جَالِساً
mā zāla ǧālisan.		**lā yazālu** ǧālisan.

He is **still** sitting. (He has not ceased to sit.)

Exercises

Practise your reading:

[1]بَدَّلْتُ [2]قَمِيصِي لِأَنَّهُ [3]وَسِخٌ.

(1) [1]I changed [2]my shirt because it was [3]dirty.

أَلدَّرْسُ [1]صَعْبٌ جِدًّا لٰكِنَّ [2]تَمْرِينَهُ [3]سَهْلٌ.

(2) The lesson is very [1]difficult but [2]its exercise (drill) is [3]easy.

إِنَّ [1]ٱلْحُكُومَةَ [2]لَيْسَتْ [3]قَادِرَةً عَلَى [4]تَنْفِيذِ [5]ٱلْمَشْرُوعِ [6]ٱلسِّيَاحِيِّ لِأَنَّهُ [7]يُكَلِّفُ كَثِيرًا.

(3) [1]The government is [2]not [3]able [4]to implement [6]the tourism [5]project because [7]it costs (too) much.

كَانَ ٱلْوَزِيرُ [1]مُسَافِرًا إِلَى دِمَشْقَ وَلٰكِنَّهُ [2]أَجَّلَ سَفَرَهُ لِأَنَّ [3]ٱلْجَوَّ [4]صَارَ [5]سَيِّئًا.

(4) The minister was going [1]to travel to Damascus but [2]he postponed his trip because [3]the weather [4]became [5]bad.

عِنْدَمَا [1]رَجَعْنَا مِنَ ٱلسُّوقِ كَانَ ٱلْأَطْفَالُ (s. طِفْلٌ) [2]مَا زَالُوا [3]نَائِمِينَ.

(5) When [1]we returned from the market the children were [2]still [3]asleep.

[1]سَمِعْتُ أَنَّ ٱلْمُدِيرَةَ [2]مَرِضَتْ [3]بِمَرَضٍ [4]خَطِيرٍ وَأَنَّهَا [5]تَرَكَتْ [6]عَمَلَهَا.

(6) [1]I heard that the director became [4]seriously [2]ill (lit. [2]became ill with [4]serious [3]illness) and [5]left [6]her job.

إِنَّ [1]ٱلْمَسَافَةَ إِلَى [2]ٱلْحُدُودِ (s. حَدٌّ) [3]قَصِيرَةٌ لٰكِنَّ [4]ٱلطَّرِيقَ [5]ضَيِّقٌ [6]وَلَيْسَ فِي [7]ٱلسَّيَّارَةِ [8]إِنَارَةٌ.

(7) [1]The distance to [2]the border(s) is [3]short, but [4]the road is [5]narrow and [7]the car [6]doesn't have [8]lights.

[1]قَرَأْتُ فِي [2]جَرِيدَةِ ٱلْيَوْمِ أَنَّهُ سَوْفَ [3]تَجْتَمِعُ [4]ٱلدَّوْلَتَانِ [5]ٱلْمُتَنَازِعَتَانِ [6]لِحَلِّ [7]مَشَاكِلِهِمَا (s. مُشْكِلٌ / مُشْكِلَةٌ) [8]دُونَ [9]تَدَخُّلٍ [10]خَارِجِيٍّ.

(8) [1]I read in today's [2]newspaper that the two [5]disputing [4]countries will [3]meet [6]to settle (solve) [7]their problems [8]without [10]outside [9]intervention.

قَالَ [1]ٱلْعَامِلُ إِنَّ [2]مَكَانَ ٱلْعَمَلِ لَيْسَ [3]بَعِيدًا عَنْ بَيْتِهِ [4]وَلِهٰذَا [5]يَذْهَبُ كُلَّ يَوْمٍ [6]مَشْيًا عَلَى [7]ٱلْأَقْدَامِ (s. قَدَمٌ).

(9) [1]The worker said that the work[2]place is not [3]far from his house [4]and therefore [5,6]he goes [7]on foot everyday.

كَانَ [1]وَرَقُ (s. وَرَقَةٌ) [2]ٱلشَّجَرِ [3]أَخْضَرَ فِي [4]ٱلرَّبِيعِ [5]فَصَارَ
[6]أَصْفَرَ فِي [7]ٱلْخَرِيفِ.

(10) [1]The leaves of [2]the trees were [3]green in [4]spring [5]and they became [6]yellow in [7]autumn.

كَانَ [1]ٱلطَّقْسُ [2]مُشْمِسًا [3]وَحَارًّا فِي [4]ٱلصَّبَاحِ [5]فَأَصْبَحَ [6]مُمْطِرًا
[7]وَبَارِدًا [8]بَعْدَ [9]ٱلظُّهْرِ.

(11) [1]The weather had been (was) [2]sunny [3]and hot in [4]the morning [5]and it became [6]rainy [7]and cold in the [8,9]afternoon.

إِنَّ [1]ٱلْمَقَالَ عَنِ [2]ٱلْحَرْبِ [3]ٱلْعَالَمِيَّةِ [4]ٱلْأُولَى لَيْسَ [5]طَوِيلاً.

(12) [1]The article about the [4]First [3]World [2]War is not [5]long.

كَانَ [1]ٱلتَّعْلِيمُ [2]ٱلْاِبْتِدَائِيُّ [3]غَيْرَ [4]شَامِلٍ فِي [5]ٱلْعَالَمِ ٱلْعَرَبِيِّ
[6]وَٱلْآنَ [7]أَصْبَحَ [8]إِجْبَارِيًّا.

(13) [2]Elementary [1]education in the Arab [5]world was [3]not [4]comprehensive, [6]and now [7]it has become [8]compulsory.

[1]لِحَدِّ [2]ٱلْآنَ [3]مَا زَالَ [4]مَرْكَزُ [5]ٱلْبَرِيدِ فِي [6]نَفْسِ [7]ٱلشَّارِعِ وَلٰكِنَّهُ سَوْفَ
[8]يُنْقَلُ إِلَى [9]شَارِعٍ [10]آخَرَ.

(14) So far ([1]until [2]now) [4]the [5]Post [4]Office has been ([3]remains) on [6]the same [7]street, but it will be [8]moved to [10]another [9]street.

[1]قَالَتْ [2]سَيِّدَةٌ إِنَّ [3]حُقُوقَ (s. حَقٌّ) [4]ٱلْمَرْأَةِ [5]مَا زَالَتْ [6]غَيْرَ [7]مُسَاوِيَةٍ
[8]لِحُقُوقِ ٱلرَّجُلِ.

(15) [2]A lady [1]said that [3]the rights [4]of women are [5]still [6,7]unequal [8]to men's rights.

[1]لَيْتَكَ / يَا لَيْتَكَ [2]تُحِبُّنِي [3]كَمَا [4]أُحِبُّكَ.

(16) [1]I wish [2]you (m.) loved me [3]as [4]I love you (m.).

[1]يَا لَيْتَ عِنْدِي [2]مَالاً أَكْثَرَ [3]لَكَانَ [4]كُلُّ [5]شَيْءٍ [6]أَسْهَلَ.

(17) [1]I wish I had more [2]money, [3]then [4,5]everything [3]would be [6]easier.

قَالَ إِنَّهُ سَوْفَ [1]يَحْضُرُ [2]عَدَدٌ كَبِيرٌ مِنَ [3]ٱلنَّاسِ [4]لِسَمَاعِ [5]مُحَاضَرَةِ [6]عَمِيدِ [7]كُلِّيَّةِ [8]ٱلْحُقُوقِ.

(18) He said that a great [2]number [3]of people [1]would attend [4]to listen to [5]the lecture by [6]the Dean of [7]the Faculty of [8]Law.

[1]لَعَلَّ [2]ٱلْعَلَاقَاتِ [3]تَتَحَسَّنُ بَيْنَ [4]ٱلشُّعُوبِ (s. شَعْبٌ) عِنْدَمَا [5]يَتَعَلَّمُونَ [6]لُغَاتِ [7]بَعْضِهِمْ.

(19) [2]Relations between [4]people [1]might [3]improve when [5]they learn [7]each other's [6]languages.

كَانَ أَبِي [1]قَلِقًا [2]عَلَيَّ عِنْدَمَا [3]تَكَلَّمَ مَعِي ٱلْيَوْمَ [4]هَاتِفِيًّا [5]مَعَ [6]أَنَّهُ كَانَ عِنْدِي [7]مَسَاءَ [8]ٱلْبَارِحَةِ / [8]أَمْسِ.

(20) My father was [1]worried [2]about me when [3]he talked to me today [4]on the phone, [5,6]although he was with me [8]yesterday [7]evening.

[1]أَخْبَرُونِي أَنَّ [2]أَخَاكَ [3]بَاعَ [4]دَرَّاجَتَهُ [5]بِسِعْرٍ [6]رَخِيصٍ [7]مَعَ [8]أَنَّهَا كَانَتْ فِي [9]حَالَةٍ جَيِّدَةٍ.

(21) [1]They told me that [2]your brother [3]sold [4]his bicycle at [6]a cheap [5]price [7,8]although it was in good [9]condition.

Translate into Arabic:

(1) Yesterday evening my brother talked to me on the phone and he was worried about his child because he had become seriously ill.

(2) They told me that the minister postponed the tourism project, because it costs too much.

(3) My father said that the market is not far away and therefore he goes there everyday on foot.

(4) The article by the Dean of the Faculty of Law about the relations between people in the Arab world was good.

(5) The minister said that elementary education is not comprehensive, and not compulsory.

(6) After the weather was cold and rainy yesterday it became sunny and hot today.

(7) I heard that the worker sold his car at a cheap price, although it was in good condition.

(8) When the children returned from the border(s), it (the weather) was rainy and cold.

(9) When I returned from the market, I changed my shirt, because it was dirty.

(10) The post office will move to another street not far from my workplace.

(11) A lady said that women's rights are not equal to men's rights.

(12) The leaves of the trees were green in spring, but they became yellow in autumn.

Chapter 27

Relative pronouns and relative clauses

27.1 Relative pronoun

The basic form (masc. sing.) of the relative pronoun أَلْاسْمُ ٱلْمَوْصُولُ is أَلَّذِي ʾallaḏī '(the one) who, which, that'. It is declined as follows:

	masculine		
	singular	dual	plural
Nom.	أَلَّذِي ʾallaḏī	أَللَّذَانِ ʾallaḏāni	أَلَّذِينَ ʾallaḏīna
Acc. and gen.	أَلَّذِي ʾallaḏī	أَللَّذَيْنِ ʾallaḏayni	أَلَّذِينَ ʾallaḏīna
	feminine		
Nom.	أَلَّتِي ʾallatī	أَللَّتَانِ ʾallatāni	أَللَّوَاتِي or أَللاَّتِي ʾallawātī ʾallātī (less used)
Acc. and gen.	أَلَّتِي ʾallatī	أَللَّتَيْنِ ʾallatayni	أَللَّوَاتِي or أَللاَّتِي ʾallawātī ʾallātī (less used)

Note a: For historical reasons, the masculine and feminine singular and masculine plural forms are written with one **lām** ...ل and the other forms with two. There is no difference in pronunciation.

Note b: The plural forms are used only for human beings.

27.2 *Definite relative clause*

The role of the relative pronoun is to link the relative clause with a definite antecedent أَلسَّابِقُ ʾas-sābiqu, which precedes it. The relative pronoun agrees with the antecedent in gender and number, e.g.

Relative clause (أَلصِّلَةُ)	***Relative pronoun*** (أَلْمَوْصُولُ)	***Antecedent*** (أَلسَّابِقُ)
سَبَحَ	أَلَّذِي	أَلْوَلَدُ

ʾal-waladu **llaḏī** sabaḥa, the boy **who** swam

مِنْ لُبْنَانَ	أَلَّتِي	أَلْكَاتِبَةُ

ʾal-kātibatu **llatī** min lubnāna, the writer (f.) **who** is from Lebanon

27.3 The relative pronoun is used only when the antecedent أَلسَّابِقُ is definite. If the antecedent is indefinite, the relative clause is introduced after the antecedent without a relative pronoun, e.g.

Definite antecedent	***Indefinite antecedent***
شَاهَدْتُ ٱلرَّجُلَ ٱلَّذِي يَتَكَلَّمُ ٱلْعَرَبِيَّةَ	شَاهَدْتُ رَجُلاً يَتَكَلَّمُ ٱلْعَرَبِيَّةَ
šāhadtu r-rağula **llaḏī** yatakallamu l-ʿarabiyyata.	šāhadtu rağulan yatakallamu l-ʿarabiyyata.
I saw the man **who** speaks Arabic.	I saw a man (who) speaks Arabic.
سَاعَدْتُ ٱلرَّجُلَ ٱلَّذِي كُسِرَتْ رِجْلُهُ	سَاعَدْتُ رَجُلاً كُسِرَتْ رِجْلُهُ
sāʿadtu r-rağula **llaḏī** kusirat riğlu-**hu**.	sāʿadtu rağulan kusirat riğlu-**hu**.
I helped the man **whose** leg was broken.	I helped a man (whose) leg was broken.
(lit. I helped the man, **who his** leg was broken.)	(lit. I helped a man, **his** leg was broken.)

Observe that, in contrast to Arabic, when you leave out the relative pronoun in English, the antecedent becomes object in the relative clause, e.g. 'This is **the man** you saw.'

27.4 An active participle may replace both the relative pronoun and the following perfect or imperfect verb, e.g.

With the perfect verb	*With the active participle*
أَلَّتِي كَتَبَتِ ٱلرِّسَالَةَ	كَاتِبَةُ ٱلرِّسَالَةِ
ʾ**allatī katabati** r-risālata	**kātibatu** r-risālati
the one **who** (f.) **wrote** the letter	the **writer** (f.) of the letter OR the one (who) wrote the letter
أَلَّذِي طَلَّقَ	أَلْمُطَلِّقُ
ʾ**allaḏī ṭallaqa**	ʾ**al-muṭalliqu**
the one **who** (m.) **divorced**	**the divorced one** (m.) OR the one (who) got divorced
With the imperfect verb	*With the active participle*
أَلرَّجُلُ ٱلَّذِي يَسْكُنُ هُنَاكَ	أَلرَّجُلُ ٱلسَّاكِنُ هُنَاكَ
ʾar-rağulu **llaḏī yaskunu** hunāka	ʾar-rağulu **s-sākinu** hunāka
the man **who lives** there	the man (who is) **living** there
أَلَّذِي يَنْتَظِرُ ٱلطَّبِيبَ	أَلْمُنْتَظِرُ ٱلطَّبِيبَ
ʾ**allaḏī yanṭaḏiru** ṭ-ṭabība	ʾ**al-muntaḏiru** ṭ-ṭabība
the one **who is waiting** for the physician	the one (who is) **waiting** for the physician

27.5 Also a passive participle placed after a noun may have the meaning of a relative clause, e.g.

جُمْلَةٌ مَكْتُوبَةٌ ğumlatun **maktūbatun**
a **written** sentence OR a sentence **which** is written

أَلْجُمْلَةُ ٱلْمَكْتُوبَةُ ʾal-ğumlatu **l-maktūbatu**
the **written** sentence OR the sentence **which** is written

أَلْمَقَالُ ٱلْمَنْشُورُ ʾal-maqālu **l-manšūru**
the **published** article OR the article **which** is published

27.6 *ʾAl-ʿāʾid* أَلْعَائِدُ, 'the returner' *(anaphoric suffix pronoun)*

If the antecedent is referred to in the relative clause as an object, or as having a preposition, or as being a genitive attribute, it is resumed by a coreferential suffix pronoun attached to the verb, preposition, or noun, respectively. This kind of anaphoric (back-referring) suffix pronoun is called أَلْعَائِد ʾal-ʿāʾid 'the returner'. The returner has no equivalent in English, because in English it is possible to use a relative pronoun as object or add a preposition or attribute to it. The following are the most common uses of **ʾal-ʿāʾid**:

(a) **ʾAl-ʿāʾid** attached to a verb

أَلْمَرْأَةُ ٱلَّتِي سَاعَدْتُهَا

ʾal-marʾatu **llatī** sāʿadtu-**hā**

the woman **whom** I helped (**her**)

(b) **ʾAl-ʿāʾid** attached to a preposition

هٰذَا هُوَ ٱلْكِتَابُ ٱلَّذِي سَأَلْتَ عَنْهُ

hāḏā huwa l-kitābu **llaḏī** saʾalta ʿan-**hu**.

This is the book **that** you asked for. (lit. . . . **that** you asked for **it**.)

(c) **ʾAl-ʿāʾid** attached to a noun

هذَا هُوَ ٱلصِّحَافِيُّ ٱلَّذِي قَرَأْتُ مَقَالَتَهُ

hāḏā huwa ṣ-ṣiḥāfiyyu **llaḏī** qaraʾtu maqālata-**hu**.

This is the journalist **whose** article I read. (lit. . . . **who** I read **his** article.)

27.7 *Interrogatives used as relative pronouns*

(a) The interrogative pronouns مَنْ man, 'who?' and مَا mā 'what?' are also used as relative pronouns in the following ways:

مَنْ (the one) who, whom (with reference to human beings)

مَا (the thing) that, which, what (with reference to non-human beings or things)

They differ, however, from the definite relative pronoun أَلَّذِي ʾallaḏī in that they never take an antecedent أَلسَّابِقُ. That is to say, the antecedent is included in their meaning. Moreover, they tend to be used with generalized or indefinite reference, e.g.

وَجَدْتُ مَنْ يَتَكَلَّمُ ٱلْعَرَبِيَّةَ
wağadtu **man** yatakallamu l-ʿarabiyyata.
I found **one who** speaks Arabic.

هٰذَا مَا أَكَلْتُ أَمْسِ
hāḏā **mā** ʾakaltu ʾamsi.
This is **what** I ate yesterday.

(b) When مَا mā 'what?' or مِمَّا mimmā 'of what?, of which?' (which is a combination of مِنْ + مَا) are used as relative pronouns, the addition of **ʾal-ʿāʾid** 'the returner' is optional, e.g.

With ʾal-ʿāʾid		***Without ʾal-ʿāʾid***
هٰذَا مَا سَمِعْنَاهُ	OR	هٰذَا مَا سَمِعْنَا
hāḏā **mā** samiʿnā-**hu**.		hāḏā **mā** samiʿnā.
This is **what** we have heard.		
لَا أَعْبُدُ مَا تَعْبُدُونَهُ	OR	لَا أَعْبُدُ مَا تَعْبُدُونَ
lā ʾaʿbudu **mā** taʿbudūna-**hu**.		lā ʾaʿbudu **mā** taʿbudūna.
I do not worship **what** you worship. (The Quran)		
هٰذَا مِمَّا كَتَبْتُهُ	OR	هٰذَا مِمَّا كَتَبْتُ
hāḏā **mimmā** katabtu-**hu**.		hāḏā **mimmā** katabtu.
This is (part) **of what** I have written.		

Exercises

Practise your reading:

[1]سَكَنْتُ [2]جَزِيرَةً [3]لَهَا [4]تَقَالِيدُ (s. تَقْلِيدٌ) [5]مُخْتَلِفَةٌ عَنْ تَقَالِيدِ [6]بِلَادِي.

(1) [1]I lived on an [2]island (which) [3]had [5]different [4]traditions from the traditions of [6]my country.

[1]ٱلْأَسْمَاءُ (s. إِسْمٌ) ٱلَّتِي [2]ذَكَرْتُهَا هِيَ أَسْمَاءُ ٱلطُّلَّابِ ٱلَّذِينَ [3]نَجَحُوا فِي [4]ٱلْامْتِحَانِ.

(2) [1]The names which [2]I mentioned are the names of the students who [3]passed [4]the exam.

[1]شَاهَدْتُ فِي يَوْمٍ [2]وَاحِدٍ [3]مَنْ [4]أَكْرَهُ وَمَنْ [5]أُحِبُّ.

(3) [1]I saw in [2]one day one [3]whom [4]I hate and one whom [5]I like.

هٰذَا [1]مَا [2]ذَكَرَ / ذَكَرَهُ ٱلْإِمَامُ فِي [3]خُطْبَةِ [4]ٱلْجُمُعَةِ.

(4) This is [1]what the imām [2]mentioned in the [4]Friday [3]speech.

[1]تَأَخَّرَ [2]فَرِيقُ [3]كُرَةِ [4]ٱلْقَدَمِ [5]نِصْفَ [6]سَاعَةٍ [7]مِمَّا (مِنْ + مَا) [8]جَعَلَهُ [9]يَخْسَرُ [10]ٱلْمُبَارَاةَ.

(5) The [4,3]football [2]team was [5]half [6]an hour [1]late, [7]which [8]made it [9]lose [10]the match (competition).

[1]أُشَاهِدُ كُلَّ يَوْمٍ [2]نَفْسَ [3]ٱلسَّائِحِ ٱلَّذِي [4]يَرْكَبُ جَمَلاً.

(6) Every day [1]I see [2]the same [3]tourist who [4]rides a camel.

قَرَأْتُ [1]ٱلْقِصَّةَ ٱلَّتِي كَتَبَهَا ٱلْكَاتِبُ ٱلَّذِي [2]حَصَلَ عَلَى [3]جَائِزَةِ نُوبِل.

(7) I read [1]the story which the writer who [2]won ([2]got) the Nobel [3]Prize wrote.

[1]سَرَقَ [2]ٱللِّصُّ [3]قِصَّةً كَتَبَهَا كَاتِبٌ [4]حَصَلَ عَلَى [5]جَوَائِزَ (s. جَائِزَةٌ) [6]عَالَمِيَّةٍ.

(8) [1]The thief has [2]stolen [3]a story (which was) written by a writer who [4]has received [6]international [5]prizes (awards).

فِي [1]وَسَطِ [2]ٱلصَّحْرَاءِ [3]شَاهَدْتُ [4]جَبَلاً [5]عَالِيًا [6]سَقَطَ [7]عَلَيْهِ [8]ٱلثَّلْجُ.

(9) In [1]the middle of [2]the desert [3]I saw [5]a high [4]mountain on which [8]snow [6]had fallen ([7]on it).

[1]أَيْنَ [2]ٱلْحِذَاءُ ٱلَّذِي [3]وَضَعْتُهُ عَلَى هٰذَا [4]ٱلرَّفِّ؟

(10) [1]Where is [2]the shoe which [3]I put on this [4]shelf?

[1]إِسْتَقْبَلَنِي فِي [2]ٱلْفُنْدُقِ [3]مَنْ [4]يَتَكَلَّمُ [5]ٱللُّغَتَيْنِ ٱلْعَرَبِيَّةَ وَٱلْإِنْجْلِيزِيَّةَ.

(11) [3]Someone who [4]speaks [5]both (lit. [5]the two languages) English and Arabic [1]received me at [2]the hotel.

[1]أَلْجُمْلَةُ [2]ٱلْمَكْتُوبَةُ فِي [3]آخِرِ [4]ٱلصَّفْحَةِ هِيَ [5]صَعْبَةٌ [6]وَمُعَقَّدَةٌ.

(12) The [1]sentence (which is) [2]written at [3]the end of [4]the page is [5]difficult [6]and complicated.

[1]أَنَا [2]ٱلَّذِي [3]عَلَّمَكُمُ ٱلْعَرَبِيَّةَ [4]وَأَنْتُمْ [5]ٱلَّذِينَ [6]تَعَلَّمْتُمُوهَا.

(13) [1]I am the one [2]who (sing.) [3]taught you (pl.) Arabic [4]and you are those [5]who [6]learned it.

هٰذَانِ هُمَا [1] ٱلسَّبَّاحَانِ ٱللَّذَانِ [2] حَصَلاَ عَلَى [3] ٱلْمِدَالِيَّتَيْنِ [4] ٱلذَّهَبِيَّةِ [5] وَٱلْفِضِّيَّةِ.

(14) These are [1]the two swimmers who [2]got [4]the gold [5]and silver [3]medals.

[1] أَلْأَجْنَبِيُّ ٱلَّذِي [2] أَخَذَ [3] دَوَاءً وَشَرِبَ كُحُولاً [4] مَرِضَ [5] وَنُقِلَ إِلَى ٱلْمُسْتَشْفَى.

(15) [1]The foreigner who [2]took [3]medicine and drank alcohol [4]became ill and [5]was taken (transported) to hospital.

[1] أَيْنَ ٱلسَّيِّدَاتُ ٱللَّوَاتِي [2] بَعَثْنَ [3] بِخَبَرِ [4] عَدَمِ [5] مُشَارَكَتِهِنَّ فِي [6] ٱلْمُؤْتَمَرِ؟

(16) [1]Where are the ladies who [2]sent [3]a message concerning their [4]non-[5]participation in [6]the congress?

هٰذِهِ هِيَ [1] ٱلْحَشَرَاتُ [2] ٱلسَّامَّةُ ٱلَّتِي [3] قَدْ [4] تُسَبِّبُ [5] لَسْعَتُهَا [6] خَطَرًا عَلَى [7] حَيَاةِ [8] ٱلْانْسَانِ.

(17) These are [2]the poisonous [1]insects whose [5]sting (bite) [3]may [4]cause [6]danger to [8]human [7]life.

[1] جَلَسْتُ مَعَ كَاتِبَيْنِ [2] سَأَلْتُهُمَا عَنْ [3] مُسْتَقْبَلِ ٱللُّغَةِ ٱلْعَرَبِيَّةِ.

(18) [1]I sat with two writers (whom) [2]I asked (them) about [3]the future of the Arabic language.

Translate into Arabic:

(1) Where is the story which I put on this shelf?

(2) Everyday I see the writer who was awarded (received) the Nobel Prize.

(3) I saw the same tourist who rides the camel every day.

(4) I saw a tourist at the hotel who speaks the two languages Arabic and English.

(5) The swimmer was half an hour late, which resulted in him losing the competition.

(6) The foreigner who taught the students English became ill and was taken to hospital.

(7) The sentence which was mentioned (it) by the imam at the end of the Friday speech was difficult and complicated.

(8) This is the football team which got the gold and silver medals.

(9) Every day I see the foreigner whom I like and the thief whom I hate.

(10) The name which the writer mentioned is a foreign name.

(11) I read a story written by a foreign writer who was awarded international prizes.

(12) I read the names of the students who passed the exam.

(13) The sentence which you wrote at the end of the page is difficult and complicated.

(14) I saw a shoe (m.) on the mountain on which snow had fallen (on it).

Chapter 28

Moods

Subjunctive, jussive (apocopatus) and imperative

28.1 We have already dealt with the verb in the indicative mood of the imperfect tense أَلْمُضَارِعُ ٱلْمَرْفُوعُ. Now we will deal with the two other moods of the imperfect, and with the imperative mood.

(a) Imperfect subjunctive mood: أَلْمُضَارِعُ ٱلْمَنْصُوبُ

(b) Imperfect jussive mood: أَلْمُضَارِعُ ٱلْمَجْزُومُ

(c) Imperative mood: أَلأَمْرُ

(See the conjugations in Appendix 2.)

28.2 *The subjunctive particles and their use*

The imperfect subjunctive mood is mostly used in subordinate clauses after the subjunctive particles listed below to indicate an externally conditioned or internally motivated action. The subjunctive particles are:

أَنْ	لَنْ	إِذَنْ	أَلاَّ	لِـ ...
ʾan	lan	ʾiḏan	ʾallā	li...
that, to	will not, never	then, in that case	that not, not to	in order to, to

لِئَلاَّ	كَيْ (لِكَيْ)	كَيْلاَ (كَيْ لاَ)
liʾallā	kay (li-kay)	kay-lā (OR kay lā)
in order not to	so that, in order to, to	so that not, in order not to

لِأَنَّ	حَتَّى	حَتَّى لاَ
li-ʾanna	ḥattā	ḥattā lā
because	so that, until, in order to	in order not to

Note: Except for لَنْ lan, these particles are, in fact, subordinating conjunctions.

28.3 The subjunctive mood is formed from the imperfect indicative by changing the final vowel /-u/ of the personal endings to /-a/ or, in the case of personal endings having the final syllable ...ـنَ /...na/, by dropping this syllable completely.

Examples of the subjunctive:

قَبِلَ أَنْ يَذْهَبَ غَدًا

qabila ʾ**an yaḏhaba** ġadan.

He agreed (accepted) **that he would go** tomorrow.

(= He agreed **to go** tomorrow.)

أَطْلُبُ مِنْكُمْ أَنْ تَفْعَلُوا ذٰلِكَ

ʾaṭlubu min-kum ʾ**an** tafʿal**ū** ḏālika. (not: تَفْعَلُونَ tafʿalū**na**)

I ask you (masc. plur.) **that you do** that.

(= I ask you **to** do that.)

هَلْ دَخَلْتِ ٱلْمَطْبَخَ لِتَشْرَبِي مَاءً؟

hal daḫalti l-maṭbaḫa **li-**tašrab**ī** māʾan? (not: لِتَشْرَبِينَ **li-**tašrabī**na**)

Did you (fem. sing.) enter the kitchen **to drink** water?

دَرَسُوا جَيِّدًا كَيْ يَنْجَحُوا فِي ٱلْاِمْتِحَانِ

darasū ǧayyidan **kay** yanǧaḥ**ū** fī l-imtiḥāni. (not: يَنْجَحُونَ yanǧaḥū**na**)

They studied well **so that they would pass** (succeed in) the examination.

(= They studied well **in order to** pass the examination.)

لَنْ أَذْهَبَ مَعَهَا

lan ʾaḏhab**a** maʿa-hā.

I **shall never** go with her. (I will not go with her.)

28.4 The subjunctive particles إِذَنْ and إِذًا ʾiḏan 'then, in that case, so' have the same meaning and pronunciation. Both are used in discourse when you draw a conclusion on the basis of a previous statement.

(a) إِذَنْ ʾiḏan is always followed by the subjunctive mood:

أَنَا أَدْرُسُ كَثِيرًا - إِذَنْ سَتَنْجَحَ غَدًا

ʾanā ʾadrusu kaṯīran – **ʾiḏan** sa-tanǧaḥ**a** ġadan.

'I study a lot.' – '**Then** (I suppose) you will succeed tomorrow!'

(b) إِذًا ʾiḏan, is used in nominal sentences:

سَتُمْطِرُ غَدًا – إِذًا أَنْتَ رَاصِدٌ جَوِّيٌّ

satumṭiru ġadan. – **ʾiḏan** ʾanta rāṣidun ǧawwiyyun.

'It will rain tomorrow.' – '**Then (I gather)** you are a meteorologist.'

28.5 The subjunctive particle أَنْ ʾan may sometimes be used after the prepositions **قَبْلَ** qabla 'before' and **بَعْدَ** baʿda 'after', i.e. أَنْ **قَبْلَ** qabla ʾan, أَنْ **بَعْدَ** baʿda ʾan. It is then followed by a verb in the subjunctive mood, e.g.

مَرِضَ قَبْلَ أَنْ يُسَافِرَ

mariḍa **qabla** **ʾan** yusāfir**a**. He became sick **before** he travelled.

سَأَدْرُسُ بَعْدَ أَنْ آكُلَ

sa-ʾadrusu **baʿda** **ʾan** ʾākul**a**. I will read (study) **after** I have eaten.

28.6 The verbal noun (**maṣdar**) can be used as a verb to replace the subjunctive mood in a subordinate clause, in the same way as the English infinitive, e.g.

Imperfect subjunctive		***Verbal noun***
طَلَبْتُ مِنْهَا أَنْ تَذْهَبَ	OR	طَلَبْتُ ذَهَابَهَا
ṭalabtu min-hā ʾan **taḏhaba**.		ṭalabtu **ḏahāba**-hā.
I asked that she **leave**.		I asked her **to leave**.
أَمَرْتُهُ بِأَنْ يَكْتُبَ لَهَا	OR	أَمَرْتُهُ بِالْكِتَابَةِ لَهَا
ʾamartu-hu bi-ʾan **yaktuba** la-hā.		ʾamartu-hu bi-l-**kitābati** la-hā.
I ordered him that he **should write** to her.		I ordered him **to write** to her.

28.7 حَتَّى ḥattā has already been described as a preposition and focus particle. Here it is introduced as a subjunctive particle, taking the subjunctive mood of the verb. The meaning of this expression is 'so that, in order to':

يَدْرُسُ حَتَّى يَنْجَحَ فِي ٱلْامْتِحَانِ

yadrusu **ḥattā** yanǧaḥa fī l-imtiḥāni.

He studies **so that** he should succeed in the examination.

(= He studies **in order to** succeed in the examination.)

حَتَّى ḥattā can be followed by the negative particle لاَ lā, i.e. حَتَّى لاَ, meaning 'so that . . . not, in order not to . . .'. It is quite commonly used nowadays, e.g.

نَظَّفَ ٱلْقَمِيصَ حَتَّى لاَ يَظْهَرَ عَلَيْهِ ٱلْوَسَخُ

naḏḏafa l-qamīṣa **ḥattā lā** yaḏhara ʿalay-hā l-wasaḫu.

He cleaned the shirt **so that** the dirt would **not** show on it.

28.8 *Imperfect jussive (apocopatus)*

The imperfect jussive mood is also called apocopatus ('cut from the end') in Arabic أَلْمُضَارِعُ ٱلْمَجْزُومُ. With some exceptions, it is formed from the subjunctive mood simply by dropping the last short vowel. (See the conjugations in Appendix 2.) The jussive mood is employed after the negative particles

لاَ lā   لَمْ lam   لَمَّا lammā

and after the exhortative particle لِـ... li... .

(a) لاَ lā 'not, no, don't', is the most common negative particle, called أَلنَّاهِيَةُ. Together with a jussive verb of the second person (sing., du., pl.; masc. and fem.), it expresses a prohibition or negative command, e.g.

لاَ تَشْرَبْ خَمْرًا! lā tašrab ḫamran! Don't drink wine ! (masc. sing.)

لاَ تَجْلِسِي هُنَا! lā taǧlisī hunā! (not: ... لاَ تَجْلِسِينَ lā taǧlisī**na**...) Don't sit here! (fem. sing.)

لاَ تَـذْهَـبُوا مَـعَـهُ! lā taḏhabū maᶜa-hu! (not: .. لاَ تَـذْهَـبُونَ lā taḏhabūna ...)

Don't go with him! (masc. pl.)

(b) The negative particle لَمْ lam 'did not' is used before a jussive verb with the same meaning as مَا mā 'not' + perfect (i.e. negative past, cf. chapter 14.11), e.g.

لَمْ يَكْتُبْ لَهُ lam yaktub la-hu. He did not write to him.

لَمْ يَكْتُبِ ٱلرِّسَالَةَ lam yaktubi r-risālata. He did not write the letter.

Remember: The **kasrah /i/** in the above phrase 'lam yaktubi ...' is the result of the rule given before that a final **sukūn** is changed to **kasrah** as a connective vowel before **hamzatu l-waṣli** (**waṣlah**).

(c) لَمْ lam is sometimes suffixed by ...مَا ...mā, becoming لَمَّا lammā, which means 'not yet'. The following verb is in the jussive mood, e.g.

لَمَّا يَكْتُبْ لَهُ lammā yaktub la-hu. He has **not** written to him **yet**.

28.9 The particle ...لِ /li.../ (also called the **lām** of imperative) expresses either a direct or indirect command, exhortation or suggestion. It can be translated as 'let . . .!, may . . .!, let's . . .!', e.g.

لِتَشْرَبْ! li-tašrab!	لِيَكْتُبْ! li-yaktub!	لِنَجْلِسْ! li-naǧlis!
May you drink! (**Drink**!)	**Let** him write!	**Let us** sit down!

Note a: The **lām** with **kasrah** ...لِ li... may be preceded by the conjunction ...فَ /fa.../ or وَ /wa../. Then the **kasrah** is replaced by **sukūn**: ...فَلْ /fa-l.../, ...وَلْ /wa-l.../.

وَلْتَشْرَبْ! wa-l-tašrab!	وَلْيَكْتُبْ! wa-l-yaktub!	فَلْنَجْلِسْ! fa-l-naǧlis!
May you drink! (**Drink**!)	**And let** him write!	**So let** us sit down!

Note b: This function of the particle ...لِ /li.../ should not be confused with its use together with the subjunctive mood, expressing intent or purpose.

28.10 *Imperative mood*

The imperative mood أَلْأَمْرُ is formed from the second person (sing., du., pl.; masc. and fem.) of the jussive mood by skipping the personal prefix ... تَـ /ta.../ and replacing it with **hamzatu l-qaṭʿi** (written on/under ʾ**alif**) and **ḍammah** أُ /ʾu/ or **kasrah** إِ /ʾi/, in accordance with the following rules:

(a) When the verb has **ḍammah** /u/ on the middle radical in the imperfect tense, the **hamzah** will take **ḍammah** in the imperative mood: أُ /ʾu/, e.g.

2nd pers. sing. jussive	***2nd pers. sing. imperative***
تَكْتُبْ tak**tub**	أُكْتُبْ ʾ**uk**tub! Write!

(b) When the verb has **fatḥah** /a/ or **kasrah** /i/ on the middle radical in the imperfect tense, the **hamzah** will take **kasrah** in the imperative mood: إِ /ʾi/, e.g.

تَذْهَبْ ta**d̲hab**	إِذْهَبْ ʾ**id̲**hab! Go!
تَجْلِسْ taǧ**lis**	إِجْلِسْ ʾ**iǧ**lis! Sit!

Exercises

Practise your reading:

لَمْ [1]يَقْبَلِ ٱلْوَزِيرُ [2]ٱلِاقْتِرَاحَ ٱلَّذِي [3]طَرَحَهُ [4]مَجْلِسُ [5]ٱلنُّوَّابِ (نَائِبٌ).

(1) The minister did not [1]accept [2]the proposal which was [3]submitted by [4,5]the Parliament ([4]council of [5]deputies).

[1]رَفَضَ [2]أَغْلَبُ [3]ٱلْمُشَارِكِينَ فِي [4]حَفْلَةِ ٱلْعُرْسِ أَنْ يَشْرَبُوا [5]نَبِيذًا.

(2) [2]Most of [3]those attending [4]the wedding party [1]refused to drink [5]wine.

[1]دَخَلْتُ [2]مَعْهَدَ [3]ٱلدِّرَاسَاتِ ٱلْعَرَبِيَّةِ فِي جَامِعَةِ هِلْسِنْكِي [4]حَتَّى أَتَعَلَّمَ [5]ٱللُّغَةَ [6]وَأَحْصُلَ عَلَى [7]شَهَادَةٍ.

(3) [1]I entered [2]the Institute of Arabic [3]Studies at the University of Helsinki [4]to study [5]the language [6]and get [7]a degree.

[1]لَمْ [2]أَقْدِرْ أَنْ [3]أَرْفَعَ [4]ٱلْمَرِيضَ عَنِ [5]ٱلْأَرْضِ [6]لِأَنْقُلَهُ إِلَى [7]سَرِيرِهِ.

(4) [1,2] I couldn't [3]lift [4]the patient (the sick man) off [5]the floor [6]to move him to [7]his bed.

لَا [1]تَتْرُكْ [2]شَنْطَتَكَ [3]بَعِيداً [4]عَنْكَ [5]لِئَلَّا [6]تُسْرَقَ.

(5) Don't [1]leave [2]your bag [3]far away ([4]from you) [5]so that it won't [6]be stolen.

لَا [1]تَخْرُجْ مِنَ [2]ٱلْفُنْدُقِ وَلَا [3]تَتْرُكْ [4]أَصْدِقَاءَكَ (صَدِيقٌ) فِي [5]ٱللَّيْلِ

[6]وَأَقْفِلْ (IV أَقْفَلَ) بَابَ [7]ٱلْغُرْفَةِ [8]جَيِّداً.

(6) Don't [1]go out of [2]the hotel, don't [3]leave [4]your friends at [5]night, [6]and lock the door of [7]the room [8]well.

[1]لِتَأْخُذْ [2]دَوَاءَكَ وَتَشْرَبْ [3]مَاءً [4]بَعْدَ أَنْ تَأْكُلَ [5]وَقَبْلَ أَنْ تَذْهَبَ إِلَى [6]ٱلنَّوْمِ.

(7) [1]Take [2]your medicine and drink [3]water [4]after you eat [5]and before you go to [6]sleep!

لَمْ [1]يَتْرُكِ [2]ٱللَّحَّامُ [3]ٱللَّحْمَ [4]خَارِجَ [5]ٱلْبَرَّادِ [6]لِئَلَّا [7]يَفْسِدَ.

(8) [2]The butcher did not [1]leave [3]the meat [4]outside [5]the refrigerator [6]in order that it should not [7]be spoiled.

[1]قَبِلَ [2]زَمِيلِي أَنْ [3]يَجْعَلَ [4]مُحَاضَرَتَهُ قَصِيرَةً [5]كَيْلَا (كَيْ لَا) [6]يَضْجَرَ

[7]ٱلْمُسْتَمِعُونَ.

(9) [2]My colleague [1]agreed [3]to make [4]his lecture short [5]in order not to [6]bore [7]the listeners ([5]in order that [7]the listeners not [6]feel boredom).

[1]فَلْنَنْتَظِرْ هُنَا حَتَّى [2]تَرْجِعَ زَوْجَتِي ثُمَّ نَذْهَبُ [3]مَعاً إِلَى ٱلْمَطْعَمِ.

(10) [1]Let us wait here till my wife [2]returns and then we will go [3]together to the restaurant.

[1]سَوْفَ لَا آكُلُ وَلَا أَشْرَبُ [2]مَا لَمْ تَأْكُلْ وَتَشْرَبْ أَنْتَ [3]أَيْضاً.

(11) [1]I will neither eat nor drink [2]unless you eat and drink [3]too.

يَا وَلَدِي! [1]إِغْسِلْ [2]وَجْهَكَ بِٱلْمَاءِ [3]ٱلسَّاخِنِ [4]وَٱلصَّابُونِ [5]وَٱلْبِسْ

[6]قَمِيصَكَ [7]ٱلنَّظِيفَ وَٱذْهَبْ إِلَى [8]حَفْلَةِ [9]ٱلْعُرْسِ.

(12) Oh son! [1]Wash [2]your face with [3]warm water [4]and soap, [5]put on (wear) your [7]clean [6]shirt, and go to the [9]wedding [8]party.

[1]وَعَدَ طَالِبٌ أُسْتَاذَهُ [2]بِأَنَّهُ [3]مِنَ [4]ٱلْآنَ [5]فَصَاعِداً سَيَدْرُسُ [6]أَكْثَرَ، قَالَ لَهُ ٱلْأُسْتَاذُ، [7]إِذَنْ [8]سَتَنْجَحُ فِي [9]ٱلِٱمْتِحَانِ.

(13) A student [1]promised his professor (teacher) [2]that [3]from [4]now [5]on he would study [6]more. The professor said to him: '[7]Then [8]you will pass (succeed in) [9]the exam.'

'هَلْ عِنْدَكَ مَاءٌ [1]بَارِدٌ لِأَشْرَبَ؟' - 'إِذًا أَنْتَ [2]عَطْشَانُ.'

(14) 'Do you have [1]cold water to drink?' – 'Then you are [2]thirsty!'

[1]سَأَلَ [2]ٱلشَّابُّ ٱلْبِنْتَ أَنْ [3]يَخْطُبَهَا، قَالَتْ: [4]إِذَنْ أَنْتَ [5]تُحِبُّنِي.

(15) [2]The young man [1]proposed to the girl (lit. he [1]asked the girl [3]to get engaged with him). She said: '[4]Then [5]you love me.'

قَالَ [1]ٱلزَّوْجُ [2]لِزَوْجَتِهِ: [3]سَأَعْمَلُ [4]كُلَّ مَا [5]يُفْرِحُكِ، فَقَالَتِ ٱلزَّوْجَةُ: إِذًا أَنْتَ زَوْجٌ [6]مُحِبٌّ.

(16) [1]The husband said to [2]his wife: '[3]I will do [4]anything that [5]pleases you.' So the wife said: 'Then you are [6]a loving husband.'

إِبْنِي [1]ٱلْحَبِيبَ! [2]لِمَاذَا لَمْ تَكْتُبْ إِلَيَّ؟ أُكْتُبْ [3]وَأَخْبِرْنِي عَنْ [4]صِحَّتِكَ!
[5]وَأَنْصَحُكَ بِأَنْ لَا تَشْرَبَ ٱلْكُحُولَ وَأَنْ [6]تُقَلِّلَ مِنَ [7]ٱلتَّدْخِينِ.

(17) [1]My beloved son! [2]Why didn't you write to me? Write [3]and tell me about [4]your health! [5]I advise you not to drink alcohol and to [6]cut down (reduce) your [7]smoking.

Translate into Arabic:

(1) My colleague refused to make his lecture short at the Institute of Arabic Studies.

(2) The Parliament did not accept the proposal which was not submitted by the minister.

(3) I could not lift the bag off the bed to move it to the floor.

(4) Take your medicine and wash your face before you go to sleep!

(5) Let us wait here in the restaurant till my son and my wife return.

(6) The sick minister will neither eat nor drink at his son's wedding.

(7) I entered the university to study the Arabic language and to get a degree.

(8) Don't go out of the hotel at night and lock the door of the room.

(9) I am thirsty. Do you have cold water?

(10) Wash your face with warm water and soap and wear your clean shirt and go to the minister's wedding party.

(11) The wife said to her husband, 'I will do anything that pleases you.' The husband said: 'Then (so) you are a loving wife.'

(12) My friend refused to drink wine at the party.

Chapter 29

Doubled verbs (mediae geminatae) and quadriliteral verbs

29.1 A doubled verb in Arabic, أَلْفِعْلُ ٱلْمُضَاعَفُ, is a triliteral verb whose second and third radicals are identical. In the basic form they are thus written as one, with **šaddah** above. This phenomenon is called إِدْغَامٌ, 'contraction', e.g.

مَرَّ marra (for: مَرَرَ marara)
to pass

فَرَّ farra (for: فَرَرَ farara)
to escape, to flee

دَلَّ dalla (for: دَلَلَ dalala)
to show

عَدَّ ʿadda (for: عَدَدَ ʿadada)
to count

29.2 *The imperfect and imperative*

The imperfect tense is vocalized in the same way as the imperfect of the regular triliteral verb, which can have any of the three vowels on the middle radical. The vowel is transferred between the first and second radical in doubled verbs.

The last consonant of the imperative of the second person masculine singular has **fatḥah**, and not **sukūn** like the regular verbs. Another difference is that the imperative does not have the initial ʾ**alif** with **hamzah**, *which is prefixed to the imperative in regular verbs*, e.g.

Perfect	***Imperfect***	***Imperative***
مَرَّ marra to pass	يَمُرُّ yam**u**rru (for: يَمْرُرُ yamruru)	مُرَّ murr**a**! pass!
فَرَّ farra, to escape, to flee	يَفِرُّ yaf**i**rru (for: يَفْرِرُ yafriru)	فِرَّ firr**a**! escape!

See table A1.2, the patterns of the doubled verb فَرَّ farra, and conjugation A2.3, the doubled verb مَرَّ marra, in the appendices.

Note: The derived verb forms are conjugated to a certain extent like the regular verbs.

29.3 The nouns of place and time for the doubled verb are formed as follows:

Noun of place	***Basic verb form***
مَحَلٌّ **ma**ḥallun place	حَلَّ ḥalla to untie, to solve
مَقَرٌّ **ma**qarrun residence, headquarters	قَرَّ qarra to settle down

29.4 *Quadriliteral verbs*

The quadriliteral or four-radical verbs, أَلْفِعْلُ ٱلرُّبَاعِي, have four consonants in the root (the pattern فَعْلَلَ faᶜlala). They are conjugated as form II فَعَّلَ faᶜᶜala (i.e. CaCCaCa) of the regular triliteral verb.

There are very few quadriliteral verbs and, apart from the basic form, they have only two derived verb forms: II and IV. The derived forms are less common and have no passive. The verbal noun (**maṣdar**) of the quadriliteral verb of the basic form follows the pattern of فَعْلَلَةٌ faᶜlalatun. The perfect, imperfect indicative and verbal noun of the quadriliteral verb are exemplified below:

Form I

Perfect	***Imperfect***	***Verbal noun (maṣdar)***
تَرْجَمَ tarǧama to translate	يُتَرْجِمُ yutarǧimu	تَرْجَمَةٌ tarǧamatun translation

دَحْرَجَ daḥraǧa to roll	يُدَحْرِجُ yudaḥriǧu	دَحْرَجَةٌ daḥraǧatun rolling
قَهْقَهَ qahqaha to laugh boisterously	يُقَهْقِهُ yuqahqihu	قَهْقَهَةٌ qahqahatun loud burst of laughter
دَهْوَرَ dahwara to hurl down	يُدَهْوِرُ yudahwiru	دَهْوَرَةٌ dahwaratun downfall
طَمْأَنَ ṭamʾana to calm, pacify	يُطَمْئِنُ yuṭamʾinu	طَمْأَنَةٌ ṭamʾanatun pacification

(See conjugation A2.4 of the verb تَرْجَمَ tarǧama in Appendix 2.)

Form II

Perfect	***Imperfect***	***Verbal noun (maṣdar)***
تَزَلْزَلَ tazalzala to shake, quake (earth)	يَتَزَلْزَلُ yatazalzalu	تَزَلْزُلٌ tazalzulun earthquake
تَفَلْسَفَ tafalsafa to philosophize	يَتَفَلْسَفُ yatafalsafu	تَفَلْسُفٌ tafalsufun philosophizing
تَشَيْطَنَ tašayṭana to act like the devil	يَتَشَيْطَنُ yatašayṭanu	تَشَيْطُنٌ tašayṭunun behaving like a devil

Form IV

Perfect	***Imperfect***	***Verbal noun (maṣdar)***
إِطْمَأَنَّ ʾiṭmaʾanna to remain quiet, to be relieved	يَطْمَئِنُّ yaṭmaʾinnu	إِطْمِئْنَانٌ ʾiṭmiʾnānun calmness, relief
إِشْمَأَزَّ ʾišmaʾazza to feel disgust, to become disgusted	يَشْمَئِزُّ yašmaʾizzu	إِشْمِئْزَازٌ ʾišmiʾzāzun disgust

Note: Observe that the derived form II of the quadriliteral verb has the pattern and meaning of form V, and form IV the pattern and meaning of form IX of triliteral verbs.

Exercises

Practise your reading:

[1]مَرَرْتُ [2]أَمْسِ بِٱمْرَأَةٍ [3]حَامِلٍ، [4]فَسَأَلَتْنِي [5]عَنْ [6]مَدْخَلِ ٱلْمُسْتَشْفَى [7]فَدَلَلْتُهَا [8]عَلَيْهِ.

(1) [2]Yesterday [1]I passed by [3]a pregnant woman [4]and she asked me the [5]whereabouts of the hospital [6]entrance, [7]so I pointed [8]it out to her.

[1]قَرَّرَتِ [2]ٱلْحُكُومَةُ بِأَنْ [3]تَشُقَّ [4]طَرِيقًا [5]عَرِيضًا [6]يَمْتَدُّ مِنَ [7]ٱلْمَطَارِ إِلَى [8]قَلْبِ [9]ٱلْعَاصِمَةِ.

(2) [2]The government [1]decided to [3]build (break open) [5]a wide [4]road [6]stretching from [7]the airport to the [8]heart of [9]the capital.

[1]هَزَّ [2]ٱلْفَلَّاحُ [3]شَجَرَةَ [4]ٱلتُّفَّاحِ (تُفَّاحَةٌ) [5]فَسَقَطَ مِنْهَا بَعْضُ ٱلتُّفَّاحِ وَلٰكِنَّهُ [6]ظَلَّ يَهُزُّهَا حَتَّى [7]كَسَرَ [8]غُصْنَهَا.

(3) [2]The peasant [1]shook [4]the apple [3]tree and some apples [5]fell, but [6]he continued shaking it until [7]he broke one of [8]its branches.

[1]هَرْوَلَ [2]ٱلْمُحَامِيُّ [3]وَأَبْلَغَ [4]ٱلسَّجِينَ [5]بِقَرَارِ [6]ٱلْإِفْرَاجِ [7]عَنْهُ.

(4) [2]The lawyer [1]rushed in [3]and informed [4]the prisoner [5]about the decision [7]regarding his [6]release.

[1]أَحْبَبْتُهَا وَأَحَبَّتْنِي [2]مُنْذُ [3]ٱلطُّفُولَةِ [4]وَمَا زَالَ حُبُّنَا [5]كَمَا [6]كَانَ.

(5) [1]I have loved her and she has loved me [2]since [3]childhood and our love is [4]still [5]as [6]it used to be.

[1]قَرَّرْتُ [2]ٱلتَّقْلِيلَ مِنَ [3]ٱلتَّدْخِينِ [4]لِأَنَّهُ [5]مُضِرٌّ [6]بِٱلصِّحَّةِ.

(6) [1]I decided [3]to smoke [2]less (lit. [2]reduce [3]smoking) [4]because [5]it is harmful [6]to one's health (lit. to the health).

[1]أَظُنُّ أَنَّ [2]قِلَّةَ [3]ٱلْأَمْطَارِ (مَطَرٌ) فِي هٰذَا [4]ٱلشِّتَاءِ [5]سَتُسَبِّبُ [6]تَقْنِينًا [7]لِمِيَاهِ ٱلشُّرْبِ [8]خِلَالَ [9]ٱلصَّيْفِ [10]ٱلْقَادِمِ.

(7) [1]I think that [2]the lack of [3]rain this [4]winter [5]will cause [6]rationing of drinking [7]water ([8]during [10]the) next [9]summer.

هَلْ [1]تَدُلُّنِي عَلَى [2]مُتَرْجِمٍ (تَرْجُمَانٍ) [3]لِلُّغَتَيْنِ ٱلْأَلْمَانِيَّةِ وَٱلْعَرَبِيَّةِ؟

(8) Will you [1]direct (show) me to [2]a translator [3]of the two languages German and Arabic.

[1]تَمَكَّنَ [2]سَجِينٌ مِنْ أَنْ [3]يَفِرَّ مِنَ [4]ٱلسِّجْنِ [5]فَلَحِقَ بِهِ شُرْطِيٌّ [6]وَقَبَضَ عَلَيْهِ [7]وَأَخَذَهُ [8]لِلتَّحْقِيقِ، فَسَأَلَهُ ٱلشُّرْطِيُّ: لِمَاذَا فَرَرْتَ مِنَ السِّجْنِ؟ [9]رَدَّ ٱلسَّجِينُ: فَرَرْتُ لِأَنِّي [10]مَلَلْتُ [11]ٱلعَيْشَ فِي ٱلسِّجْنِ.

فَقَالَ ٱلشُّرْطِيُّ هٰذَا لَيْسَ [12]مُبَرِّرًا وَسَوْفَ [13]أَرُدُّكَ إِلَيْهِ.

(9) [2]A prisoner [1]was able [3]to escape from [4]jail. A policeman [5]chased him, [6]caught him [7]and took him in [8]for interrogation. The policeman asked him: 'Why did you escape from jail?' The prisoner [9]answered: 'I escaped because I [10]was fed up [11]with life in jail.'

The policeman said, 'That is not [12]an excuse and I will [13]take you back there.'

[1]بِسَبَبِ [2]ٱلزِّلْزَالِ أَمْسِ [3]تَشَقَّقَتْ [4]جُدْرَانُ (جِدَارٌ) ٱلْمَنَازِلِ (مَنْزِلٌ) [5]وَٱلْجُسُورِ (جِسْرٌ) [6]وَدَبَّ [7]ٱلْخَوْفُ [8]وَٱلذُّعْرُ بَيْنَ [9]ٱلْمُوَاطِنِينَ.

وَلَوْ كَانَ ٱلزِّلْزَالُ [10]أَشَدَّ [11]بِقَلِيلٍ، [12]لَٱنْفَجَرَ [13]ٱلسَّدُّ [14]وَجَرَفَتِ ٱلْمِيَاهُ ٱلْمَنَازِلَ [15]وَٱلْمَزَارِعَ (مَزْرَعَةٌ).

(10) [1]Due to [2]the earthquake yesterday, the [4]walls of houses [5]and bridges [3]cracked [7]and fear [8]and panic [6]spread among the [9]citizens.

Had the earthquake been [11]a bit [10]stronger, [13]the dam would [12]have burst, and the water would [14]have swept away houses [15]and farms.

هَلْ [1]تَشُكُّ فِي [2]حُكْمِ [3]ٱلْقَاضِي؟ لَا، لَيْسَ عِنْدِي [4]أَيُّ [5]شَكٍّ وَلَكِنْ [6]أَظُنُّ أَنَّ ٱلْحُكْمَ عَلَى [7]ٱلْمُتَّهَمِ كَانَ [8]شَدِيدًا.

(11) Do you [1]doubt [3]the judge's [2]decision (decree)? No, I do not have [4]any [5]doubt but [6]I think that the decision against [7]the accused was [8]severe.

[1]مَدَّ رَجُلٌ [2]يَدَهُ [3]لِيُصَافِحَ ٱمْرَأَةً وَكَانَ مَعَهَا [4]كَلْبٌ [5]فَظَنَّ ٱلْكَلْبُ أَنَّهُ [6]سَيَضْرِبُهَا [7]فَقَفَزَ/ فَنَطَّ عَلَى ٱلرَّجُلِ [8]وَعَضَّهُ فِي [9]رِجْلِهِ.

(12) A man [1]stretched out [2]his hand [3]to shake the hand of a woman who had

[4]a dog with her. The dog [5]thought [6]he was going to hit her, [7]so he jumped on the man [8]and bit [9]his leg.

1سَاعَدْتُ صَدِيقَتِي فِي 2حَلِّ 3ٱلْمَسَائِلِ (مَسْأَلَةٌ) 4ٱلرِّيَاضِيَّةِ حَتَّى 5تَنْجَحَ فِي 6ٱمْتِحَانِ 7دُخُولِ 8كُلِّيَّةِ 9ٱلْهَنْدَسَةِ. 10وَظَلَلْتُ 11أُسَاعِدُهَا حَتَّى 12تَخَرَّجَتْ 13وَصَارَتْ 14مُهَنْدِسًا / مُهَنْدِسَةً.

(13) [1]I helped my friend (f.) in [2]solving [4]the mathematical [3]problems so that she [5]would pass (succeed in) [7]the entrance [6]exam of [9]the engineering [8]faculty. [10]And I kept on [11]helping her until [12]she graduated [13]and became [14]an engineer.

Translate into Arabic:

(1) I helped my friend (f.) until she graduated and became an engineer.

(2) Yesterday I passed by the judge. He asked me where the entrance of the jail was and I showed it to him.

(3) The peasant shook the apple tree and so broke one of its branches.

(4) Do you doubt that smoking is harmful to health?

(5) Due to the earthquake yesterday bridges and the walls of houses cracked.

(6) The dog jumped on the pregnant woman and bit her hand.

(7) The lawyer and the judge informed the prisoner about the decision regarding his release (that he be released).

(8) I do not have any doubt that the judge's decision against the accused was too severe.

(9) I have loved her since childhood and my love for her is still as it used to be.

(10) A prisoner was able to escape from the jail. The policeman chased him and caught him.

(11) Yesterday I passed by the translator (f.) of the two languages Arabic and German, and she had a policeman with her.

Chapter 30

Verbs with hamzah

There are verbs where **hamzah** occurs as one of the radicals. These are called, أَلْفِعْلُ ٱلْمَهْمُوزُ , ʾal-fiʿlu l-mahmūzu.

30.1 *Verbs with initial hamzah*

Verbs with **hamzah** as the first radical, أَلْفِعْلُ ٱلْمَهْمُوزُ ٱلْأَوَّلُ, are conjugated on the same principles as the regular strong verbs, with some exceptions. (See below and the conjugations in Appendix 2.)

Perfect	***Imperfect***	***Imperative***	
أَذِنَ ʾaḏina, to allow	يَأْذَنُ yaʾḏanu	إِيذَنْ! ʾīḏan	(for: إِئْذَنْ ʾiʾḏan)
أَسَرَ ʾasara, to capture	يَأْسِرُ yaʾsiru	إِيسِرْ! ʾīsir	(for: إِئْسِرْ ʾiʾsir)
أَمَلَ ʾamala, to hope	يَأْمُلُ yaʾmulu	أُومُلْ! ʾūmul	(for: أُؤْمُلْ ʾuʾmul)

30.2 When the imperative is preceded by the conjunction وَ wa... or ... فَـ fa..., the long vowel after the initial **hamzah** disappears, i.e. is replaced by **sukūn**: ... وَأْ wa-ʾ..., ... فَأْ faʾ..., e.g.

وَأْذَنْ! **wa-**ʾḏan! and allow!	(for: وَإِيذَنْ **wa-**ʾīḏan)
وَأْسِرْ! **wa-**ʾsir! and capture!	(for: وَإِيسِرْ **wa-**ʾīsir)
فَأْمُلْ! **fa-**ʾmul! and hope!	(for: فَأُومُلْ **fa-**ʾūmul)

30.3 In some verbs, such as أَخَذَ ʾaḫaḏa, 'to take', and أَكَلَ ʾakala 'to eat', the initial **hamzah** is elided in the imperative, e.g.

Imperative

	Singular		***Dual***	***Plural***	
Form I	***Masc.***	***Fem.***	***Masc. and Fem.***	***Masc.***	***Fem.***
أَخَذَ	خُذْ	خُذِي	خُذَا	خُذُوا	خُذْنَ
ʾaḫaḏa	ḫuḏ, take!	ḫuḏī	ḫuḏā	ḫuḏū	ḫuḏna
أَكَلَ	كُلْ	كُلِي	كُلاَ	كُلُوا	كُلْنَ
ʾakala	kul, eat!	kulī	kulā	kulū	kulna

30.4 *Assimilation process*

If the initial radical of the basic verb form is أ ʾa, as أَخَذَ ʾaḫaḏa 'to take', then the initial **hamzah** in verb form VIII is assimilated to the infix /-t-/, producing a doubled ...ـتّـ. /-tt-/, e.g.

إِتَّخَذَ ʾittaḫaḏa, to take up, to adopt (instead of إِأْتَخَذَ ʾiʾtaḫaḏa)

30.5 *Verbs with hamzah as the middle radical*

(a) The medial **hamzah**, أَلْفِعْلُ ٱلْمَهْمُوزُ ٱلْوَسَط, can be written on ʾ**alif** (.. أ..), **wāw** (..ـؤ..) or **yāʾ** (..ـئـ..). (Follow the rules for writing **hamzah** provided in chapter 20.) These verbs are conjugated on the same principle as the regular verbs, with the exception of the two verbs سَأَلَ saʾala 'to ask' and رَأَى raʾā 'to see', which lose their medial **hamzah.** (See the conjugation of the verb رَأَى raʾā (A2.16 in Appendix 2) and chapter 33.)

Perfect	***Imperfect***	***Imperative (rare)***
بَؤُسَ baʾusa, to be brave	يَبْؤُسُ yabʾusu	أُبْؤُسْ ʾubʾus!
سَئِمَ saʾima, to be weary	يَسْأَمُ yasʾamu	إِسْأَمْ ʾisʾam!

(b) The irregular verb سَأَلَ saʾala 'to ask' can drop its medial **hamzah** in the imperfect jussive and imperative. Thus it has two alternative sets of forms for the jussive and two alternative sets of forms for the imperative:

Perfect	Imperfect jussive	Imperative
سَأَلَ	يَسْأَلْ OR يَسَلْ	إِسْأَلْ OR سَلْ
sa'ala	yas'al yasal	'is'al sal

(c) سَأَلَ sa'ala is conjugated regularly in the passive like other verbs with **hamzah** as the middle radical, e.g.

Active	Passive	
Perfect	Perfect	Imperfect
سَأَلَ sa'ala	سُئِلَ su'ila	يُسْأَلُ yus'alu

30.6 Verbs with hamzah as the final radical

(a) **Hamzah** as the final radical, أَلْفِعْلُ ٱلْمَهْمُوزُ ٱلْآخِرِ: These types of verb are also conjugated like regular strong verbs, e.g.

Perfect	Imperfect	Imperative
قَرَأَ qara'a, to read	يَقْرَأُ yaqra'u	إِقْرَأْ 'iqra'!
بَطُؤَ baṭu'a, to be slow	يَبْطُؤُ yabṭu'u	أُبْطُؤْ 'ubṭu'!
خَطِئَ ḫaṭi'a, to be mistaken	يَخْطَأُ yaḫṭa'u	إِخْطَأْ 'iḫṭa'!

(b) In the verb دَفِيءَ dafi'a 'to be warm', the infix ت /-t-/ of verb form VIII ('ifta'ala إِفْتَعَلَ) is assimilated to the initial radical د /d/, which is doubled, i.e. إِدَّفَأَ '**id**dafa'a 'to warm oneself' instead of إِدْتَفَأَ 'idtafa'a.

Note: The derived verb forms (II–X) of all verbs with **hamzah** mentioned above are conjugated in the active and passive more or less on the same principles as the derived verb forms (II–X) of strong verbs.

Exercises

Practise your reading:

[1]هَنَّأَ [2]جَلَالَةُ ٱلْمَلِكِ [3]ٱلْمُؤَرِّخَ عَلَى [4]أَعْمَالِهِ (عَمَلٌ) [5]ٱلشَّهِيرَةِ [6]وَقَدَّمَ لَهُ
[7]مُكَافَأَةً [8]مَالِيَّةً.

(1) [2]His Majesty the King [1]congratulated [3]the historian on his [5]famous [4]works [6]and gave him [8]a financial [7]reward.

ذَهَبْتُ مَعَ [1]وَفْدٍ [2]لِنُهَنِّئَ (هَنَّأَ) [3]رُؤَسَاءَ (رَئِيسٌ) [4]ٱلْأَدْيَانِ (دِينٌ)
[5]بِمُنَاسَبَةِ [6]ٱلْأَعْيَادِ (عِيدٌ).

(2) I went with [1]a delegation [2]to congratulate [4]the religious [3]leaders [5]on the occasion of [6]the holidays.

[1]طَلَبَ رَئِيسُ [2]ٱلنِّقَابَةِ [3]تَأْجِيلَ [4]ٱلْمُؤْتَمَرِ [5]ٱلسَّنَوِيِّ لِأَنَّ [6]أَحَدَ [7]ٱلْأَعْضَاءِ
(عُضْوٌ) [8]ٱلْمَسْؤُولِينَ [9]وَٱلْمُؤَسِّسِينَ [10]لِلنِّقَابَةِ قَدْ [11]مَرِضَ [12]فَجْأَةً
[13]وَنُقِلَ إِلَى [14]عِيَادَةِ [15]ٱلطَّبِيبِ.

(3) The chairman (the head) of [2]the trade union [1]requested [3]postponement of [5]the annual [4]congress (conference), because [6]one of [8]the responsible [7]members [9]and founders [10]of the trade union had [12]suddenly [11]become ill [13]and been taken ([13]transported) to [14,15]the clinic (lit. [15]doctor's [14]reception).

[1]مَعَ ٱلْأَسَفِ أَنَّ [2]عَدَدَ قُرَّاءِ (قَارِئٌ) [3]ٱلْقِصَصِ (قِصَّةٌ) [4]وَٱلرِّوَايَاتِ [5]يَقِلُّ
يَوْمًا بَعْدَ يَوْمٍ [6]وَلِهٰذَا فَإِنَّ [7]ٱتِّخَاذَ [8]تَأْلِيفِ ٱلْكُتُبِ [9]كَمِهْنَةٍ [10]أَصْبَحَ
[11]غَيْرَ [12]مُرْبِحٍ.

(4) [1]Unfortunately, [2]the number of readers of [3]short stories [4]and novels [5]is decreasing day by day. [6]Therefore [7]taking up [8]writing (composing) books [9]as a profession [10]has become [11,12]unprofitable.

إِنَّ [1]مَسْؤُولِيَّاتِ [2]ٱلْمَرْأَةِ فِي ٱلْمَنْزِلِ [3]أَكْثَرُ [4]أَهَمِّيَّةً مِنْ مَسْؤُولِيَّاتِ
ٱلرَّجُلِ، فَهِيَ ٱلْمَسْؤُولَةُ عَنْ [5]بُؤْسِ [6]ٱلْعَائِلَةِ [7]وَهَنَائِهَا.

(5) [1]The responsibilities of [2]women at home [3]are more [4]important than the

responsibilities of men. They are responsible for both the [5]misery [7]and the happiness of the [6]family.

¹سَيَبْتَدِئُ ٱلْإِمَامُ بَعْدَ ²أُسْبُوعٍ فِي تَدْرِيسِ ³طَرِيقَةِ قِرَاءَةِ ٱلْقُرْآنِ ⁴ٱلْكَرِيمِ.

(6) After [2]a week the imam will [1]start teaching [3]the way (the correct method) of reading [4]the Holy Quran.

أَنَا ¹مُتَأَكِّدٌ أَنَّ هٰذَا ٱلْأَكْلَ وَٱلشَّرَابَ عَلَى ²حِسَابِ ³ٱلْمُؤْتَمَرِ ⁴فَكُلْ وَٱشْرَبْ ⁵بِحُرِّيَّةٍ!

(7) I am [1]sure that this food and drink is on [3]the conference (congress) [2]account, [4]so feel [5]free to [4]eat and drink!

¹أَنْشَأَتِ ٱلْحُكُومَةُ ²مَرْفَأً ³وَمَطَارًا جَدِيدَيْنِ وَفِي هٰذَا ⁴ٱلْعَامِ ⁵سَيَبْدَآنِ ⁶بِٱسْتِقْبَالِ ⁷ٱلْمُسَافِرِينَ ⁸وَٱلْبَضَائِعِ (بِضَاعَةٌ). ⁹وَتَأْمُلُ ٱلْحُكُومَةُ أَنْ يَكُونَ هٰذَانِ ¹⁰ٱلْمَشْرُوعَانِ ¹¹سَيُؤَثِّرَانِ عَلَى ¹²تَحْسِينِ ¹³ٱلْاقْتِصَادِ ¹⁴وَفُرَصِ (فُرْصَةٌ) ¹⁵ٱلْعَمَلِ.

(8) The government [1]built a new [2]harbour [3]and a new airport, and this [4]year [5]they will start [6]to accommodate [7]passengers [6]and receive [8]goods. The government [9]hopes that these [10]two projects [11]will have an influence on [12]the improvement of [13]the economy and [15]job [14]opportunities.

¹أُجِّلَ ²تَأْسِيسُ ³ٱلْمُؤَسَّسَةِ ⁴ٱلتِّجَارِيَّةِ، حَتَّى ⁵يُسْتَأْجَرَ ⁶لَهَا ⁷قَاعَةٌ ⁸مُنَاسِبَةٌ.

(9) [2]The establishment of [4]the commercial [3]enterprise (establishment) has been [1]postponed until [8]an appropriate [7]hall [5]is rented ([6]for it).

¹آمُلُ مِنْكَ أَنْ لَا / أَلَّا ²تَتَأَخَّرَ عَنْ ³دَفْعِ ⁴فَاتُورَةِ ⁵تَأْمِينِ ⁶ٱلسَّيَّارَةِ ⁷وَإِلَّا ⁸تَتَعَرَّضُ ⁹لِمَسْؤُولِيَّةٍ.

(10) [1]I hope (from you) that you will not [2]be late in [3]paying [6]the car [5]insurance [4]bill, [7]otherwise [8]you will be held [9]responsible.

[1]سُئِلَ أَحَدُ [2]ٱلْمَسْؤُولِينَ فِي ٱلشَّرِكَةِ عَنْ [3]مَسْأَلَةٍ [4]تَتَعَلَّقُ [5]بِشَأْنِ
[6]ٱلنُّفَايَاتِ الَّتِي [7]تُسَبِّبُهَا ٱلشَّرِكَةُ، [8]فَمَا [9]جَرُؤَ ٱلْمَسْؤُولُ أَنْ
[10]يَرُدَّ عَلَى أَيِّ [11]سُؤَالٍ [12]حَوْلَ [13]ٱلْمَوْضُوعِ.

(11) [2]A company official (one of the responsible persons at the company) [1]was asked about [3]an issue [4]concerning ([5]the matter of) [6]waste products which [7]are generated by the company, but he (the responsible person) [8]did not [9]dare [10]to answer any [11]question [12]about [13]the subject.

[1]أُسْتُؤْنِفَتِ [2]ٱلْمُفَاوَضَاتُ بَيْنَ [3]ٱلْحُكُومَةِ [4]وَٱلْمُتَظَاهِرِينَ [5]لِحَلِّ [6]أَزْمَةِ
[7]ٱلْبِطَالَةِ.

(12) (The) [2]negotiations [1]have been resumed between [3]the government [4]and the demonstrators [5]to solve [7]the unemployment [6] crisis.

[1]أُنْشِئَتْ [2]أَوَّلُ [3]صَحِيفَةٍ عَرَبِيَّةٍ فِي مِصْرَ [4]عَلَى يَدِ [5]مُهَاجِرِينَ لُبْنَانِيِّينَ
وَكَانَ ذٰلِكَ [6]مُنْذُ أَكْثَرَ مِنْ [7]مِئَةِ سَنَةٍ.

(13) [2]The first Arabic [3]newspaper [1]was established in Egypt [4]by (lit. [4]at the hand of) Lebanese [5]immigrants, and that was more than [7]one hundred years [6]ago.

[1]لَا تَزَالُ [2]مَسْأَلَةُ [3]ٱللَّاجِئِينَ (لَاجِىءٌ) [4]حَتَّى ٱلْيَوْمِ [5]مُعَقَّدَةً فِي [6]ٱلْعَالَمِ.

(14) [2]The matter of [3]refugees [1]has remained (is still) [5]a complicated issue in [6]the world ([4]until) today.

Translate into Arabic:

(1) Today I went with the chairman (the head) of the trade union to congratulate His Majesty the King on the occasion of the holidays.

(2) A government official was asked to postpone the annual women's conference (congress).

(3) Unfortunately, the chairman (president) of the trade union suddenly became ill.

(4) The matter of waste products which are generated by the company is still a complicated issue.

(5) At the conference one of the members of the delegation congratulated the historian on his famous works.

(6) The number of refugees is decreasing day by day.

(7) The official did not dare to answer any question about the matter concerning (the) waste.

(8) Unfortunately, the number of readers of short stories and novels is decreasing day by day.

(9) I am sure that the responsibilities of women at home are more important than the responsibilities of men.

(10) The first commercial company was established in Egypt, and that was more than one hundred years ago.

(11) This year the new harbour and airport will start to accommodate passengers and receive goods, and these two projects will influence the improvement of the economy and job opportunities.

Chapter 31

Verbs with a weak initial radical

31.1 The weak verbs, أَلْأَفْعَالُ ٱلْمُعْتَلَّةُ, which literally means 'sick verbs' are verbs whose roots contain one or more weak radicals, حُرُوفُ ٱلْعِلَّة. The weak radicals are the semivowels و /w/ and ي /y/. They are called 'weak' because they are dropped or assimilated with vowels according to certain rules in many conjugational forms. The weak verbs are also called assimilated verbs.

Note: A verb is called strong, if none of its radicals is dropped or assimilated with a vowel in the conjugation of the verb.

31.2 Weak verbs fall into four main categories:

(a) Initial weak radical (assimilated verb) أَلْفِعْلُ ٱلْمِثَالُ *see below*;

(b) Middle weak radical (hollow verb) أَلْفِعْلُ ٱلْأَجْوَفُ *chap. 32*;

(c) Final weak radical (defective verb) أَلْفِعْلُ ٱلنَّاقِصُ *chap. 33*;

(d) Doubly and trebly weak verbs أَلْفِعْلُ ٱللَّفِيفُ *chap. 33*.

31.3 *Verbs with the weak initial radical* و */w/*

(a) Verbs with the weak initial radical و /w/ drop this radical in the active imperfect and imperative. In the passive imperfect it is assimilated to the preceding vowel, e.g.

Active		Passive	
Perfect	*Imperfect*	*Imperfect*	*Imperative*
وَضَعَ waḍaʿa to put (down)	يَضَعُ yaḍaʿu (for: يَوْضَعُ yawḍaʿu)	يُوضَعُ yūḍaʿu	ضَعْ ḍaʿ! put!
وَقَفَ waqafa to stand (still)	يَقِفُ yaqifu (for: يَوْقِفُ yawqifu)	يُوقَفُ yūqafu	قِفْ qif! stop!
وَثِقَ waṯiqa to trust	يَثِقُ yaṯiqu (for: يَوْثِقُ yawṯiqu)	يُوثَقُ yūṯaqu	ثِقْ ṯiq! trust!

Note: It may be difficult to find the root in the dictionary when the first initial weak radical of the imperfect and imperative is missing.

(b) In a small number of verbs the initial weak radical وَ /w/ is also retained in the imperfect. These verbs have **kasrah** ـِـ /i/ as the middle vowel in the perfect, and **fatḥah** ـَـ /a/ in the imperfect, e.g.

Perfect	*Imperfect*
وَجِعَ waǧiʿa, to feel pain	يَوْجَعُ yawǧaʿu
وَجِلَ waǧila, to be afraid	يَوْجَلُ yawǧalu

31.4 *Assimilation of the weak radical* و */w/ in the derived verb forms*

(a) The initial و /w/ of the basic verb form وَصَلَ waṣala 'to arrive' in verb form VIII is assimilated to the infix ت /t/, which then appears as doubled ـتّـَ /..tt../, e.g.

إِتَّصَلَ ʾittaṣala, to be joined, to contact (for: إِوْتَصَلَ ʾiwtaṣala)

(b) The IVth form أَوْقَعَ ʾawqaʿa 'to drop' is derived from the verb وَقَعَ waqaʿa 'to fall'. Its verbal noun (**maṣdar**) is إِيقَاعٌ ʾīqāʿun 'rhythm' (for: إِوْقَاعٌ ʾiwqāʿun).

(c) The Xth form of وَدَعَ wadaʿa 'to put down' is إِسْتَوْدَعَ ʾistawdaʿa 'to deposit'. Its verbal noun (**maṣdar**) is إِسْتِيدَاعٌ ʾistīdāʿun 'lodging, depositing' (for: إِسْتِوْدَاعٌ ʾistiwdāʿun).

31.5 The nouns of place and time are formed as follows.

Nouns of place and time	***Basic verb form***
مِيلَادٌ mīlādun, birth	وَلَدَ walada, to give birth
مَوْعِدٌ mawʿidun, appointment	وَعَدَ waʿada, to promise
مَوْقِفٌ mawqifun, parking lot	وَقَفَ waqafa, to stand, to stand still

31.6 *Verbs with the initial weak radical* ي /y/

There are very few verbs with the initial weak radical ي /y/. These verbs are mostly conjugated like strong verbs. The imperative and the passive of the basic verb form are rare, e.g.

Perfect		***Imperfect***
يَبِسَ yabisa, to become dry		يَيْبَسُ yaybasu
يَئِسَ yaʾisa, to despair		يَيْأَسُ yayʾasu
يَقِظَ yaqiḏa, to wake up		يَيْقَظُ yayqaḏu
	OR	
يَقُظَ yaquḏa, to wake up		يَيْقُظُ yayquḏu

See table A1.3, the pattern of the derived verb forms with a weak initial radical و /w/, and conjugation A2.8 of the weak verb وَضَعَ waḍaʿa 'to put' in the appendices.

Exercises

Practise your reading:

¹يَقَعُ (ا وقع) ²جُزْءٌ مِنْ ³بُلْدَانِ (بَلَدٌ) ⁴ٱلْعَالَمِ ٱلْعَرَبِيِّ فِي آسْيَا ⁵وَيَقَعُ ٱلْجُزْءُ ⁶ٱلْآخَرُ فِي ⁷شَمَالِ إِفْرِيقْيَا .

(1) [2]Some (lit. [2]one part) of the [3]countries of the Arab [4]world [1]are (lit. is) located in Asia and [6]the others [5]are situated in [7]north Africa.

[1]بَعْدَ أَنِ [2]ٱسْتَيْقَظْتُ (X يقظ) فِي [3]ٱلصَّبَاحِ، [4]إِتَّصَلْتُ (VIII وَصَلَ) بِصَدِيقَتِي [5]هَاتِفِيًّا [6]وَٱتَّفَقْنَا (VIII وَفِقَ) عَلَى [7]مَوْعِدٍ (I وَعَدَ) فِي [8]وَسَطِ ٱلْمَدِينَةِ، [9]وَعِنْدَمَا ذَهَبْتُ إِلَى هُنَاكَ [10]وَصَلْتُ [11]مُتَأَخِّرًا [12]نِصْفَ [13]سَاعَةٍ [14]تَقْرِيبًا، [15]فَبَحَثْتُ عَنْهَا فَلَمْ [16]أَجِدْهَا (I وَجَدَ) [17]تَوَقَّعْتُ (V وَقَعَ) بِأَنْ [18]تَنْتَظِرَنِي.

(2) [1]After [2]I woke up in [3]the morning, [4]I contacted my girlfriend [5]by telephone [6]and we agreed to meet (lit. on [7]an appointment), in the [8]city centre. [9]When I went there, [10]I arrived [14]about [12]half an [13]hour [11]late. [15]I looked for her but I did not [16]find her. [17]I expected her to [18]wait for me.

[1]تَوَجَّهَ (V وَجُهَ) [2]وَفْدٌ مِنَ [3]ٱلتُّجَّارِ (تَاجِرٌ) إِلَى [4]وِزَارَةِ [5]ٱلتِّجَارَةِ [6]لِتَوْقِيعِ (II وَقَعَ) [7]ٱتِّفَاقِيَّةٍ (VIII وَفِقَ) جَدِيدَةٍ مَعَ رَئِيسِ [8]قِسْمِ [9]ٱلاِسْتِيرَادِ (X وَرَدَ) [10]وَٱلتَّصْدِيرِ فِي ٱلْوِزَارَةِ.

(3) [2]A delegation of [3]businessmen [1]went to [4]the Ministry of [5]Trade [6]to sign a new [7]agreement with the head of the [8]Department of [9]Imports [10]and Exports at the ministry.

[1]وَقَعَ [2]صُنْدُوقٌ [3]ثَقِيلٌ عَلَى [4]عَامِلٍ فِي [5]ٱلْمُسْتَوْدَعِ (X وَدَعَ) [6]فَٱتَّصَلْتُ (VIII وَصَلَ) [7]بِٱلْمَرْكَزِ [8]ٱلطِّبِّيِّ [9]ٱلْوَحِيدِ فِي [10]ٱلْمِنْطَقَةِ، [11]وَنُقِلَ إِلَيْهِ فِي [12]سَيَّارَةِ [13]ٱلإِسْعَافِ، [14]مُوَرَّمَ (II وَرِمَ) [15]ٱلْجِسْمِ [16]وَمَوْجُوعًا (I وَجِعَ) / مُتَأَلِّمًا وَأَنَا مَعَهُمْ، وَعِنْدَ [17]وُصُولِنَا (I وَصَلَ) [18]فَحَصَهُ ٱلطَّبِيبُ وَقَالَ إِنَّهُ لَمْ [19]يَجِدْ (I وَجَدَ) [20]أَيَّةَ [21]كُسُورٍ (كَسْرٌ) وَلَا [22]خَطَرَ عَلَى [23]حَيَاتِهِ.

(4) [3]A heavy [2]box [1]fell on [4]a worker in [5]the warehouse. [6]I contacted [9]the only [8]medical (health) [7]centre in [10]the area, [11]and he was taken (lit. transported) there by [12,13]ambulance (lit. [13]aid [12]car) with his [15]body [14]swollen [16]and in pain. I went (lit. I am) with them. When we [17]arrived, the physician (doctor) [18]examined him and said that he did not [19]find [20]any [21]fractures and that [23]his life was not in [22]danger.

[1]يَصِلُ (V وَصَلَ) إِلَى بَيْرُوتَ [2]غَدًا وَفْدٌ كُوَيْتِيٌّ [3]يُمَثِّلُ وِزَارَةَ [4]ٱلنَّفْطِ [5]وَفَوْرَ وُصُولِهِ [6]سَيُقَابِلُ ٱلْمَسْؤُولِينَ فِي ٱلْحُكُومَةِ ٱللُّبْنَانِيَّةِ [7]لِلتَّوْقِيعِ (II وَقَعَ) عَلَى [8]ٱتِّفَاقِيَّةٍ (VIII وَفِقَ) [9]تَتَعَلَّقُ [10]بِٱلتَّبَادُلِ [11]ٱلتِّجَارِيِّ بَيْنَ ٱلْبَلَدَيْنِ. [12]كَمَا [13]سَيَضَعُ (I وَضَعَ) ٱلْوَفْدُ ٱلْكُوَيْتِيُّ [14]تَقْرِيرًا [15]يَشْرَحُ فِيهِ [16]وِجْهَةَ [17]نَظَرِ حُكُومَةِ بِلَادِهِ [18]حَوْلَ [19]مَسْأَلَةِ [20]تَصْدِيرِ [21]ٱلنَّفْطِ [22]ٱلْخَامِ إِلَى لُبْنَانَ.

(5) A Kuwaiti delegation [3]representing the Ministry of [4]Oil [1]will arrive [2]tomorrow in Beirut, [5]and immediately after its arrival [6]will meet the officials in the Lebanese government [7]to sign [8]an agreement [9]concerning [11]trade [10]exchange between the two countries. The Kuwaiti delegation will [12]also [13]draw up [14]a report [15]explaining [16,17]the position (lit. [16]point of [17]view) of its country's government [18] on [19]the issue of [22]crude [21]oil [20]exports to Lebanon.

[1]سَأَفْقِدُ [2]ثِقَتِي (I وَثِقَ) [3]بِكَ فِي [4]حَالِ [5]عَدَمِ [6]تَوْقِيعِكَ (II وَقَعَ) عَلَى [7]ٱلِاتِّفَاقِيَّةِ (VIII وَفِقَ) [8]ٱلْمُتَّفَقِ عَلَيْهَا بَيْنَنَا، [9]وَلَنْ [10]أَتَّصِلَ (VIII وَصَلَ) بِكَ [11]ثَانِيَةً.

(6) [1]I shall lose [2]my trust [3]in you [4]if (lit. [4]in case) you [5]do not [6]sign [7]the agreement (contract) that we [8]agreed between us, [9]and I will [9]never [10]contact you [11]again.

[1]يَجِبُ أَنْ [2]تَنْظُرَ [3]يَمِينًا [4]وَيَسَارًا عِنْدَمَا [5]تَصِلُ (I وَصَلَ) بِٱلسَّيَّارَةِ إِلَى [6]مُفْتَرَقِ [7]طُرُقٍ (طَرِيقٌ) وَأَنْ [8]تَقِفَ (I وَقَفَ) عِنْدَ [9]إِشَارَةِ، [10]'قِفْ!'

(7) [1]You must [2]look [3]right [4]and left when [5]you reach [6,7]a junction (cross-roads) by car, [8]and stop at [9]the [10]'STOP!' sign.

لَا [1]تَيْأَسْ [2](I يَئِسَ) يَاعَزِيزِي إِنَّ [3]ثِقَتَكَ (I وَثِقَ) بِٱللّٰهِ [4]وَٱتِّكَالَكَ (VIII وَكَلَ) عَلَيْهِ [5]يُسَاعِدَانِكَ [6]لِلتَّغَلُّبِ عَلَى [7]هُمُومِكَ (هَمٌّ).

(8) ([2]Oh!) [2]My dear do not [1]feel hopeless. [3]Your trust in God [4]and reliance on Him [5]will help you [6]overcome [7]your worries.

‏¹إِسْتَيْقَظَ (X يَقِظَ) ²ٱلسُّوَّاحُ (سَائِحٌ) ³بَاكِرًا فِي ⁴ٱلصَّبَاحِ ⁵لِيُوَدِّعُوا
(II وَدَعَ) ⁶أَصْدِقَاءَهُمْ (صَدِيقٌ) ⁷وَيَسْتَعِدُّوا ⁸لِرِحْلَةٍ ⁹بَعِيدَةٍ ¹⁰بِٱتِّجَاهِ
(VIII وَجَّهَ) ¹¹ٱلْجُزْءِ ¹²ٱلشَّمَالِيِّ لِلْبِلَادِ.

(9) ²The tourists ¹woke up ³early in ⁴the morning ⁵to bid farewell to ⁶their friends ⁷and to get ready for ⁹a long ⁸journey ¹⁰to (¹⁰towards) ¹²the northern ¹¹part of the country.

Translate into Arabic:

(1)   Part of the Ministry of Trade is situated in the city centre.

(2)   You must stop at the 'STOP!' sign and look left and right when you reach a junction.

(3)   Part of the Arab world is situated in Asia and the other part is situated in north Africa.

(4)   The businessmen's delegation woke up early in the morning and went by car on a long journey to (towards) the northern part of Lebanon.

(5)   I contacted the head of the Department of Imports and Exports at the Ministry of Trade to sign a new agreement concerning trade exchange.

(6)   A heavy box fell on my friend (m.). I contacted the only physician in the area. The physician examined him and said that his life was not in danger.

(7)   The physician arrived about half an hour late at the medical centre.

(8)   I will never trust you or contact you again, if (in case) you sign the agreement.

(9)   A delegation from the Kuwaiti Ministry of Oil went to the Lebanese Ministry of Trade to sign an agreement to export crude oil to Lebanon and to have a trade exchange between the two countries.

Chapter 32

Verbs with a weak middle radical

32.1 Verbs with a weak middle radical, أَلْفِعْلُ ٱلْأَجْوَفُ, are those which have ʾ**alif** (.. ا..) as the middle letter of the basic verb form. This middle ʾ**alif** (.. ا..) is derived from the weak radical و /w/ or ي /y/. These types of verb are also called 'hollow' because their middle radical is lost in the basic (and many other) verb forms, e.g.

قَالَ q**ā**la, to say (for: قَوَلَ qawala) from the root قول q**w**l

بَاعَ b**ā**ʿa, to sell (for: بَيَعَ bayaʿa) from the root بيع b**y**ʿ

32.2 The first radical in the first and second persons of the basic verb form in the perfect tense receives the related vowel of the middle radical, which is itself lost, according to the rules below.

(About the three vowels and their three related consonants, see chapter 20.)

(a) If the middle radical is و /w/, then the first and second persons take **ḍammah** /u/ on the first radical in the perfect:

Perfect	***Root***	***1st pers. sing.***
قَالَ qāla, he said	(قول q**w**l)	قُلْتُ q**u**ltu, I said
كَانَ kāna, he was	(كون k**w**n)	كُنْتُ k**u**ntu, I was

(Remember from chapter 20 that و is related to **ḍammah** /u/.)

(b) If the middle radical is ي /y/, then the first and second persons take **kasrah** /i/ on the first radical in the perfect:

Perfect	*Root*	*1st pers. sing.*
بَاعَ bāʿa, he sold	(بيع byʿ)	بِعْتُ biʿtu, I sold
سَارَ sāra, he walked	(سير syr)	سِرْتُ sirtu, I walked

(Remember from chapter 20 that ي is related to **kasrah** /i/.)

32.3 In the imperfect indicative and subjunctive, the weak middle radical ..ـو.. /w/ or ..ـيـ.. /y/ reappears, but it disappears in the jussive and some of the imperative forms, e.g.

		Imperfect			*Imperative*			
Perfect	*Root*	*Ind.*	*Subj.*	*Juss.*	*Sing.*	*Plur.*	*Sing.*	*Plur.*
			Masculine		*Masculine*		*Feminine*	
قَالَ	(قول)	يَقُولُ	يَقُولَ	يَقُلْ	قُلْ	قُولُوا	قُولِي	قُلْنَ
qāla to say	(qwl)	yaqūlu	yaqūla	yaqul	qul say!	qūlū	qūlī	qulna
بَاعَ	(بيع)	يَبِيعُ	يَبِيعَ	يَبِعْ	بِعْ	بِيعُوا	بِيعِي	بِعْنَ
bāʿa to sell	(byʿ)	yabīʿu	yabīʿa	yabiʿ	biʿ sell!	bīʿū	bīʿī	biʿna

See table A1.4 for the patterns of the derived verb forms with a weak middle radical و. See paradigms A2.9 and A2.10 for the verbs قَالَ 'to say' and بَاعَ 'to sell' in Appendix 2.

32.4 A very small number of verbs with a weak middle radical و /w/ or ي /y/ also change the و or ي to ʾ**alif** (ا) in the imperfect and some forms of the imperative, e.g.

		Imperfect			*Imperative*			
Perfect	*Root*	*Ind.*	*Subj.*	*Juss.*	*Sing.*	*Plur.*	*Sing.*	*Plur.*
			Masculine		*Masculine*		*Feminine*	
نَامَ	(نوم)	يَنَامُ	يَنَامَ	يَنَمْ	نَمْ	نَامُوا	نَامِي	نِمْنَ
nāma to sleep	(nwm)	yanāmu	yanāma	yanam	nam sleep!	nāmū	nāmī	nimna
خَافَ	(خوف)	يَخَافُ	يَخَافَ	يَخَفْ	خَفْ	خَافُوا	خَافِي	خِفْنَ
ḫāfa to be afraid	(ḫwf)	yaḫāfu	yaḫāfa	yaḫaf	ḫaf be afraid!	ḫāfū	ḫāfī	ḫifna

نَالَ	(نيل)	يَنَالُ	يَنَالَ	يَنَلْ	نَلْ	نَالُوا	نَالِي	نِلْنَ
nāla	(nyl)	yanālu	yanāla	yanal	nal	nālū	nālī	nilna
to obtain					obtain!			

See conjugation A2.11 of the verb خَافَ in Appendix 2.

32.5 The weak middle radical ..و.. /w/ also becomes ..يـ... /y/ in the perfect passive. This ..يـ... /y/ is then assimilated to the preceding **kasrah**, producing the long vowel ī. See the table and the conjugation in the appendices.

Form	*Perfect* Active	Root	Passive	*Imperfect* Active	Passive
I	قَالَ qāla, to say	(قول) (qwl)	قِيلَ qīla, it was said	يَقُولُ yaqūlu	يُقَالُ yuqālu
I	بَاعَ bāᶜa, to sell	(بيع) (byᶜ)	بِيعَ bīᶜa, it was sold	يَبِيعُ yabīᶜu	يُبَاعُ yubāᶜu
IV	أَمَالَ ʾamāla, to bend	(ميل) (myl)	أُمِيلَ ʾumīla, it was bent	يُمِيلُ yumīlu	يُمَالُ yumālu
X	إِسْتَعَادَ ʾistaᶜāda, to recall	(عود) (ᶜwd)	أُسْتُعِيدَ ʾustuᶜīda, it was recalled	يَسْتَعِيدُ yastaᶜīdu	يُسْتَعَادُ yustaᶜādu

Note: The two verbs كَانَ kāna 'he was' and لَيْسَ laysa 'is not, are not' have no passive forms.

32.6 In the active participle of the basic verb form (I), the weak middle radical .ـو... /w/ or ..يـ.. /y/ is changed to **hamzah** with **kasrah** ..ئـِ..., /ʾi/, e.g.

Perfect	*Active participle*	
قَالَ qāla, to say	قَائِلٌ qāʾilun, teller, saying	(for: قَاوِلٌ qāwilun)

بَاعَ bāʿa, to sell	بَائِعٌ bāʾiʿun, seller, salesman	(for: بَايِعٌ bāyiʿun)
نَامَ nāma, to sleep	نَائِمٌ nāʾimun, sleeping	(for: نَاوِمٌ nāwimun)

Note: The passive participle of such verbs is rare.

32.7 The verbal nouns of roots with a weak middle radical are similar to the verbal nouns of the strong verbs, e.g.

Perfect	*Verbal noun*
قَالَ qāla, to say	قَوْلٌ qawlun, speech, saying
بَاعَ bāʿa, to sell	بَيْعٌ bayʿun, selling
نَامَ nāma, to sleep	نَوْمٌ nawmun, sleep

32.8 The nouns of place and time are formed as follows:

مَكَانٌ makānun, place	(v. كَانَ kāna 'to be', root **kwn**)
مَنَامٌ manāmun, place to sleep	(v. نَامَ nāma 'to sleep', root: **nwm**)
مَسَارٌ masārun, lane, route, trajectory	(v. سَارَ sāra 'to walk', root: **syr**)

32.9 The derived verb forms II, III, V and VI of roots with weak middle radicals are conjugated regularly like the derived verb forms of strong verbs. But there are exceptions in the verb forms IV, VII, VIII and X, where the weak radicals reappear.

See table A1.4 for the patterns of derived verb forms of roots with a weak middle radical و or ي in Appendix 1.

32.10 *Tenses formed with* كَانَ *kāna*

The verb كَانَ kāna 'to be' (lit. 'he was') can be used in the perfect or imperfect tense as an auxiliary preceding another verb in the perfect or imperfect tense:

(a) Past perfect (pluperfect)

كَانَ (قَدْ) كَتَبَ kāna (qad) kataba, he had written

لَمَّا شَاهَدْتُهُ كَانَ (قَدْ) كَتَبَ ٱلرِّسَالَةَ

lammā šāhadtu-hu **kāna** (qad) **kataba** r-risālata.

When I saw him, **he had** (already) **written** the letter.

Remember: قَدْ qad is inserted to emphasize the finality of the action or for reasons of style.

(b) Past progressive or habitual

كَانَ يَكْتُبُ kāna yaktubu, he was writing, he has been writing
he had been writing, he used to write (everyday)

لَمَّا شَاهَدْتُهُ كَانَ يَشْرَبُ قَهْوَةً lammā šāhadtu-hu **kāna yašrabu** qahwatan.
When I saw him, he **was drinking** coffee.

كَانَ يَشْرَبُ شَايًا كُلَّ يَوْمٍ kāna **yašrabu** šāyan kulla yawmin.
He **used to drink** tea every day.

(c) Future in the past (future of perfect)

كَانَ سَيَكْتُبُ kāna sa-yaktubu, he was going to write

Note: سَوْفَ sawfa is not used after كَانَ kāna.

(d) Past in the future (perfect of future)

يَكُونُ (قَدْ) كَتَبَ yakūnu (qad) kataba, he will have written

عِنْدَمَا أَصِلُ إِلَيْهِ يَكُونُ (قَدْ) كَتَبَ ٱلرِّسَالَةَ

ʿindamā ʾaṣilu ʾilayhi yakūnu (qad) kataba r-risālata.

When I reach him, **he will have written** the letter.

Exercises

Practise your reading:

لَمَّا [1]خَرَجَ [2]ٱلْمُعَاقُ مِنَ [3]ٱلطَّائِرَةِ كَانَ [4]مُتَّكِئًا (VIII وَكَأَ) عَلَى [5]عَصًا
وَمَعَهُ [6]مُضِيفَتَانِ [7]تُسَاعِدَانِهِ.

(1) When [2]the disabled (handicapped) person [1]left the [3]aeroplane, [4]he was leaning on [5]a walking stick, and there were [6]two stewardesses ([6]flight attendants) [7]helping him.

[1]لَيْتَكَ [2]زُرْتَنِي (I زَارَ) قَبْلَ أَنْ [3]تُسَافِرَ لِأَنَّنِي [4]مُشْتَاقَةٌ إِلَيْكَ. وَعِنْدَمَا يَكُونُ
[5]بِٱسْتِطَاعَتِكَ فَٱكْتُبْ لِي [6]رِسَالَةً [7]وَضَعْ (I وَضَعَ) فِيهَا [8]صُورَتَكَ!

(2) [1]I wish you had [2]visited me before [3]you left, because [4]I miss you. Whenever [5]you can, write me [6]a letter [7]and put [8]your photograph in it!

[1]أَنْصَحُكَ أَنْ لَا [2]تَأْكُلَ قَبْلَ ٱلذَّهَابِ إِلَى [3]ٱلنَّوْمِ لِأَنَّهُ [4]قَدْ [5]يُسَبِّبُ لَكَ
[6]زِيَادَةً فِي [7]ٱلْوَزْنِ.

(3) [1]I advise you not [2]to eat before going [3]to sleep because [4]it might [5]cause you [6]to gain [7]weight.

[1]عِنْدِي سَيَّارَةٌ [2]قَدِيمَةٌ لٰكِنَّهَا [3]دَائِمًا فِي [4]ٱلتَّصْلِيحِ [5]فَأُرِيدُ أَنْ [6]أَبِيعَهَا أَوْ
[7]أُبْدِلَهَا بِسَيَّارَةٍ [8]أُخْرَى [9]وَلٰكِنِّي لَمْ [10]أَخْتَرِ [11]ٱلصِّنْفَ [12]بَعْدُ [13]لِأَنَّ ذٰلِكَ
[14]يَتَوَقَّفُ عَلَى [15]بَيْعِ سَيَّارَتِي [16]أَوَّلًا.

(4) [1]I have [2]an old car but it [3]is always being [4]repaired. [5]I want [6]to sell it or [7]exchange it for [8]another car [9]but I have not [10]chosen [11]the type [12]yet [13]because that [14]depends on [15]selling my car [16]first.

[1]قُمْ يَا شَابُّ عَنِ [2]ٱلْكُرْسِيِّ [3]وَٱسْمَحْ [4]لِلضَّيْفِ بِأَنْ [5]يَجْلِسَ فِي [6]مَكَانِكَ!

(5) Oh young man! [1]Stand up (from [2]the chair) [3]and let [4]the guest [5]sit down [6]instead (in [6]your place)!

ذَهَبْتُ [1]لِزِيَارَةِ [2]جَدِّي فِي مَنْزِلِهِ فَكَانَ [3]نَائِمًا فِي [4]غُرْفَةِ ٱلنَّوْمِ، [5]فَجَلَسْتُ
[6]بَعْضَ [7]ٱلْوَقْتِ فِي [8]غُرْفَةِ ٱلْجُلُوسِ [9]مَعَ [10]جَدَّتِي حَتَّى [11]قَامَ مِنَ [12]ٱلنَّوْمِ.
[13]فَفَرِحَ [14]بِمُشَاهَدَتِي [15]وَجَلَسَ [16]بِجِوَارِي، [17]يَتَحَدَّثُ عَنْ [18]سُوءِ [19]حَالَتِهِ

[20]ٱلصِّحِّيَّةِ، [21]وَصَارَ [22]يَخَافُ مِنَ [23]ٱلْمَوْتِ [24]فَقُلْتُ لَهُ: لاَ [25]تَخَفْ فَإِنَّ [26]ٱلْعُمْرَ [27]بِيَدِ ٱللّٰهِ [28]وَحْدَهُ.

(6) I went [1]to visit [2]my grandfather at his house. He was [3]asleep in [4]the bedroom, so [5]I sat in [8]the sitting room for [6,7]a while (lit. [6]for some [7]time) [9]with [10]my grandmother until [11]he got up (from [12]sleep). [13]He was pleased [14]to see me [15]and sat [16]next to me, [17]talking about his [18]bad ([19]state of) [20]health. [21]He began [22]to be afraid of [23]dying, so [24]I said to him: 'Don't [25]be afraid – the [26]lifespan is [27]in the hands of God [28]alone.'

[1]لَوْ [2]لَمْ [3]يَكُنِ [4]ٱلْقَانُونُ فِي [5]ٱلدُّوَلِ (دَوْلَةٌ) [6]ٱلْمُتَحَضِّرَةِ [7]مُطَبَّقًا [8]وَمُحْتَرَمًا، [9]لَمَا [10]سَادَ [11]ٱلْأَمْنُ [12]وَٱلْعَدَالَةُ.

(7) [1]If [4]the law in (the) [6]civilized [5]countries [3]was [2]not [7]applied [8]and respected, then [11]safety [12]and justice [9]would not [10]prevail.

[1]يُقَالُ إِنَّ هُنَاكَ [2]إِشَاعَةً [3]تَقُولُ إِنَّ [4]غِيَابَ ٱلرَّئِيسِ [5]ٱلطَّوِيلَ عَنِ [6]ٱجْتِمَاعَاتِ [7]مَجْلِسِ ٱلْوُزَرَاءِ (وَزِيرٌ) [8]سَبَبُهُ [9]مَرَضُهُ [10]ٱلْخَطِيرُ، وَأَنَّ [11]مَوْتَهُ [12]قَدْ [13]يُسَبِّبُ [14]أَزْمَةً [15]سِيَاسِيَّةً فِي ٱلْبِلَادِ.

(8) [2]Rumour has it (lit. [1]it is said that there is a [2]rumour [3]saying) that the president's [5]long [4]absence from the cabinet (lit. [7]the Council of Ministers) [6]meetings is [8]because of his [10]serious [9]illness, and that [11]his death [12]might [13]cause [15]a political [14]crisis in the country.

[1]قَادَ / سَاقَ ٱلسَّيَّارَةَ وَكَانَ قَدْ [2]نَسِيَ [3]رُخْصَةَ / إِجَازَةَ [4]ٱلسَّوْقِ فِي ٱلْبَيْتِ [5]فَأَوْقَفَتْهُ [6]دَوْرِيَّةٌ مِنَ [7]ٱلشُّرْطَةِ. [8]فَسَأَلُوهُ عَنِ ٱلرُّخْصَةِ.

[9]أَجَابَ أَنَّهُ قَدْ [10]نَسِيَهَا فِي ٱلْبَيْتِ. [11]فَلَمْ [12]يُصَدِّقُوهُ [13]حَتَّى [14]أَعَادُوهُ إِلَى ٱلْبَيْتِ [15]وَشَاهَدُوا [16]ٱلْإِجَازَةَ [17]بِأَعْيُنِهِمْ (عَيْنٌ).

(9) [1]He drove the car, but had [2]left (lit. [2]forgotten) [4]the driving [3]licence at home. A [7]police [6]patrol [5]stopped him and [8]asked him for his licence. [9]He replied that [10]he had left it (lit. [10]forgot it) at home, but they [11]did not [12]believe him [13]until [14]they had taken (lit. returned) him home [15]and seen [16]the licence [17]with their own eyes.

[1]سَافَرْتُ إِلَى عَمَّانَ [2]لأَزُورَ [3]صَدِيقًا [4]لِي [5]يَسْكُنُ هُنَاكَ وَقَدْ [6]قُمْنَا [7]مَعًا
[8]بِزِيَارَةٍ إِلَى مَدِينَةِ ٱلْعَقَبَةِ عَلَى [9]ٱلْبَحْرِ [10]ٱلْأَحْمَرِ. [11]فَأَخَذْنَا [12]حَافِلَةً
[13]سِيَاحِيَّةً، وَفِي [14]طَرِيقِنَا [15]مَرَرْنَا عَلَى ٱلْمَدِينَةِ [16]ٱلْأَثَرِيَّةِ أَلْبَتْرَاءَ.
[17]فَتَجَوَّلْنَا فِيهَا [18]أَكْثَرَ مِنْ [19]سَاعَتَيْنِ. [20]ثُمَّ [21]تَابَعْنَا [22]طَرِيقَنَا إِلَى
ٱلْعَقَبَةِ. [23]وَبَعْدَ أَنْ [24]أَقَمْنَا [25]لِمُدَّةِ [26]أُسْبُوعٍ فِي ٱلْعَقَبَةِ [27]عُدْنَا إِلَى
عَمَّانَ [28]وَمِنْ هُنَاكَ [29]عُدْتُ إِلَى بَيْرُوتَ.

(10) [1]I travelled to Amman [2]to visit [3]a friend [4]of mine who [5]lives there, and [7]together [6]we went [8]to visit the city of Aqaba on the [10]Red [9]Sea. [11]We took [13]a tour ([13]tourism) [12]bus and on [14]our way [15]we passed by the [16]ancient city of Petra, so [17]we wandered around it (trekked through it) for [18]more than [19]two hours. [20]Then [21]we continued on [22]our way to Aqaba. [23]After [24]we had stayed for [26]a week (lit. for one week's [25]time) in Aqaba, [27]we went back to Amman, [28]and from there [29]I returned to Beirut.

Translate into Arabic:

(1) The law is applied and respected in the country.

(2) I travelled by aeroplane with a friend to Beirut, Amman and Aqaba.

(3) I wish you had visited my grandfather before his serious illness.

(4) I advise you to sit for some time in the sitting room with my grandmother.

(5) I have an old chair that I want to sell (it) to a friend of mine who lives in Amman.

(6) The young man left (forgot) his driving licence, letter and (his) photograph on the bus.

(7) Write to me whenever you can because I miss you.

(8) (إِنَّ) The death of the president might cause a political crisis in the country.

(9) I travelled by coach (a tour bus) with a friend, who sat beside me talking about his bad state of health.

(10) The stewardess helped my grandfather when he left the aeroplane.

(11) The young man let the guest sit on a chair in the sitting room.

(12) My grandmother began to be afraid of death. I told her not to be afraid since one's lifespan is in the hands of God alone.

(13) When the young disabled man got out of the car, he was leaning on a walking stick.

(14) Rumour has it that the president was stopped by a police patrol and asked for his driving licence.

(15) My guest and I took a coach (a tour bus) to the ancient city of Petra. We wandered around it (trekked through it) for more than two hours.

Chapter 33

Verbs with a weak final radical, doubly weak verbs and weak verbs with hamzah

33.1 Verbs with a weak final radical و /w/ or ي /y/ are called defective verbs أَلْفِعْلُ ٱلنَّاقِص. The final weak radical appears as ʾ**alif** ا /ā/ or ʾ**alif maqṣūrah** ى /ā/ in the basic verb form (perfect, third person masc. sing.) upon combining with the personal ending. The defective verbs fall into the following categories according to their vocalization.

33.2 If the final radical is و /w/, then the basic form (perfect, third person masc. sing.) ends in ʾ**alif** ا... /...ā/ (contraction of...a-**w**-a), and the imperfect (in most persons) ends in ...وُ /...ū/ (contraction of...u-**w**-u), e.g.

Perfect *(3. masc. sing.)*		**Imperfect** *(3. masc. sing.)*
دَعَا	(for: دَعَوَ	يَدْعُو
daʿā, to invite	daʿawa)	yadʿū
غَزَا	(for: غَزَوَ	يَغْزُو
ġazā, to raid	ġazawa)	yaġzū

33.3 If the final radical is ي /y/ and the middle radical has the vowel **kasrah** /i/, then the basic form ends quite regularly in ...ِيَ /...iya/, but the imperfect ends in ʾ**alif maqṣūrah** ...َى /...ā/ (contraction of ...a-y-u), e.g.

Perfect *(3. masc. sing.)*	**Imperfect** *(3. masc. sing.)*	
لَقِيَ	يَلْقَى	(for: يَلْقَيُ
laqiya, to meet	yalqā	yalqayu)

نَسِيَ nasiya, to forget	يَنْسَى yansā	(for: يَنْسَيُ yansayu)

33.4 If the final radical is ي /y/ and the middle radical has the vowel **fatḥah** /a/, then the basic form ends in ʾ**alif maqṣūrah** ى.... /...ā/ (contraction of ...a-y-a), and the imperfect ends in ...ِي /...ī/ (contraction of ...i-y-u):

Perfect *(3. masc. sing.)*		***Imperfect*** *(3. masc. sing.)*
قَضَى qaḍā, to judge	(for: قَضَيَ qaḍaya)	يَقْضِي yaqḍī
رَمَى ramā, to throw	(for: رَمَيَ ramaya)	يَرْمِي yarmī

33.5 A very small number of verbs, of the type discussed above in paragraph 33.4, have ʾ**alif maqṣūrah** ـَى... /...ā/ (contraction of ...a-y-u) also in the imperfect tense, e.g.

Perfect *(3. masc. sing.)*		***Imperfect*** *(3. masc. sing.)*	
سَعَى saʿā, to strive	(for: سَعَيَ saʿaya)	يَسْعَى yasʿā	(for: يَسْعَيُ yasʿayu)
نَهَى nahā, to forbid	(for: نَهَيَ nahaya)	يَنْهَى yanhā	(for: يَنْهَيُ yanhayu)

33.6 All verb forms I–X of roots with a weak final radical ـو.... /w/ or ي... /y/ omit this final radical in the jussive and imperative, e.g.

Perfect	***Imperf. ind.***	***Imperf. juss.***	***Imperative***
رَمَى ramā, to throw	يَرْمِي yarmī	يَرْمِ yarmi	!إِرْمِ ʾirmi!
رَجَا raǧā, to hope	يَرْجُو yarǧū	يَرْجُ yarǧu	!أُرْجُ ʾurǧu!
إِرْتَضَى (VIII) ʾirtaḍā, to be satisfied	يَرْتَضِي yartaḍī	يَرْتَضِ yartaḍi	!إِرْتَضِ ʾirtaḍi!

33.7 The passive of all verbs with a weak final radical و... /w/ or ي... /y/ is conjugated according to the same pattern as the strong verbs, e.g.

Active Perfect	Passive Perfect	Passive Imperfect Ind.	Subj.	Juss.
دَعَا daʿā, to invite	دُعِيَ duʿiya	يُدْعَى yudʿā	يُدْعَى yudʿā	يُدْعَ yudʿa
لَقِيَ laqiya, to meet	لُقِيَ luqiya	يُلْقَى yulqā	يُلْقَى yulqā	يُلْقَ yulqa
رَمَى ramā, to throw	رُمِيَ rumiya	يُرْمَى yurmā	يُرْمَى yurmā	يُرْمَ yurma
سَعَى saʿā, to strive	سُعِيَ suʿiya	يُسْعَى yusʿā	يُسْعَى yusʿā	يُسْعَ yusʿa

33.8 The conjugation of the derived verb forms II–X of verbs with a weak final radical و... /...w/ or ي... /...y/ is identical to that of the derived verb forms of strong verbs. There is an exception with some verbal nouns where the weak final radical after the **ʾalif** is changed to **hamzah**, e.g. لِقَاءٌ liqāʾun 'meeting' (for: لِقَايٌ liqāyun) from the root لقي lqy 'to meet'.

See the pattern tables of verbs with a weak final radical و /w/ or ي /y/ and their conjugations in the appendices.

33.9 The declension of the active participle of verbs with a weak final radical و... /w/ or ي... /y/ is illustrated below with the help of the active participle قَاضٍ qāḍin 'judge', from the verb قَضَى qaḍā 'to judge'. It should be noted that the active participle has only two case endings in the masculine singular: /...in/ for both the nominative and genitive and /...an/ for the accusative:

	masc. indef.	masc. def.	fem. indef.
		singular	
Nom.	قَاضٍ (for: قَاضِيٌ) qāḍ**in** qāḍiy**un**)	أَلْقَاضِي (for: أَلْقَاضِيُ ʾal-qāḍ**ī** ʾal-qāḍ**iyu**)	قَاضِيَةٌ qāḍiyat**un**
Gen.	قَاضٍ (for: قَاضِيٍ) qāḍ**in** qāḍiy**in**)	أَلْقَاضِي (for: أَلْقَاضِيِ ʾal-qāḍ**ī** ʾal-qāḍ**iyi**)	قَاضِيَةٍ qāḍiyat**in**
Acc.	قَاضِيًا qāḍiy**an**	أَلْقَاضِيَ ʾal-qāḍi**ya**	قَاضِيَةً qāḍiyat**an**
		dual	
Nom.	قَاضِيَانِ qāḍiy**āni**	أَلْقَاضِيَانِ ʾal-qāḍiy**āni**	قَاضِيَتَانِ qāḍiyat**āni**
Acc. and gen.	قَاضِيَيْنِ qāḍiy**ayni**	أَلْقَاضِيَيْنِ ʾal-qāḍiy**ayni**	قَاضِيَتَيْنِ qāḍiyat**ayni**
		plural	
Nom.	قَاضُونَ qāḍ**ūna**	أَلْقَاضُونَ ʾal-qāḍ**ūna**	قَاضِيَاتٌ qāḍiyāt**un**
Acc. and gen.	قَاضِينَ qāḍ**īna**	أَلْقَاضِينَ ʾal-qāḍ**īna**	قَاضِيَاتٍ qāḍiyāt**in**

Note: A common plural for both masc. and fem. is the broken plural قُضَاةٌ quḍātun.

33.10 *Doubly weak verbs*

Some of the most common verbs have the two weak radicals و /w/ and ي /y/. They are called in Arabic أَللَّفِيفُ. The following are the most common types:

(a) Verbs with و /w/ or ي /y/ as initial and final radical: These verbs obey both the rules for verbs with a weak initial radical as well as the rules for verbs with a weak final radical, e.g.

Perfect	***Imperfect***			***Imperative***			
	Ind.	***Subj.***	***Juss.***	***Singular***		***Plural***	
				Masc.	***Fem.***	***Masc.***	***Fem.***
وَقَى	يَقِي	يَقِيَ	يَقِ	قِ	قِي	قُوا	قِينَ
waqā	yaqī	yaqiya	yaqi	qi!	qī!	qū!	qīna!
to protect, prevent							

The active participle is وَاقٍ wāqin 'protective, preservative' and is declined like قَاضٍ qāḍin 'judge'. The verbal noun (**maṣdar**) is وِقَاءٌ wiqāʾun or وِقَايَةٌ wiqāyatun 'protection, prevention'.

Note: Verb form VIII is very common for the above-mentioned verb, being إِتَّقَى ʾittaqā 'to fear God' (Quranic), for إِوْتَقَى ʾiwtaqā. The verbal noun (**maṣdar**) of form VIII of this verb is إِتِّقَاءٌ ʾittiqāʾun.

(b) Verbs with **wāw** و /w/ and **yāʾ** ي /y/ as second and third radical, respectively, are conjugated in the same way as verbs with a weak final radical. The weak middle radical و /w/ or ي /y/ is fully pronounced, e.g.

Perfect	***Imperfect***
شَوَى šawā, to grill, barbecue (for: شَوَيَ šawaya)	يَشْوِي yašwī
(conjugated like v. رَمَى ramā, to throw	يَرْمِي yarmī)
قَوِيَ qawiya, to be strong	يَقْوَى yaqwā
(conjugated like v. نَسِيَ nasiya, to forget	يَنْسَى yansā)

33.11 *Weak verbs with hamzah*

Verbs with a weak middle radical ...و... /w/ or ...يـ... /y/ and final **hamzah** are very common, e.g.

Perfect	*Imperfect*
جَاءَ ǧāʾa, to come (for: جَيَأَ ǧayaʾa)	يَجِيءُ yaǧīʾu
شَاءَ šāʾa, to wish (for: شَيَءَ šayaʾa)	يَشَاءُ yašāʾu
سَاءَ sāʾa, to be bad (for: سَوَأَ sawaʾa)	يَسُوءُ yasūʾu

33.12 Verbs with a middle **hamzah** and final **ʾalif-maqṣūrah** ى (in the basic form) are rare, but include the common verb رَأَى raʾā 'to see'. In the perfect it is conjugated like verbs with a final **ʾalif maqṣūrah** ...ى, but in the imperfect the middle **hamzah** أَ /...ʾa.../ is, exceptionally, omitted:

Perfect	*Imperfect*
رَأَى raʾā, to see (for: رَأَيَ raʾaya)	يَرَى yarā (for: يَرْأَى)
(conjugated like v. رَمَى ramā, 'to throw')	

Note: The middle **hamzah** is also omitted in form IV: أَرَى ʾarā 'he showed', which in the imperfect is يُرِي yurī. (See paradigm A2.16 in Appendix 2.)

Exercises

Practise your reading:

هٰؤُلَاءِ ¹ٱلتُّجَّارُ (تَاجِرٌ) ²يَشْتَرُونَ ³وَيَبِيعُونَ ⁴بَضَائِعَ (بِضَاعَةٌ) ⁵مُهَرَّبَةً فِي ⁶ٱلسُّوقِ.

(1) These ¹traders (merchants) are ²buying ³and selling ⁵smuggled ⁴goods in ⁶the market.

¹بَعْدَ أَنْ ²أَمْضَيْنَا ³حَوَالَيْ ⁴أَرْبَعِ سَاعَاتٍ ⁵نَتَمَشَّى فِي ⁶ٱلْغَابَةِ ⁷دَعَانَا ⁸أَحَدُ ⁹زُمَلَائِنَا (زَمِيلٌ) إِلَى ¹⁰ٱلْعَشَاءِ فِي مَنْزِلِهِ.

(2) ¹After ²we spent ³around ⁴four hours ⁵walking (strolling) in ⁶the forest, ⁸one of ⁹our colleagues ⁷invited us to ¹⁰dinner at his home.

هَلْ ¹أَتَيْتَ مِنَ ²ٱلشَّارِعِ؟ لَا، أَتَيْتُ مِنَ ³ٱلدُّكَّانِ.

(3) Did ¹you come (in) from ²the street? No, I came from ³the shop.

[1]لَمْ [2]أَرَ فِي [3]عُمْرِي [4]أَجْمَلَ مِنْ هٰذِهِ [5]ٱلْفَتَاةِ.

(4) I have [1]never in [3]my life [2]seen [4]a more beautiful [5]young girl than this.

[1]نَلْتَقِي فِي [2]ٱلْأُسْبُوعِ [3]ٱلْآتِي، [4]إِنْ [5]شَاءَ ٱللّٰهُ.

(5) [1]We will meet [3]next [2]week, God [5]willing (lit. [4]if God [5]wills).

[1]حُكِيَ أَنَّ مُعَلِّمَ [2]ٱلرِّيَاضَةِ فِي مَدْرَسَةِ [3]قَرْيَتِي، [4]وَيُدْعَى عَلِيًّا، [5]قَدْ
[6]يُسْتَدْعَى لِيَكُونَ [7]أَحَدَ [8]ٱلْحُكَّامِ (حَكَمٌ) فِي [9]مُبَارَيَاتِ (مُبَارَاةٌ)
[10]ٱلْأَنْدِيَةِ (نَادٍ) [11]لِلْمُصَارَعَةِ ٱلَّتِي [12]سَتُقَامُ (قَامَ) فِي ٱلْعَاصِمَةِ.

(6) [1]It was said that [2]the sports teacher at [3]my village school, [4]who is called Ali, [5]may [6]be invited to be [7]one of [8]the judges at the [11]wrestling [9]matches that are [12]taking place in [10]clubs in the capital.

[1]إِسْتَأْتُ جِدّاً ٱلْيَومَ [2]عِنْدَمَا [3]ٱلْتَقَيْتُ [4]فَجْأَةً فِي [5]ٱلشَّارِعِ بِصَدِيقٍ [6]لَمْ
[7]أَرَهُ [8]مُنْذُ [9]زَمَنٍ [10]طَوِيلٍ، [11]فَاجَأَنِي [12]بِسُؤَالٍ عَنْ [13]صِحَّةِ [14]إِشَاعَةٍ
[15]تَرْوِي أَنِّي [16]طَلَّقْتُ زَوْجَتِي [17]نَفَيْتُ ذٰلِكَ [18]طَبْعاً وَقُلْتُ لَهُ [19]إِنَّهَا [20]فَقَطْ
[21]إِشَاعَةٌ [22]كَاذِبَةٌ.

(7) Today I was very much [1]offended, [2]when I [4]suddenly [3]met a friend in [5]the street whom I have [6]not [7]seen [8]for a [10]long [9]time. [11]He surprised me when he [12]asked about [13]the truth of [14]a rumour (that [15]says) that [16]I have divorced my wife. [18]Of course [17]I denied it and told him [19]that it is [20]only a [22]false [21]rumour.

لَا [1]تَنْسَ أَنْ [2]تَأْتِيَ ٱلْيَوْمَ [3]لِسَمَاعِ [4]ٱلْمُحَاضَرَةِ ٱلَّتِي [5]سَيُلْقِيهَا [6]بَاحِثٌ
فِي [7]قَضِيَّةِ [8]ٱللَّاجِئِينَ (لَاجِئٌ). [9]آسِفٌ جِدّاً أَنَا [10]لَسْتُ (v. لَيْسَ)
[11]آتِيًا لِأَنِّي عَلَى [12]مَوْعِدٍ [13]لِشِرَاءِ [14]شِقَّةٍ جَدِيدَةٍ.

(8) Do not [1]forget [2]to come today [3]to hear [4]the lecture which [5]will be delivered by [6]a researcher on the [8]refugee [7]issue. [9]I am very sorry [10]I am not [11]coming because I have [12]an appointment [13]to buy a new [14]flat (apartment).

[1]عَفْوًا لَا [2]أُرِيدُ أَنْ [3]أَبْقَى فِي [4]ٱلدَّاخِلِ [5]وَٱلْجَوُّ جَمِيلٌ [6]وَصَافٍ. [7]تَعَالَ [8]نَتَمَشَّى فِي ٱلسُّوقِ وَفِي [9]نَفْسِ [10]ٱلْوَقْتِ [11]أَشْتَرِي [12]هَدِيَّةً [13]أَوْصَتْنِي عَلَيْهَا [14]أُخْتِي.

(9) [1]Sorry, I do not [2]want [3]to stay [4]indoors (inside) in this nice [6]clear [5]weather. [7]Come and [8]walk in the market and at [9]the same [10]time [11]I will buy [12]a gift which [14]my sister [13]has asked me for.

[1]دَعَوْتُ [2]ٱلْبَارِحَةَ بَعْضَ [3]ٱلْأَصْدِقَاءِ (صَدِيقٌ) عَلَى فِنْجَانِ قَهْوَةٍ فِي [4]أَحَدِ ٱلْمَقَاهِي (مَقْهًى)، وَلٰكِنِّي [5]لِسُوءِ [6]ٱلْحَظِّ [7]نَسِيتُ [8]نُقُودِي فِي ٱلْبَيْتِ، [9]فَدَفَعَ أَحَدُهُمْ [10]ٱلْحِسَابَ. [11]كَمَا [12]أَعْطَانِي [13]مَبْلَغًا صَغِيرًا [14]لِأَشْتَرِيَ بَعْضَ [15]ٱلْأَشْيَاءِ (شَيْءٌ) ٱلَّتِي [16]أَحْتَاجُهَا فِي ٱلْبَيْتِ.

(10) [2]Yesterday [1]I invited some [3]friends for a cup of coffee in [4]a cafe (lit. in [4]one of the coffee shops), but [5]unfortunately (lit. [5]bad [6]luck, fortune) [7]I left (lit. [7]I forgot) [8]my money at home, so one of them [9]paid [10]the bill. He [11]also [12]gave me a small [13]sum [14]to buy some [15]things which [16]I need at home.

[1]ضَابِطٌ [2]ذُو [3]رُتْبَةٍ [4]عَالِيَةٍ فِي [5]ٱلْجَيْشِ، [6]دَنَا فِي [7]ٱلْمَأْتَمِ مِنْ [8]جُثْمَانِ [9]ٱلْجُنْدِيِّ [10]ٱلشَّهِيدِ، [11]فَحَيَّاهُ [12]تَحِيَّةً [13]عَسْكَرِيَّةً [14]وَحَنَى [15]رَأْسَهُ لَهُ.

(11) At [7]the funeral [4]a high-[2,3]ranking [1]officer in [5]the army [6]approached [10]the martyred [9]soldier's [8]body. [11]He [11]saluted him with [13]a military [12]salute [14]and bowed [15]his head towards him.

[1]تُوُفِّيَ وَالِدُ أَحَدِ أَصْدِقَائِي [2]فَأَرْسَلْتُ لِصَدِيقِي [3]رِسَالَةَ [4]ٱلتَّعْزِيَةِ [5]ٱلتَّالِيَةَ: [6]أُؤَكِّدُ [7]لَكَ أَنَّ [8]ٱلْخَبَرَ [9]ٱلْمُحْزِنَ [10]بِوَفَاةِ وَالِدِكَ [11]جَعَلَنِي [12]مُشَارِكًا [13]لِأَحْزَانِكَ (حُزْنٌ) فِي هٰذِهِ [14]ٱلْمَأْسَاةِ.

(12) The father of one of my friends [1]died [2]so I sent my friend [5]the following [3]letter of [4]condolence: "[6]I assure [7]you that [9]the sad [8]news of your father's [10]death [11]made me [12]share [13]the sadness of [14]your tragedy with you.'

ذَهَبْتُ [1]مَسَافَةً طَوِيلَةً عَلَى [2]ٱلْأَقْدَامِ (قَدَمٌ) [3]لِأُصَلِّيَ [4]صَلَاةَ [5]ٱلظُّهْرِ فِي
[6]ٱلْجَامِعِ [7]وَلِأَسْتَمِعَ [8]لِتِلَاوَاتٍ جَمِيلَةٍ مِنَ ٱلْقُرْآنِ [9]ٱلْكَرِيمِ.

(13) I went a long [1]way (distance) [2]on foot [3]to pray (perform) [5]the noon [4]prayer in [6]the mosque [7]and to hear (some) beautiful [8]recitations from the [9]Holy Quran.

لَمْ [1]نَرَ [2]أَخَاكَ [3]سِوَى [4]مَرَّةٍ [5]وَاحِدَةٍ [6]طِيلَةَ [7]ٱلْفَتْرَةِ ٱلَّتِي [8]قَضَيْنَاهَا
[9]هُنَا، [10]أُدْعُهُ مَرَّةً إِلَى [11]ٱلْغَدَاءِ أَوِ [12]ٱلْعَشَاءِ!

(14) We only saw your brother [4,5]once (lit. we did not [1]see [2]your brother [3]except [5]one [4]time) [6]during [7]the time [8]we spent [9]here. [10]Invite him some time (lit. once) to [11]lunch or [12]dinner!

[1]جَاءَ [2]ٱلْمُشَاهِدُونَ [3]لِيَرَوْا [4]ٱلْمُبَارَاةَ [5]ٱلنِّهَائِيَّةَ فِي [6]كُرَةِ [7]ٱلْقَدَمِ [8]بَيْنَ
[9]ٱلسُّوَيْدِ [10]وَأَلْمَانْيَا.

(15) [2]The spectators [1]came [3]to see the [5]final [6,7]football [4]match [8]between [9]Sweden and [10]Germany.

لَقَدْ [1]أَخْطَأْتُ مَعَكِ يَا أُمِّي، [2]فَلَا [3]تَبْكِي! [4]وَٱلَّذِي [5]جَرَى [6]قَدْ [7]مَضَى
[8]وَأَرْجُو [9]ٱلْمَعْذِرَةَ.

(16) [1]I have wronged you, mother, [2]don't [3]cry! [4]What [5]happened [7]is [6]already [7]passed [8]and I ask (your) [9]forgiveness.

Translate into Arabic:

(1) Next week is the army officer's funeral.

(2) My brother invited me to dinner at his new flat.

(3) In all my life I have never seen a cafe more beautiful than this one.

(4) Have you come from the lecture? No, I came with my wife from the forest.

(5) A researcher from Germany will deliver a lecture on the refugee issue.

(6) Rumour has it (says) that the martyred soldier died yesterday.

(7) Sorry, I don't want to stay inside the shop in this nice clear weather.

(8) A high ranking officer in the army might be invited to be the referee in the final football match between Sweden and Germany.

(9) Today, I met a colleague whom I had not seen for a long time.

(10) Do not forget to come with me today to the mosque to hear some beautiful recitations from the Holy Quran.

(11) I went a long way on foot with my girlfriend to have lunch at the football club in the capital.

(12) After I spent around four hours walking in the market with the sports teacher he invited me to dinner at the village school.

(13) Unfortunately, this trader (merchant) is buying smuggled goods and selling them in the market.

Chapter 34

Cardinal numbers

34.1 The Arabic cardinal numbers, أَلْأَعْدَادُ ٱلْأَصْلِيَّةُ, are rather complicated and even native speakers make errors in using them. It is important to remember that the numbers 3–10 take the feminine form with **tāʾ marbūṭah** (ة...) when they qualify a masculine noun, but the masculine form when they qualify a feminine noun.

34.2 With the exception of the feminine form إِحْدَى ʾiḥdā, 'one', the cardinal numbers 1–10 are inflected for all three cases in the same way as nouns and adjectives.

The nominative forms of the cardinal numbers 1–10 are:

		Used with a masculine noun	Used with a feminine noun
0	.	صِفْرٌ ṣifrun	صِفْرٌ ṣifrun
1	١	أَحَدٌ ʾaḥadun (noun)	إِحْدَى ʾiḥdā (indecl.)
1	١	وَاحِدٌ wāḥidun (adj.)	وَاحِدَةٌ wāḥidatun
2	٢	إِثْنَانِ ʾiṯnāni	إِثْنَتَانِ ʾiṯnatāni
3	٣	ثَلَاثَةٌ ṯalāṯatun	ثَلَاثٌ ṯalāṯun
4	٤	أَرْبَعَةٌ ʾarbaʿatun	أَرْبَعٌ ʾarbaʿun
5	٥	خَمْسَةٌ ḫamsatun	خَمْسٌ ḫamsun
6	٦	سِتَّةٌ sittatun	سِتٌّ sittun
7	٧	سَبْعَةٌ sabʿatun	سَبْعٌ sabʿun
8	٨	ثَمَانِيَةٌ ṯamāniyatun	ثَمَانٍ ṯamānin

9	٩	تِسْعَةٌ tisʿatun	تِسْعٌ tisʿun
10	١٠	عَشَرَةٌ ʿašaratun	عَشْرٌ ʿašrun

Note a: صِفْرٌ ṣifrun 'zero' comes from the verb صَفَرَ, which means 'to be empty'.

Note b: The combined accusative-genitive forms of إِثْنَانِ ʾiṯnāni (m.) and إِثْنَتَانِ ʾiṯnatāni (f.) 'two' are: إِثْنَيْنِ ʾiṯnayni (m.) and إِثْنَتَيْنِ ʾiṯnatayni (f.), respectively.

Note c: The number ثَمَانٍ 'eight' is declined like the participle قَاضٍ (see chapter 33 for verbs with a weak final radical).

Note d: The middle consonant ش /š/ in عَشَرَةٌ / عَشْرٌ 'ten' takes **fatḥah** in the masculine: عَشَرَةٌ, but **sukūn** in the feminine: عَشْرٌ.

34.3 The Arabic cardinal numbers differ from English cardinal numbers in that they are nouns and not adjectives (except 2, which has both noun and adjective forms). Therefore the noun following the number is not in the nominative, but takes different case endings according to the number.

The numbers 3–10 are followed by a noun in the indefinite genitive plural.

Remember: The gender of the numbers is decided by the gender of the noun in the singular and not in the plural.

Masculine	***Singular***	***Feminine***	***Singular***
خَمْسَةُ رِجَالٍ	(رَجُلٌ)	لِخَمْسِ بَنَاتٍ	(بِنْتٌ)
ḫamsatu riǧālin	(raǧulun)	li-ḫamsi banātin	(bintun)
five men	(man)	for five girls	(girl)
مِنْ سَبْعَةِ مُعَلِّمِينَ	(مُعَلِّمٌ)	سَبْعُ مُعَلِّمَاتٍ	(مُعَلِّمَةٌ)
min sabʿ**ati** muʿallimīna	(muʿallimun)	sabʿu muʿallimātin	(muʿallimatun)
from seven teachers	(teacher)	seven teachers	(teacher)
ثَلاَثَةُ أَيَّامٍ	(يَوْمٌ)	ثَلاَثُ لَيَالٍ	(لَيْلَةٌ)
ṯalāṯatu ʾayyāmin	(yawmun)	ṯalāṯu layālin	(laylatun)
three days	(day)	three nights	(night)

34.4 The first two cardinal numbers (1, 2) are used as appositive adjectives to emphasize the amount:

Masculine		*Feminine*
وَاحِدٌ wāḥidun, one		وَاحِدَةٌ wāḥidatun
إِثْنَانِ ʾitnāni, two		إِثْنَتَانِ ʾitnatāni
وَصَلَ طَالِبٌ وَاحِدٌ		زَارَنِي مَرَّةً وَاحِدَةً
waṣala ṭālibun **wāḥidun**.		zāranī marratan **wāḥidatan**.
(Only) **one** student arrived.		He visited me **once** (only).
شَاهَدْتُ بِنْتَيْنِ		شَاهَدْتُ بِنْتَيْنِ ٱثْنَتَيْنِ
šāhadtu bintayni.	OR	šāhadtu bintayni **t̲natayni**.
I saw (only) two girls.		(less commonly used as an adjective)

Note: These numbers never precede the noun adjectivally, because the singular and dual forms of the nouns are sufficient to indicate the number of referents.

وَصَلَ طَالِبٌ	(Not: وَصَلَ وَاحِدٌ طَالِبٌ
waṣala ṭālibun.	waṣala wāḥidun ṭālibun.)
One student arrived.	
وَصَلَتْ طَالِبَتَانِ	(Not: وَصَلَتْ ٱثْنَتَانِ طَالِبَتَانِ
waṣalat ṭālibatāni.	waṣalat t̲natāni ṭālibatāni.)
Two female students arrived.	

34.5 The nouns أَحَدٌ ʾaḥadun 'one' (masc.) and إِحْدَى ʾiḥdā 'one' (fem.) are used in the ʾ**iḍāfah** construction with a noun or a pronoun, e.g.

Masculine	*Feminine*
أَحَدُ ٱلْأَوْلَادِ. ʾaḥadu l-ʾawlādi	إِحْدَى ٱلْبَنَاتِ. ʾiḥdā l-banāti
one of the children	one of the girls
أَحَدُهُمْ ʾaḥadu-hum	إِحْدَاهُنَّ ʾiḥdā-hunna
one of them	one of them

أَحَدٌ ʾaḥadun is also used after a negative particle to mean 'not . . . anyone, nobody, no one, none', but the feminine form إِحْدَى ʾiḥdā cannot be used for the same purpose, e.g.

مَا شَاهَدْتُ أَحَدًا	لاَ أَحَدَ فِي ٱلْبَيْتِ
mā šāhadtu ʾaḥadan.	lā ʾaḥada fī l-bayti.
I didn't see anyone.	Nobody is at home.

34.6 بِضْعُ biḍʿu, whose feminine is بِضْعَةُ biḍʿatu, means '(a) few, some, several'. It follows the rules for the numbers 3–10, e.g.

Masc: بِضْعَةُ أَيَّامٍ biḍʿatu ʾayyāmin several days (يَوْمٌ yawmun, masc. sing.)

Fem: بِضْعُ لَيَالٍ biḍʿu layālin several nights (لَيْلَةٌ laylatun, fem. sing.)

34.7 The compound numbers 11–19 are followed by a noun in the indefinite accusative singular. Except for the number 12, they are indeclinable. Both parts of the compound number are vocalized with **fatḥah** at the end. The masculine form of the number 10 is used with masculine nouns and the feminine form of the number 10 is used with feminine nouns.

	Used with a masculine noun	*Used with a feminine noun*
11 ١١	أَحَدَ عَشَرَ ʾaḥada ʿašara	إِحْدَى عَشْرَةَ ʾiḥdā ʿašrata bintan
12 ١٢	إِثْنَا عَشَرَ ʾiṯnā ʿašara	إِثْنَتَا عَشْرَةَ ʾiṯnatā ʿašrata
13 ١٣	ثَلاَثَةَ عَشَرَ ṯalāṯata ʿašara	ثَلاَثَ عَشْرَةَ ṯalāṯa ʿašrata
14 ١٤	أَرْبَعَةَ عَشَرَ ʾarbaʿata ʿašara	أَرْبَعَ عَشْرَةَ ʾarbaʿa ʿašrata
15 ١٥	خَمْسَةَ عَشَرَ ḫamsata ʿašara	خَمْسَ عَشْرَةَ ḫamsa ʿašrata
16 ١٦	سِتَّةَ عَشَرَ sittata ʿašara	سِتَّ عَشْرَةَ sitta ʿašrata
17 ١٧	سَبْعَةَ عَشَرَ sabʿata ʿašara	سَبْعَ عَشْرَةَ sabʿa ʿašrata
18 ١٨	ثَمَانِيَةَ عَشَرَ ṯamāniyata ʿašara	ثَمَانِيَ عَشْرَةَ ṯamāniya ʿašrata
19 ١٩	تِسْعَةَ عَشَرَ tisʿata ʿašara	تِسْعَ عَشْرَةَ tisʿa ʿašrata bintan

Note: The accusative-genitive forms of the number 12 are: إِثْنَيْ عَشَرَ ʾiṯnay ʿašara (masc.) and إِثْنَتَيْ عَشْرَةَ ʾiṯnatay ʿašrata (fem.).

Examples:

Masculine	*Feminine*
أَحَدَ عَشَرَ وَلَدًا	إِحْدَى عَشْرَةَ بِنْتًا
ʾaḥada ʿašara waladan	ʾiḥdā ʿašrata bintan
eleven boys (lit. boy)	eleven girls (lit. girl)
مِنْ أَحَدَ عَشَرَ رَجُلًا	مَعَ إِحْدَى عَشْرَةَ بِنْتًا
min ʾaḥada ʿašara rağulan	maʿa ʾiḥdā ʿašrata bintan
from eleven men (lit. man)	with eleven girls (lit. girl)
لِخَمْسَةَ عَشَرَ مُعَلِّمًا	مِنْ خَمْسَ عَشْرَةَ مُعَلِّمَةً
li-ḫamsata ʿašara muʿalliman	min ḫamsa ʿašrata muʿallimatan
for fifteen teachers (lit. teacher, m.)	from fifteen teachers (lit. teacher, f.)

34.8 The cardinal numbers of the tens أَلْعُقُودُ, i.e. 20, 30, 40, 50, 60, 70, 80, 90, are treated as sound plurals. They are followed by the masculine or feminine noun in the indefinite accusative singular.

Used with both masculine and feminine nouns:

		Acc. and gen. / Nom.	
20	٢٠	عِشْرُونَ / عِشْرِينَ	ʿišrūna / ʿišrīna
30	٣٠	ثَلَاثُونَ / ثَلَاثِينَ	t̲alāt̲ūna / t̲alāt̲īna
40	٤٠	أَرْبَعُونَ / أَرْبَعِينَ	ʾarbaʿūna / ʾarbaʿīna
50	٥٠	خَمْسُونَ / خَمْسِينَ	ḫamsūna / ḫamsīna
60	٦٠	سِتُّونَ / سِتِّينَ	sittūna / sittīna
70	٧٠	سَبْعُونَ / سَبْعِينَ	sabʿūna / sabʿīna
80	٨٠	ثَمَانُونَ / ثَمَانِينَ	t̲amānūna / t̲amānīna
90	٩٠	تِسْعُونَ / تِسْعِينَ	tisʿūna / tisʿīna

Examples:

Nominative	***Accusative and genitive***
عِشْرُونَ وَلَدًا / بِنْتًا	عِشْرِينَ وَلَدًا / بِنْتًا
ʿišrūna waladan / bintan	ʿišrīna waladan / bintan
twenty boys/girls (lit. boy/girl)	
تِسْعُونَ وَلَدًا / بِنْتًا	تِسْعِينَ وَلَدًا / بِنْتًا
tisʿūna waladan / bintan	tisʿīna waladan / bintan
ninety boys/girls (lit. boy/girl)	

34.9 The compound numbers 20–99 are followed by the noun in the indefinite accusative singular, like the numbers 11–19. These compound numbers are fully declined. The conjunction وَ is inserted between the two parts, for example خَمْسَةٌ وَعِشْرُونَ ḫamsatun **wa**-ʿišrūna 'twenty-five', literally 'five and twenty', e.g.

	masculine	feminine
Nom.	خَمْسَةٌ وَعِشْرُونَ وَلَدًا ḫamsat**un** **wa**-ʿišrūna walad**an** twenty-five boys (lit. boy)	خَمْسٌ وَعِشْرُونَ بِنْتًا ḫams**un** **wa**-ʿišrūna bint**an** twenty-five girls (lit. girl)
Acc.	خَمْسَةً وَعِشْرِينَ وَلَدًا ḫamsat**an** **wa**-ʿišrīna walad**an**	خَمْسًا وَعِشْرِينَ بِنْتًا ḫams**an** **wa**-ʿišrīna bint**an**
Gen.	خَمْسَةٍ وَعِشْرِينَ وَلَدًا ḫamsat**in** **wa**-ʿišrīna walad**an**	خَمْسٍ وَعِشْرِينَ بِنْتًا ḫams**in** **wa**-ʿišrīna bint**an**

34.10 The hundreds, 100–900, are followed by the noun in the indefinite genitive singular. The noun can be masculine or feminine. The combinations of the compound numbers are written in two different ways.

100	١٠٠	مِئَةٌ miʾatun OR مِائَةٌ miʾatun
200	٢٠٠	مِئَتَانِ miʾatāni (dual, nom.)
200	٢٠٠	مِئَتَيْنِ miʾatayni (dual, acc. and gen.)
300	٣٠٠	ثَلَاثُ مِئَةٍ ṯalāṯu miʾatin

400	٤٠٠	أَرْبَعُ مِئَةٍ ʾarbaʿu miʾatin
500	٥٠٠	خَمْسُ مِئَةٍ ḫamsu miʾatin
600	٦٠٠	سِتُّ مِئَةٍ sittu miʾatin
700	٧٠٠	سَبْعُ مِئَةٍ sabʿu miʾatin
800	٨٠٠	ثَمَانِ مِئَةٍ ṯamāni miʾatin
900	٩٠٠	تِسْعُ مِئَةٍ tisʿu miʾatin

Note: Observe that the middle **ʾalif** (ا) in مِائَةٌ miʾatun, as an alternative form of مِئَةٌ miʾatun, is not pronounced.

Examples:

مِئَةُ رَجُلٍ / امْرَأَةٍ
miʾatu rağulin / mraʾatin
one hundred men / women
(lit. man / woman)

مِنْ تِسْعِ مِئَةِ أُمٍّ / أَبٍ
min tisʿi miʾati ʾummin / ʾabin
from nine hundred mothers / fathers
(lit. mother / father)

مِئَتَا وَلَدٍ / بِنْتٍ
miʾatā waladin / bintin
two hundred boys / girls
(lit. two hundred boy / girl)

لِمِئَتَيْ وَلَدٍ / بِنْتٍ
li-miʾatay waladin / bintin
for two hundred boys / girls
(lit. for two hundred boy / girl)

34.11 The plural of مِئَةٌ miʾatun is مِئَاتٌ miʾātun, which is an exception. In compound numbers it is always singular, not plural like the words for a thousand and a million, e.g.

تِسْعُ مِئَةٍ tisʿu miʾatin, nine hundred (not: تِسْعُ مِئَاتٍ tisʿu miʾātin)

34.12 The number thousand (1,000) in Arabic is أَلْفٌ ʾalfun. The dual of it is أَلْفَانِ ʾalfāni in the nominative, and أَلْفَيْنِ ʾalfayni in the accusative and genitive. The plural is أُلُوفٌ ʾulūfun or آلَافٌ ʾālāfun.

34.13 The number million (1,000,000) is مِلْيُونٌ, milyūnu. The dual forms are: مِلْيُونَانِ milyūnāni (nom.) and مِلْيُونَيْنِ milyūnayni (acc. and gen.). The plural is مَلَايِينُ malāyīnu (diptote).

34.14 The numbers thousand and million are used with both masculine and feminine and followed by the noun in the indefinite genitive singular, e.g.

Nom. أَلْفُ وَلَدٍ / بِنْتٍ ʾalfu waladin / bintin, 1,000 boys / girls

Nom. أَلْفَا وَلَدٍ / بِنْتٍ ʾalfā waladin / bintin, 2,000 boys / girls

Nom. مَلْيُونُ وَلَدٍ / بِنْتٍ milyūnu waladin / bintin, 1,000,000 boys / girls

Acc. and gen. أَلْفَيْ وَلَدٍ / بِنْتٍ ʾalfay waladin / bintin, 2,000 boys / girls

34.15 With compound numbers over 100, the following noun is declined according to the last number or last two numbers. For example, take the number 125: the last two numbers are 25, so the following noun will be according to the rule of 25, i.e. it is in the indefinite accusative singular, e.g.

مِئَةٌ وَخَمْسَةٌ وَعِشْرُونَ رَجُلاً

miʾatun wa-**ḫamsatun wa-ʿišrūna rağulan**, **125** men

مِئَةٌ وَثَلاثٌ وَثَلاثُونَ بِنْتاً

miʾatun wa-**ṯalāṯun wa-ṯalāṯūna bintan**, **133** girls

If the number is 105, the final number is 5 and it will be according to the rule of 5, i.e. the following noun is in the indefinite genitive plural, e.g.

مِئَةٌ وَخَمْسَةُ رِجَالٍ

miʾatun wa-**ḫamsatu riğālin**

105 girls

مِئَةٌ وَتِسْعُ بَنَاتٍ

miʾatun wa-**tisʿu banātin**

109 men

34.16 If the number is preceded by the definite article أَلْـ /ʾal.../, it can be placed after the definite noun, which follows the general rules of agreement for numbers, e.g.

Masculine

أَلرِّجَالُ الْخَمْسَةُ

ʾar-riğālu l-ḫamsatu

the five men

Feminine

أَلْبَنَاتُ ٱلْخَمْسُ

ʾal-banātu l-ḫamsu

the five girls

أَلشَّبَابُ ٱلثَّلَاثَةَ عَشَرَ
ʾaš-šabābu t-talātata ʿašara
the thirteen young men

أَلشَّابَّاتُ ٱلثَّلَاثَ عَشْرَةَ
ʾaš-šabbātu t-talāta ʿašrata
the thirteen young girls

Note: The preceding noun can also be made definite by occurring in the ʾ**iḍāfah** construction, e.g.

كُتُبُ ٱلْمُعَلِّمِ ٱلثَّلَاثَةُ
kutubu l-muʿallimi t-talātatu
the three books of the teacher

34.17 To express numerical subsets, such as 'one/two/three etc. of (a given set)', one uses the preposition مِنْ min 'from, (out) of' before the plural genitive form of the noun, e.g.

كِتَابٌ مِنْ كُتُبِ ٱلْمُعَلِّمِ
kitābun min kutubi l-muʿallimi
one of the teacher's books

ثَلَاثَةُ كُتُبٍ مِنْ كُتُبِ ٱلْمُعَلِّمِ
talātatu kutubin min kutubi l-muʿallimi
three of the teacher's books

34.18 The following are the most common ways of reading a sequence of compound numbers. Reading the sequence numbers of the year: The synonyms عَامٌ ʿāmun 'year' (masc.) and سَنَةٌ sanatun 'year' (fem.) have the accusative forms عَامَ ʿāma and سَنَةَ sanata, respectively, which are used *in adverbial phrases of time*. Then they follow the rules of the ʾ**iḍāfah** construction, where the following noun is in the genitive case, e.g.

عَامَ أَلْفٍ وَتِسْعِ مِئَةٍ وَتِسْعَةٍ وَتِسْعِينَ (masc. acc.)
ʿām**a** ʾalf**in** wa-tisʿi miʾatin wa-tisʿ**atin** wa-tisʿ**īna**
in the **year 1999**

سَنَةَ أَلْفٍ وَتِسْعِ مِئَةٍ وَتِسْعٍ وَتِسْعِينَ (fem. acc.)
sanat**a** ʾalfin wa-tisʿi miʾatin wa-tisʿ**in** wa-tisʿ**īna**
in the **year 1999**

Note: Normally the year in such a sequence is preceded by the preposition فِي, e.g.

فِي عَامِ أَلْفٍ وَتِسْعِ مِئَةٍ وَوَاحِدٍ وَثَمَانِينَ (masc. gen.)
fī ʿām**i** ʾalfin wa-tisʿi miʾatin wa-**wāḥidin** wa-ṯamānīna
in the **year 1981**

فِي سَنَةِ أَلْفٍ وَتِسْعِ مِئَةٍ وَإِحْدَى وَثَمَانِينَ (fem. gen.)
fī **sanati** ʾalfin wa-tisʿi miʾatin wa-ʾ**iḥdā** wa-ṯamānīna
in the **year 1981**

فِي عَامِ أَلْفٍ وَسَبْعِ مِئَةٍ وَاثْنَيْنِ وَسِتِّينَ (masc. gen.)
fī ʿ**āmi** ʾalfin wa-sabʿi miʾatin wa-**ṯnayni** wa-sittīna
in the **year 1762**

فِي سَنَةِ أَلْفٍ وَسَبْعِ مِئَةٍ وَاثْنَتَيْنِ وَسِتِّينَ (fem. gen.)
fī **sanati** ʾalfin wa-sabʿi miʾatin wa-**ṯnatayni** wa-sittīna
in the **year 1762**

فِي عَامِ أَلْفٍ وَخَمْسِ مِئَةٍ وَثَلَاثَةٍ وَأَرْبَعِينَ (masc. gen.)
fī ʿ**āmi** ʾalfin wa-ḫamsi miʾatin wa-**ṯalāṯatin** wa-ʾarbaʿīna
in the **year 1543**

فِي سَنَةِ أَلْفٍ وَخَمْسِ مِئَةٍ وَثَلَاثٍ وَأَرْبَعِينَ (fem. gen.)
fī **sanati** ʾalfin wa-ḫamsi miʾatin wa-**ṯalāṯin** wa-ʾarbaʿīna
in the **year 1543**

Compare:

أَرْبَعَةُ آلَافٍ وَتِسْعُ مِئَةٍ وَسَبْعَةٌ وَثَمَانُونَ وَلَدًا (masc. nom.)
ʾarbaʿatu ʾālāfin wa-tisʿu miʾatin wa-**sabʿatun** wa-ṯamānūna waladan
4,987 boys

أَرْبَعَةُ آلَافٍ وَتِسْعُ مِئَةٍ وَسَبْعٌ وَثَمَانُونَ بِنْتًا (fem. nom.)
ʾarbaʿatu ʾālāfin wa-tisʿu miʾatin wa-**sab**ʿ**un** wa-ṯamānūna bintan
4,987 girls

Exercises

Practise your reading:

[1]رَبِحَ [2]فَرِيقُ ٱلْجَامِعَةِ [3]ٱلرِّيَاضِيُّ، إِحْدَى عَشْرَةَ مِنْ [4]ٱثْنَتَيْ عَشْرَةَ [5]مُبَارَاةً [6]لَعِبَهَا خِلَالَ ٱلسَّنَتَيْنِ [7]ٱلْمَاضِيَتَيْنِ.

(1) The university [3]sports [2]team [1]won eleven of [4]the twelve [5]matches it [6]played during the [7]last two years.

[1]كَمْ [2]عُمْرُكَ؟ عُمْرِي ثَمَانٍ وَعِشْرُونَ سَنَةً. وَكَمْ عُمْرُكِ أَنْتِ؟ عُمْرِي ثَلَاثُونَ عَامًا.

(2) [1]How [2]old are you (m.)? (lit. What age are you?) I am (lit. my age is) 28 years old. And how old are you (f.)? I am 30 years old.

كَانَ فِي [1]ٱلِامْتِحَانِ أَحَدَ عَشَرَ [2]سُؤَالًا، خَمْسَةٌ مِنْهَا كَانَتْ [3]خَطِّيَّةً، وَٱلسِّتَّةُ ٱلْأُخْرَى كَانَتْ [4]شَفَهِيَّةً. [5]عَرَفَ ٱلطَّالِبُ [6]جَوَابَ ثَمَانِيَةٍ مِنْهَا.

(3) There were eleven [2]questions in [1]the examination. Five of them were [3]written and the other six were [4]oral. The student [5]knew [6]the answers to eight of them.

[1]تَدُورُ ٱلْأَرْضُ [2]حَوْلَ [3]مِحْوَرِهَا [4]دَوْرَةً [5]وَاحِدَةً كُلَّ أَرْبَعٍ وَعِشْرِينَ سَاعَةً، وَتَدُورُ حَوْلَ [6]ٱلشَّمْسِ [7]دَوْرَةً [8]وَاحِدَةً كُلَّ ثَلَاثِ مِئَةٍ وَخَمْسَةٍ وَسِتِّينَ يَوْمًا وَسِتِّ سَاعَاتٍ.

(4) The earth [1]rotates [2]around [3]its axis once (lit. [5,4]only one revolution) every 24 hours, and [7]rotates around [6]the sun [8]only once (lit. [7]one revolution) every 365 days and six hours.

[1]قَامَتْ أَرْبَعُ [2]طَائِرَاتٍ [3]حَرْبِيَّةٍ بِعَشْرِ [4]غَارَاتٍ [5]جَوِّيَّةٍ [6]وَرَمَتْ [7]مَا يَزِيدُ عَلَى مِئَةٍ وَخَمْسٍ وَعِشْرِينَ [8]قُنْبُلَةً، وَسِتَّةَ عَشَرَ [9]صَارُوخًا، [10]فَهَدَمَتِ ٱثْنَيْ عَشَرَ مَنْزِلًا، [11]وَقَتَلَتْ ثَمَانِيَةَ [12]أَشْخَاصٍ (شَخْصٌ) [13]وَجَرَحَتْ مِئَتَيْنِ وَأَرْبَعَةَ عَشَرَ [14]آخَرِينَ.

(5) Four [3]war [2]planes [1]made 10 [5,4]air raids [6]and dropped [7]more than 125 [8]bombs and 16 [9]rockets. [10]They destroyed 12 houses, [11]killed 8 [12]people [13]and wounded 214 [14]others.

كَانَتْ [1]هِجْرَةُ [2]ٱلنَّبِيِّ مُحَمَّدٍ مِنَ مَكَّةَ إِلَى ٱلْمَدِينَةِ فِي سَنَةِ سِتِّ مِئَةٍ
وَٱثْنَيْنِ وَعِشْرِينَ [3]بَعْدَ [4]ٱلْمِيلَادِ. [5]وَٱتُّخِذَ هٰذَا [6]ٱلتَّارِيخُ عِنْدَ ٱلْمُسْلِمِينَ
[7]كَبِدَايَةٍ لِلسَّنَةِ [8]ٱلْهِجْرِيَّةِ

(6) [1]The emigration of [2]the Prophet Muhammad from Mecca to Medina took place in the year [3,4] AD 622 ([3]after [4]the birth). This [6]date [5]was taken by the Muslims [7]as the beginning of the Hiğrah ([8]calendar) year.

فِي يَوْمٍ وَاحِدٍ [1]بَاعَ [2]تَاجِرُ [3]ٱلْخُضَارِ [4]وَٱلْفَاكِهَةِ ثَلَاثَةَ عَشَرَ [5]صُنْدُوقًا
مِنَ [6]ٱلْعِنَبِ، فَبَاعَ [7]كُلَّ وَاحِدٍ مِنْهَا بِأَحَدَ عَشَرَ دِينَارًا. وَبَاعَ [8]أَيْضًا مِئَةً
وَأَرْبَعَةَ صَنَادِيقَ (صُنْدُوقٍ) مِنَ [9]ٱلتُّفَّاحِ، وَخَمْسَةً وَخَمْسِينَ صُنْدُوقًا مِنَ
[10]ٱلْبُرْتُقَالِ، بَاعَ كُلَّ وَاحِدٍ مِنْهَا بِسَبْعَةِ دَنَانِيرَ [11]وَنِصْفِ ٱلدِّينَارِ وَكَانَ
[12]رِبْحُهُ مِئَةً وَعَشَرَةَ دَنَانِيرَ.

(7) In one day [3]the greengrocer ([4]and fruit [2]merchant) [1]sold thirteen [5]boxes of [6]grapes, selling them for eleven dinars [7]each. He [8]also sold 104 boxes of [9]apples and 55 of [10]oranges, which he sold for seven [11]and a half dinars each. [12]His profit was 110 dinars.

[1]إِذَا [2]جَمَعْنَا مِئَتَيْ [3]خَرُوفٍ وَخَرُوفٍ، وَأَرْبَعَ مِئَةٍ وَوَاحِدٍ وَثَلَاثِينَ
[4]حِصَانًا، وَثَمَانِيَ عَشْرَةَ [5]بَقَرَةً، وَأَلْفًا وَسِتَّ مِئَةٍ وَعِشْرِينَ جَمَلًا، وَثَلَاثَةً
وَثَلَاثِينَ [6]حِمَارًا، وَتِسْعًا وَتِسْعِينَ [7]دَجَاجَةً [8]وَقِطَّتَيْنِ [9]وَكَلْبًا
وَاحِدًا، فَكَمْ يَكُونُ [10]مَجْمُوعُ [11]عَدَدِ هٰذِهِ [12]ٱلْحَيَوَانَاتِ؟

(8) [1]If [2]we add 201 [3]sheep, 431 [4]horses, 18 [5]cows, 1,620 camels, 33 [6]donkeys, 99 [7]hens, [8]2 cats [9]and 1 dog, what will the [10]total [11]number of [12]animals be?

لَوِ [1]ٱفْتَرَضْنَا أَنَّ [2]ٱلْقِطَارَ [3]يَسِيرُ [4]لَيْلَ [5]نَهَارَ [6]بِسُرْعَةِ خَمْسَةٍ وَسِتِّينَ مِيلًا
فِي ٱلسَّاعَةِ، [7]فَيَحْتَاجُ [8]لِوُصُولِهِ إِلَى ٱلشَّمْسِ [9]حَوَالَيْ مِئَةٍ وَأَرْبَعٍ وَسِتِّينَ
سَنَةً. أَمَّا [10]سُرْعَةُ [11]قَذِيفَةِ [12]ٱلْمِدْفَعِ فَهِيَ أَلْفٌ وَمِئَتَانِ وَتِسْعَةُ أَمْيَالٍ فِي
ٱلسَّاعَةِ، [13]فَتَحْتَاجُ لِثَمَانِي سَنَوَاتٍ [14]وَنِصْفِ ٱلسَّنَةِ لِتَصِلَ إِلَى ٱلشَّمْسِ،

أَمَّا [15]ٱلنُّورُ [16]فَيَجْتَازُ هٰذِهِ [17]ٱلْمَسَافَةَ بِثَمَانِي [18]دَقَائِقَ وَتِسْعَ عَشْرَةَ
[19]ثَانِيَةً.

(9) If we [1]suppose that [2]a train [3]travels [6]at a speed of 65 miles per hour, [5]day and [4]night, [7]it would need [9]around 164 years [8]to reach the sun. However, the [10]speed of [12]the cannon-[11]ball is 1,209 miles per hour. [13]It would need eight and a [14]half years to reach the sun; but [15]light [16]traverses this [17]distance in eight [18]minutes and nineteen [19]seconds.

Translate into Arabic:

(1) The sports team won thirteen of the fifteen matches it played during (the) last year.

(2) How old are you (m.) ? I am 22 years old.

(3) In the exam there were thirteen questions: two of them were written and the other eleven were oral. The student knew the answers to five of them.

(4) At the beginning of the year three war planes made ten air raids and dropped 165 bombs and 16 rockets.

(5) A cannon-ball killed the greengrocer and a teacher with five of his students, wounded seven others and destroyed two houses.

(6) In one day the merchant sold 16 boxes of grapes, 108 boxes of apples and 57 of oranges. His profit was 121 dinars.

(7) If we add 101 sheep, 331 horses, 17 cows, 33 donkeys, 89 hens and 1 cat, what will the total number of animals be?

(8) If we suppose that a train travels day and night at a speed of 77 miles per hour, it would need around 164 days for one revolution around the earth.

Chapter 35

Ordinal numbers, fractions, expressions of time and calendars

35.1 The ordinal numbers, أَلْعَدَدُ ٱلتَّرْتِيبِيُّ, 2nd–10th are based on the corresponding cardinal numbers. They are formed on the pattern for active participles: فَاعِلٌ fāʿilun. The ordinal number 'first' is formed from an independent root ʾ-w-l on the pattern أَفْعَلُ ʾafʿalu. The ordinal numbers agree with the gender and case of the head noun, i.e. the masculine forms are used with reference to masculine nouns, and the feminine forms are used with reference to feminine nouns. They take the definite article أَلْـ... and are inflected for all three cases. Like any other adjective, the ordinal number usually follows the noun it qualifies.

	Used with masculine	***Used with feminine***
1st	أَلْأَوَّلُ ʾal-ʾawwalu	أَلْأُولَى ʾal-ʾūlā
2nd	أَلثَّانِي ʾaṯ-ṯānī	أَلثَّانِيَةُ ʾaṯ-ṯāniyatu
3rd	أَلثَّالِثُ ʾaṯ-ṯāliṯu	أَلثَّالِثَةُ ʾaṯ-ṯāliṯatu
4th	أَلرَّابِعُ ʾar-rābiʿu	أَلرَّابِعَةُ ʾar-rābiʿatu
5th	أَلْخَامِسُ ʾal-ḫāmisu	أَلْخَامِسَةُ ʾal-ḫāmisatu
6th	أَلسَّادِسُ ʾas-sādisu	أَلسَّادِسَةُ ʾas-sādisatu
7th	أَلسَّابِعُ ʾas-sābiʿu	أَلسَّابِعَةُ ʾas-sābiʿatu
8th	أَلثَّامِنُ ʾaṯ-ṯāminu	أَلثَّامِنَةُ ʾaṯ-ṯāminatu
9th	أَلتَّاسِعُ ʾat-tāsiʿu	أَلتَّاسِعَةُ ʾat-tāsiʿatu
10th	أَلْعَاشِرُ ʾal-ʿāširu	أَلْعَاشِرَةُ ʾal-ʿāširatu

Note: The double /tt/ (tāʾ with šaddah) in the cardinal number سِتَّةٌ sittatun 'six' is resolved as /d/ + /s/ in the ordinal number سَادِسٌ sādisun 'sixth'.

Examples:

Masculine	***Feminine***
أَلْوَلَدُ ٱلْأَوَّلُ ʾal-waladu l-ʾawwalu, the first boy	أَلْبِنْتُ ٱلْأُولَى ʾal-bintu l-ʾūlā, the first girl
هُوَ ٱلْأَوَّلُ huwa l-ʾawwalu. He is the first.	هِيَ ٱلْأُولَى hiya l-ʾūlā. She is the first.
هُوَ خَامِسُهُمْ huwa ḫāmisu-hum. He is the fifth of them.	هِيَ خَامِسَتُهُنَّ hiya ḫāmisatu-hunna. She is the fifth of them.
أَلدَّرْسُ ٱلثَّانِي ʾad-darsu t-tānī, the second lesson	أَلسَّنَةُ ٱلثَّانِيَةُ ʾas-sanatu t-tāniyatu, the second year
أَلْكِتَابُ ٱلرَّابِعُ ʾal-kitābu r-rābiʿu, the fourth book	أَلسَّاعَةُ ٱلْخَامِسَةُ ʾas-sāʿatu l-ḫāmisatu, five o'clock (lit. the fifth hour)

35.2 The ordinal numbers أَلْأَوَّلُ ʾal-ʾawwalu (masc.) and أَلْأُولَى ʾal-ʾūlā (fem.) 'first' have the following plurals:

	singular	broken plural			sound plural
Masc.	أَلْأَوَّلُ ʾal-ʾawwalu	أَلْأُوَلُ ʾal-ʾuwalu	OR	أَلْأَوَائِلُ ʾal-ʾawāʾilu	أَلْأَوَّلُونَ ʾal-ʾawwalūna
Fem.	أَلْأُولَى ʾal-ʾūlā	أَلْأُوَلُ ʾal-ʾuwalu	OR	أَلْأَوَائِلُ ʾal-ʾawāʾilu	أَلْأُولَاتُ ʾal-ʾūlātu

35.3 Ordinal numbers can also be used in the ʾ**iḍāfah** construction with a following genitive noun or with a suffixed personal pronoun, e.g.

أَوَّلُ ٱلنَّاسِ ʾawwalu n-nāsi the first of the people	أَوَّلُهُمْ ʾawwalu-hum the first of them (masc.)
خَامِسُ وَلَدٍ ḫāmisu waladin (the) fifth boy	خَامِسُهُمْ ḫāmisu-hum the fifth of them (masc.)
فَاطِمَةُ خَامِسَةُ بِنْتٍ fāṭimatu ḫāmisatu bintin. Fatima is the fifth girl.	هِيَ خَامِسَتُهُنَّ hiya ḫāmisatu-hunna. She is the fifth of them.

Note: In this construction the ordinal number is in the masculine even when the following noun or suffix pronoun is feminine, unless the ordinal number is preceded by a feminine subject. (Even so, the feminine ordinal number أُولَى ʾūlā 'first' is less often used in the ʾ**iḍāfah** construction.)

Masculine	***Feminine***	
أَوَّلُ وَلَدٍ ʾawwalu waladin the first boy	أَوَّلُ بِنْتٍ ʾawwalu bintin the first girl	(Not: أُولَى بِنْتٍ ʾūlā bintin)
ثَانِي وَلَدٍ t̲āniya waladin the second boy	ثَانِي مَرَّةٍ t̲āniya marratin the second time	(Not: ثَانِيَةُ مَرَّةٍ t̲āniyatu marratin)
خَامِسُ وَلَدٍ ḫāmisu waladin the fifth boy	خَامِسُ بِنْتٍ ḫāmisu bintin the fifth girl	(Not: خَامِسَةُ بِنْتٍ ḫāmisatu bintin)
أَوَّلُهُمْ ʾawwalu-hum the first of them	أَوَّلُهُنَّ ʾawwalu-hunna the first of them	(Not: أُولاهُنَّ ʾūlā-hunna)
خَامِسُهُمْ ḫāmisu-hum the fifth of them	خَامِسُهُنَّ ḫāmisu-hunna the fifth of them	(Not: خَامِسَتُهُنَّ ḫāmisatu-hunna)

35.4 The ordinal numbers 11th–19th are inflected for gender but not for case. In forming the ordinal number meaning 'eleventh', it should be observed that:

أَلْحَادِيَ ʾal-ḥādiya (m.) is used instead of أَلْأَوَّلُ ʾal-ʾawwalu 'first' (m.), and

أَلْحَادِيَةَ ʾal-ḥādiyata (f.) is used instead of أَلْأُولَى ʾal-ʾūlā 'first' (f.).

	Used with masculine	***Used with feminine***
	أَلْوَلَدُ ٱلْحَادِيَ عَشَرَ	أَلْبِنْتُ ٱلْحَادِيَةَ عَشْرَةَ
11th	ʾal-waladu l-ḥādiya ʿašara	ʾal-bintu l-ḥādiyata ʿašrata
	the eleventh boy	the eleventh girl
	أَلْوَلَدُ ٱلثَّانِيَ عَشَرَ	أَلْبِنْتُ ٱلثَّانِيَةَ عَشْرَةَ
12th	ʾal-waladuʾ t-tāniya ʿašara	ʾal-bintu t-tāniyata ʿašrata
	أَلْوَلَدُ ٱلثَّالِثَ عَشَرَ	أَلْبِنْتُ ٱلثَّالِثَةَ عَشْرَةَ
13th	ʾal-waladu t-tālita ʿašara	ʾal-bintu t-tālitata ʿašrata
	أَلْوَلَدُ ٱلرَّابِعَ عَشَرَ	أَلْبِنْتُ ٱلرَّابِعَةَ عَشْرَةَ
14th	ʾal-waladu r-rābiʿa ʿašara	ʾal-bintu r-rābiʿata ʿašrata

35.5 *Telling the time*

وَقْتٌ waqtun, time (plural: أَوْقَاتٌ ʾawqātun)

The ordinal numbers are used in telling the time, but 'one o'clock' can also be expressed by a cardinal number:

أَلسَّاعَةُ ٱلْوَاحِدَةُ / ٱلْأُولَى ʾas-sāʿatu l-wāḥidatu OR l-ʾūlā, one o'clock

أَلسَّاعَةُ ٱلثَّانِيَةُ ʾas-sāʿatu t-tāniyatu, two o'clock

أَلسَّاعَةُ ٱلثَّالِثَةُ ʾas-sāʿatu t-tālitatu, three o'clock

أَلسَّاعَةُ ٱلرَّابِعَةُ ʾas-sāʿatu r-rābiʿatu, four o'clock

etc.

Note: The classical meaning of the word سَاعَةٌ sāʿatun is '(short) time, hour', but nowadays it also has the meaning 'clock, timepiece, watch'.

35.6 The ordinal numbers for the even tens, أَلْعِشْرُونَ ʾal-ʿišrūna '20th', أَلثَّلَاثُونَ ʾat-talātūna '30th', أَلْأَرْبَعُونَ ʾal-ʾarbaʿūna '40th', etc., are formed by prefixing the definite article ..ألْ to the corresponding cardinal numbers. They are inflected for case but not for gender, e.g.

أَلْوَلَدُ / أَلْبِنْتُ ٱلْعِشْرُونَ ʾal-waladu / ʾal-bintu l-ʿišrūna, the 20th boy / girl

35.7 Ordinal adverbs are derived from ordinal numbers simply by inflecting them for the indefinite accusative case (see chapter 38 on adverbs), e.g.

أَوَّلاً ʾawwalan, firstly   ثَانِياً ṯāniyan, secondly   ثَالِثاً ṯāliṯan, thirdly

etc.

35.8 The fractions from $\frac{1}{2}$ to $\frac{1}{10}$ are formed mostly according to the pattern فُعْلٌ fuʿlun, for the singular, and أَفْعَالٌ ʾafʿālun, for the plural:

	Singular	***Plural***
$\frac{1}{2}$	نِصْفٌ niṣfun	أَنْصَافٌ ʾanṣāfun
$\frac{1}{3}$	ثُلْثٌ ṯulṯun	أَثْلَاثٌ ʾaṯlāṯun
$\frac{1}{4}$	رُبْعٌ rubʿun	أَرْبَاعٌ ʾarbāʿun
$\frac{1}{5}$	خُمْسٌ ḫumsun	أَخْمَاسٌ ʾaḫmāsun
$\frac{1}{6}$	سُدْسٌ sudsun	أَسْدَاسٌ ʾasdāsun
$\frac{1}{7}$	سُبْعٌ subʿun	أَسْبَاعٌ ʾasbāʿun
$\frac{1}{8}$	ثُمْنٌ ṯumnun	أَثْمَانٌ ʾaṯmānun
$\frac{1}{9}$	تُسْعٌ tusʿun	أَتْسَاعٌ ʾatsāʿun
$\frac{1}{10}$	عُشْرٌ ʿušrun	أَعْشَارٌ ʾaʿšārun

Examples:

ثُلْثَانِ
ṯulṯāni (dual), $\frac{2}{3}$

ثَلَاثَةُ أَخْمَاسٍ
ṯalāṯatu ʾaḫmāsin, $\frac{3}{5}$

خَمْسَةُ أَثْمَانٍ
ḫamsatu ʾaṯmānin, $\frac{5}{8}$

تِسْعَةٌ وَثَلَاثَةُ أَرْبَاعٍ
tisʿatun wa-ṯalāṯatu ʾarbāʿin, $9\frac{3}{4}$

أَرْبَعَةٌ وَخَمْسَةُ أَسْدَاسٍ
ʾarbaʿatun wa-ḫamsatu ʾasdāsin, $4\frac{5}{6}$

35.9 The word for percentage is أَلنِّسْبَةُ ٱلْمِئَوِيَّةُ ʾan-nisbatu l-miʾawiyyatu. Percentage figures (%) are expressed by adding the numeral phrase بِٱلْمِئَةِ bi-l-mi'ati or فِي ٱلْمِئَةِ fī l-mi'ati to the cardinal number, e.g.

ثَلَاثَةٌ بِٱلْمِئَةِ talātatun bi-l-mi'ati, 3%	أَرْبَعُونَ بِٱلْمِئَةِ 'arba'ūna bi-l-mi'ati, 40%	مِئَةٌ بِٱلْمِئَةِ mi'atun bi-l-mi'ati, 100%

35.10 *Days of the week*

The names of the days of the week, أَيَّامُ ٱلْأُسْبُوعِ 'ayyāmu l-'usbū'i, are formed by combining the word for 'day', يَوْمٌ yawmun (masc. sing.), with nominal forms of the numerals (except for Friday and Saturday, which have their own names) in the 'iḍāfah construction. Sometimes the word يَوْمٌ is, in fact, left out.

يَوْمُ ٱلْأَحَدِ yawmu l-'aḥadi, Sunday
يَوْمُ ٱلْاِثْنَيْنِ yawmu l-iṯnayni, Monday
يَوْمُ ٱلثُّلَاثَاءِ yawmu ṯ-ṯulāṯā'i, Tuesday
يَوْمُ ٱلْأَرْبِعَاءِ yawmu l-'arbi'ā'i, Wednesday
يَوْمُ ٱلْخَمِيسِ yawmu l-ḫamīsi, Thursday
يَوْمُ ٱلْجُمُعَةِ yawmu l-ǧumu'ati, Friday
يَوْمُ ٱلسَّبْتِ yawmu s-sabti, Saturday

35.11 *The calendars and names of the months*

The names of the months of the year, أَشْهُرُ ٱلسَّنَةِ (sing.: شَهْرٌ), according to the different prevalent calendars are:

	used in Egypt, Sudan and North Africa	used in eastern Arab world	the Islamic or lunar months
(1) January	يَنَايِرُ	كَانُونُ ٱلثَّانِي kānūnu ṯ-ṯānī	مُحَرَّمٌ muḥarramu

	used in Egypt, Sudan and North Africa	used in eastern Arab world	the Islamic or lunar months
(2) February	فَبْرَايِرُ	شُبَاطُ šubāṭu	صَفَرٌ ṣafarun
(3) March	مَارْسُ	آذَارُ ʾād̲āru	رَبِيعُ ٱلْأَوَّلُ rabīʿu l-ʾawwalu
(4) April	أَبْرِيلُ	نَيْسَانُ naysānu	رَبِيعُ ٱلثَّانِي rabīʿu t̲-t̲ānī
(5) May	مَايُو	أَيَّارُ ʾayyāru	جُمَادَى ٱلْأُولَى ǧumādā l-ʾūlā
(6) June	يُونِيُو	حَزِيرَانُ ḥazīrānu	جُمَادَى ٱلْآخِرَةُ ǧumāda l-ʾāḫiratu
(7) July	يُولِيُو	تَمُّوزُ tammūzu	رَجَبٌ rağabun
(8) August	أُغُسْطُسُ	آبُ ʾābu	شَعْبَانُ šaʿbānu
(9) September	سَبْتَمْبَرُ	أَيْلُولُ ʾaylūlu	رَمَضَانُ ramaḍānu
(10) October	أُكْتُوبَرُ	تِشْرِينُ ٱلْأَوَّلُ tišrīnu l-ʾawwalu	شَوَّالُ šawwālu
(11) November	نُوفَمْبَرُ	تِشْرِينُ ٱلثَّانِي tišrīnu t̲-t̲ānī	ذُو ٱلْقَعْدَةِ d̲ū l-qiʿdati
(12) December	دِيسَمْبَرُ	كَانُونُ ٱلْأَوَّلُ kānūnu l-ʾawwalu	ذُو ٱلْحِجَّةِ d̲ū l-ḥiğğati

Note: The months of the Islamic lunar calendar rotate backwards, because the lunar year is about 11 days shorter than the solar year.

35.12 *Seasons of the year*

أَلرَّبِيعُ ʾar-rabīʿu, spring

أَلصَّيْفُ ʾaṣ-ṣayfu, summer

أَلْخَرِيفُ ʾal-ḫarīfu, autumn

أَلشِّتَاءُ ʾaš-šitāʾu, winter

35.13 *The Islamic era and the Muslim festivals*

عِيدٌ ʿīdun, festival, pl.: أَعْيَادٌ ʾaʿyādun

(a) The **hiğrah** year, أَلسَّنَةُ ٱلْهِجْرِيَّةُ ʾas-sanatu l-hiğriyyatu, is the year in which the Prophet Muḥammad emigrated from Mecca to Medina, i.e. 622 AD (16 July). This year is counted as year 1 of the Islamic era. The Muslim year is a lunar year, أَلسَّنَةُ ٱلْقَمَرِيَّةُ ʾas-sanatu l-qamariyyatu, and counts only 354 days. The lunar year is not so often used but when it is used, the Christian year is also mentioned.

(b) The holy month of رَمَضَانُ Ramaḍān(u) has no regular corresponding date in the Christian year, because the lunar months rotate backwards. It is the month of fasting from dawn to sunset. The festivities at the end of Ramadan have two names: عِيدُ ٱلْفِطْرِ ʿīdu l-fiṭri 'The festival of the breaking of the fast' and أَلْعِيدُ ٱلصَّغِيرُ ʾal-ʿīdu ṣ-ṣaġīru 'The small festival'. The common festival greeting is: عِيدٌ مُبَارَكٌ ʿīdun mubārakun 'Blessed feast!' or رَمَضَانُ مُبَارَكٌ Ramaḍānu mubārakun 'Blessed Ramadan!'

(c) عِيدُ ٱلْأَضْحَى ʿīdu l-ʾaḍḥā means 'The festival of sacrifice', which consists of different ceremonies on the days of the pilgrimage (أَلْحَجُّ ʾal-ḥağğu) to Mecca. It takes place on the tenth day of the month of ذُو ٱلْحِجَّةِ ḏū l-ḥiğğati (the last month of the Islamic calendar), when the pilgrims sacrifice sheep and give some of the meat to the poor. It has another name, أَلْعِيدُ ٱلْكَبِيرُ ʾal-ʿīdu l-kabīru, which means 'The great festival'.

(d) The birthday of the Prophet Muhammad is called عِيدُ ٱلْمَوْلِدِ ٱلنَّبَوِيِّ ʿīdu l-mawlidi n-nabawiyyi, but it is not much celebrated as a festival.

35.14 *Christian festivals*

The Christian year is called أَلسَّنَةُ ٱلْمِيلَادِيَّةُ ʾas-sanatu l-mīlādiyyatu 'the year of the birth (of Christ)'.

Christmas is عِيدُ ٱلْمِيلَادِ ʿīdu l-mīlādi.

Easter is عِيدُ ٱلْفِصْحِ ʿīdu l-fiṣḥi or عِيدُ ٱلْقِيَامَةِ ʿīdu l-qiyāmati.

BC قَبْلَ ٱلْمِيلَادِ qabla l-mīlādi   AD بَعْدَ ٱلْمِيلَادِ baʿda l-mīlādi

Note: One of the most common festival greetings for both Muslims and Christians is عِيدٌ مُبَارَكٌ ʿīdun mubārakun, which means 'A blessed feast'.

Exercises

Practise your reading:

[1]حَفِظْتُ [2]غَيْبًا دَرْسَ [3]ٱلْعَدَدِ [4]ٱلتَّرْتِيبِيِّ فِي [5]ٱلصَّفْحَةِ ٱلْحَادِيَةِ وَٱلْأَرْبَعِينَ مِنَ [6]ٱلْجُزْءِ [7]ٱلْأَوَّلِ لِكِتَابِ [8]قَوَاعِدِ [9]ٱللُّغَةِ ٱلْعَرَبِيَّةِ.

(1) [1]I learned [2]by heart (memorized) the lesson on [4]ordinal [3]numbers on [5]page 41 in the [7]first [6]part of the book on Arabic [9]language [8]grammar.

خَمْسَةٌ [1]بِٱلْمِئَةِ مِنْ [2]سُكَّانِ (سَاكِنٌ) ٱلْمَدِينَةِ [3]أَجَانِبُ (أَجْنَبِيٌّ)، مِنْ عَشْرِ [4]جِنْسِيَّاتٍ [5]مُخْتَلِفَةٍ، إِثْنَانِ بِٱلْمِئَةِ مِنْهُمْ مِنْ [6]دُوَلٍ (دَوْلَةٌ) لَيْسَتْ [7]تَابِعَةً [8]لِلْاِتِّحَادِ ٱلْأُورُبِّي.

(2) Five [1]per cent of [2]the inhabitants of the city are [3]foreigners of ten [5]different [4]nationalities. Two per cent of them are from [6]countries not [7]belonging to the European [8]Union.

[1]يَتَأَلَّفُ كِتَابُ [2]تَارِيخِ ٱلْعَرَبِ [3]ٱلْحَدِيثِ مِنْ أَرْبَعَةِ [4]أَجْزَاءٍ (جُزْءٌ) قَرَأْتُ مِنْهُ [5]ٱلْجُزْأَيْنِ [6]ٱلْأَوَّلَ وَٱلثَّانِيَ [7]فَقَطْ.

(3) The [3]modern Arab [2]history book [1]consists of four [4]volumes. I read [7]only [6]the first and the second [5]parts (volumes).

كَانَتْ أَوَّلُ [1] حَمْلَةٍ [2] صَلِيبِيَّةٍ إِلَى [3] ٱلشَّرْقِ فِي [4] ٱلْقَرْنِ ٱلْحَادِي عَشَرَ

[5] وَٱحْتَلُّوا [6] ٱلْقُدْسَ فِي [7] عَامِ أَلْفٍ وَتِسْعَةٍ وَتِسْعِينَ.

(4) The first [2]Crusade (lit. [2]Crusaders' [1]expedition) to [3]the East was in the eleventh [4]century, [5]and they conquered [6]Jerusalem in (the [7]year) 1099.

[1] دَفَعْتُ [2] ٱلثُّلْثَيْنِ مِنْ [3] ثَمَنِ [4] ٱلسَّيَّارَةِ [5] وَسَأَدْفَعُ ٱلثُّلْثَ [6] ٱلْبَاقِي فِي

[7] بِدَايَةِ ٱلسَّنَةِ [8] ٱلْقَادِمَةِ [9] إِضَافَةً إِلَى [10] فَائِدَةٍ هِيَ ثَمَانٍ بِٱلْمِئَةِ.

(5) [1]I paid [2]two thirds of [3]the price of [4]the car [5]and I will pay [6]the remaining third at [7]the beginning of [8]next year, [9]in addition to [10]interest of eight per cent.

ذَهَبْتُ مَعَ صَدِيقَيَّ [1] لِزِيَارَتِكُمْ فِي مَنْزِلِكُمِ [2] ٱلرِّيفِي فِي ٱلسَّاعَةِ ٱلثَّامِنَةِ

[3] وَٱلنِّصْفِ مِنْ [4] صَبَاحِ [5] يَوْمِ ٱلاثْنَيْنِ [6] ٱلْمَاضِي. وَلٰكِنْ [7] مَعَ ٱلْأَسَفِ [8] لَمْ

[9] يَكُنْ [10] أَحَدٌ [11] هُنَاكَ، [12] فَٱنْتَظَرْنَاكُمْ [13] أَكْثَرَ مِنْ ثَلَاثَةِ [14] أَرْبَاعِ (رُبْعُ)

ٱلسَّاعَةِ ثُمَّ [15] ذَهَبْنَا.

(6) I went with two friends of mine [1]to visit you (plur.) in your [2]country house at 8.30 a.m. (lit. eight o'clock [3]and half) [6]last [5]Monday [4]morning. [7]Unfortunately [8,10]nobody [9]was [11]there. [12]We waited for you for [13]more than three [14]quarters of an hour, then [15]we went (left).

[1] إِبْتَدَأْتُ فِي هٰذَا [2] ٱلْأُسْبُوعِ فِي أَوَّلِ دَرْسٍ فِي [3] ٱللُّغَةِ ٱلْعَرَبِيَّةِ، فَفِي

ٱلسَّاعَةِ [4] ٱلْأُولَى عَلَّمَنَا ٱلْمُعَلِّمُ كِتَابَةَ [5] ٱلْأَحْرُفِ (حَرْفٌ) وَفِي ٱلسَّاعَةِ

[6] ٱلثَّانِيَةِ [7] لَفْظَهَا.

(7) This [2]week [1]I began the first lesson in the Arabic [3]language. In [4]the first hour the teacher taught us how to write [5]the letters, and in [6]the second hour how to [7]pronounce them (lit. the writing of [5]the letters – [7]their pronunciation).

[1] كَمِ [2] ٱلسَّاعَةُ [3] ٱلْآنَ؟

(8) [1]What [2]time (hour) is it [3]now?

أَلسَّاعَةُ [1] ٱلْآنَ [2] ٱلثَّالِثَةُ [3] وَخَمْسَ عَشْرَةَ [4] دَقِيقَةً مِنْ [5] بَعْدِ [6] ٱلظُّهْرِ.

(9) The time (hour) [1]now is [3]15 [4]minutes past [2]three in the [5,6]afternoon (p.m.).

أَلسَّاعَةُ [1] ٱلعَاشِرَةُ [2] وَٱلدَّقِيقَةُ [3] ٱلْخَامِسَةُ مِنْ [4] قَبْلِ [5] ٱلظُّهْرِ.

(10) It is [3]five ([2]minutes) past [1]ten a.m. (lit. [4]before [5]noon).

أَلسَّاعَةُ [1] ٱلسَّابِعَةُ [2] وَٱلرُّبْعُ [3] صَبَاحًا.

(11) It is [2]quarter past [1]seven in [3]the morning.

أَلسَّاعَةُ [1] ٱلثَّامِنَةُ [2] وَٱلدَّقِيقَةُ [3] ٱلْعَاشِرَةُ [4] صَبَاحًا.

(12) It is [3]ten ([2]minutes) past [1]eight [4]in the morning.

أَلسَّاعَةُ [1] ٱلْحَادِيَةَ عَشْرَةَ [2] إِلاَّ رُبْعًا مِنْ [3] قَبْلِ [4] ٱلظُّهْرِ.

(13) It is quarter to [1]eleven a.m. (lit. a quarter [2]less than eleven [3]before [4]noon).

أَلسَّاعَةُ ٱلثَّانِيَةَ عَشْرَةَ إِلاَّ ثُلُثًا مَسَاءً.

(14) It is twenty to (lit. a third less than) twelve in the evening.

أَلسَّاعَةُ [1] ٱلثَّانِيَةَ عَشْرَةَ [2] ظُهْرًا.

(15) It is [1]twelve (o'clock) [2]noon.

[1] قَرَّرَتِ [2] ٱلْحُكُومَةُ [3] رَفْعَ [4] ٱلضَّرِيبَةِ عَلَى [5] ٱلْبَضَائِعِ (s. بِضَاعَةٌ)
[6] ٱلْمُسْتَوْرَدَةِ [7] بِنِسْبَةِ أَرْبَعَةٍ بِٱلْمِئَةِ، [8] إِبْتِدَاءً مِنْ [9] أَوَّلِ [10] كَانُونَ ٱلثَّانِي
/ يَنَايِرُ [11] لِعَامِ أَلْفٍ وَتِسْعِ مِئَةٍ وَتِسْعَةٍ وَتِسْعِينَ.

(16) [2]The government [1]decided [3]to raise [4]the taxes on [6]imported [5]goods [7]by four per cent, [8]starting from the [9]first of [10]January ([11]for the year) 1999.

[1] وَقَعَ [2] عَامِلٌ مِنَ [3] ٱلشُّبَّاكِ فِي [4] ٱلطَّابِقِ [5] ٱلثَّالِثِ [6] وَكَسَرَ [7] رِجْلَيْهِ
[8] ٱلِاثْنَتَيْنِ.

(17) [2]A worker [1]fell from [3]the window of (on) [5]the third [4]floor [6]and broke [8]both [7]his legs.

هَلْ [1]تُشَرِّفُنَا [2]بِزِيَارَتِكَ [3]يَوْمَ ٱلسَّبْتِ [4]ٱلْمُقْبِلِ [5]لِمُنَاسَبَةِ [6]عِيدِ [7]مِيلَادِي ٱلْخَمْسِينَ؟ [8]آسِفٌ جِدّاً، إِنِّي [9]مَشْغُولٌ فِي ذٰلِكَ ٱلْيَوْمِ وَلٰكِنِّي [10]سَأَزُورُكُمْ [11]يَوْمَ ٱلْأَحَدِ. [12]أَتَجِيءُ [13]صَبَاحًا أَوْ [14]مَسَاءً؟ أَجِيءُ [15]بَعْدَ [16]ٱلظُّهْرِ إِنْ [17]شَاءَ ٱللّٰهُ.

(18) Will you [1]honour us [2]with a (lit. your) visit [4]next [3]Saturday [5]on the occasion of my 50th [6,7]birthday? [8]I am very sorry, [9]I am busy that day, but [10]I will visit you on [11]Sunday. [12]Will you come in the [13]morning or in [14]the evening? I will come in the [15,16]afternoon, God [17]willing.

[1]عِيدُ [2]رَأْسِ ٱلسَّنَةِ ٱلْهِجْرِيَّةِ فِي [3]أَوَائِلِ (أَوَّلُ) ٱلشَّهْرِ ٱلرَّابِعِ [4]وَلَيْسَ فِي [5]أَوَاخِرِ (آخِرِ) ٱلشَّهْرِ ٱلثَّالِثِ [6]كَمَا [7]ذُكِرَ.

(19) [1,2]The Hiğrah New Year (lit. [1]the occasion of [2]the head of the Hiğrah year) is at [3]the beginning of the fourth month (i.e. rabīʿ t-tānī) [4]and not at [5]the end of the third month [6]as had been [7]mentioned.

أَلسُّورَةُ ٱلْأُولَى مِنَ ٱلْقُرْآنِ ٱلْكَرِيمِ ٱسْمُهَا ‹[1]ٱلْفَاتِحَةُ›، وَٱلسُّورَةُ ٱلْمِئَةُ وَٱلرَّابِعَةَ عَشْرَةَ هِيَ [2]ٱلْأَخِيرَةُ [3]وَٱسْمُهَا ‹[4]ٱلنَّاسُ›.

(20) The first sūrah (chapter) of the Holy Quran is called [1]*The Opening*, and the 114th is [2]the last sūrah and it [3]is called [4]*Mankind*.

[1]إِنْتَهَيْنَا مِنَ [2]ٱلْقَرْنِ ٱلْعِشْرِينَ [3]وَٱبْتَدَأْنَا فِي ٱلْقَرْنِ ٱلْحَادِي وَٱلْعِشْرِينَ.

(21) [1]We have finished the twentieth [2]century [3]and we have begun the twenty-first century.

[1]أَلصَّلَاةُ [2]وَصَوْمُ شَهْرِ رَمَضَانَ، إِثْنَانِ [3]مِنْ [4]أَرْكَانِ (رُكْنٌ) ٱلْإِسْلَامِ ٱلْخَمْسَةِ، [5]وَيَجِبُ عَلَى كُلِّ مُسْلِمٍ [6]قَادِرٍ أَنْ [7]يُؤَدِّيَهَا.

(22) [1]Prayer [2]and fasting in the month of Ramadan [3]are two of the five [4]pillars (principles) of Islam. Every Muslim [5]must [7]perform them if he [6]can.

Translate into Arabic:

(1) The book on the Crusades to the East in the eleventh century consists of five parts (volumes), and I read only the first and the second parts (volumes).

(2) This week I learned by heart the first volume of the Modern Arab History.

(3) Last Monday I paid one third of the price of my country house and I will pay the two remaining thirds at the beginning of this week, in addition to interest of nine per cent.

(4) At the beginning of this year I began the first lesson in the Arabic language. In the first hour the teacher taught us how to pronounce the letters and in the second hour how to write them.

(5) The government decided to raise the tax on imported goods by 7 per cent, starting from the fifth month of the year 2005.

(6) Eight per cent of the inhabitants of the city are foreigners of 22 different nationalities, and four per cent of them are from countries not belonging to the European Union.

(7) Will you come on Saturday or Sunday? I will come on Sunday morning or in the afternoon, God willing.

(8) The 65th sūrah of the Holy Quran is called *Sūratu ṭ-ṭalāqi* ('The Divorce'), and the 89th sūrah is called *Sūratu l-fağri* ('The Dawn').

(9) Fasting in the month of Ramaḍān is one of the five pillars of Islam.

(10) What time is it now?

(11) The time now is 13 minutes past three p.m. (in the afternoon).

(12) It is ten minutes past eleven a.m. (before noon).

(13) It is quarter past seven a.m. (in the morning).

(14) It is five minutes past eight a.m. (in the morning).

(15) It is quarter to ten a.m.

(16) It is twenty (a third) to ten.

(17) It is twelve (o'clock) noon.

(18) Last Saturday a foreigner fell from the window of (on) the second floor and broke both his legs.

(19) I read about the ordinal numbers on page thirty-one in the Arabic language grammar book.

Chapter 36

Exception

36.1 Exception in Arabic: أَلْاِسْتِثْنَاءُ

The following are the four most common words or particles used in the sense 'except (for), excepting, with the exception of, apart from, excluding, barring':

إِلاَّ	غَيْرُ	سِوَى	(مَا عَدَا) عَدَا
ʾillā	ġayrun	siwā	ʿadā (mā ʿadā)

An exceptive sentence contains the following four central elements:

(a) the predicate, expressing the action or situation to which the exception refers;

(b) the first noun, أَلْمُسْتَثْنَى مِنْهُ, i.e. (the set) from which the exception is made;

(c) the subtractive or exceptive particle, أَدَاةُ ٱلاِسْتِثْنَاءِ;

(d) the second noun, أَلْمُسْتَثْنَى, i.e. the excepted or excluded member.

36.2 The particle إِلاَّ ʾillā, is most commonly used. It takes the following noun in any of the three cases as follows:

(a) إِلاَّ ʾillā, in a positive sentence

In a positive sentence the second noun that follows إِلاَّ is in the accusative case, e.g.

The 2nd noun (the excepted member)	*The exceptive particle*	*The 1st noun* (the set from which the exception is made)	*Predicate*
وَاحِدًا	إِلَّا	ٱلطُّلَّابُ	خَرَجَ

ḫaraǧa ṭ-ṭullābu **ʾillā** wāḥid**an**. (All) the students went out **except** one.

ٱلرَّئِيسَ	إِلَّا	ٱلْأَعْضَاءُ	حَضَرَ

ḥaḍara l-ʾaʿḍāʾu **ʾillā** r-raʾīs**a**. (All) the members came **except** the president.

(b) إِلَّا ʾillā, in a negative sentence with the first noun expressed

In a negative sentence the second noun that follows إِلَّا ʾillā can be in either the nominative or accusative, e.g.

مَا جَاءَ ٱلطُّلَّابُ إِلَّا وَاحِدًا / وَاحِدٌ

mā ǧāʾa ṭ-ṭullābu **ʾillā** wāḥid**an** / wāḥid**un**.

Only one student came. (lit. No students came **except** one.)

لَمْ يَقْرَأْ مِنَ ٱلْجَرَائِدِ إِلَّا جَرِيدَةً / جَرِيدَةٌ

lam yaqraʾ mina l-ǧarāʾidi **ʾillā** ǧarīdat**an** / ǧarīdat**un**.

He read only one of the newspapers.

(lit. He didn't read from the newspapers **except** one newspaper.)

لَا إِلٰهَ إِلَّا ٱللّٰهَ / ٱللّٰهُ **lā** ʾilāha **ʾillā** llāh**a** / llāh**u**.

There is no god except God (Allah). OR There is only one God.

(c) إِلَّا ʾillā, in a negative sentence without the first noun

In a negative sentence the first noun may be dropped before إِلَّا ʾillā. Then the noun that follows إِلَّا may take any of the three cases, according to the case assignment (rection) determined by the verb, e.g.

لَمْ يَأْكُلْ إِلَّا قَلِيلًا lam yaʾkul **ʾillā** qalīl**an**.

He ate only a little. (lit. He did not eat **except** a little.)

مَا جَاءَ إِلاَّ رَجُلٌ **mā** ğāʾa **ʾillā** rağul**un**.

Only one man came. (lit. Nobody came **except** one man.)

مَا مَرَرْتُ إِلاَّ بِرَجُلٍ **mā** marartu **ʾillā** bi-rağul**in**. I passed by only one man.

(lit. I didn't pass by **except** one man.)

لاَ أَحْتَرِمُ إِلاَّ ٱلصَّادِقَ **lā** ʾaḥtarimu **ʾillā** ṣ-ṣādiqa.

I respect only the honest. (lit. I don't respect **except** the honest.)

لاَ يُوجَدُ إِلاَّ كِتَابٌ **lā** yūğadu **ʾillā** kitāb**un**.

There is only one book. (lit. There does not exist **except** one book.)

36.3 The particles غَيْرُ ġayru, سِوَى siwā and عَدَا ʿadā may replace إِلاَّ ʾillā, but they take the following noun in the genitive case, e.g.

مَا جَاءَ غَيْرُ / سِوَى وَاحِدٍ **mā** ğāʾa **ġayru** / **siwā** wāḥid**in**.

Only one came. (lit. Nobody came **except for** one.)

جَاءَ ٱلرِّجَالُ عَدَا وَاحِدٍ ğāʾa r-riğālu ʿ**adā** wāḥid**in**.

The men came **except for** one (of them).

عَدَا ʿadā may be preceded by the relative pronoun مَا mā: مَا عَدَا mā ʿadā, when it is regarded as a verb. It is then followed by a noun in the accusative case, e.g.

جَاءَ ٱلرِّجَالُ مَا عَدَا وَاحِداً ğāʾa r-riğālu **mā** ʿ**adā** wāḥid**an**.

The men came **except(ing)** one (of them).

36.4 **إِلاَّ أَنَّ ʾillā ʾanna and غَيْرَ أَنَّ ġayra ʾanna**

The particle إِلاَّ ʾillā, and the accusative of غَيْرُ ġayru may be followed by the subordinating conjunction أَنَّ ʾanna 'that'. The meaning then becomes 'except that, nevertheless, but, however', e.g.

[1]تَبَاحَثُوا فِي [2]ٱلْأَمرِ [3]إِلاَّ أَنَّهُمْ / غَيْرَ أَنَّهُمْ [4]لَمْ [5]يَجِدُوا [6]حَلاًّ

tabāḥaṯū fī l-ʾamri ʾ**illā** ʾ**anna**-hum / **ġayra** ʾ**anna**-hum lam yağidū ḥallan.
[1]They discussed [2]the matter, [3]**but** they did [4]not [5]find [6]a solution.

[1]غَيْرَ أَنَّهُ [2]رَفَضَ [3]ٱلْإِجَابَةَ

ġayra ʾ**anna**-hu rafaḍa l-ʾIğābata.
[1]**But** (nevertheless) [2]he refused to [3]answer.

Exercises

Practise your reading:

[1]نَامَ كُلُّ [2]أَفْرَادِ (فَرْدٌ) [3]ٱلْعَائِلَةِ فِي ٱلْبَيْتِ [4]ٱلرِّيفِيِّ [5]إِلاَّ وَاحِداً [6]عَادَ إِلَى ٱلْمَدِينَةِ.

(1) All [3]family [2]members [1]slept in [4]the country house [5]except one who [6]returned to the city.

ذَهَبَتْ [1]فِرْقَةٌ مِنَ [2]ٱلْجَيْشِ إِلَى [3]ٱلْحُدُودِ (حَدٌّ) [4]مَا عَدَا [5]جُنْدِيَّيْنِ كَانَا [6]مَرِيضَيْنِ.

(2) An [2]army [1]division (group) went to [3]the border [4]except [5]two soldiers (who) were [6]ill.

[1]أَطْفَأَتْ أُخْتِي [2]كُلَّ [3]ٱلْمَصَابِيحِ (مِصْبَاحٌ) [4]مَا عَدَا مِصْبَاحَيِ [5]ٱلْحَمَّامِ [6]وَغُرْفَةِ [7]ٱلْجُلُوسِ.

(3) My sister [1]put out [2]all the [3]lights (lamps) [4]except the two lights in [5]the bathroom and the [7]sitting [6]room.

[1]نَاقَشَ [2]أَعْضَاءُ (عُضْوٌ) [3]مَجْلِسِ [4]ٱلْأَمْنِ [5]ٱلنِّزَاعَ بَيْنَ [6]ٱلدَّوْلَتَيْنِ [7]إِلاَّ أَنَّهُمْ لَمْ [8]يَتَّفِقُوا عَلَى [9]رَأْيٍ [10]مُوَحَّدٍ.

(4) [2]The members of [4]the Security [3]Council [1]discussed [5]the conflict between [6]the two countries, [7]but they did not [8]agree on a [10]single [9]opinion.

[1]مَا [2]أَنَا [3]إِلاَّ [4]بَشَرٌ [5]مِثْلُكُمْ.

(5) [1,2]I am nothing [3]but (except) [4]a human being [5]like you. (Quran)

[1]آمَنَ تَلَامِذَةُ (تِلْمِيذٌ) [2]ٱلسَّيِّدِ [3]ٱلْمَسِيحِ ٱلاِثْنَا عَشَرَ [4]بِرِسَالَتِهِ إِلاَّ وَاحِدًا.

(6) (All of) the twelve disciples of [2]the Lord [3]Jesus/Messiah [1]believed [4]in his message apart from one.

كُلُّ [1]ٱلنَّاسِ (إِنْسَانٌ)، [2]سِوَى [3]ٱلْقَلِيلِينَ، لاَ [4]يَهْتَمُّونَ [5]بِٱلسِّيَاسَةِ [6]ٱلدُّوَلِيَّةِ.

(7) All [1]people, [2]apart from a [3]few, [4]are not interested in [6]international [5]politics.

[1]لِكُلِّ [2]دَاءٍ [3]دَوَاءٌ إِلاَّ [4]ٱلْمَوْتَ.

(8) [1]For every [2]disease there is [3]a medicine (cure) except [4]death.

[1]زَارَ [2]ٱلسَّائِحُ [3]جِبَالَ لُبْنَانَ [4]كُلَّهَا [5]مَاعَدَا جَبَلَ [6]ٱلأَرْزِ.

(9) [2]The tourist [1]visited [4]all the Lebanese [3]mountains [5]except [6]the mountain of the cedars.

[1]سَقَيْتُ كُلَّ [2]أَشْجَارِ (شَجَرَةٌ) [3]ٱلْبُسْتَانِ [4]مَاعَدَا [5]شَجَرَةَ [6]تُفَّاحٍ [7]يَابِسَةً.

(10) [1]I irrigated all [2]the trees of [3]the orchard (garden) [4]except one [7]dried-up [6]apple [5]tree.

[1]حَضَرَ كُلُّ ٱلطُّلاَّبِ (طَالِبٌ) [2]ٱلْمُحَاضَرَةَ إِلاَّ أَخِي وَأَخَاكَ.

(11) All students [1]attended [2]the lecture except my brother and yours.

[1]مَا [2]نَجَحَ أَحَدٌ فِي [3]ٱلاِمْتِحَانِ إِلاَّ طَالِبٌ وَاحِدٌ / طَالِبًا وَاحِدًا.

(12) Only one student [2]passed the exam. (lit. [1]No one [2]passed [3]the exam except one student.)

[1]هَرَبَ كُلُّ [2]ٱلْجُنُودِ مِنَ [3]ٱلثُّكْنَةِ [4]سِوَى [5]قَائِدِهِمْ [6]وَجُنْدِيٍّ وَاحِدٍ.

(13) All [2]soldiers [1]ran away (escaped) from [3]the barracks [4]except [5]their commander and one [6]soldier.

مَا [1]عَرَفْتُ مِنَ [2]ٱلأَعْضَاءِ ٱلَّذِينَ [3]حَضَرُوا [4]ٱلاِجْتِمَاعَ [5]سِوَى ٱلرَّئِيسِ [6]وَعُضْوٍ وَاحِدٍ.

(14) I did not [1]know any of [2]the members who [3]attended [4]the meeting [5]except the chairman and one [6]member.

سَوْفَ لاَ [1]أَشْتَرِي [2]شَيْئًا مِنَ [3]ٱلْمَكْتَبَةِ إِلاَّ [4]ٱلْجَرِيدَةَ [5]وَٱلْمَجَلَّةَ ٱلْعَرَبِيَّتَيْنِ.

(15) I will not [1]buy [2]anything from [3]the bookshop except the Arabic [4]newspaper [5]and the magazine.

[1]خَرَجَ [2]ٱلْمُسْتَمِعُونَ مِنَ [3]قَاعَةِ [4]ٱلْمُحَاضَرَاتِ إِلاَّ [5]ٱلْمُحَاضِرَ وطَالِبَةً جَدِيدَةً.

(16) [2]The audience (listeners) [1]went out of [4]the lecture [3]hall except [5]the lecturer and one new student (f.).

[1]زَرَعْتُ فِي ٱلْجُنَيْنَةِ [2]أَزْهَارًا (زَهْرَةٌ) [3]مُتَنَوِّعَةً [4]عَدَا [5]ٱلْوَرْدِ (وَرْدَةٌ).

(17) [1]I planted [3]a variety of [2]flowers in the garden but no (lit. [4]except) [5]roses.

[1]نَجَحَ [2]جَمِيعُ ٱلطُّلاَّبِ فِي [3]ٱلاِمْتِحَانِ [4]ٱلنِّهَائِيِّ [5]مَاعَدَا طَالِبًا [6]كَسْلاَنَ.

(18) [2]All the students [1]passed [4]the final [3]exam [5]except one [6]lazy student.

لاَ [1]أَكْرَهُ [2]شَيْئًا إِلاَّ [3]ٱلطَّقْسَ [4]ٱلْبَارِدَ.

(19) I [1]hate [2]nothing except [4]cold [3]weather.

[1]لَيْسَ فِي [2]حَقْلِنَا إِلاَّ [3]شَجَرُ (شَجَرَةٌ) [4]ٱلْعِنَبِ [5]وَٱلتِّينِ [6]وَٱلزَّيْتُونِ.

(20) There are only [4]grape, [5]fig [6]and olive trees in [2]our field.
(lit. [1]There is [1]nothing in [2]our field except [4]grape, [5]fig [6]and olive [3]trees.)

[1]لَيْسَ [2]عِنْدَ [3]ٱلنَّاسِ [4]حَدِيثٌ إِلاَّ ٱلْحَدِيثَ عَنْ [5]أَزْمَةِ [6]ٱلشَّرْقِ [7]ٱلأَوْسَطِ.

(21) [3]People [4]talk only about the crisis in the [7]Middle [6]East.
(lit. [1]There is no (other) [4]talk [2]by [3]the people except talk about [5]the crisis in [7]the Middle [6]East.)

[1]تَكَلَّمَ [2]ٱلْخَبِيرُ [3]ٱلْعَسْكَرِيُّ [4]لِمُرَاسِلِي [5]ٱلصُّحُفِ (صَحِيفَةٌ) [6]غَيْرَ أَنَّهُ [7]رَفَضَ [8]ٱلإِجَابَةَ عَنْ [9]جَمِيعِ [10]ٱلأَسْئِلَةِ (سُؤَالٌ).

(22) [3]The military [2]expert [1]talked to [5]newspaper [4]correspondents [6]but [7]he refused [8]to answer [9]all the [10]questions.

Translate into Arabic:

(1) All the family members except one, who was ill, visited the mountain of the cedars.

(2) All the students slept in the country house except my sister who returned to the city.

(3) All the soldiers went to the border except the commander and one soldier who were ill.

(4) All the members of the Security Council went out of the hall except one new member.

(5) In the final exam I did not know the answers to any of the questions except one.

(6) All the members attended the meeting except the military expert and one member.

(7) All the audience went out of the hall except the chairman of the meeting and the newspaper correspondents.

(8) My brother put out all the lights in the house except the light in the bathroom.

(9) I will not buy anything except roses, the newspaper and a magazine.

(10) The lecturer talked to an army division about the conflict between the two countries but he refused to answer all the questions.

(11) In the garden I planted a variety of flowers and trees but no (lit. except) olive trees.

(12) The members who attended the meeting discussed the crisis in the Middle East, but they didn't agree on a single opinion.

Chapter 37

Verbs of wonder, the negative copula لَيْسَ laysa, verbs with special uses and some special uses of the preposition ..بِـ bi...

37.1 *Verbs of wonder,* أَفْعَالُ ٱلتَّعَجُّبِ

Exclamatory phrases such as 'How beautiful!', 'How tall!', 'How black he/she/it is!', 'What a rich man he is!', etc., are expressed by using the interrogative pronoun مَا mā 'what?', followed by a verb form which looks like the derived verb form IV in the perfect tense third person singular masculine (pattern: أَفْعَلَ ʾafʿala) and a noun in the accusative case or a suffixed pronoun, e.g.

مَا أَجْمَلَ ٱلْبِنْتَ
mā ʾağmala l-binta!
How beautiful the girl is!

مَا أَجْمَلَهَا
mā ʾağmala-hā!
How beautiful she / it is!

مَا أَكْذَبَ هٰذَا ٱلرَّجُلَ
mā ʾakḏaba hāḏā r-rağula!
What a liar this man is!

مَا أَكْذَبَهُ
mā ʾakḏaba-hu!
What a liar he is!

مَا ¹أَشَدَّ ²سَوَادَ هٰذِهِ ³ٱلْغَيْمَةِ
mā ʾašadda sawāda hāḏihi l-ġaymati!
What a black cloud this is!
(lit. **How** ¹strong is the ²blackness of this ³cloud! OR
What ¹a strength of ²blackness this ³cloud has!)

مَا أَشَدَّ سَوَادَهَا
mā ʾašadda sawāda-hā!
How black it is!

37.2 If two verbs of wonder refer to the same noun, the second verb is placed after the noun and takes a suffix pronoun, e.g.

مَا أَطْوَلَ ٱلدَّرْسَ وَمَا أَصْعَبَهُ!	(not: مَا أَطْوَلَ وَمَا أَصْعَبَ ٱلدَّرْسَ
mā ʾaṭwala d-darsa wa-mā **ʾaṣʿaba-hu!**	mā ʾaṭwala wa-mā ʾaṣʿaba d-darsa)
What a long and difficult lesson!	

37.3 *Verbs with special uses*

(a) The negative copula لَيْسَ laysa 'is not' is counted among the sisters of كَانَ kāna. It is peculiar in that it is inflected only for the perfect tense but with the meaning of the imperfect tense (referring to present time).

(b) Conjugation of لَيْسَ laysa:

	singular	dual	plural
3. masc.	لَيْسَ laysa, he is not	لَيْسَا laysā, they (2) are not	لَيْسُوا laysū, they are not
3. fem.	لَيْسَتْ laysat, she is not	لَيْسَتَا laysatā, they (2) are not	لَسْنَ lasna, they are not
2. masc.	لَسْتَ lasta, you are not	لَسْتُمَا lastumā, you (2) are not	لَسْتُمْ lastum, you are not
2. fem.	لَسْتِ lasti, you are not	لَسْتُمَا lastumā, you (2) are not	لَسْتُنَّ lastunna, you are not
1.	لَسْتُ lastu, I am not	(as in plural)	لَسْنَا lasnā, we are not

Note: Regarding the expression of the predicative complement of لَيْسَ laysa, see below (37.10b).

Remember from chapter 32 that the two verbs كَانَ kāna 'he was' and لَيْسَ laysa 'is not, are not', have no passive forms.

37.4 The verb زَالَ zāla (imperfect: يَزَالُ yazālu) 'to cease, to disappear, to go away' is another sister of كَانَ kāna. It can be used as an aspectual auxiliary in the perfect or imperfect tense, preceded by the negative particle مَا mā, لَا lā or لَمْ lam, and followed either by a verb in the imperfect tense or by a verbal adjective or a noun in the accusative case. Both these constructions signify that the action has not ceased, the activity or state is still continuing, e.g.

مَا زَالَ/ لَا يَزَالُ/ لَمْ يَزَلْ يَدْرُسُ فِي ٱلْجَامِعَةِ

mā zāla / lā yazālu / lam yazal yadrusu fī l-ǧāmiʿati.

He is **still** (lit. did not cease) studying at the university.

مَا زَالَ/ لَا يَزَالُ/ لَمْ يَزَلْ حَيًّا

mā zāla / lā yazālu / lam yazal ḥayyan.

He is **still** alive. (lit. He did not cease being alive.)

37.5 The verb عَادَ ʿāda (imperf.: يَعُودُ yaʿūdu) 'to return, to do again, to resume' is somewhat similar to the above verb زَالَ zāla.

(a) When it is preceded by the negative particle مَا mā or لَمْ lam, the meaning is: 'not again, no longer', e.g.

عَادَ يَدْرُسُ فِي ٱلْجَامِعَةِ

ʿāda yadrusu fī l-ǧāmiʿati.

He **resumed** studying at the university.

مَا عَادَ / لَمْ يَعُدْ يَدْرُسُ فِي ٱلْجَامِعَةِ

mā ʿāda / lam yaʿud yadrusu fī l-ǧāmiʿati.

He **is no longer** studying at the university. OR

He **no longer** studies at the university.

(b) The IVth form of the above verb عَادَ ʿāda is أَعَادَ ʾaʿāda. When it is followed by a defined noun in the accusative case, it will have the meaning 'to do again, to give back, re-', e.g.

أَعَادَ ٱلْكِتَابَ

ʾaʿāda l-kitāba. He **returned / gave back** the book.

أَعَادَ ٱلْاِمْتِحَانَ

ʾaʿāda l-ʾimtiḥāna. He **repeated** (**re**-took) the exam. (He **re**-examined.)

أَعَادَ ٱلنَّظَرَ فِي ٱلْقَضِيَّةِ

ʾaʿāda n-naḏara fī l-qaḍiyyati. He **re-**considered the case.

إِقْتَرَحَ إِعَادَةَ ٱلنَّظَرِ فِي ٱلْقَضِيَّةِ

ʾiqtaraḥa **ʾiʿādata** n-naḏari fī l-qaḍiyyati. He proposed to **re-**consider the case.

Note: The above إِعَادَةٌ is the verbal noun of form IV.

37.6 The verb كَادَ kāda (imperfect: يَكَادُ yakādu) 'to be about to . . ., almost, (nearly) . . .' is used as an auxiliary with the following verb in the imperfect indicative or, alternatively, imperfect subjunctive (after أَنْ), e.g.

Main verb: imperfect indicative		***Main verb: imperfect* subjunctive**
كَادَ ٱلْوَلَدُ يَقَعُ kāda l-walad**u** yaqaʿ**u.** The boy **was about** to fall over.	OR	كَادَ ٱلْوَلَدُ أَنْ يَقَعَ kāda l-walad**u** **ʾan** yaqaʿ**a.**
كِدْتُ أَمُوتُ مِنَ ٱلْعَطَشِ kidtu ʾamūtu mina l-ʿaṭaši. I **almost** died of thirst.	OR	كِدْتُ أَنْ أَمُوتَ مِنَ ٱلْعَطَشِ kidtu **ʾan** ʾamūt**a** mina l-ʿaṭaši. I was **almost** going to die of thirst.
يَكَادُ يَمُوتُ مِنَ ٱلْجُوعِ yakādu yamūt**u** mina l-ǧūʿi. He is **almost** dying of hunger.	OR	يَكَادُ أَنْ يَمُوتَ مِنَ ٱلْجُوعِ yakādu **ʾan** yamūt**a** mina l-ǧūʿi. He is **almost** going to die of hunger.

When كَادَ kāda is in the perfect or imperfect tense, preceded by the negative particle مَا mā or لَمْ lam, both tenses have almost the same meaning: 'just, barely, hardly, almost not', e.g.

مَا كَادَ / لَمْ يَكَدْ يَقِفُ حَتَّى وَقَعَ

mā kāda / **lam** yakad yaqifu ḥattā waqaʿa. He **barely** stood up before he fell down.

37.7 The verb دَامَ dāma 'to last, to continue, to go on' can be used in temporal clauses meaning 'as long as . . . (something is happening or going on)'. It is then preceded by the conjunction مَا mā 'as long as' and followed by a verb in the imperfect tense or a participle in the accusative case, e.g.

مَا دَامَ جَالِسًا

mā dāma ǧālisan, **as long as** he is sitting

مَا دَامَ يَجْلِسُ

mā dāma yaǧlisu, **as long as** he sits

37.8 The verb قَلَّ qalla 'to be little, to diminish, to be rare' can take the suffix ..ـمَا /...mā/, as قَلَّمَا qallamā meaning 'seldom', e.g.

قَلَّمَا نَلْتَقِي

qallamā naltaqī. We **seldom** meet.

37.9 *Verbs with the meaning* **'to start, to begin'**

In addition to the verb بَدَأَ bada'a 'to start, to begin' there are a few other verbs which have this same meaning as well as their major meaning. The following are the most common of them: صَارَ ṣāra 'to become', قَامَ qāma 'to stand up', أَخَذَ 'aḫaḏa, 'to take', e.g.

بَدَأَ / أَخَذَ يَرْكُضُ

bada'a / 'aḫaḏa yarkuḍu. He began to run.

قَامَ يَمْشِي

qāma yamšī. He rose/began to walk.

صَارَ يَضْحَكُ

ṣāra yaḍḥaku. He began to laugh.

37.10 *Some special uses of the prefixed preposition* ..بِـ *bi...*

The preposition ..بِـ **bi...**, which normally means 'by, with', etc., can also be used in certain types of complements:

(a) بِـ.. bi... preceding *a direct object*

Certain triliteral transitive verbs, such as سَمِعَ samiʿa 'to hear' and بَعَثَ baʿata 'to send', may take the preposition بِـ.. bi... before the direct object, which then appears in the genitive case. This construction is merely a stylistic alternative to the regular construction with an accusative direct object, e.g.

سَمِعْتُ بِٱلْخَبَرِ	OR	سَمِعْتُ ٱلْخَبَرَ
samiʿtu **bi**-l-ḫabari. I heard the piece of news / about the news.		samiʿtu l-ḫabara.
بَعَثَ إِلَيْهِ بِرِسَالَةٍ	OR	بَعَثَ إِلَيْهِ رِسَالَةً
baʿaṯa ʾilay-hi **bi**-risālatin. He sent him a letter.		baʿaṯa ʾilay-hi risālatan.

Compare:

أَكَلَ ٱللَّحْمَ بِٱلشَّوْكَةِ

ʾakala l-laḥma **bi**-š-šawkati. He ate the meat with the fork.

(b) بِـ.. bi ... before the complement of a negative predicate

After the negative copula لَيْسَ laysa 'is not', and after the negative particle مَا mā 'not', the predicative complement may take the preposition بِـ... bi.. (+ genitive). Again, this construction is merely a stylistic alternative to the regular construction with an accusative predicative complement, e.g.

لَسْتُ بِقَصِيرٍ	OR	لَسْتُ قَصِيرًا
lastu **bi**-qaṣīrin. I am not short.		lastu qaṣīran
لَيْسَ بِقَبِيحٍ	OR	لَيْسَ قَبِيحًا
laysa **bi**-qabīḥin. He / it is not ugly.		laysa qabīḥan
مَا كُنَّا بِنَائِمِينَ	OR	مَا كُنَّا نَائِمِينَ
mā kunnā **bi**-nāʾimīna. We were not sleeping.		mā kunnā nāʾimīna
مَا هُوَ بِبَخِيلٍ	OR	مَا هُوَ بَخِيلاً
mā huwa **bi**-baḫīlin. He is not stingy.		mā huwa baḫīlan

Note: ما mā has the function of لَيْسَ laysa, which is a sister of كَانَ kāna.

(c) بِـ.. bi... preceding the conjunctions أَنْ ʾan and أَنَّ ʾanna

The preposition بِـ.. bi... can be prefixed to the subordinating conjunctions أَنْ ʾan and أَنَّ ʾanna 'that' without any change of meaning, e.g.

طَلَبَ مِنِّي بِأَنْ أَذْهَبَ مَعَهُ ṭalaba min-nī **bi**-ʾan ʾaḏhaba maʿa-hu. He asked me to go with him.	OR	طَلَبَ مِنِّي أَنْ أَذْهَبَ مَعَهُ ṭalaba min-nī ʾan ʾaḏhaba maʿa-hu.
أَخْبَرَنِي بِأَنَّ وَالِدَهُ مَرِيضٌ ʾaḫbara-nī **bi**-ʾanna wālida-hu marīḍun. He told me that his father is ill.	OR	أَخْبَرَنِي أَنَّ وَالِدَهُ مَرِيضٌ ʾaḫbara-nī ʾanna wālida-hu marīḍun.

(d) Sometimes the particle إِذْ ʾiḏ 'when' is used with the meaning 'and then suddenly . . . !', indicating surprise or sudden appearance. In that case the subject may take the preposition بِـ.. bi.... The particle قَدْ qad is then normally added after the subject before the verb.

إِذْ بِٱلرَّئِيسِ قَدْ وَصَلَ ʾiḏ **bi**-r-raʾīsi qad waṣala! Then / suddenly the president arrived!	OR	إِذْ وَصَلَ ٱلرَّئِيسُ ʾiḏ waṣala r-raʾīsu

Exercises

Practise your reading:

¹مَا ²أَبْعَدَ هٰذِهِ ٱلْقَرْيَةَ وَمَا ³أَضْيَقَ ⁴شَوَارِعَهَا (شَارِعٌ).

(1) ¹ How ²far away this village is and how ³narrow its ⁴streets!

مَا ¹أَقْصَرَ ٱلرَّئِيسَ وَمَا ²أَطْوَلَ ³زَوْجَتَهُ.

(2) How ¹short the president is and how ²tall ³his wife!

[1]قَلَّمَا [2]يَأْتِي مُدِيرُ ٱلشَّرِكَةِ إِلَى [3]عَمَلِهِ فِي [4]يَوْمَيِ [5]ٱلسَّبْتِ [6]وَٱلْأَحَدِ.

(3) It is [1]seldom that the manager (director) of the company [2]comes to [3]work on ([4]days) [5]Saturdays [6]and Sundays.

مَا [1]أَضْعَفَ هٰذَا [2]ٱلْمَرِيضَ وَمَا [3]أَشَدَّ [4]ٱصْفِرَارَ [5] (IX) وَجْهِهِ.

(4) How [1]weak this [2]patient is and how [4]pale (lit. how [3]strong [4]yellow) [5]his face!

[1]لَسْتُ [2]فَرْحَانًا ٱلْيَوْمَ لِأَنِّي لَمْ [3]أَنْجَحْ فِي [4]ٱلْاِمْتِحَانِ.

(5) [1]I am not [2]happy today because I didn't [3]pass [4]the exam.

[1]أَلَيْسَ ٱلطَّبِيبُ فِي [2]عُطْلَتِهِ فِي [3]ٱلْأُسْبُوعِ [4]ٱلْقَادِمِ؟

(6) [1]Isn't the physician on [2]holiday (vacation) [4]next [3]week?

هٰذَا [1]ٱلْعِقْدُ لَيْسَ [2]قَدِيمًا جِدًّا.

(7) This [1]necklace is not very [2]old.

[1]أَلَيْسَ [2]يُوجَدُ فِي ٱلْجَامِعَةِ [3]مَنْ هُوَ [4]أَجْدَرُ / أَشْطَرُ مِنْكَ فِي [5]ٱللُّغَةِ ٱلْعَرَبِيَّةِ؟

(8) [1]Isn't [2]there anyone at the university [3]who is [4]more competent (clever) than you in the Arabic [5]language?

[1]لَا نَكَادُ [2]نَسْمَعُ مَاذَا [3]يَقُولُ [4]مُذِيعُ [5]نَشْرَةِ [6]ٱلْأَخْبَارِ (خَبَرٌ).

(9) [1]We can hardly [2]hear what [4]the reporter of [6]the news [5]bulletin is [3]saying.

[1]لَمْ أَكَدْ [2]أَفْتَحُ بَابَ غُرْفَةِ [3]ٱلنَّوْمِ فِي [4]ٱلْعَتْمَةِ [5]حَتَّى [6]قَفَزَ [7]ٱلْقِطُّ عَلَى [8]صَدْرِي [9]فَكِدْتُ [10]أَمُوتُ مِنَ [11]ٱلْخَوْفِ.

(10) [1]I had hardly (almost) [2]opened the door of [3]the bedroom (lit. [3]sleeping room) [5]when suddenly in [4]the darkness [7]the cat [6]jumped on to [8]my chest. [9]I was [11]scared [10]to death (lit. [9]I almost [10]died [11]of fright).

[1]لَمْ يَزَلْ (هُنَاكَ) بَعْضُ [2]ٱلْوَقْتِ حَتَّى [3]تَطِيرَ [4]ٱلطَّائِرَةُ.

(11) [1]There is still some [2]time before the [4]aeroplane [3]takes off (flies).

[1]مَا دَامَ [2]جَدُّكَ مَرِيضًا [3]فَيَجِبُ أَنْ [4]يَبْقَى [5]شَهْرًا [6]آخَرَ فِي [7]ٱلْفِرَاشِ.

(12) [1]As long as [2]your grandfather is ill (so) [3]he should [4]stay in [7]bed for [6]another [5]month.

[1]بَعْدَ [2]نِصْفِ [3]شَهْرٍ فِي [4]ٱلصَّحْرَاءِ [5]كَادَتِ ٱلْجِمَالُ (جَمَلٌ) [6]تَمُوتُ مِنَ [7]ٱلْعَطَشِ.

(13) [1]After [2]half [3]a month in [4]the desert the camels [5]almost [6]died of [7]thirst.

[1]عَادَ [2]ٱلْأَهْلُ [3]ثَانِيَةً [4]يَبْحَثُونَ عَنِ ٱلطِّفْلِ [5]ٱلضَّائِعِ فِي [6]ٱلْغَابَةِ.

(14) [2]The family [1]resumed ([3]again) [4]searching for the [5]lost child in [6]the forest.

[1]إِنَّنِي [2]مَا زِلْتُ [3]أَحْتَرِمُ [4]وَأُقَدِّرُ [5]جَلَالَةَ ٱلْمَلِكِ [6]مُنْذُ يَوْمِ [7]تَتْوِيجِهِ.

(15) [1]I [2]have [3]respected [4]and admired [5]His Majesty the King [6]since the day of his [7]coronation.

أَلَسْتَ أَنْتَ ٱلَّذِي كَانَ [1]نَائِبًا لِرَئِيسِ [2]مَجْلِسِ [3]إِدَارَةِ شَرِكَةِ [4]ٱلنَّفْطِ؟

(16) Aren't you the one who was the [1]vice-chairman of [4]the oil company's [3]administrative [2]board ([2]council)?

[1]أَلْمُدَّةُ [2]ٱلْمُعْطَاةُ لَيْسَتْ [3]كَافِيَةً [4]لِلْإِجَابَةِ عَلَى كُلِّ [5]أَسْئِلَةِ (سُؤَالٌ) [6]ٱلِامْتِحَانِ.

(17) The [1]time [2]given is not [3]enough [4]to answer all [6]the exam [5]questions.

[1]مَا زَالَتِ [2]ٱلْحُكُومَةُ [3]تَرْفُضُ [4]تَخْفِيضَ [5]رُسُومِ (s. رَسْمٌ) [6]ٱلضَّرَائِبِ (ضَرِيبَةٌ) عَنْ [7]أَصْحَابِ (صَاحِبٌ) [8]ٱلدَّخْلِ [9]ٱلْقَلِيلِ.

(18) [2]The government [1]still [3]refuses [4]to reduce [6]tax (lit. [5]fee, due) for [7]those on [9]low (lit. [9]little) [8]incomes.

ذَهَبَ [1]ٱلضَّيْفُ [2]لِيَتَمَشَّى فِي [3]ٱلْغَابَةِ [4]وَلَمْ [5]يَرْجِعْ.

(19) [1]The guest went [2]for a walk in [3]the forest [4]and did not [5]return.

Translate into Arabic:

(1) How tall the manager of the company is and how short his wife!

(2) The patient seldom comes to the physician on Saturdays and Sundays.

(3) How pale (yellow) the face of the president is and how weak he is!

(4) We can hardly hear what His Majesty the King is saying.

(5) I am not happy today because the director's child is still lost in the forest.

(6) Isn't your grandfather ill and shouldn't he stay in bed for another week?

(7) The cat jumped on my chest and I was almost scared to death.

(8) The cat almost died of thirst in the bedroom.

(9) There is still half a day before the aeroplane departs (flies).

(10) How narrow the streets of this village are!

(11) Isn't the family on holiday next month?

(12) After half a month the family resumed searching for the lost child in the desert.

(13) The vice-chairman of the board of the oil company still refuses to pay the taxes.

(14) The time given is not enough to answer all the questions in the news bulletin.

Chapter 38

Adverbs and adverbials, absolute or inner object, ḥāl (circumstantial clause) and tamyīz (accusative of specification)

38.1 Adverbs

Arabic adverbs are mostly derived from nominals. The majority of the derived adverbs are, in fact, indefinite accusative nouns or adjectives, although there are also many derived adverbs with **ḍammah** without nunation or article. Compared to European languages, Arabic has few underived (original) adverbs. The underived adverbs may end in **sukūn** or **fatḥah,** less often in **kasrah** or **ḍammah** without nunation.

38.2 In Arabic grammars, adverbs are classified by meaning as follows:

(a) adverbs of time, ظَرْفُ زَمَانٍ (answer the question: مَتَى matā 'when?')

(b) adverbs of place, ظَرْفُ مَكَانٍ (answer the question: أَيْنَ ʾayna 'where?' or 'whence?').

Note: Of course, there are also adverbs of manner, degree, reason, restriction, etc., e.g. the underived adverb فَقَطْ faqaṭ 'only'.

38.3 All adverbs of time are derived from verbal roots or pronominal bases. The common adverb مَتَى matā 'when?' (also used as the temporal conjunction 'when') is apparently etymologically connected with the interrogative pronouns مَا mā 'what?' and مَنْ man 'who?'.

مَتَى matā can be preceeded by the particle أَيْ ʾay, as أَيْ مَتَى ʾaymatā, without any change of meaning, e.g.

مَتَى جِئْتَ؟ **matā** ği͗ta? OR أَيْ مَتَى جِئْتَ؟ ʾ**ay matā** ği͗ta?
When did you come?

38.4 Adverbs of time often have the definite article أَلْـ... and take the accusative or, rarely, nominative case, e.g.

With article:

أَلْيَوْمَ	أَلْجُمْعَةَ	أَلْآنَ	أَللَّيْلَةَ	أَلسَّاعَةَ	أَلسَّنَةَ
ʾal-yawma	ʾal-ğumʿata	ʾal-ʾāna	ʾal-laylata	ʾas-sāʿata	ʾas-sanata
today	on Friday	now	tonight	now, at this time	in this year

Without article:

بَعْدُ	قَبْلُ	حِينَ	أَمْسِ	غَدًا
baʿdu	qablu	ḥīna	ʾamsi	ġadan
afterwards, still, yet	before, earlier	when (conj.)	yesterday	tomorrow

Note: Adverbs ending in **ḍammah**, like بَعْدُ and قَبْلُ, may take a preposition. Nevertheless they do not change the ending into **kasrah**, e.g. مِنْ بَعْدُ min baʿdu 'afterwards'.

Examples:

مَا جَاءَ ٱلْيَوْمَ mā ğāʾa **l-yawma**. He did not come **today**.

مَا جَاءَ بَعْدُ mā ğāʾa **baʿdu**. He has not come **yet**.

سَافَرَ أَمْسِ sāfara ʾ**amsi**. He travelled **yesterday**.

Note: The **kasrah** in أَمْسِ ʾamsi 'yesterday' is not an indication of the genitive case, but is only used for smoothing the pronunciation. Observe also that أَمْسِ ʾamsi 'yesterday' has definite reference, although lacking the article. The noun أَلْأَمْسُ ʾal-ʾamsu, which is definite, means 'the past' (not: 'yesterday'). Similarly, غَدًا ġadan 'tomorrow' has definite reference but indefinite form. Compare the prepositional expression فِي ٱلْغَدِ fī l-ġadi 'in the future' (not 'tomorrow').

38.5 Certain nouns in the accusative without the article أَلْـ... are used as adverbs when followed by a year, e.g.

سَنَةَ ٢٠٠٣	في سَنَةِ ٢٠٠٣
sanata 2003, in the year 2003 OR	fī sanati 2003

38.6 Underived adverbs of place, ظَرْفُ زَمَانٍ, are very few, e.g.

تَحْتُ	هُنَا	هُنَاكَ	حَيْثُ
taḥtu	hunā	hunāka	ḥaytu
beneath	here	there	where, whither, whereas, due to the fact that

Examples:

إِجْلِسْ هُنَا !

ʾiǧlis **hunā**! Sit **here**! (masc. sing.)

إِذْهَبْ مِنْ حَيْثُ جِئْتَ !

ʾiḏhab min **ḥayṯu** ǧiʾta! Go **whence** you came!

38.7 Derived adverbs of place are common, e.g., فَوْقُ fawqu 'up(stairs), on top, above', وَرَاءُ warāʾu 'behind, in the rear, at the back'.

38.8 Other common adverbs having the form of accusative adjectives or nouns are:

تَقْرِيبًا	لَيْلاً	غَدًا	أَحْيَانًا	جِدًّا	حَالاً
taqrīban	laylan	ġadan	ʾaḥyānan	ǧiddan	ḥālan
almost	by night	tomorrow	sometimes	very	immediately
حَدِيثًا	دَائِمًا	أَخِيرًا	مَثَلاً	ثَانِيًا	أَوَّلاً
ḥadīṯan	dāʾiman	ʾaḫīran	maṯalan	ṯāniyan	ʾawwalan
recently	always	finally, lately	for example	secondly	firstly, first
شَرْقًا	شَمَالاً	يَمِينًا	يَوْمًا	كَثِيرًا	قَلِيلاً
šarqan	šamālan	yamīnan	yawman	kaṯīran	qalīlan
eastward	on the left, to the north	on the right	one day	much, very	little, few

Examples:

أُسَافِرُ غَدًا

ʾusāfiru **ġadan**. I will travel **tomorrow**.

وَصَلَتِ ٱلطَّائِرَةُ لَيْلًا

waṣalati ṭ-ṭāʾiratu **laylan**. The aeroplane arrived **at night**.

تَوَجَّهَتِ ٱلْبَاخِرَةُ جَنُوبًا

tawağğahati l-bāḫiratu **ğanūban**. The ship set out (headed) **southwards**.

38.9 English adverbs are often rendered by prepositional phrases in Arabic, e.g.

فَهِمَ بِسُهُولَةٍ

fahima **bi-suhūlatin**. He understood **easily** (lit. with ease).

قَرَأَ عَلَى مَهْلٍ

qaraʾa **ʿalā mahlin**. He read **slowly**.

38.10 *Absolute or inner object*

The so-called absolute or inner object, أَلْمَفْعُولُ ٱلْمُطْلَقُ, is used to emphasize the manner of action or the number of instances. It consists of a verbal noun (derived from the same root as the main verb) in the indefinite accusative form, followed by an accusative adjective.

رَكَضَ رَكْضًا سَرِيعًا

rakaḍa **rakḍan** sarīʿan. He ran swiftly. (lit. He ran a swift **running**.)

فَرِحَ فَرَحًا كَبِيرًا

fariḥa **faraḥan** kabīran. He rejoiced greatly. (lit. He rejoiced **a great joy**.)

Note: Sometimes the inner object consists only of a dual verbal noun:

دَقَّتِ ٱلسَّاعَةُ دَقَّتَيْنِ

daqqati s-sāʿatu **daqqatayni**. The clock struck twice (**two strikes**).

38.11 Ḥāl clause (phrase)

Ḥāl حَالٌ means 'circumstance, condition, or state'. It is added to an already complete sentence as a kind of supplementive adverbial clause or phrase, answering the question كَيْفَ kayfa 'how?' or 'in which manner or condition?'. In English it corresponds mostly to a (co)predicative or adverbial participle (referring to the subject or object), as in 'He came laughing. I saw him standing.'

Ḥāl حَالٌ is mostly an adjective or active participle in the indefinite accusative, agreeing in gender and number with the noun to which it refers, e.g.

عَادَ ٱلسَّائِحُ مَرِيضًا ʿāda s-sāʾiḥu **marīḍan**. The tourist returned **ill**.

(In which **ḥāl** 'condition' has the tourist returned? He returned **marīḍan** 'ill'. Thus, **marīḍan** is **ḥāl**, because it describes the circumstance or condition of the tourist.)

لاَ تَشْرَبِ ٱلْقَهْوَةَ سَاخِنَةً!

lā tašrabi l-qahwata **sāḫinatan**! Don't drink the coffee (while it is) **hot**!

ذَهَبَ صَدِيقِي بَاكِيًا

ḏahaba ṣadīqī **bākiyan**. My friend left **weeping**. (My friend wept as he left.)

ذَهَبَ ٱلْأَوْلَادُ بَاكِينَ

ḏahaba l-ʾawlādu **bākīna**. The boys left **weeping**. (The boys wept as they left.)

ذَهَبَتِ ٱلْبَنَاتُ بَاكِيَاتٍ

ḏahabati l-banātu **bākiyātin**. The girls left **weeping**. (The girls wept as they left.)

Remember that the above بَاكِيَاتٍ is in the accusative indefinite form, although it has two **kasrahs**. See chapter 13 on the sound feminine plural!

38.12 Ḥāl حَالٌ can be in the definite form only when followed by a suffixed possessive pronoun. **Ḥāl** is never defined by the definite article أَلْ, e.g.

جَاءَ ٱلْمَبْعُوثُ وَحْدَهُ

ǧāʾa l-mabʿūṯu **waḥda-hu**. The delegate came alone (by himself).

38.13 *The wāw of ḥāl,* وَاوُ ٱلْحَالِ

The conjunction وَ 'and' can be used to introduce a **ḥāl** clause based on an active participle (which then remains in the nominative case). This وَ is called the **wāw** of **ḥāl**, وَاوُ ٱلْحَالِ, and can be translated as 'while, as'. The **wāw** of **ḥāl** can be connected to a personal pronoun or a noun in the nominative (referring to a separate subject), e.g.

تَكَلَّمَ وَهُوَ وَاقِفٌ

takallama **wa**-huwa wāqif**un**. He spoke **while** (he was) standing.

هَرَبَ وَٱلْحَارِسُ نَائِمٌ

haraba **wa-**l-ḥārisu nāʾim**un**. He escaped **while** the guard was sleeping.

38.14 Ḥāl, حَالٌ, may replace the participle with a finite verb in the imperfect tense, preceded by the **wāw** of **ḥāl** وَ and a pronoun, e.g.

ذَهَبَ وَهُوَ يَبْكِي

ḏahaba **wa**-huwa **yabkī**. He left **weeping**. (He was **weeping** as he left.)

38.15 *Tamyīz (accusative of specification)*

The word **tamyīz**, تَمْيِيزٌ, means 'specification, discrimination, clarification'. In grammar it refers to a nominal attribute in the accusative indefinite form that expresses the substance or content after measure words, or the item counted after the cardinal numbers 11–99. In addition, it is used after the elative form in periphrastic comparative and superlative expressions. Examples:

إِشْتُرِيَ لِتْرٌ زَيْتًا

ʾišturiya litrun **zaytan**.

One litre of **oil** was bought.

(**zaytan** is **tamyīz**, because it specifies that the measured substance is oil and not something else)

اِشْتَرَى وَالِدِي لِتْرًا زَيْتًا

ᵓištarā wālid-ī litran **zaytan**.

My father bought one litre of **oil**.

عِنْدِي عِشْرُونَ قَمِيصًا

ᶜind-ī ᶜišrūna **qamīṣan**.

I have twenty **shirts**.

أَلْبِنْتُ أَقَلُّ جَمَالاً مِنْ أُمِّهَا

ᵓal-bintu ᵓaqallu **ǧamālan** min ᵓummi-hā.

The girl is less beautiful than her mother.

(lit. The girl is less **with regard to beauty** than her mother.)

Exercises

Practise your reading:

[1]حَفِظْتُ [2]غَيْبًا دُرُوسَ (دَرْسٌ) [3]قَوَاعِدِ (قَاعِدَةٌ) [4]أَللُّغَةِ ٱلْعَرَبِيَّةِ دَرْسًا دَرْسًا.

(1) [1]I learned the Arabic [3]grammar (lessons) [2]by heart, lesson by lesson (lit. the [3]rules of the Arabic [4]language).

[1]سَهِرْتُ [2]ٱللَّيْلَ [3]كُلَّهُ [4]لِوَحْدِي [6,5]وَٱلنَّاسُ [7]نَائِمُونَ.

(2) [1]I stayed [1]awake [3]all [2]night [4]alone (by myself) [5]while [6]the people were [7]asleep.

فِي [1]ٱلْغَرْبِ [2]يَصْنَعُونَ [3]ٱلْحَدِيدَ [4]سِلَاحًا وَفِي [5]ٱلشَّرْقِ [6]يَقْطَعُونَ [7]ٱلْأَشْجَارَ (شَجَرَةٌ) [8]حَطَبًا.

(3) In [1]the West [2]they make [3]iron into [4]weapons and in [5]the East [6]they cut [7]trees for [8]wood.

[1]هَاجَرَ [2]جَارِي مِنَ [3]ٱلْقَرْيَةِ [5,4]وَهُوَ كَبِيرٌ [6]وَلَمْ [7]نَعُدْ [8]نَسْمَعُ [9]عَنْهُ [10]شَيْئًا [11]مُنْذُ ذٰلِكَ ٱلْحِينِ.

(4) [2]My neighbour [1]emigrated from [3]the village [4]when [5]he was old and [11]since then we have [8]heard [6,7,10]nothing [9]about him.

[1]أَتَانِي [2]ضَيْفٌ [3]فَجْأَةً [4,5]وَأَنَا [6]أَسْتَعِدُّ [7]لِلذَّهَابِ فِي [8]سَيَّارَةٍ [9]أُجْرَةٍ كَانَتْ [10]تَنْتَظِرُنِي فِي [11]ٱلْخَارِجِ.

(5) [2]A guest dropped in (lit. [1]came to me [3]suddenly) [4,5]while I [6]was preparing [7]to go out in [8,9]a taxi ([9]hired [8]car) which was [10]waiting for me [11]outside.

[1]أَلزَّوْجُ [2]مُخْلِصٌ [3]أَمَّا [4]زَوْجَتُهُ [5]فَهِيَ [6]أَكْثَرُ [7]مِنْهُ [8]إِخْلَاصًا.

(6) [1]The husband [2]is faithful [3]but [4]his wife [5]is [6]more [8]faithful [7]than he.

أَلْمَمْلَكَةُ ٱلْعَرَبِيَّةُ ٱلسَّعُودِيَّةُ [1]مِنْ [2]أَكْثَرِ [3]دُوَلِ (دَوْلَةٌ) [4]ٱلْعَالَمِ [5]إِنْتَاجًا [6]لِلنَّفْطِ.

(7) The Kingdom of Saudi Arabia is [1]one of [2]the greatest [6]oil-[5]producing [3]countries in [4]the world.

[1]نَبَحَ ٱلْكَلْبُ عَلَى [2]ٱللِّصِّ [3]نُبَاحًا [4]عَالِيًا [5]فَخَافَ ٱللِّصُّ [6]وَهَرَبَ.

(8) The dog [1]barked [3,4]loudly (lit. a [4]high [3]barking) at [2]the thief. The thief [5]was scared [6]and ran away.

[1]إِسْتَقْبَلَ رَئِيسُ ٱلْجُمْهُورِيَّةِ [2]ٱلْوُزَرَاءَ (وَزِيرٌ) [3]وَٱلنُّوَّابَ (نَائِبٌ) [4]وَسَلَّمَ عَلَيْهِمْ [5]بِالْيَدِ وَاحِدًا وَاحِدًا.

(9) The president of the republic [1]received [2]the ministers [3]and parliamentary members [4]and shook their [5]hands one by one.

[1]بَاعَ [2]ٱلتَّاجِرُ [3]حَقِيبَةَ [4]سَفَرٍ وَعِشْرِينَ [5]قَمِيصًا وَأَحَدَ عَشَرَ [6]حِذَاءً.

(10) [2]The merchant [1]sold one ([4]travelling) [3]suitcase, 20 [5]shirts and 11 [6]shoes.

[1]إِشْتَرَيْتُ [2]ٱلْقُمْصَانَ (قَمِيصٌ) [3]بَيْضَاءَ، [4]وَٱلْقُبَّعَةَ [5]سَوْدَاءَ، [6]وَسَاعَةً [7]ذَهَبِيَّةً، [8]وَخَاتَمًا [9]فِضِّيًّا.

(11) [1]I bought the [3]white [2]shirts and the [5]black [4]hat, and [7]a gold [6]watch and [9]a silver [8]ring. (lit. the shirts white and the hat black)

[1]لَا شَكَّ أَنَّ ٱلطَّبِيبَ أَكْثَرُ [2]خِبْرَةً مِنَ [3]ٱلْمُمَرِّضَةِ.

(12) There is [1]no doubt that the physician is more [2]experienced than [3]the nurse.

[1]أَعْجَبَنِي أَنْ [2]أَرَى ٱلرَّئِيسَ [3]مَاشِيًا [4]لِوَحْدِهِ فِي [5]ٱلشَّارِعِ [6]ٱلرَّئِيسِي.

(13) [1]I was pleased [2]to see the president [3]walking [4]alone on [6]the main [5]street.

[1]كُلَّمَا [2]ٱزْدَادَ [3]ٱلْإِنْسَانُ [4]غَرَامًا [5]قَلَّ [6]مَنَامًا.

(14) [1,2]The more [3]a man is in [4]love, [5]the less [6]sleep he gets. (lit. [1]Whenever [3]the man's [4]love [2]increases, his [6]sleep [5]decreases.)

[1]سَكَنْتُ مَعَهُ [2]أُسْبُوعًا فِي [3]نَفْسِ [4]ٱلشَّقَّةِ وَمَا [5]أَحْبَبْتُهُ [6]أَبَدًا.

(15) [1]I lived with him for [2]one week in [3]the same [4]apartment and I did not [5]like him [6]at all.

[1]أُسَافِرُ [2]غَدًا إِلَى [3]ٱلشَّرْقِ [4]ٱلْأَوْسَطِ [5]وَأَغِيبُ عَنِ ٱلْبِلَادِ [6]شَهْرًا [7]كَامِلًا.

(16) [1]I will travel [2]tomorrow to [4]the Middle [3]East and [5]I will be away from the country for a [7]whole [6]month.

[1]دَخَلَ [2]ٱلْمُحَاضِرُ [3]قَاعَةَ [4]ٱلْمُحَاضَرَاتِ [5]وَهُوَ يَضْحَكُ/ ضَاحِكًا.

(17) [2]The lecturer [1]entered [4]the lecture [3]hall ([5]while he was) laughing.

لَا تَشْرَبِ [1]ٱلْعَصِيرَ [2]سَاخِنًا وَلَا تَشْرَبِ [3]ٱلشَّايَ [4]بَارِدًا.

(18) Don't drink [1]juice [2]hot and don't drink [3]tea [4]cold!

[1]مَشَيْتُ [2]لِمُدَّةِ سَاعَتَيْنِ [3]مَشْيًا [4]سَرِيعًا [5]فَتَعِبْتُ.

(19) [1]I walked [4]quickly (lit. a [4]quick [3]walk) for two hours ([2]time) [5]and got tired.

[1]طَلَعَ [2]ٱلْقَمَرُ [3]بَغْتَةً مِنْ [4]خَلْفِ [5]ٱلْجَبَلِ.

(20) [2]The moon [1]rose [3]suddenly from [4]behind [5]the mountain.

[1]قَرَّرْتُ أَنْ [2]أَعُودَ إِلَى [3]وَطَنِي لُبْنَانَ [4]عَاجِلًا [5]أَمْ [6]آجِلًا.

(21) [1]I decided [2]I would return to [3]my homeland Lebanon [4]sooner [5]or [6]later.

Translate into Arabic:

(1) There is no doubt that I will return to my village sooner or later.

(2) The wife is more faithful than her husband.

(3) The dog barked suddenly at the guest and (so) the guest got scared and ran away.

(4) The West is more experienced than the East.

(5) I decided to drink the tea hot and the juice cold.

(6) The thief sold a black shirt, a white hat, a gold ring and a silver watch.

(7) I liked to see the lecturer laughing on the main street.

(8) The merchant emigrated to the Kingdom of Saudi Arabia and we have not heard anything about him.

(9) People cut trees for wood and from iron they make weapons.

(10) I lived alone for a month and a week on the mountain.

(11) I will be away tomorrow from the Arabic grammar lesson.

(12) I stayed awake all night alone in the apartment and I learned by heart the lessons about the Middle East.

(13) The president of the republic received the ministers and parliamentary members in the hall and shook their hands one by one.

Chapter 39

Conditional sentences

39.1 A conditional sentence contains two parts. The first part of the conditional sentence expresses a condition or contingency. It is called protasis and the Arabic term is أَلشَّرْط, 'the condition'. The second part expresses the consequence or result of the condition and is called apodosis, جَوَابُ ٱلشَّرْط, 'the answer to the condition'.

39.2 Conditional sentences are mostly introduced by one of the three conditional particles, which are إِنْ ʾin, إِذَا ʾiḏā and لَوْ law, all meaning 'if'. The following outlines the differences in their use.

39.3 إِنْ ʾin 'if', is followed by a verb in the perfect or imperfect jussive (apocopatus). In the following examples the second part has the perfect or imperfect jussive, e.g.

(a)

ʾ***in + perf. + perf.***	ʾ***in + perf. + imperf. jussive***	ʾ***in + imperf. jussive + imperf. jussive***
إِنْ دَرَسَ نَجَحَ	إِنْ دَرَسَ يَنْجَحْ	إِنْ يَدْرُسْ يَنْجَحْ
ʾin darasa naǧaḥa.	ʾin darasa yanǧa**ḥ**.	ʾin yadrus yanǧaḥ.

If he studies, ***he succeeds*** (OR ***he will succeed***).

(b) The imperative can be used in the second part and must be preceded by فَـ.., e.g.

ʾ***in + perf. + imperative***	ʾ***in + imperf. jussive + imperative***
إِنْ ذَهَبَ فَٱذْهَبْ	إِنْ يَذْهَبْ فَٱذْهَبْ
ʾin ḏahaba fa-**ḏhab**!	ʾin yaḏhab fa-**ḏhab**!

If he goes, then **you go**! OR If he goes, then **you should go**!

Note: In spite of being in the perfect tense, the above verb ذَهَبَ refers to the future here (see chapter 17).

39.4 إِذَا ʾiḏā 'if' is a synonym of إِنْ ʾin, with the nuance of eventuality. It is followed by the perfect tense in the first part and the perfect or imperfect indicative in the second part. If the second part is a nominal sentence or contains an imperative or one of the words below, then the second part must be preceded by the particle فَـ ... fa 'then':

the particle قَدْ qad

the future particles سَوْفَ sawfa or سَـ ... sa...

the interrogative particle هَلْ hal

the negative particle مَا mā, لَنْ lan, or لَا lā

the negative copula لَيْسَ laysa.

Note: The imperfect jussive and the imperative cannot be used after إِذَا.

Examples:

(a) فَـ ... /fa.../ preceding the second part when it is a nominal sentence:

إِنْ تَعْمَلْ فَٱلْعَمَلُ صِحِّيٌّ ʾin taʿmal **fa-l-ʿamalu** ṣiḥḥiyyun.

If you work, (then) work is healthy.

(b) فَـ ... /fa.../ preceding the second part when it contains an imperative verb:

إِنْ سَأَلَكَ فَأَجِبْهُ ʾin saʾalaka **fa-ʾağib-hu**.

If he asks you, (then) you answer him!

(c) فَـ ... /fa.../ preceding the particle قَدْ qad:

إِنْ / إِذَا وَعَدَكَ فَقَدْ صَدَقَ ʾin/ʾiḏā waʿadaka **fa-qad** ṣadaqa.

If he promises you, (then) he is sincere.

(d) فَـ ... /fa.../ preceding the future particle سَوْفَ sawfa or سَـ ... sa:

إِنْ / إِذَا أَسَأْتَ فَسَوْفَ تَنْدَمُ / فَسَتَنْدَمُ

ʾin/ʾiḏā ʾasaʾta **fa-sawfa** tandamu OR **fa-sa**tandamu.

If you cause harm, (then) you will regret it.

(e) ... فَـ /fa.../ preceding the interrogative particle هَلْ hal:

إِنْ / إِذَا قُلْتُ لَكَ سِرّاً فَهَلْ تَكْتُمُهُ؟

ʾin/ʾiḏā qultu laka sirran **fa-hal** taktumu-hu?

If I **tell** you a secret, **will** you keep it confidential? OR

If I **told** you a secret, **would** you keep it confidential?

(f) ... فَـ /fa.../, preceding the negative particle مَا mā, لَنْ lan or لاَ lā:

إِنْ / إِذَا زَارَنِي عَدُوٌّ فَمَا أَطْرُدُهُ / فَلاَ أَطْرُدُهُ / فَلَنْ أَطْرُدَهُ

ʾin / ʾiḏā zāranī ʿaduwwun **fa-mā** ʾaṭrudu-hu / **fa-lā** ʾaṭrudu-hu / **fa-lan** ʾaṭruda-hu.

If an enemy visits me, I shall **not** dismiss him.

(g) ... فَـ /fa.../ preceding the negative copula لَيْسَ laysa:

إِنْ تَذْهَبْ فَلَسْتُ بِذَاهِبٍ ʾin taḏhab **fa-lastu** bi-ḏāhibin.

If you go, (then) I am not going.

39.5 لَوْ law 'if', for unreal condition, takes the perfect in both parts and refers to the past or future. The second part is often preceded by the particle ... لَـ, e.g.

لَوْ دَرَسَ لَنَجَحَ law darasa **la-**nağaḥa.

If he had studied, he **would** have succeeded. OR

If he studied, he **would** succeed.

لَوْ كَانَ عِنْدِي نُقُودٌ لَسَافَرْتُ law kāna ʿindī nuqūdun **la-**sāfartu.

If I had had money, I **would** have travelled.

39.6 لَوْلاَ *law-lā and* لَوْلَمْ *law-lam 'if not'*

لَوْلاَ law-lā is followed by a nominal predicate or suffix pronoun. لَوْلَمْ law-lam is followed by the verb in the imperfect jussive, e.g.

لَوْلاَ رَغْبَةُ ٱلْوَزِيرِ لاَسْتَقَالَ ٱلسَّفِيرُ law-lā rağbatu l-wazīri la-staqāla s-safīru.

If it had not been the minister's wish, the ambassador would have resigned.

لَوْلَاهُ لَاسْتَقَالَ ٱلسَّفِيرُ law-lā-**hu la-**staqāla s-safīru.

Were it not for him, the ambassador would have resigned.

لَوْ لَمْ يَكُنْ مُجْتَهِدًا لَمَا نَجَحَ **law-lam** yakun muǧtahidan la-mā naǧaḥa.

If he had not been industrious, he would not have succeeded.

39.7 All three conditional particles can be followed by the verb كَانَ kāna, to confirm the perfect tense (past), e.g.

لَوْ كَانَ قَدْ أَتَى لَرَآهُمْ **law kāna** qad ʾatā la-raʾā-hum.

If he had come, he would have seen them.

إِنْ / إِذَا كَانَ قَدْ قَالَ ذٰلِكَ لَصَدَقَ **ʾin** / **ʾiḏā kāna** qad qāla ḏālika la-ṣadaqa.

If he (has) said that, (then) he will keep his word.

39.8 The second part of the conditional sentence may precede the first part:

سَأُقَابِلُكَ إِذَا زُرْتُ دِمَشْقَ sa-ʾuqābiluka **ʾiḏā** zurtu Dimašqa.

I will meet you, **if** I visit Damascus.

أُسَاعِدُكَ غَدًا إِنْ تُسَاعِدْنِي ٱلْيَوْمَ ʾusāʿiduka ġadan **ʾin** tusāʿidnī l-yawma.

I will help you tomorrow, **if** you help me today.

39.9 The following interrogative pronouns can be used in generalized relative clauses with conditional implication. The verb in both parts of the sentence is then in the imperfect jussive (apocopatus) mood:

مَنْ man, whoever	مَهْمَا mahmā, whatever
أَيْنَمَا ʾaynamā, wherever	حَيْثُمَا ḥayṯumā, wherever

Examples:

مَنْ يَطْلُبْ يَجِدْ **man** yaṭlub yağid. He who seeks, finds.

مَهْمَا تَطْلُبْ أَدْفَعْ **mahmā** taṭlub ʾadfaʿ. Whatever you ask, I will pay.

أَيْنَمَا / حَيْثُمَا تَذْهَبْ أَذْهَبْ **ʾayna-mā / ḥayṯu-mā** taḏhab ʾaḏhab.

Wherever you go, I will go.

39.10 *Concessive particles*

The combined particles and expressions below correspond to the English concessive conjunctions and prepositions: ‘although, even if, in spite of, despite’.

حَتَّى وَلَوْ ḥattā wa-law, even if, even supposing that

مَعَ أَنَّ maʿa ʾanna, even though, although

وَلَوْ wa-law, whatever, even if, even though

رَغْمَ raġma, (prep.) in spite of

بِٱلرَّغْمِ مِنْ bi-r-raġmi min..., (prep.) in spite of, despite

رَغْمَ أَنَّ raġma ʾanna, although, even though

وَإِنْ wa-ʾin, even though

Examples:

حَتَّى وَلَوْ دَرَسَ سَوْفَ يَسْقُطُ

ḥattā wa-law darasa sawfa yasquṭu.

Even if he were to study, he'll fail.

مَعَ أَنَّهُ دَرَسَ جَيِّداً، سَقَطَ فِي ٱلْاِمْتِحَانِ

maʿa ʾanna-hu darasa ǧayyidan, saqaṭa fī l-imtiḥāni.

Although he studied well, he failed in the exam.

سَأَذْهَبُ رَغْمَ ٱلْمَطَرِ

sa-ʾaḏhabu raġma l-maṭari.

I will go in spite of the rain.

ذَهَبَ إِلَى عَمَلِهِ رَغْمَ مَرَضِهِ / بِٱلرَّغْمِ مِنْ مَرَضِهِ

ḏahaba ʾilā ʿamali-hi raġma maraḍi-hi / bi-r-raġmi min maraḍi-hi.

He went to his work in spite of his illness.

ذَهَبَ إِلَى عَمَلِهِ رَغْمَ أَنَّهُ مَرِيضٌ

ḏahaba ʾilā ʿamali-hi raġma ʾanna-hu marīḍun.

He went to his work, although he is ill.

سَوْفَ أُسَافِرُ وَإِنْ وَقَعَتِ ٱلسَّمَاءُ

sawfa ʾusāfiru wa-ʾin waqaʿat-i s-samāʾu.

I will travel, even if heaven were to fall.

Exercises

Practise your reading:

إِنْ لَمْ [1]تَزُرْنِي فِي مَنْزِلِي [2]أَغْضَبْ عَلَيْكَ وَإِنْ [3]زُرْتَنِي ٱلْيَوْمَ [4]أَزُرْكَ [5]غَدًا.

(1) If you don't [1]visit me at (my) home [2]I will be angry with you, but if you [3]visit me today [4]I will visit you [5]tomorrow.

[1]لَوْلَا [2]مُسَاعَدَةُ ٱلْحُكُومَةِ [3]وَٱلصَّلِيبِ ٱلْأَحْمَرِ [4]وَٱلْهِلَالِ ٱلْأَحْمَرِ [5]لِلْمُصَابِينَ [6]بِٱلزِّلْزَالِ [7]لَمَاتَ كَثِيرٌ مِنَ ٱلنَّاسِ [8]جُوعًا [9]وَعَطَشًا.

(2) [1]Had there not been [2]the help (support) of the government, Red [3]Cross and Red [4]Crescent [5]for the victims [6]of the earthquake, many people would [7]have died of [8]hunger [9]and thirst.

إِنْ [1]تَخْرُجِ [2]ٱلْكَلِمَةُ مِنَ [3]ٱلْعَقْلِ [4]تَدْخُلِ ٱلْعَقْلَ [5]وَٱلْقَلْبَ وَإِنْ تَخْرُجْ مِنَ [6]ٱللِّسَانِ تَدْخُلْ فِي [7]أُذُنٍ وَتَخْرُجُ مِنْ أُذُنٍ [8]أُخْرَى.

(3) If a [2]word [1]comes from [3]the mind, [4]it enters the mind [5]and heart. If it comes from [6]the tongue, it goes in [7]one ear and out [8]the other.

لَوْ كَانَ [1]ٱلْفَرْدُ [2]قَادِرًا أَنْ [3]يَحْكُمَ [4]نَفْسَهُ بِنَفْسِهِ [5]بِدُونِ [6]قَانُونٍ، [7]لَمَا [8]ٱحْتَاجَ إِلَى [9]حُكُومَةٍ.

(4) If an [1]individual were [2]able [3]to govern [4]himself by himself [5]without the [6]law, [7]there would be no [8]need for [9]government.

لَوْ كَانَ مِنْ [1]تَعَاوُنٍ [2]وَتَفَاهُمٍ [3]مُتَبَادَلَيْنِ بَيْنَ [4]ٱلدُّوَلِ (دَوْلَةٌ) [5]وَٱلشُّعُوبِ (شَعْبٌ) [6]لَقَلَّتْ [7]أَسْبَابُ (سَبَبٌ) [8]ٱلْحُرُوبِ (حَرْبٌ) [9]وَٱلْإِرْهَابِ.

(5) If there were [3]mutual [1]cooperation and [2]understanding between [4]countries [5]and people, [6]then there would [6]be less [7]cause for [8]war [9]and terrorism.

مَنْ [1]يَعْمَلْ فِي [2]صِغَرِهِ [3]وَشَبَابِهِ [4]فَسَوْفَ [5]يَرْتَاحُ فِي كِبَرِهِ.

(6) He who [1]works in [2]his childhood [3]and youth [4]will [5]relax in old age.

لَوْ تَعَلَّمْتَ [1] مِهْنَةً فِي صِغَرِكَ [2] لَنَفَعَتْكَ فِي [3] مُسْتَقْبَلِكَ.

(7) Had you learned [1]a profession in your childhood, [2]it would have been useful for [3]your future.

لَوْ لاَ [1] وُصُولُ [2] سَيَّارَةِ [3] ٱلْإِسْعَافِ [4] بِسُرْعَةٍ [5] لَنَزَفَ [6] دَمُ [7] ٱلْجَرِيحِ [8] وَمَاتَ.

(8) Had the [2,3]ambulance (lit. [3]aid [2]car) not [1]arrived [4]quickly, (then) [7]the wounded (man) [5,6]would have bled to [8]death (lit. [6]his blood would have [5]drained [8]and he would [8]have died).

إِنْ تَذْهَبْ مَعَهُ فِي [1] نَفْسِ ٱلسَّيَّارَةِ [2] فَلَسْتُ بِذَاهِبٍ مَعَكُمْ.

(9) If you go with him in [1]the same car, [2]I won't go with you.

لَوْ [1] يَهْتَمُّ كُلُّ أَبٍ وَأُمٍّ [2] بِتَرْبِيَةِ أَبْنَائِهِمَا (إِبْنٌ) تَرْبِيَةً جَيِّدَةً [3] لَقَلَّ [4] ٱلْمُجْرِمُونَ.

(10) If every father and mother [1]were concerned for the proper (good) [2]education of their children, [4]there would [3]be fewer [4]criminals.

لَوْلاَ ٱلْمَدَارِسُ وَٱلْجَامِعَاتُ [1] لَسَادَ [2] ٱلْجَهْلُ [3] وَكَثُرَ [4] ٱلْإِجْرَامُ [5] وَٱزْدَحَمَتِ [6] ٱلسُّجُونُ (سِجْنٌ).

(11) Had there not been schools and universities, [2]ignorance [1]would have prevailed, [4]crime would [3]have increased and [6]jails would [5]have been crowded.

إِذَا [1] سَأَلَكَ [2] ٱلْقَاضِي [3] أَسْئِلَةً (سُؤَالاً) [4] فَأَجِبْهُ [5] عَلَى كُلِّ [6] حَالٍ.

(12) If [2]the judge [1]asks you [3]questions, [4]answer him [5,6]in any case ([5,6]anyway, always)!

إِنْ [1] تَكْسَلْ فِي دِرَاسَتِكَ ٱلْيَوْمَ [2] تَرْسُبْ فِي [3] ٱلاِمْتِحَانِ [4] غَداً.

(13) If [1]you are lazy today in your studies, [2]you will flunk (fail) [3]the exam [4]tomorrow.

لَوْ دَرَسَ [1] دُرُوسَهُ (دَرْسٌ) جَيِّداً [2] وَقَلَّلَ مِنْ [3] غِيَابِهِ مِنَ [4] ٱلْمُحَاضَرَاتِ [5] لَنَجَحَ فِي [6] ٱلاِمْتِحَانِ.

(14) Had he studied [1]his lessons well [2]and reduced his [3]absence from [4] the lectures, [5]he would have passed [6]the exam.

لَوْ [1]عُولِجَ [2]ٱلْجَرِيحُ [3]عِلَاجًا [4]أَحْسَنَ، [5]لَشُفِيَ مِنْ [6]جُرُوحِهِ (جُرْحٌ) فِي [7]مُدَّةٍ [8]أَقْصَرَ.

(15) Had [2]the wounded (man) [1]received [4]better [3]treatment (lit. [1]been treated with a [4]better [3]treatment), (then) his wounds [5]would have healed [7,8]more quickly (lit. [5]then he would have [5]recovered from [6]his wounds in [8]a shorter [7]time).

إِنْ لَمْ [1]تَعْمَلْ [2]وَتُنْتِجْ [3]كَغَيْرِكَ [4]طَرَدْتُكَ مِنَ ٱلْعَمَلِ.

(16) If you don't [1]work [2]and be productive [3]like the others (lit. others than you), [4]I will fire you (lit. I will dismiss you from work).

إِنْ تَعْمَلْ أَوْ [1]تُمَارِسْ [2]أَيَّ [3]نَوْعٍ مِنَ [4]ٱلرِّيَاضَةِ، [5]فَٱلْعَمَلُ [6]وَٱلرِّيَاضَةُ [7]يُرِيحَانِ [8]ٱلْجِسْمَ [9]وَيُنْسِيَانِ [10]ٱلْهُمُومَ (هَمٌّ).

(17) If you work or [1]practise [2]any [3]type of [4]sport(s), [5]work [6]and sport(s) [7]will relax [8]the body [9]and make you forget [10]your worries.

[1]أَيْنَمَا [2]تَذْهَبْ أَذْهَبْ [3]مَعَكَ وَأَيْنَمَا [4]تَنَمْ [5]أَنَمْ.

(18) [1]Wherever [2]you go I will go [3]with you and wherever [4]you sleep [5]I will sleep.

إِنِ [1]ٱحْتَرَمَكَ [2]أَحَدٌ [3]فَٱحْتَرِمْهُ وَإِنْ لَمْ يَحْتَرِمْكَ فَلَا [4]تَحْتَرِمْهُ.

(19) If [2]a person [1]respects you (then) [3]respect him, and if he doesn't respect you, then don't [4]respect him.

لَوْ لَمْ [1]يَكُنِ [2]ٱلطَّقْسُ [3]حَارًّا فِي [4]ٱلْأُسْبُوعِ [5]ٱلْمَاضِي [6]لَمَا [7]صَعِدْتُ / [7]طَلَعْتُ إِلَى [8]ٱلْجَبَلِ.

(20) Had the [2]weather not [1]been [3]hot [5]last [4]week, I [6]would not [7]have gone up to [8]the mountain.

Translate into Arabic:

(1) Wherever you sleep I will sleep and wherever you go I will go (with you).

(2) If the physician had not arrived quickly, the wounded (man) would have died.

(3) If you don't visit the wounded (man) today, I will be angry with you and I will not visit you tomorrow.

(4) If you practise or do any type of sports like the others, you will relax in old age.

(5) If the wounded (man) had been treated well, he would have recovered from his wounds in a shorter time.

(6) If you had learned any type of sport in your childhood, (then) sports would have relaxed your body and made you forget your worries.

(7) If your father asks you questions about your studies, answer him always (anyway)!

(8) If you are lazy at your work and are not productive like the others, I will fire you (lit. dismiss you from work).

(9) If he had reduced his absence from the lessons and lectures, he would have passed the exam.

(10) Had it not been for the Red Cross and Red Crescent, many people would have died of hunger and thirst.

(11) If the ambulance hadn't arrived quickly, many of the victims of the earthquake would have died.

(12) If my father had not been ill last week, I would not have gone up to him on the mountain.

(13) If a word comes from the tongue it goes in one ear and out the other, but if a word comes out from the heart (then) it goes into the mind.

(14) If there were mutual cooperation between the government and the people, the causes of crime would be reduced.

(15) Had the government not supported (helped) young people (the youth), crimes would have increased, and jails would have been crowded.

Appendix 1

Tables of verb forms

Table A1.1. The patterns of the ten forms of the strong triliteral verb فَعَلَ faʿala 'to do, to act'

	Active									
	I	II	III	IV	V	VI	VII	VIII	IX	X
	فَعَلَ	فَعَّلَ	فَاعَلَ	أَفْعَلَ	تَفَعَّلَ	تَفَاعَلَ	إِنْفَعَلَ	إِفْتَعَلَ	إِفْعَلَّ	إِسْتَفْعَلَ
Perfect	faʿala	faʿʿala	fāʿala	ʾafʿala	tafaʿʿala	tafāʿala	ʾinfaʿala	ʾiftaʿala	ʾifʿalla	ʾistafʿala
	يَفْعَلُ	يُفَعِّلُ	يُفَاعِلُ	يُفْعِلُ	يَتَفَعَّلُ	يَتَفَاعَلُ	يَنْفَعِلُ	يَفْتَعِلُ	يَفْعَلُّ	يَسْتَفْعِلُ
Imperf.	yafʿalu	yufaʿʿilu	yufāʿilu	yufʿilu	yatafaʿʿalu	yatafāʿalu	yanfaʿilu	yaftaʿilu	yafʿallu	yastafʿilu
	إِفْعَلْ	فَعِّلْ	فَاعِلْ	أَفْعِلْ	تَفَعَّلْ	تَفَاعَلْ	إِنْفَعِلْ	إِفْتَعِلْ	إِفْعَلَّ	إِسْتَفْعِلْ
Imperat.	ʾifʿal	faʿʿil	fāʿil	ʾafʿil	tafaʿʿal	tafāʿal	ʾinfaʿil	ʾiftaʿil	ʾifʿalla	ʾistafʿil
	فَاعِلٌ	مُفَعِّلٌ	مُفَاعِلٌ	مُفْعِلٌ	مُتَفَعِّلٌ	مُتَفَاعِلٌ	مُنْفَعِلٌ	مُفْتَعِلٌ	مُفْعَلٌّ	مُسْتَفْعِلٌ
Particip.	fāʿilun	mufaʿʿilun	mufāʿilun	mufʿilun	mutafaʿʿilun	mutafāʿilun	munfaʿilun	muftaʿilun	mufʿallun	mustafʿilun

الفِعلُ المجهولُ

Passive

Perfect	فُعِلَ fuʿila	فُعِّلَ fuʿʿila	فُوعِلَ fūʿila	أُفْعِلَ ʾufʿila	تُفُعِّلَ tufuʿʿila	تُفُوعِلَ tufūʿila	أُنْفُعِلَ ʾunfuʿila	أُفْتُعِلَ ʾuftuʿila		أُسْتُفْعِلَ ʾustufʿila
Imperf.	يُفْعَلُ yufʿalu	يُفَعَّلُ yufaʿʿalu	يُفَاعَلُ yufāʿalu	يُفْعَلُ yufʿalu	يُتَفَعَّلُ yutafaʿʿalu	يُتَفَاعَلُ yutafāʿalu	يُنْفَعَلُ yunfaʿalu	يُفْتَعَلُ yuftaʿalu		يُسْتَفْعَلُ yustafʿalu
Particip.	مَفْعُولٌ mafʿūlun	مُفَعَّلٌ mufaʿʿalun	مُفَاعَلٌ mufāʿalun	مُفْعَلٌ mufʿalun	مُتَفَعَّلٌ mutafaʿʿalun	مُتَفَاعَلٌ mutafāʿalun	مُنْفَعَلٌ munfaʿalun	مُفْتَعَلٌ muftaʿalun		مُسْتَفْعَلٌ mustafʿalun
Verbal noun (maṣdar)	فَعْلٌ faʿlun	تَفْعِيلٌ tafʿīlun تَفْعِلَةٌ tafʿilatun	فِعَالٌ fiʿālun مُفَاعَلَةٌ mufāʿalatun	إِفْعَالٌ ʾifʿālun	تَفَعُّلٌ tafaʿʿulun	تَفَاعُلٌ tafāʿulun	إِنْفِعَالٌ ʾinfiʿālun	إِفْتِعَالٌ ʾiftiʿālun	إِفْعِلَالٌ ʾifʿilālun	إِسْتِفْعَالٌ ʾistifʿālun

Note: There are dozens of verbal nouns (maṣdar) for form I.

Table A1.2. The patterns of the derived forms of the doubled verb فَرَّ farra 'to escape, to flee'

	Active									
	I	II	III	IV	V	VI	VII	VIII	IX	X
	فَرَّ		فَارَّ	أَفَرَّ		تَفَارَّ	إِنْفَرَّ	إِفْتَرَّ		إِسْتَفَرَّ
Perfect	farra		fārra	ʾafarra		tafārra	ʾinfarra	ʾiftarra		ʾistafarra
	يَفِرُّ		يُفَارُّ	يُفِرُّ		يَتَفَارُّ	يَنْفَرُّ	يَفْتَرُّ		يَسْتَفِرُّ
Imperfect	yafirru		yufārru	yufirru		yatafārru	yanfarru	yaftarru		yastafirru
	إِفْرِرْ		فَارِرْ	أَفْرِرْ		تَفَارَرْ	إِنْفَرِرْ	إِفْتَرِرْ		إِسْتَفْرِرْ
Imperative	ʾifrir		fārir	ʾafrir		tafārar	ʾinfarir	ʾiftarir		ʾistafrir
	فَارٌّ		مُفَارٌّ	مُفِرٌّ		مُتَفَارٌّ	مُنْفَرٌّ	مُفْتَرٌّ		مُسْتَفِرٌّ
Participle	fārrun		mufārrun	mufirrun		mutafārrun	munfarrun	muftarrun		mustafirrun

Passive

	فُرَّ		فُورِرَ	أُفِرَّ		تُفُورِرَ	أُنْفُرَّ	أُفْتُرَّ		أُسْتُفِرَّ
Perfect	furra		fūrira	ʾufirra		tufūrira	ʾunfurra	ʾufturra		ʾustufirra
	يُفَرُّ		يُفَارُّ	يُفَرُّ		يُتَفَارُّ	يُنْفَرُّ	يُفْتَرُّ		يُسْتَفَرُّ
Imperfect	yufarru		yufārru	yufarru		yutafārru	yunfarru	yuftarru		yustafarru
	مَفْرُورٌ		مُفَارٌّ	مُفَرٌّ		مُتَفَارٌّ	مُنْفَرٌّ	مُفْتَرٌّ		مُسْتَفَرٌّ
Participle	mafrūrun		mufārrun	mufarrun		mutafārrun	munfarrun	muftarrun		mustafarrun
Verbal	فَرٌّ		فِرَارٌ	إِفْرَارٌ		تَفَارٌّ	إِنْفِرَارٌ	إِفْتِرَارٌ		إِسْتِفْرَارٌ
noun (maṣdar)	farrun		firārun	ʾifrārun		tafārrun	infirārun	ʾiftirārun		ʾistifrārun

Table A1.3 The patterns of the derived forms of verbs with a weak initial radical و: وَصَلَ waṣala, 'to arrive'

	Active									
	I	II	III	IV	V	VI	VII	VIII	IX	X
	وَصَلَ	وَصَّلَ	وَاصَلَ	أَوْصَلَ	تَوَصَّلَ	تَوَاصَلَ	إِنْوَصَلَ	إِتَّصَلَ		إِسْتَوْصَلَ
Perfect	waṣala	waṣṣala	wāṣala	ʾawṣala	tawaṣṣala	tawāṣala	ʾinwaṣala	ʾittaṣala		ʾistawṣala
	يَصِلُ	يُوَصِّلُ	يُوَاصِلُ	يُوصِلُ	يَتَوَصَّلُ	يَتَوَاصَلُ	يَنْوَصِلُ	يَتَّصِلُ		يَسْتَوْصِلُ
Imperf.	yaṣilu	yuwaṣṣilu	yuwāṣilu	yūṣilu	yatawaṣṣalu	yatawāṣalu	yanwaṣilu	yattaṣilu		yastawṣilu
	صِلْ	وَصِّلْ	وَاصِلْ	أَوْصِلْ	تَوَصَّلْ	تَوَاصَلْ	إِنْوَصِلْ	إِتَّصِلْ		إِسْتَوْصِلْ
Imperat.	ṣil	waṣṣil	wāṣil	ʾawṣil	tawaṣṣal	tawāṣal	ʾinwaṣil	ʾittaṣil		ʾistawṣil
	وَاصِلٌ	مُوَصِّلٌ	مُوَاصِلٌ	مُوصِلٌ	مُتَوَصِّلٌ	مُتَوَاصِلٌ	مُنْوَصِلٌ	مُتَّصِلٌ		مُسْتَوْصِلٌ
Particip.	wāṣilun	muwaṣṣilun	muwāṣilun	mūṣilun	mutawaṣṣilun	mutawāṣilun	munwaṣilun	muttaṣilun		mustawṣilun

Passive

Perfect	وُصِلَ wuṣila	وُصِّلَ wuṣṣila	وُوصِلَ wūṣila	أُوصِلَ ʾūṣila	تُوُصِّلَ tuwuṣṣila	تُووصِلَ tuwūṣila	أُنْوُصِلَ ʾunwuṣila	أُتُّصِلَ ʾuttuṣila	أُسْتُوصِلَ ʾustūṣila
Imperf.	يُوصَلُ yūṣalu	يُوَصَّلُ yuwaṣṣalu	يُوَاصَلُ yuwāṣalu	يُوصَلُ yūṣalu	يُتَوَصَّلُ yutawaṣṣalu	يُتَوَاصَلُ yutawāṣalu	يُنْوَصَلُ yunwaṣalu	يُتَّصَلُ yuttaṣalu	يُسْتَوْصَلُ yustawṣalu
Particip.	مَوْصُولٌ mawṣūlun	مُوَصَّلٌ muwaṣṣalun	مُوَاصَلٌ muwāṣalun	مُوصَلٌ mūṣalun	مُتَوَصَّلٌ mutawaṣṣalun	مُتَوَاصَلٌ mutawāṣalun	مُنْوَصَلٌ munwaṣalun	مُتَّصَلٌ muttaṣalun	مُسْتَوْصَلٌ mustawṣalun
Verbal noun (maṣdar)	وَصْلٌ waṣlun	تَوْصِيلٌ tawṣīlun	وِصَالٌ wiṣālun مُوَاصَلَةٌ muwāṣalatun	إِيصَالٌ ʾīṣālun	تَوَصُّلٌ tawaṣṣulun	تَوَاصُلٌ tawāṣulun	إِنْوِصَالٌ inwiṣālun	إِتِّصَالٌ ʾittiṣālun	إِسْتِيصَالٌ ʾistīṣālun

Table A1.4 The patterns I–X of verbs with a weak middle radical و: قَامَ qāma 'to stand up' (from قوم qwm)

Active

	I	II	III	IV	V	VI	VII	VIII	IX	X
Perfect	قَامَ qāma	قَوَّمَ qawwama	قَاوَمَ qāwama	أَقَامَ ʾaqāma	تَقَوَّمَ taqawwama	تَقَاوَمَ taqāwama	إِنْقَامَ ʾinqāma	إِقْتَامَ ʾiqtāma		إِسْتَقَامَ ʾistaqāma
Imperf.	يَقُومُ yaqūmu	يُقَوِّمُ yuqawwimu	يُقَاوِمُ yuqāwimu	يُقِيمُ yuqīmu	يَتَقَوَّمُ yataqawwamu	يَتَقَاوَمُ yataqāwamu	يَنْقَامُ yanqāmu	يَقْتَامُ yaqtāmu		يَسْتَقِيمُ yastaqīmu
Imperat.	قُمْ qum	قَوِّمْ qawwim	قَاوِمْ qāwim	أَقِمْ ʾaqim	تَقَوَّمْ taqawwam	تَقَاوَمْ taqāwam	إِنْقَمْ ʾinqam	إِقْتَمْ ʾiqtam		إِسْتَقِمْ ʾistaqim
Particip.	قَائِمٌ qāʾimun	مُقَوِّمٌ muqawwimun	مُقَاوِمٌ muqāwimun	مُقِيمٌ muqīmun	مُتَقَوِّمٌ mutaqawwimun	مُتَقَاوِمٌ mutaqāwimun	مُنْقَامٌ munqāmun	مُقْتَامٌ muqtāmun		مُسْتَقِيمٌ mustaqīmun

Passive

	قِيمَ	قُوِّمَ	قُووِمَ	أُقِيمَ	تُقُوِّمَ	تُقُووِمَ	أُنْقِيمَ	أُقْتِيمَ	أُسْتُقِيمَ
Perfect	qīma	quwwima	qūwima	ʾuqīma	tuquwwima	tuqūwima	ʾunqīma	ʾuqtīma	ʾustuqīma
	يُقَامُ	يُقَوَّمُ	يُقَاوَمُ	يُقَامُ	يُتَقَوَّمُ	يُتَقَاوَمُ	يُنْقَامُ	يُقْتَامُ	يُسْتَقَامُ
Imperf.	yuqāmu	yuqawwamu	yuqāwamu	yuqāmu	yutaqawwamu	yutaqāwamu	yunqāmu	yuqtāmu	yustaqāmu
	مَقُومٌ	مُقَوَّمٌ	مُقَاوَمٌ	مُقَامٌ	مُتَقَوَّمٌ	مُتَقَاوَمٌ	مُنْقَامٌ	مُقْتَامٌ	مُسْتَقَامٌ
Particip.	maqūmun	muqawwamun	muqāwamun	muqāmun	mutaqawwamun	mutaqāwamun	munqāmun	muqtāmun	mustaqāmun
Verbal	قَوْمٌ	تَقْوِيمٌ	مُقَاوَمَةٌ	إِقَامَةٌ	تَقَوُّمٌ	تَقَاوُمٌ	إِنْقِيَامٌ	إِقْتِيَامٌ	إِسْتِقَامَةٌ
noun	qawmun	taqwīmun	muqāwamatun	ʾiqāmatun	taqawwumun	taqāwumun	inqiyāmun	ʾiqtiyāmun	ʾistiqāmatun
(maṣdar)									

Appendix 2

Verb conjugation paradigms

A2.1 Strong verb كَتَبَ 'to write' (perf. /a/ imperf. /u/)

	Active				Passive		
Person	Perf.	Imperf. indic.	Imperf. subj.	Imperf. jussive	Perf.	Imperf. indic.	Imperat.
				Singular			
3. m.	كَتَبَ	يَكْتُبُ	يَكْتُبَ	يَكْتُبْ	كُتِبَ	يُكْتَبُ	
3. f.	كَتَبَتْ	تَكْتُبُ	تَكْتُبَ	تَكْتُبْ	كُتِبَتْ	تُكْتَبُ	
2. m.	كَتَبْتَ	تَكْتُبُ	تَكْتُبَ	تَكْتُبْ	كُتِبْتَ	تُكْتَبُ	أُكْتُبْ
2. f.	كَتَبْتِ	تَكْتُبِينَ	تَكْتُبِي	تَكْتُبِي	كُتِبْتِ	تُكْتَبِينَ	أُكْتُبِي
1. m. f.	كَتَبْتُ	أَكْتُبُ	أَكْتُبَ	أَكْتُبْ	كُتِبْتُ	أُكْتَبُ	
				Dual			
3. m.	كَتَبَا	يَكْتُبَانِ	يَكْتُبَا	يَكْتُبَا	كُتِبَا	يُكْتَبَانِ	
3. f.	كَتَبَتَا	تَكْتُبَانِ	تَكْتُبَا	تَكْتُبَا	كُتِبَتَا	تُكْتَبَانِ	
2. m. f.	كَتَبْتُمَا	تَكْتُبَانِ	تَكْتُبَا	تَكْتُبَا	كُتِبْتُمَا	تُكْتَبَانِ	أُكْتُبَا

Person	Active Perf.	Imperf. indic.	Imperf. subj.	Imperf. jussive	Passive Perf.	Imperf. indic.	Imperat.
				Plural			
3. m.	كَتَبُوا	يَكْتُبُونَ	يَكْتُبُوا	يَكْتُبُوا	كُتِبُوا	يُكْتَبُونَ	
3. f.	كَتَبْنَ	يَكْتُبْنَ	يَكْتُبْنَ	يَكْتُبْنَ	كُتِبْنَ	يُكْتَبْنَ	
2. m.	كَتَبْتُمْ	تَكْتُبُونَ	تَكْتُبُوا	تَكْتُبُوا	كُتِبْتُمْ	تُكْتَبُونَ	أُكْتُبُوا
2. f.	كَتَبْتُنَّ	تَكْتُبْنَ	تَكْتُبْنَ	تَكْتُبْنَ	كُتِبْتُنَّ	تُكْتَبْنَ	أُكْتُبْنَ
1. m. f.	كَتَبْنَا	نَكْتُبُ	نَكْتُبَ	نَكْتُبْ	كُتِبْنَا	نُكْتَبُ	

Act. part. كَاتِبٌ Pass. part. مَكْتُوبٌ Verbal noun (maṣdar) كَتْبٌ or كِتَابَةٌ

A2.2 Conjugations of the derived verb forms II–X

The conjugations of the derived verb forms II–X below serve as models for other derived verbs. Here they are conjugated only in the singular. The dual and plural are conjugated regularly.

II كَسَّرَ 'to smash, to break into pieces'

	Active Perf.	Imperf.	Passive Perf.	Imperf.	Imperat.
3. m.	كَسَّرَ	يُكَسِّرُ	كُسِّرَ	يُكَسَّرُ	
3. f.	كَسَّرَتْ	تُكَسِّرُ	كُسِّرَتْ	تُكَسَّرُ	
2. m.	كَسَّرْتَ	تُكَسِّرُ	كُسِّرْتَ	تُكَسَّرُ	كَسِّرْ
2. f.	كَسَّرْتِ	تُكَسِّرِينَ	كُسِّرْتِ	تُكَسَّرِينَ	كَسِّرِي
1. m. f.	كَسَّرْتُ	أُكَسِّرُ	كُسِّرْتُ	أُكَسَّرُ	

Active participle: مُكَسِّرٌ Passive participle: مُكَسَّرٌ

Verbal noun (maṣdar): تَكْسِيرٌ or تَكْسِرَةٌ (as تَجْرِبَةٌ 'a test, trial')

III كَاتَبَ 'to correspond with'

	Active Perf.	Active Imperf.	Passive Perf.	Passive Imperf.	Imperat.
3. m.	كَاتَبَ	يُكَاتِبُ	كُوتِبَ	يُكَاتَبُ	
3. f.	كَاتَبَتْ	تُكَاتِبُ	كُوتِبَتْ	تُكَاتَبُ	
2. m.	كَاتَبْتَ	تُكَاتِبُ	كُوتِبْتَ	تُكَاتَبُ	كَاتِبْ
2. f.	كَاتَبْتِ	تُكَاتِبِينَ	كُتِبْتِ	تُكَاتَبِينَ	كَاتِبِي
1. m. f.	كَاتَبْتُ	أُكَاتِبُ	كُوتِبْتُ	أُكَاتَبُ	

Act. part. مُكَاتِبٌ Pass. part. مُكَاتَبٌ Verbal noun (maṣdar): كِتَابٌ or مُكَاتَبَةٌ

IV أَعْلَمَ 'to inform'

	Active Perf.	Active Imperf.	Passive Perf.	Passive Imperf.	Imperat.
3. m.	أَعْلَمَ	يُعْلِمُ	أُعْلِمَ	يُعْلَمُ	
3. f.	أَعْلَمَتْ	تُعْلِمُ	أُعْلِمَتْ	تُعْلَمُ	
2. m.	أَعْلَمْتَ	تُعْلِمُ	أُعْلِمْتَ	تُعْلَمُ	أَعْلِمْ
2. f.	أَعْلَمْتِ	تُعْلِمِينَ	أُعْلِمْتِ	تُعْلَمِينَ	أَعْلِمِي
1. m. f.	أَعْلَمْتُ	أُعْلِمُ	أُعْلِمْتُ	أُعْلَمُ	

Act. part. مُعْلِمٌ Pass. part. مُعْلَمٌ Verbal noun (maṣdar): إِعْلَامٌ

V تَعَلَّمَ 'to learn, to be taught'

	Active Perf.	Active Imperf.	Passive Perf.	Passive Imperf.	Imperat.
3. m.	تَعَلَّمَ	يَتَعَلَّمُ	تُعُلِّمَ	يُتَعَلَّمُ	
3. f.	تَعَلَّمَتْ	تَتَعَلَّمُ	تُعُلِّمَتْ	تُتَعَلَّمُ	
2. m.	تَعَلَّمْتَ	تَتَعَلَّمُ	تُعُلِّمْتَ	تُتَعَلَّمُ	تَعَلَّمْ
2. f.	تَعَلَّمْتِ	تَتَعَلَّمِينَ	تُعُلِّمْتِ	تُتَعَلَّمِينَ	تَعَلَّمِي
1. m. f.	تَعَلَّمْتُ	أَتَعَلَّمُ	تُعُلِّمْتُ	أُتَعَلَّمُ	

Act. part. مُتَعَلِّمٌ Pass. part. مُتَعَلَّمٌ Verbal noun (maṣdar): تَعَلُّمٌ

VI تَقَاتَلَ 'to fight one another'

	Active Perf.	Active Imperf.	Passive Perf.	Passive Imperf.	Imperat.
3. m.	تَقَاتَلَ	يَتَقَاتَلُ	تُقُوتِلَ	يُتَقَاتَلُ	
3. f.	تَقَاتَلَتْ	تَتَقَاتَلُ	تُقُوتِلَتْ	تُتَقَاتَلُ	
2. m.	تَقَاتَلْتَ	تَتَقَاتَلُ	تُقُوتِلْتَ	تُتَقَاتَلُ	تَقَاتَلْ
2. f.	تَقَاتَلْتِ	تَتَقَاتَلِينَ	تُقُوتِلْتِ	تُتَقَاتَلِينَ	تَقَاتَلِي
1. m. f.	تَقَاتَلْتُ	أَتَقَاتَلُ	تُقُوتِلْتُ	أُتَقَاتَلُ	

Act. part. مُتَقَاتِلٌ Pass. part. مُتَقَاتَلٌ Verbal noun (maṣdar): تَقَاتُلٌ

VII إِنْكَسَرَ 'to be broken'

	Active Perf.	Active Imperf.	Passive Perf.	Passive Imperf.	Imperat.
3. m.	إِنْكَسَرَ	يَنْكَسِرُ	(The passive is not used, because form VII has intransitive-passive meaning.)		
3. f.	إِنْكَسَرَتْ	تَنْكَسِرُ			
2. m.	إِنْكَسَرْتَ	تَنْكَسِرُ			إِنْكَسِرْ
2. f.	إِنْكَسَرْتِ	تَنْكَسِرِينَ			إِنْكَسِرِي
1. m. f.	إِنْكَسَرْتُ	أَنْكَسِرُ			

Act. part. مُنْكَسِرٌ Verbal noun (maṣdar) إِنْكِسَارٌ

VIII إِحْتَرَقَ 'to burn, to be burned'

	Active Perf.	Active Imperf.	Passive Perf.	Passive Imperf.	Imperat.
3. m.	إِحْتَرَقَ	يَحْتَرِقُ	أُحْتُرِقَ	يُحْتَرَقُ	
3. f.	إِحْتَرَقَتْ	تَحْتَرِقُ	أُحْتُرِقَتْ	تُحْتَرَقُ	
2. m.	إِحْتَرَقْتَ	تَحْتَرِقُ	أُحْتُرِقْتَ	تُحْتَرَقُ	إِحْتَرِقْ
2. f.	إِحْتَرَقْتِ	تَحْتَرِقِينَ	أُحْتُرِقْتِ	تُحْتَرَقِينَ	إِحْتَرِقِي
1. m. f.	إِحْتَرَقْتُ	أَحْتَرِقُ	أُحْتُرِقْتُ	أُحْتَرَقُ	

Act. part. مُحْتَرِقٌ Pass. part. مُحْتَرَقٌ Verbal noun (maṣdar): إِحْتِرَاقٌ

IX إِصْفَرَّ 'to become yellow'

	Active		Passive		
	Perf.	Imperf.	Perf.	Imperf.	Imperat.
3. m.	إِصْفَرَّ	يَصْفَرُّ	(The passive is not used.)		
3. f.	إِصْفَرَّتْ	تَصْفَرُّ			
2. m.	إِصْفَرَرْتَ	تَصْفَرُّ			إِصْفَرَّ
2. f.	إِصْفَرَرْتِ	تَصْفَرِّينَ			إِصْفَرِّي
1. m. f.	إِصْفَرَرْتُ	أَصْفَرُّ			

Act. part. مُصْفَرٌّ Verbal noun (maṣdar): إِصْفِرَارٌ

X إِسْتَعْمَلَ 'to use'

	Active		Passive		
	Perf.	Imperf.	Perf.	Imperf.	Imperat.
3. m.	إِسْتَعْمَلَ	يَسْتَعْمِلُ	أُسْتُعْمِلَ	يُسْتَعْمَلُ	
3. f.	إِسْتَعْمَلَتْ	تَسْتَعْمِلُ	أُسْتُعْمِلَتْ	تُسْتَعْمَلُ	
2. m.	إِسْتَعْمَلْتَ	تَسْتَعْمِلُ	أُسْتُعْمِلْتَ	تُسْتَعْمَلُ	إِسْتَعْمِلْ
2. f.	إِسْتَعْمَلْتِ	تَسْتَعْمِلِينَ	أُسْتُعْمِلْتِ	تُسْتَعْمَلِينَ	إِسْتَعْمِلِي
1. m. f.	إِسْتَعْمَلْتُ	أَسْتَعْمِلُ	أُسْتُعْمِلْتُ	أُسْتَعْمَلُ	

Act. part. مُسْتَعْمِلٌ Pass. part. مُسْتَعْمَلٌ Verbal noun (maṣdar): إِسْتِعْمَالٌ

A2.3 **Doubled verb مَرَّ 'to pass' (*perf. /a/ imperf. /u/*)**

Person	Active				Passive		
	Perf.	Imperf. indic.	Imperf. subj.	Imperf. jussive	Perf.	Imperf. indic.	Imperat.
	Singular						
3.m.	مَرَّ	يَمُرُّ	يَمُرَّ	يَمُرَّ	مُرَّ	يُمَرُّ	
3.f.	مَرَّتْ	تَمُرُّ	تَمُرَّ	تَمُرَّ	مُرَّتْ	تُمَرُّ	
2.m.	مَرَرْتَ	تَمُرُّ	تَمُرَّ	تَمُرَّ	مُرِرْتَ	تُمَرُّ	مُرَّ
2.f.	مَرَرْتِ	تَمُرِّينَ	تَمُرِّي	تَمُرِّي	مُرِرْتِ	تُمَرِّينَ	مُرِّي
1.m.f.	مَرَرْتُ	أَمُرُّ	أَمُرَّ	أَمُرَّ	مُرِرْتُ	أُمَرُّ	
	Dual						
3.m.	مَرَّا	يَمُرَّانِ	يَمُرَّا	يَمُرَّا	مُرَّا	يُمَرَّانِ	
3.f.	مَرَّتَا	تَمُرَّانِ	تَمُرَّا	تَمُرَّا	مُرَّتَا	تُمَرَّانِ	
2.m.f.	مَرَرْتُمَا	تَمُرَّانِ	تَمُرَّا	تَمُرَّا	مُرِرْتُمَا	تُمَرَّانِ	مُرَّا
	Plural						
3.m.	مَرُّوا	يَمُرُّونَ	يَمُرُّوا	يَمُرُّوا	مُرُّوا	يُمَرُّونَ	
3.f.	مَرَرْنَ	يَمْرُرْنَ	يَمْرُرْنَ	يَمْرُرْنَ	مُرِرْنَ	يُمْرَرْنَ	
2.m.	مَرَرْتُمْ	تَمُرُّونَ	تَمُرُّوا	تَمُرُّوا	مُرِرْتُمْ	تُمَرُّونَ	مُرُّوا
2.f.	مَرَرْتُنَّ	تَمْرُرْنَ	تَمْرُرْنَ	تَمْرُرْنَ	مُرِرْتُنَّ	تُمْرَرْنَ	أُمْرُرْنَ
1.m.f.	مَرَرْنَا	نَمُرُّ	نَمُرَّ	نَمُرَّ	مُرِرْنَا	نُمَرُّ	

Act. part. مَارٌّ   Pass. part. مَمْرُورٌ   Verbal noun (maṣdar) مَرٌّ

A2.4 ***Quadriliteral verb*** **تَرْجَمَ 'to translate'**

Person	Active Perf.	Imperf. indic.	Imperf. subj.	Imperf. jussive	Passive Perf.	Imperf. indic.	Imperat.
				Singular			
3. m.	تَرْجَمَ	يُتَرْجِمُ	يُتَرْجِمَ	يُتَرْجِمْ	تُرْجِمَ	يُتَرْجَمُ	
3. f.	تَرْجَمَتْ	تُتَرْجِمُ	تُتَرْجِمَ	تُتَرْجِمْ	تُرْجِمَتْ	تُتَرْجَمُ	
2. m.	تَرْجَمْتَ	تُتَرْجِمُ	تُتَرْجِمَ	تُتَرْجِمْ	تُرْجِمْتَ	تُتَرْجَمُ	تَرْجِمْ
2. f.	تَرْجَمْتِ	تُتَرْجِمِينَ	تُتَرْجِمِي	تُتَرْجِمِي	تُرْجِمْتِ	تُتَرْجَمِينَ	تَرْجِمِي
1. m. f.	تَرْجَمْتُ	أُتَرْجِمُ	أُتَرْجِمَ	أُتَرْجِمْ	تُرْجِمْتُ	أُتَرْجَمُ	

Person	Active Perf.	Imperf. indic.	Imperf. subj.	Imperf. jussive	Passive Perf.	Imperf. indic.	Imperat.
				Dual			
3. m.	تَرْجَمَا	يُتَرْجِمَانِ	يُتَرْجِمَا	يُتَرْجِمَا	تُرْجِمَا	يُتَرْجَمَانِ	
3. f.	تَرْجَمَتَا	تُتَرْجِمَانِ	تُتَرْجِمَا	تُتَرْجِمَا	تُرْجِمَتَا	تُتَرْجَمَانِ	
2. m. f.	تَرْجَمْتُمَا	تُتَرْجِمَانِ	تُتَرْجِمَا	تُتَرْجِمَا	تُرْجِمْتُمَا	تُتَرْجَمَانِ	تَرْجِمَا
				Plural			
3. m.	تَرْجَمُوا	يُتَرْجِمُونَ	يُتَرْجِمُوا	يُتَرْجِمُوا	تُرْجِمُوا	يُتَرْجَمُونَ	
3. f.	تَرْجَمْنَ	يُتَرْجِمْنَ	يُتَرْجِمْنَ	يُتَرْجِمْنَ	تُرْجِمْنَ	يُتَرْجَمْنَ	
2. m.	تَرْجَمْتُمْ	تُتَرْجِمُونَ	تُتَرْجِمُوا	تُتَرْجِمُوا	تُرْجِمْتُمْ	تُتَرْجَمُونَ	تَرْجِمُوا
2. f.	تَرْجَمْتُنَّ	تُتَرْجِمْنَ	تُتَرْجِمْنَ	تُتَرْجِمْنَ	تُرْجِمْتُنَّ	تُتَرْجَمْنَ	تَرْجِمْنَ
1. m. f.	تَرْجَمْنَا	نُتَرْجِمُ	نُتَرْجِمَ	نُتَرْجِمْ	تُرْجِمْنَا	نُتَرْجَمُ	

Act. part. مُتَرْجِمٌ Pass. part. مُتَرْجَمٌ Verbal noun (maṣdar) تَرْجَمَةٌ

A2.5 *Verb with initial hamzah:* أَخَذَ *'to take' (perf. /a/ imperf. /u/)*

Person	Active Perf.	Imperf. indic.	Imperf. subj.	Imperf. jussive	Passive Perf.	Imperf. indic.	Imperat.
			Singular				
3. m.	أَخَذَ	يَأْخُذُ	يَأْخُذَ	يَأْخُذْ	أُخِذَ	يُؤْخَذُ	
3. f.	أَخَذَتْ	تَأْخُذُ	تَأْخُذَ	تَأْخُذْ	أُخِذَتْ	تُؤْخَذُ	
2. m.	أَخَذْتَ	تَأْخُذُ	تَأْخُذَ	تَأْخُذْ	أُخِذْتَ	تُؤْخَذُ	خُذْ
2. f.	أَخَذْتِ	تَأْخُذِينَ	تَأْخُذِي	تَأْخُذِي	أُخِذْتِ	تُؤْخَذِينَ	خُذِي
1. m. f.	أَخَذْتُ	آخُذُ	آخُذَ	آخُذْ	أُخِذْتُ	أُوخَذُ	
			Dual				
3. m.	أَخَذَا	يَأْخُذَانِ	يَأْخُذَا	يَأْخُذَا	أُخِذَا	يُؤْخَذَانِ	
3. f.	أَخَذَتَا	تَأْخُذَانِ	تَأْخُذَا	تَأْخُذَا	أُخِذَتَا	تُؤْخَذَانِ	
2. m. f.	أَخَذْتُمَا	تَأْخُذَانِ	تَأْخُذَا	تَأْخُذَا	أُخِذْتُمَا	تُؤْخَذَانِ	خُذَا
			Plural				
3. m.	أَخَذُوا	يَأْخُذُونَ	يَأْخُذُوا	يَأْخُذُوا	أُخِذُوا	يُؤْخَذُونَ	
3. f.	أَخَذْنَ	يَأْخُذْنَ	يَأْخُذْنَ	يَأْخُذْنَ	أُخِذْنَ	يُؤْخَذْنَ	
2. m.	أَخَذْتُمْ	تَأْخُذُونَ	تَأْخُذُوا	تَأْخُذُوا	أُخِذْتُمْ	تُؤْخَذُونَ	خُذُوا
2. f.	أَخَذْتُنَّ	تَأْخُذْنَ	تَأْخُذْنَ	تَأْخُذْنَ	أُخِذْتُنَّ	تُؤْخَذْنَ	خُذْنَ
1. m. f.	أَخَذْنَا	نَأْخُذُ	نَأْخُذَ	نَأْخُذْ	أُخِذْنَا	نُؤْخَذُ	

Act. part. آخِذٌ   Pass. part. مَأْخُوذٌ   Verbal noun (maṣdar) أَخْذٌ

A2.6 *Verb with middle hamzah:* سَأَلَ *'to ask' (perf. /a/ imperf. /a/)*

	Active				Passive		
Person	Perf.	Imperf. indic.	Imperf. subj.	Imperf. jussive	Perf.	Imperf. indic.	Imperat.
				Singular			
3. m.	سَأَلَ	يَسْأَلُ	يَسْأَلَ	يَسْأَلْ	سُئِلَ	يُسْأَلُ	
3. f.	سَأَلَتْ	تَسْأَلُ	تَسْأَلَ	تَسْأَلْ	سُئِلَتْ	تُسْأَلُ	
2. m.	سَأَلْتَ	تَسْأَلُ	تَسْأَلَ	تَسْأَلْ	سُئِلْتَ	تُسْأَلُ	إِسْأَلْ
2. f.	سَأَلْتِ	تَسْأَلِينَ	تَسْأَلِي	تَسْأَلِي	سُئِلْتِ	تُسْأَلِينَ	إِسْأَلِي
1. m. f.	سَأَلْتُ	أَسْأَلُ	أَسْأَلَ	أَسْأَلْ	سُئِلْتُ	أُسْأَلُ	
				Dual			
3. m.	سَأَلَا	يَسْأَلَانِ	يَسْأَلَا	يَسْأَلَا	سُئِلَا	يُسْأَلَانِ	
3. f.	سَأَلَتَا	تَسْأَلَانِ	تَسْأَلَا	تَسْأَلَا	سُئِلَتَا	تُسْأَلَانِ	
2. m. f.	سَأَلْتُمَا	تَسْأَلَانِ	تَسْأَلَا	تَسْأَلَا	سُئِلْتُمَا	تُسْأَلَانِ	إِسْأَلَا
				Plural			
3. m.	سَأَلُوا	يَسْأَلُونَ	يَسْأَلُوا	يَسْأَلُوا	سُئِلُوا	يُسْأَلُونَ	
3. f.	سَأَلْنَ	يَسْأَلْنَ	يَسْأَلْنَ	يَسْأَلْنَ	سُئِلْنَ	يُسْأَلْنَ	
2. m.	سَأَلْتُمْ	تَسْأَلُونَ	تَسْأَلُوا	تَسْأَلُوا	سُئِلْتُمْ	تُسْأَلُونَ	إِسْأَلُوا
2. f.	سَأَلْتُنَّ	تَسْأَلْنَ	تَسْأَلْنَ	تَسْأَلْنَ	سُئِلْتُنَّ	تُسْأَلْنَ	إِسْأَلْنَ
1. m. f.	سَأَلْنَا	نَسْأَلُ	نَسْأَلَ	نَسْأَلْ	سُئِلْنَا	نُسْأَلُ	

Act. part. سَائِلٌ   Pass. part. مَسْؤُولٌ   Verbal noun (maṣdar) سُؤَالٌ

Note: سَأَلَ has alternative forms in the jussive and imperative (see chapter 30).

A2.7 *Verb with final hamzah:* قَرَأَ *'to read' (perf. /a/ imperf. /a/)*

Person	Active Perf.	Imperf. indic.	Imperf. subj.	Imperf. jussive	Passive Perf.	Imperf. indic.	Imperat.
				Singular			
3. m.	قَرَأَ	يَقْرَأُ	يَقْرَأَ	يَقْرَأْ	قُرِىءَ	يُقْرَأُ	
3. f.	قَرَأَتْ	تَقْرَأُ	تَقْرَأَ	تَقْرَأْ	قُرِئَتْ	تُقْرَأُ	
2. m.	قَرَأْتَ	تَقْرَأُ	تَقْرَأَ	تَقْرَأْ	قُرِئْتَ	تُقْرَأُ	إِقْرَأْ
2. f.	قَرَأْتِ	تَقْرَئِينَ	تَقْرَئِي	تَقْرَئِي	قُرِئْتِ	تُقْرَئِينَ	إِقْرَئِي
1. m. f.	قَرَأْتُ	أَقْرَأُ	أَقْرَأَ	أَقْرَأْ	قُرِئْتُ	أُقْرَأُ	
				Dual			
3. m.	قَرَآ	يَقْرَآنِ	يَقْرَآ	يَقْرَآ	قُرِآ	يُقْرَآنِ	
3. f.	قَرَأَتَا	تَقْرَآنِ	تَقْرَآ	تَقْرَآ	قُرِئَتَا	تُقْرَآنِ	
2. m. f.	قَرَأْتُمَا	تَقْرَآنِ	تَقْرَآ	تَقْرَآ	قُرِئْتُمَا	تُقْرَآنِ	إِقْرَآ
				Plural			
3. m.	قَرَؤُوا	يَقْرَؤُونَ	يَقْرَؤُوا	يَقْرَؤُوا	قُرِئُوا	يُقْرَؤُونَ	
3. f.	قَرَأْنَ	يَقْرَأْنَ	يَقْرَأْنَ	يَقْرَأْنَ	قُرِئْنَ	يُقْرَأْنَ	
2. m.	قَرَأْتُمْ	تَقْرَؤُونَ	تَقْرَؤُوا	تَقْرَؤُوا	قُرِئْتُمْ	تُقْرَؤُونَ	إِقْرَؤُوا
2. f.	قَرَأْتُنَّ	تَقْرَأْنَ	تَقْرَأْنَ	تَقْرَأْنَ	قُرِئْتُنَّ	تُقْرَأْنَ	إِقْرَأْنَ
1. m. f.	قَرَأْنَا	نَقْرَأُ	نَقْرَأَ	نَقْرَأْ	قُرِئْنَا	نُقْرَأُ	

Act. part. قَارِئٌ Pass. part. مَقْرُوءٌ Verbal noun (maṣdar) قِرَاءَةٌ

A2.8 *Verb with weak initial* و*:* وَضَعَ *'to put' (perf. /a/ imperf. /a/)*

	Active				Passive		
	Perf.	Imperf.	Imperf.	Imperf.	Perf.	Imperf.	Imperat.
Person		indic.	subj.	jussive		indic.	
				Singular			
3. m.	وَضَعَ	يَضَعُ	يَضَعَ	يَضَعْ	وُضِعَ	يُوضَعُ	
3. f.	وَضَعَتْ	تَضَعُ	تَضَعَ	تَضَعْ	وُضِعَتْ	تُوضَعُ	
2. m.	وَضَعْتَ	تَضَعُ	تَضَعَ	تَضَعْ	وُضِعْتَ	تُوضَعُ	ضَعْ
2. f.	وَضَعْتِ	تَضَعِينَ	تَضَعِي	تَضَعِي	وُضِعْتِ	تُوضَعِينَ	ضَعِي
1. m. f.	وَضَعْتُ	أَضَعُ	أَضَعَ	أَضَعْ	وُضِعْتُ	أُوضَعُ	
				Dual			
3. m.	وَضَعَا	يَضَعَانِ	يَضَعَا	يَضَعَا	وُضِعَا	يُوضَعَانِ	
3. f.	وَضَعَتَا	تَضَعَانِ	تَضَعَا	تَضَعَا	وُضِعَتَا	تُوضَعَانِ	
2. m. f.	وَضَعْتُمَا	تَضَعَانِ	تَضَعَا	تَضَعَا	وُضِعْتُمَا	تُوضَعَانِ	ضَعَا
				Plural			
3. m.	وَضَعُوا	يَضَعُونَ	يَضَعُوا	يَضَعُوا	وُضِعُوا	يُوضَعُونَ	
3. f.	وَضَعْنَ	يَضَعْنَ	يَضَعْنَ	يَضَعْنَ	وُضِعْنَ	يُوضَعْنَ	
2. m.	وَضَعْتُمْ	تَضَعُونَ	تَضَعُوا	تَضَعُوا	وُضِعْتُمْ	تُوضَعُونَ	ضَعُوا
2. f.	وَضَعْتُنَّ	تَضَعْنَ	تَضَعْنَ	تَضَعْنَ	وُضِعْتُنَّ	تُوضَعْنَ	ضَعْنَ
1. m. f.	وَضَعْنَا	نَضَعُ	نَضَعَ	نَضَعْ	وُضِعْنَا	نُوضَعُ	

Act. part. وَاضِعٌ   Pass. part. مَوْضُوعٌ   Verbal noun (maṣdar) وَضْعٌ

A2.9 ***Verb with weak middle*** **و:قَالَ *'to say' (from*** **قول** ***) (perf. /a/ imperf. /u/)***

Person	Active Perf.	Imperf. indic.	Imperf. subj.	Imperf. jussive	Passive Perf.	Imperf. indic.	Imperat.
				Singular			
3. m.	قَالَ	يَقُولُ	يَقُولَ	يَقُلْ	قِيلَ	يُقَالُ	
3. f.	قَالَتْ	تَقُولُ	تَقُولَ	تَقُلْ	قِيلَتْ	تُقَالُ	
2. m.	قُلْتَ	تَقُولُ	تَقُولَ	تَقُلْ	قِلْتَ	تُقَالُ	قُلْ
2. f.	قُلْتِ	تَقُولِينَ	تَقُولِي	تَقُولِي	قِلْتِ	تُقَالِينَ	قُولِي
1. m. f.	قُلْتُ	أَقُولُ	أَقُولَ	أَقُلْ	قِلْتُ	أُقَالُ	
				Dual			
3. m.	قَالاَ	يَقُولاَنِ	يَقُولاَ	يَقُولاَ	قِيلاَ	يُقَالاَنِ	
3. f.	قَالَتَا	تَقُولاَنِ	تَقُولاَ	تَقُولاَ	قِيلَتَا	تُقَالاَنِ	
2. m. f.	قُلْتُمَا	تَقُولاَنِ	تَقُولاَ	تَقُولاَ	قِلْتُمَا	تُقَالاَنِ	قُولاَ
				Plural			
3. m.	قَالُوا	يَقُولُونَ	يَقُولُوا	يَقُولُوا	قِيلُوا	يُقَالُونَ	
3. f.	قُلْنَ	يَقُلْنَ	يَقُلْنَ	يَقُلْنَ	قِلْنَ	يُقَلْنَ	
2. m.	قُلْتُمْ	تَقُولُونَ	تَقُولُوا	تَقُولُوا	قِلْتُمْ	تُقَالُونَ	قُولُوا
2. f.	قُلْتُنَّ	تَقُلْنَ	تَقُلْنَ	تَقُلْنَ	قِلْتُنَّ	تُقَلْنَ	قُلْنَ
1. m. f.	قُلْنَا	نَقُولُ	نَقُولَ	نَقُلْ	قِلْنَا	نُقَالُ	

Act. part. قَائِلٌ　Pass. part. مَقُولٌ　Verbal noun (maṣdar) قَوْلٌ

A2.10 ***Verb with weak middle*** **ي:** **بَاعَ** ***'to sell' (from*** **بيع*****) (perf. /a/ imperf. /i/)***

Person	Active Perf.	Imperf. indic.	Imperf. subj.	Imperf. jussive	Passive Perf.	Imperf. indic.	Imperat.
				Singular			
3. m.	بَاعَ	يَبِيعُ	يَبِيعَ	يَبِعْ	بِيعَ	يُبَاعُ	
3. f.	بَاعَتْ	تَبِيعُ	تَبِيعَ	تَبِعْ	بِيعَتْ	تُبَاعُ	
2. m.	بِعْتَ	تَبِيعُ	تَبِيعَ	تَبِعْ	بِعْتَ	تُبَاعُ	بِعْ
2. f.	بِعْتِ	تَبِيعِينَ	تَبِيعِي	تَبِيعِي	بِعْتِ	تُبَاعِينَ	بِيعِي
1. m. f.	بِعْتُ	أَبِيعُ	أَبِيعَ	أَبِعْ	بِعْتُ	أُبَاعُ	
				Dual			
3. m.	بَاعَا	يَبِيعَانِ	يَبِيعَا	يَبِيعَا	بِيعَا	يُبَاعَانِ	
3. f.	بَاعَتَا	تَبِيعَانِ	تَبِيعَا	تَبِيعَا	بِيعَتَا	تُبَاعَانِ	
2. m. f.	بِعْتُمَا	تَبِيعَانِ	تَبِيعَا	تَبِيعَا	بِعْتُمَا	تُبَاعَانِ	بِيعَا
				Plural			
3.	بَاعُوا	يَبِيعُونَ	يَبِيعُوا	يَبِيعُوا	بِيعُوا	يُبَاعُونَ	
3. f.	بِعْنَ	يَبِعْنَ	يَبِعْنَ	يَبِعْنَ	بِعْنَ	يُبَعْنَ	
2. m.	بِعْتُمْ	تَبِيعُونَ	تَبِيعُوا	تَبِيعُوا	بِعْتُمْ	تُبَاعُونَ	بِيعُوا
2. f.	بِعْتُنَّ	تَبِعْنَ	تَبِعْنَ	تَبِعْنَ	بِعْتُنَّ	تُبَعْنَ	بِعْنَ
1. m. f.	بِعْنَا	نَبِيعُ	نَبِيعَ	نَبِعْ	بِعْنَا	نُبَاعُ	

Act. part. بَائِعٌ Pass. part. مَبِيعٌ Verbal noun (maṣdar) بَيْعٌ

A2.11 ***Verb with weak middle*** و***:*** خَافَ **'to fear'** ***(from*** خوف***) (perf. /i/ imperf. /a/)***

Person	Active Perf.	Imperf. indic.	Imperf. subj.	Imperf. jussive	Passive Perf.	Imperf. indic.	Imperat.
			Singular				
3. m.	خَافَ	يَخَافُ	يَخَافَ	يَخَفْ	خِيفَ	يُخَافُ	
3. f.	خَافَتْ	تَخَافُ	تَخَافَ	تَخَفْ	خِيفَتْ	تُخَافُ	
2. m.	خِفْتَ	تَخَافُ	تَخَافَ	تَخَفْ			خَفْ
2. f.	خِفْتِ	تَخَافِينَ	تَخَافِي	تَخَافِي			خَافِي
1. m. f.	خِفْتُ	أَخَافُ	أَخَافَ	أَخَفْ			
			Dual				
3. m.	خَافَا	يَخَافَانِ	يَخَافَا	يَخَافَا	خِيفَا	يُخَافَانِ	
3. f.	خَافَتَا	تَخَافَانِ	تَخَافَا	تَخَافَا	خِيفَتَا	تُخَافَانِ	
2. m. f.	خِفْتُمَا	تَخَافَانِ	تَخَافَا	تَخَافَا			خَافَا
			Plural				
3.	خَافُوا	يَخَافُونَ	يَخَافُوا	يَخَافُوا			
3. f.	خِفْنَ	يَخَفْنَ	يَخَفْنَ	يَخَفْنَ			
2. m.	خِفْتُمْ	تَخَافُونَ	تَخَافُوا	تَخَافُوا			خَافُوا
2. f.	خِفْتُنَّ	تَخَفْنَ	تَخَفْنَ	تَخَفْنَ			خَفْنَ
1. m. f.	خِفْنَا	نَخَافُ	نَخَافَ	نَخَفْ			

Act. part. خَائِفٌ Pass. part. مَخُوفٌ Verbal noun (maṣdar) خَوْفٌ

A2.12 ***Verb with weak final و: دَعَا 'to invite' (from دعو) (perf. /a/ imperf. /u/)***

Person	Active Perf.	Imperf. indic.	Imperf. subj.	Imperf. jussive	Passive Perf.	Imperf. indic.	Imperat.
			Singular				
3. m.	دَعَا	يَدْعُو	يَدْعُوَ	يَدْعُ	دُعِيَ	يُدْعَى	
3. f.	دَعَتْ	تَدْعُو	تَدْعُوَ	تَدْعُ	دُعِيَتْ	تُدْعَى	
2. m.	دَعَوْتَ	تَدْعُو	تَدْعُوَ	تَدْعُ	دُعِيتَ	تُدْعَى	أُدْعُ
2. f.	دَعَوْتِ	تَدْعِينَ	تَدْعِي	تَدْعِي	دُعِيتِ	تُدْعَيْنَ	أُدْعِي
1. m. f.	دَعَوْتُ	أَدْعُو	أَدْعُوَ	أَدْعُ	دُعِيتُ	أُدْعَى	
			Dual				
3. m.	دَعَوَا	يَدْعُوَانِ	يَدْعُوَا	يَدْعُوَا	دُعِيَا	يُدْعَيَانِ	
3. f.	دَعَتَا	تَدْعُوَانِ	تَدْعُوَانِ	تَدْعُوَا	دُعِيَتَا	تُدْعَيَانِ	
2. m. f.	دَعَوْتُمَا	تَدْعُوَانِ	تَدْعُوَا	تَدْعُوَا	دُعِيتُمَا	تُدْعَيَانِ	أُدْعُوَا
			Plural				
3. m.	دَعَوْا	يَدْعُونَ	يَدْعُوا	يَدْعُوا	دُعُوا	يُدْعَوْنَ	
3. f.	دَعَوْنَ	يَدْعُونَ	يَدْعُونَ	يَدْعُونَ	دُعِينَ	يُدْعَيْنَ	
2. m.	دَعَوْتُمْ	تَدْعُونَ	تَدْعُوا	تَدْعُوا	دُعِيتُمْ	تُدْعَوْنَ	أُدْعُوا
2. f.	دَعَوْتُنَّ	تَدْعُونَ	تَدْعُونَ	تَدْعُونَ	دُعِيتُنَّ	تُدْعَيْنَ	أُدْعُونَ
1. m. f.	دَعَوْنَا	نَدْعُو	نَدْعُوَ	نَدْعُ	دُعِينَا	نُدْعَى	

Act. part. دَاعٍ   Pass. part. مَدْعُوٌّ   Verbal noun (maṣdar) دَعْوَةٌ or دُعَاءٌ

A2.13 *Verb with weak final* ي: لَقِيَ *'to meet' (perf. /i/ imperf. /a/)*

Person	Active Perf.	Imperf. indic.	Imperf. subj.	Imperf. jussive	Passive Perf.	Imperf. indic.	Imperat.
			Singular				
3. m.	لَقِيَ	يَلْقَى	يَلْقَى	يَلْقَ	لُقِيَ	يُلْقَى	
3. f.	لَقِيَتْ	تَلْقَى	تَلْقَى	تَلْقَ	لُقِيَتْ	تُلْقَى	
2. m.	لَقِيتَ	تَلْقَى	تَلْقَى	تَلْقَ	لُقِيتَ	تُلْقَى	إِلْقَ
2. f.	لَقِيتِ	تَلْقَيْنَ	تَلْقَيْ	تَلْقَيْ	لُقِيتِ	تُلْقَيْنَ	إِلْقَيْ
1. m. f.	لَقِيتُ	أَلْقَى	أَلْقَى	أَلْقَ	لُقِيتُ	أُلْقَى	
			Dual				
3. m.	لَقِيَا	يَلْقَيَانِ	يَلْقَيَا	يَلْقَيَا	لُقِيَا	يُلْقَيَانِ	
3. f.	لَقِيَتَا	تَلْقَيَانِ	تَلْقَيَا	تَلْقَيَا	لُقِيَتَا	تُلْقَيَانِ	
2. m. f.	لَقِيتُمَا	تَلْقَيَانِ	تَلْقَيَا	تَلْقَيَا	لُقِيتُمَا	تُلْقَيَانِ	إِلْقَيَا
			Plural				
3. m.	لَقُوا	يَلْقَوْنَ	يَلْقَوْا	يَلْقَوْا	لُقُوا	يُلْقَوْنَ	
3. f.	لَقِينَ	يَلْقَيْنَ	يَلْقَيْنَ	يَلْقَيْنَ	لُقِينَ	يُلْقَيْنَ	
2. m.	لَقِيتُمْ	تَلْقَوْنَ	تَلْقَوْا	تَلْقَوْا	لُقِيتُمْ	تُلْقَوْنَ	إِلْقَوْا
2. f.	لَقِيتُنَّ	تَلْقَيْنَ	تَلْقَيْنَ	تَلْقَيْنَ	لُقِيتُنَّ	تُلْقَيْنَ	إِلْقَيْنَ
1. m. f.	لَقِينَا	نَلْقَى	نَلْقَى	نَلْقَ	لُقِينَا	نُلْقَى	

Act. part. لاَقٍ   Pass. part. مَلْقِيٌّ ,   Verbal noun (maṣdar) لِقَاءٌ

A2.14 ***Verb with final weak ى: رَمَى 'to throw' (from رمي) (perf. /a/ imperf. /i/)***

Person	Active Perf.	Imperf. indic.	Imperf. subj.	Imperf. jussive	Passive Perf.	Imperf. indic.	Imperat.
				Singular			
3. m.	رَمَى	يَرْمِي	يَرْمِيَ	يَرْمِ	رُمِيَ	يُرْمَى	
3. f.	رَمَتْ	تَرْمِي	تَرْمِيَ	تَرْمِ	رُمِيَتْ	تُرْمَى	
2. m.	رَمَيْتَ	تَرْمِي	تَرْمِيَ	تَرْمِ	رُمِيتَ	تُرْمَى	إِرْمِ
2. f.	رَمَيْتِ	تَرْمِينَ	تَرْمِي	تَرْمِي	رُمِيتِ	تُرْمَيْنَ	إِرْمِي
1. m. f.	رَمَيْتُ	أَرْمِي	أَرْمِيَ	أَرْمِ	رُمِيتُ	أُرْمَى	
				Dual			
3. m.	رَمَيَا	يَرْمِيَانِ	يَرْمِيَا	يَرْمِيَا	رُمِيَا	يُرْمَيَانِ	
3. f.	رَمَتَا	تَرْمِيَانِ	تَرْمِيَا	تَرْمِيَا	رُمِيَتَا	تُرْمَيَانِ	
2. m. f.	رَمَيْتُمَا	تَرْمِيَانِ	تَرْمِيَا	تَرْمِيَا	رُمِيتُمَا	تُرْمَيَانِ	إِرْمِيَا
				Plural			
3. m.	رَمَوْا	يَرْمُونَ	يَرْمُوا	يَرْمُوا	رُمُوا	يُرْمَوْنَ	
3. f.	رَمَيْنَ	يَرْمِينَ	يَرْمِينَ	يَرْمِينَ	رُمِينَ	يُرْمَيْنَ	
2. m.	رَمَيْتُمْ	تَرْمُونَ	تَرْمُوا	تَرْمُوا	رُمِيتُمْ	تُرْمَوْنَ	إِرْمُوا
2. f.	رَمَيْتُنَّ	تَرْمِينَ	تَرْمِينَ	تَرْمِينَ	رُمِيتُنَّ	تُرْمَيْنَ	إِرْمِينَ
1. m. f.	رَمَيْنَا	نَرْمِي	نَرْمِيَ	نَرْمِ	رُمِينَا	نُرْمَى	

Act. part. رَامٍ Pass. part. مَرْمِيٌّ Verbal noun (maṣdar) رَمْيٌ

A2.15 *Weak verbs with middle* ي *and final hamzah:* جَاءَ *'to come'*

	Active		Passive		
Person	Perf.	Imperf.	Perf.	Imperf.	Imperat.
			Singular		
3. m.	جَاءَ	يَجِيءُ	جِيءَ	يُجَاءُ	
3. f.	جَاءَتْ	تَجِيءُ	جِيئَتْ	تُجَاءُ	
2. m.	جِئْتَ	تَجِيءُ	جِئْتَ	تُجَاءُ	جِئْ
2. f.	جِئْتِ	تَجِيئِينَ	جِئْتِ	تُجَائِينَ	جِيئِي
1. m. f.	جِئْتُ	أَجِيءُ	جِئْتُ	أُجَاءُ	
			Dual		
3. m.	جَاءَا	يَجِيئَانِ	جِيئَا	يُجَاءَانِ	
3. f.	جَاءَتَا	تَجِيئَانِ	جِئْتُمَا	تُجَاءَانِ	
2. m. f.	جِئْتُمَا	تَجِيئَانِ	جِئْتُمَا	تُجَاءَانِ	جِيئَا
			Plural		
3. m.	جَاؤُوا	يَجِيئُونَ	جِيئُوا	يُجَاؤُونَ	
3. f.	جِئْنَ	يَجِئْنَ	جِئْنَ	يُجَأْنَ	
2. m.	جِئْتُمْ	تَجِيئُونَ	جِئْتُمْ	تُجَاؤُونَ	جِيئُوا
2. f.	جِئْتُنَّ	تَجِئْنَ	جِئْتُنَّ	تُجَأْنَ	جِئْنَ
1. m. f.	جِئْنَا	نَجِيءُ	جِئْنَا	نُجَاءُ	

Act. part. جَاءٍ   Pass. part. مَجِيءٌ   Verbal noun (maṣdar) جَيْءٌ

A2.16 ***Verb with final ʾalif maqṣūrah ى: رَأَى 'to see' (perf. /a/ imperf. /a/) (This is a common verb with certain irregularities of its own.)***

Person	Active Perf.	Imperf. indic.	Imperf. subj.	Imperf. jussive	Passive Perf.	Imperf. indic.	Imperat.
				Singular			
3. m.	رَأَى	يَرَى	يَرَى	يَرَ	رُئِيَ	يُرَى	
3. f.	رَأَتْ	تَرَى	تَرَى	تَرَ	رُئِيَتْ	تُرَى	
2. m.	رَأَيْتَ	تَرَى	تَرَى	تَرَ	رُئِيتَ	تُرَى	رَ
2. f.	رَأَيْتِ	تَرَيْنَ	تَرَيْ	تَرَيْ	رُئِيتِ	تُرَيْنَ	رَيْ
1. m. f.	رَأَيْتُ	أَرَى	أَرَى	أَرَ	رُئِيتُ	أُرَى	
				Dual			
3. m.	رَأَيَا	يَرَيَانِ	يَرَيَا	يَرَيَا	رُئِيَا	يُرَيَانِ	
3. f.	رَأَتَا	تَرَيَانِ	تَرَيَا	تَرَيَا	رُئِيَتَا	تُرَيَانِ	
2. m. f.	رَأَيْتُمَا	تَرَيَانِ	تَرَيَا	تَرَيَا	رُئِيتُمَا	تُرَيَانِ	رَيَا
				Plural			
3. m.	رَأَوْا	يَرَوْنَ	يَرَوْا	يَرَوْا	رُؤُوا	يُرَوْنَ	
3. f.	رَأَيْنَ	يَرَيْنَ	يَرَيْنَ	يَرَيْنَ	رُئِينَ	يُرَيْنَ	
2. m.	رَأَيْتُمْ	تَرَوْنَ	تَرَوْا	تَرَوْا	رُئِيتُمْ	تُرَوْنَ	رَوْا
2. f.	رَأَيْتُنَّ	تَرَيْنَ	تَرَيْنَ	تَرَيْنَ	رُئِيتُنَّ	تُرَيْنَ	رَيْنَ
1. m. f.	رَأَيْنَا	نَرَى	نَرَى	نَرَ	رُئِينَا	نُرَى	

Act. part. رَاءٍ (as قَاضٍ) Pass. part. مَرْئِيٌّ Verbal noun (maṣdar) رَأْيٌ

A2.17 Doubly weak verbs with weak middle و and weak final ى: رَوَى 'to tell'

	Active				Passive		
Person	Perf.	Imperf. indic.	Imperf. subj.	Imperf. jussive	Perf.	Imperf. indic.	Imperat.
				Singular			
3. m.	رَوَى	يَرْوِي	يَرْوِيَ	يَرْوِ	رُوِيَ	يُرْوَى	
3. f.	رَوَتْ	تَرْوِي	تَرْوِيَ	تَرْوِ	رُوِيَتْ	تُرْوَى	
2. m.	رَوَيْتَ	تَرْوِي	تَرْوِيَ	تَرْوِ	رُوِيتَ	تُرْوَى	إِرْوِ
2. f.	رَوَيْتِ	تَرْوِينَ	تَرْوِي	تَرْوِي	رُوِيتِ	تُرْوَيْنَ	إِرْوِي
1. m. f.	رَوَيْتُ	أَرْوِي	أَرْوِيَ	أَرْوِ	رُوِيتُ	أُرْوَى	
				Dual			
3. m.	رَوَيَا	يَرْوِيَانِ	يَرْوِيَا	يَرْوِيَا	رُوِيَا	يُرْوَيَانِ	
3. f.	رَوَتَا	تَرْوِيَانِ	تَرْوِيَا	تَرْوِيَا	رُوِيَتَا	تُرْوَيَانِ	
2. m. f.	رَوَيْتُمَا	تَرْوِيَانِ	تَرْوِيَا	تَرْوِيَا	رُوِيتُمَا	تُرْوَيَانِ	إِرْوِيَا
				Plural			
3. m.	رَوَوْا	يَرْوُونَ	يَرْوُوا	يَرْوُوا	رُوُوا	يُرْوَوْنَ	
3. f.	رَوَيْنَ	يَرْوِينَ	يَرْوِينَ	يَرْوِينَ	رُوِينَ	يُرْوَيْنَ	
2. m.	رَوَيْتُمْ	تَرْوُونَ	تَرْوُوا	تَرْوُوا	رُوِيتُمْ	تُرْوَوْنَ	إِرْوُوا
2. f.	رَوَيْتُنَّ	تَرْوِينَ	تَرْوِينَ	تَرْوِينَ	رُوِيتُنَّ	تُرْوَيْنَ	إِرْوِينَ
1. m. f.	رَوَيْنَا	نَرْوِي	نَرْوِيَ	نَرْوِ	رُوِينَا	نُرْوَى	

Act. part. رَاوٍ (as قَاضٍ) Pass. part. مَرْوِيٌّ Verbal noun (maṣdar) رِوَايَةٌ

Index

Related titles from Routledge

Colloquial Arabic of Egypt
Second Edition

By Jane Wightwick and Mahmound Gafaar

The second edition of this course in Arabic of Egypt for beginners has been completely revised and updated to make learning Arabic of Egypt easier and more enjoyable than ever before.

Specially written by experienced teachers for self-study and class use, the course offers you a step-by-step approach to written and spoken Arabic of Egypt. No prior knowledge of the language is required.

What makes *Colloquial Arabic of Egypt* your best choice in personal language learning?

- The Arabic presented in this course is given in romanised form throughout
- The Arabic script is introduced progressively to aid familiarity with the standard written language
- Emphasis on modern conversational language with clear pronunciation guidance
- Grammar section for easy reference
- Stimulating exercises with lively illustrations

By the end of this rewarding course you will be able to communicate confidently and effectively in Arabic of Egypt in a broad range of everyday situations. This title is available to purchase as a paperback with accompanying CDs to be bought separately, or alternatively as a great value pack containing both book and audio.

ISBN: 978–0–415–276894 (pbk)
ISBN: 978–0–415–276917 (pack)